PLAYING
FOR KEEPS

PLAYING FOR KEEPS

THE MAKING OF THE PRIME MINISTER, 1988

GRAHAM FRASER

M&S

McClelland & Stewart Inc.
The Canadian Publishers
481 University Avenue
Toronto, Ontario
M5G 2E9

Canadian Cataloguing in Publication Data

Fraser, Graham, 1946–
  Playing for keeps

Bibliography: p.
Includes index.
ISBN 0-7710-3208-0

1. Canada.   Parliament – Election, 1988.*
2. Canada – Politics and government – 1984 –   .*
I. Title.

JL193.F73 1989   324.971'0647   C89–89–094451–2

Printed and bound in Canada

Queries regarding radio broadcasting, motion picture, video cassette, television, translation and related rights should be directed to
the Author's representative, Peter Livingston Associates, 120
Carlton Street, Suite 304, Toronto, M5A 4K2, Canada (416) 928–
1019.

CONTENTS

For Barbara, with love
Never a dull moment

CHAPTER ONE

Election Day

"Such pattern as the tale may have is largely imposed by hindsight. Events as they occur in the Eternal Now seem even more confused than they really are; the Moving Finger writes in characters too large to be deciphered from close up."

Blair Fraser

Shortly after seven o'clock in the morning on November 21 in St. John's, Ross Reid, the Progressive Conservative candidate in St. John's East, came downstairs at his parents' house to be picked up by a friend and driven to the Bell Island ferry. It was a steep hill down to Portugal Cove, where the aged ferries came in; they parked the car, and waited for the *Catherine* to pull in to the dock. He stood there, shivering in the chilly early morning, looking west across the water, and chatted with a couple of NDP volunteers who were going to man the polls as scrutineers. Reid was beginning his tour of the polls: a candidate's ritual on election day. It was close to the easternmost extremity of Canada, and the democratic exercise was about to begin. In just over seventeen hours, the polls would close in British Columbia, five thousand kilometres and four and a half time zones away.

That morning, fifty-one days after he had called the election, Brian Mulroney slept in. He and his family had arrived in Baie-Comeau the night before from Trois-Rivières, and the last rally of the campaign. He woke up at the guest house of Le

Manoir, once the home of the mill managers of the Quebec North Shore Paper Co. – what Mulroney remembered from his childhood as Jim Lane's or Charlie Newman's house – beside the stone inn built by the company for executives visiting Baie-Comeau. At ten o'clock, he emerged after breakfast with his family and said "Les jeux sont fait." It was the croupier's line: the bets are placed, the wheel is about to spin. It's over now. "We're going to vote."

It had snowed the night before, and there was snow on the ground when the Mulroneys emerged and headed over to Ste Amélie School on the campaign bus, not far away: the primary school he had attended, named for the wife of Colonel McCormick, publisher of the Chicago *Tribune* and creator of the company and the town. He was sentimental about his childhood and his family, and he enjoyed the nostalgic flavour of visits to his home town, where he could bask in the affectionate reminiscences of the people who remembered him as a boy, and point out the house on Champlain Street where he had lived then.

There was a crowd there, and someone shouted, "Il y aura pas de Rouges icitte, Brian! On est en charge des boîtes, à part de ça!" (There are no Grits here – besides, we're in charge of the ballot boxes!)

They came back to the house – people were coming and going; the kids were there. Mulroney had a quick lunch, went upstairs, and slept for a couple of hours as everyone waited for the results.

An hour after Mulroney had voted, a time zone further west, Ed Broadbent arrived in Oshawa to vote. The campaign had spent the night before at the Hilton in Toronto, and travelled to Oshawa, sixty kilometres to the east, so that Broadbent could vote at a high school on Harmony Street. He told reporters he felt confident and content.

"I'm not nervous," he told the scrum of reporters and cameramen who had gathered to watch him vote in the high-school gymnasium and collect a few comments for early newscasts or early-edition stories. "I tend in these situations to get quite calm, actually, and I feel the campaign has ended up on a very high note."

But he made it clear that what he was hoping for was a breakthrough in Quebec, and predicted that the NDP would win more than one seat there. He would not be satisfied with less. "I'm looking for significant breakthroughs," he said.

For lunch, Broadbent took his staff, the RCMP officers, and the flight crew to Fazio's. It was a long, leisurely lunch; Broadbent toasted everyone, and thanked the people who had accompanied him on the tour, making a particular point of thanking the tour director, his chief of staff, George Nakitsas.

Three hours after Broadbent, John Turner left the Hotel Vancouver, drove to Emily Carr School to vote, and then toured the polls. More than once, he stopped and chatted with school children, explaining who Captain Quadra – the Spanish sea captain his constituency was named after – had been. "I feel great, I feel first class," he told reporters. "I dreamed we'd do well today."

Then he toured the polls, shaking hands and chatting, before coming back to his campaign headquarters to talk to the volunteers. Down the street, Gerry Scott, the NDP candidate, was complaining that he was getting reports that officials at polling stations were explaining to voters that John Turner's name was the last on the ballot. This had been one worrisome problem for the Liberals: the Rhino candidate was also called John Turner.

For politicians, election day is strangely anti-climactic: there is almost nothing they can do. An election-day organization is in full swing in their committee rooms, and there is little place for the candidate, who has done everything he or she can. Some tour the polls, some join the E-day operation and help get out the vote; others find both exercises tacky, and, like Lynn McDonald of the NDP, stay home, and work on their speeches for the rally that night.

On November 21, 1988, 13,168,329 Canadians went to polling stations – usually in a church basement or a school basement – and cast valid ballots. Each person whose name was on the voters' list was given a ballot – a ballot with as few as three names, or as many as twelve. (In Rosemont, there were three independents, a Rhino, a Communist, a Green Party candidate, a Social Credit candidate, and a candidate for the Party for Commonwealth-Republic. Benoît Tremblay, the Progressive Conservative, won, the Liberal Jacques Guilbault came second, Giuseppe Sciortino of the NDP came third, Suzanne Blais-Grenier fourth, the Rhino came fifth, the Green candidate sixth, and none of the other candidates got more than 159 votes.) On a table nearby stood a cardboard shield, behind which was a pencil. Each voter was free to fill the white circle opposite one of the names with a mark: an x, or a check mark. The ballot was given back to the returning officer, who tore off a coupon at the end of the piece of paper, and deposited the ballot in a ballot box.

With that simple action, a fifty-one-day ritual was completed. For the thirty-fourth time since 1867, Canadians chose a new Parliament. For the first time this century – and only the second time since John A. Macdonald did it – a Conservative majority government was re-elected. Because of the free-trade issue, a crucial decision was made about Canada's future. In re-electing the government of Brian Mulroney, forty-three per cent of the electorate chose to endorse a Free Trade Agreement with the United States: an agreement that would change the course of Canadian economic development, and the future role of government. A substantial majority who opposed the agreement divided their votes between the Liberal Party and the New Democratic Party.

An election in Canada is both very simple, and extremely complicated. Unlike the Americans, we do not vote for our leaders; we vote for their surrogates. Unlike the British, our leaders are forced to campaign across a continent, across five and a half time zones.

At times, a Canadian election campaign resembles a chuckwagon race at the Calgary Stampede: holding on for dear life as the chuckwagon careers across the course, the team members have to leap out and perform before jumping back on the wagon and tearing off again. It is not accidental that the Conservative tour director, Stuart Murray, started out in the music business, organizing rock shows – or that the manager of the Liberal tour (a job universally known now as "The Wagonmaster"), Andy Shaw, had handled the communications duties for bike races.

Canadians have set the bar extremely high in their electoral steeplechase. To be successful, a Canadian party leader has to have the stamina to endure a 51-day election campaign, the managerial skills to put together a team that can stick together through the rigours, the intellect to respond to a variety of policy questions on short notice, the skill to deal with the demands of television, and the capacity to perform in two three-hour television debates, one in French and one in English.

There are few Western democracies that put such heavy, and such varied, demands on their leaders. As time goes on, Canadians have raised their standards of performance, or increased the requirements. It is only ten years since the first televised leaders' debate in French in Canada; now, it would be unthinkable to have a televised debate in English only.

But while the demands have increased, the resources and techniques have increased even more dramatically, as each party adjusts to the reality that Canadians, for the most part, participate in political campaigns by watching television.

The 1988 election was remarkable, however, for the way it challenged a series of conventional assumptions about modern campaigns. Conventional wisdom has it that politics is so shaped by television, and the techniques of image-creation that substantive debate over issues is difficult or impossible, as eight-second clips become the vehicle for communicating policy. However, millions of Canadians watched three hours of uninterrupted debate, and their reflection transformed the campaign.

Conventional wisdom has it that the "winner" of a television debate emerges only two or three days later. And yet Liberal candidates insist that the next morning they could see a spontaneous response to John Turner's performance the night before.

Conventional wisdom suggests that television has brought campaigns without issues, only personalities. However, in 1867, during the first election campaign under the British North America Act, Sir John A. Macdonald declared that Confederation had dissolved the old parties, and he had the right, under the circumstances, to a fair trial. A coalition of Liberals and Conservatives had come together to form Confederation; it was as a leader of a coalition that he ran in the first election, claiming that there were no political issues before the country.

While television may naturally focus more on personality than on policy, the 1988 election was rich in policy debate. In fact, however fervently Prime Minister Brian Mulroney might have wanted to emulate Sir John A.'s neat trick of claiming the slate had been wiped clean and he was starting over without issues, the free-trade issue captured the electorate, and the election. It provided the context in which candidates and voters discussed and debated the direction the country should take, the role of the state in the economy, the nature of the Canadian identity, the kind of social programs Canada should have and preserve.

But no election consists simply of leaders debating issues, regardless of how riveting the debate becomes. In 1988, there were 295 constituencies where the campaign played itself out, and candidates scrambled to persuade voters to support them.

These candidates were variously organizing meetings, participating in debates with their opponents, campaigning door-to-door, standing on street corners with signs waving at drivers, shaking hands with commuters at stations and bus stops. While pollsters were carrying on nightly telephone polling, and polls were being published to an unprecedented degree throughout the campaign, each candidate was a single-handed barometer of public opinion. They were all gauging the ebb and flow of the public mood as they shook hands with voters.

Thus, the Liberal candidate George Rideout in Moncton, the Conservative Terry Clifford, the member for London-Middlesex in the last House, and the New Democratic candidate Len Taylor in The Battlefords – Meadow Lake were hearing what voters thought about the issues and the national campaigns as they went from door to door, and responding as best they could to the changes in public concern. Any examination of the election runs the risk of losing sight of a crucial element if too much attention is focused on national strategists, advisers, and tacticians, and too little on the local candidate whose success or failure in winning votes is the ultimately deciding factor.

The intensity of the 1988 election, the degree to which it became transformed by the televised debates, the concentration on leadership, the way in which the free-trade question swept all other issues away, the contrast in the nature of the campaign in Quebec and in the other provinces, the role of television, the importance of polls, the volatility of the electorate, all combined to make it a fascinating event in Canadian political history.

In many ways, the 1988 election shattered the mould of brokerage politics in Canadian elections. For generations, political observers concluded that there was little difference between the two major parties. James Bryce summed up a widely held view in 1921 when he wrote "In Canada, ideas are not needed to make parties, for these can live by heredity and, like the Guelfs and Ghibellines of mediaeval Italy, by memories of past combats."

In their study of the 1974, 1979, and 1980 elections, *Absent Mandate*, Harold D. Clarke, Jane Jenson, Lawrence LeDuc, and John H. Pammett concluded that the nature of Canadian brokerage politics was that "it is extremely difficult for any government to obtain a true policy mandate." They gave a gloomy analysis: "Elections may focus the attention of public and politicians alike on important societal problems and reflect or even generate issue conflicts, but their ability to produce policy mandates is doubtful," they concluded. "Given the prevailing tendencies toward brokerage politics in the Canadian political system, absent mandates are likely to be the rule, not the exception. Elections decide who shall govern, but not the substance of public policy."

On at least one substantial issue, this was not the case in 1988. For it was clear that, in casting their ballots, Canadians were making a clear policy choice on the Free Trade Agreement, and a policy choice that had unmistakable implications. However, to the extent that the government had sought and received a mandate, it was exercised before the end of the year, when the House of Commons and the Senate ratified the Agreement.

Nevertheless, while the policy choice involved was unusual, and the combination of factors at play was unique, the elements of the 1988 election included some of the constant themes of Canadian politics.

After observing the Canadian election of 1904, the French political scientist André Siegfried concluded that the four arguments Canadian election organizers used most often, "and which ensure victory to their party when they can make out their claim with sufficient plausibility," were "the defence of one of the two races or of one of the two religions against the other; the prosperity of the country; the promise of public works or material local advantages; and the personal prestige of the party leader."

There is a consistency to that observation (if one replaces "religion" with "language") which is revealing, and a caution against too extravagant claims about the uniqueness of the last election.

Siegfried also points out that Canadians make their electoral choice on the basis of which party they believe will best offer prosperity – and make that decision, to an overwhelming degree, on the basis of their conclusion about the party leader.

"Admirers, like the English, of strong individualities, they love to put in the place of honour a man of authority and prestige," he wrote. "Their commercial idea of credit, which they carry into politics, makes them feel that their reputation cannot fail to be strengthened if they have at their head a personage of distinction, calculated to impress people with a sense of his worth.

"That is why it is of the first importance to the success of a party that it should be led by someone who inspires confidence, and whose name is a programme in itself," he continued. "As long as the Conservatives had Macdonald for their leader, they voted for him rather than for the party. So it is with Laurier and the Liberals of today."

Again, the concentration on leaders and leadership, while perhaps greater than in the past, is a fundamental part of the Canadian political tradition.

In 1987, when I decided to undertake this project, I had a sense that this would be an extraordinary election, unique in some ways, and unusual in others. For the first time, there was the prospect of a genuine three-way race. For the first time, a governing party would have spent a substantial part of its mandate in third place in the polls. For the first time in a long time, there was the prospect of a clear policy division between the government and the opposition that would mark the election as a fork in the road, a policy choice that could create a very different regional division in Canada from any in decades.

At the same time, there was the likelihood of two colliding, almost contradictory factors, which would make the election particularly interesting.

On the one hand, there would be an increasingly sophisticated use of television, polling, direct mail, political consultants and communications advisers, all using the techniques of marketing and media control to adjust their campaigns to the climate of public opinion. But at the same time there would be a traditional confrontation of ideas: a choice that has run through the fabric of Canadian history. Free trade had the potential to be the symbol of a larger ideological division over the role of the state and the private sector.

That was my starting point, as I prepared for the campaign. As it turned out, the election campaign fell into place in a way that enabled me to structure this narrative in a chronological fashion: the period before the writs were issued, the initial part of the campaign before the television debates, the debates themselves, and the post-debate period.

However, the simplicity of the chronological pattern is deceptive. An extremely wide range of factors came into play:

the personalities of the leaders, the wealth of the parties, the television advertisements, the leaders' tours, the personal chemistry between each leader and his campaign team, and the relative success that each campaign achieved in being clear and coherent in defending its policy decisions. Even those most intimately involved in the strategic planning of the national campaigns saw different elements as being determining factors in victory or defeat.

At the same time, each national campaign had to be translated into 295 constituency campaigns, where questions that never touched the national news became local firestorms. The challenge has been to sort out these elements, and give each one an appropriate weight.

There has been a tendency on the part of journalists to spend more and more time and energy writing about election planners, strategists, organizers, pollsters, and advertisers – and less and less time and energy writing about what the politicians say. The insiders have gradually begun to acquire a primacy over the outsiders. There are a number of reasons for this: political strategy is more fun to write about than economic policy, and polling numbers are more exciting than deficit projections.

It is also part of a flawed but persistent journalistic assumption that I think of as the Campaign Correlative: If a party can't run an efficient campaign, it can't hope to run the government. In this analogy, the campaign tour becomes a metaphor for government.

However, it is improbable that the voters re-elected the Mulroney government because its tour operation was so smooth. It seems, on reflection, that the election campaign merely served to expose the strengths and weaknesses of the three parties: strengths and weaknesses that were well rooted in the culture of each of the three. The seeds of victory and defeat were planted long before the writs were issued.

Nevertheless, much of André Siegfried's observation on the importance of leadership holds true. The campaign was a supreme test of the political-management skills of the three leaders. Of the three, only one would survive; only the winner would continue in politics. The three men had to symbolize their parties' different identities, while shaping and directing the messages each party was trying to deliver. Each one would be held responsible for the errors and successes of the campaign. They were playing for keeps.

In addition to marking a watershed in political leadership, the election would also be a turning point in public policy. The directions established by the Progressive Conservatives in the first mandate would be reversed, or confirmed; the Free Trade Agreement would be ratified or die; the degree of government involvement in the economy would tilt in one direction or another, depending on the government reflexes on the questions of privatization, deregulation, decentralization, government ownership, and foreign investment. Tory economic management, however faltering and indecisive some businessmen considered it to have been, would either be wiped away or continue. The high-stakes game was not merely an exercise in political careerism; the direction of the country would be decided in a critical fashion.

In describing the campaign, I have tried to keep in mind a warning from Richard Brookhiser, who argues in a book on the 1984 American campaign that political journalism has become too preoccupied with "inside" stories about strategists and handlers, and has tended to forget the "outside story" of what politicians are actually saying to voters. I have also kept in mind a comment by the American columnist George Will: "Politicians' words – the most public acts of public people – matter and should be taken seriously by serious students of politics." For, in the final analysis, the voters watch, listen, and choose.

CHAPTER TWO

Mulroney Rounds the Edges

"In every party, there are two sorts of men, the rigid and the supple."
Richard Steele
The Tatler, No. 214
Aug 19–22, 1710

On Wednesday June 8, shortly before noon, Brian Mulroney left the railway-committee room of the House of Commons, where the weekly meeting of the Progressive Conservative caucus was held, and walked up to his office, which looked out over the lawns of Parliament Hill. A few days later, it would be the fifth anniversary of his winning the Tory leadership, and in his weekly speech to caucus he had talked of some of the changes that had occurred in the party since he had become leader.

Roch LaSalle, the veteran Quebec Tory who had resigned as Minister of Public Works under a cloud, was there that morning, and, spotting him, Mulroney reminded the caucus that in the 1980 election, of the 102 seats in Canada with a francophone component of more than 15 per cent, the Tories had won one, Roch LaSalle's seat in Joliette.

Mulroney rarely missed a caucus meeting; it was, in the jargon of opinion polling, a huge focus group: a chance to listen to opinions from across the country.

"The caucus is the heart of the machine," he said a few

minutes later. "It's the heart of our movement, because the caucus is the genuine microcosm of the country. I'm not violating caucus secrecy by telling you that this morning the principal discussion was about the incredible situation in Western Canada with our farmers. The heat, the drought, the interest rates. . . . People get up and talk about the impact with great emotion.

"This is not a theoretical point of view, this is a man or a woman standing up and saying 'Hey! I'm from Swift Current, and here's what happened yesterday at Millie's farm.' Now, if you've been around Millie's farm yourself in some way, you understand that Millie has the same problems as your mother or your father, so you listen, and this is the way that you get a great sense of the country."

The caucus in a parliamentary democracy is a crucial, but difficult phenomenon. When a prime minister chooses his cabinet, he has created the executive; in its crudest form, the rest of the caucus exists to ratify the decisions made by the cabinet. But an unhappy caucus is a threat to any leader: demoralized MPs will blame their leaders, seek alternatives, and, even if they remain outwardly loyal, lose heart and support in their constituency, and risk defeat. As a result, caucus is a sounding board, a gripe session, a barometer of public opinion, and a key to the future success of any political leader and his party.

As a result, Mulroney's speech to caucus was one of the key events of his week, and he devoted a great deal of effort and energy to reaching out to the huge group: reassuring, cajoling, correcting, encouraging, flattering. Sometimes shamelessly theatrical, he would use birthdays, anniversaries, personal anecdotes, and the tough, funny, locker-room talk of political partisans to keep his sprawling caucus united, optimistic, and enthusiastic. Constantly, week after week, he would hammer at a central theme: victory and power depended upon caucus unity; division would lead to defeat and opposition.

Coming back to his office, damp with exertion, he changed his shirt before ushering me into his office to discuss his fifth anniversary as party leader, and reflect on the changes that had taken place. Was it a different party from the one he had taken over in 1983?

"Yeah, I think it is, but I think it is in the stream of progressive, modern thought that Bob Stanfield and Joe Clark pursued in general measure," he said. "I think what we have done is make a number of significant changes. The most obvious is our breakthrough in French Canada."

Repeating the observation he had made to caucus about the Tory failure to win francophone support in 1980, he observed that there were two results of this failure.

"First of all, you give the government to the Liberals. For openers, you make of the Liberals a natural governing party, when obviously they don't deserve it. You forfeit the leadership of the country in those circumstances," he said. "But secondly, the absence of an influence can be sometimes as damaging as the wrong kind of influence. And for the Progressive Conservative caucus to have evolved over a long period of time without the influence on the day-to-day basis in the caucus, in the formulation of policy, of the sensitivities and attitudes of French-speaking members, was quite harmful."

Thus, Mulroney saw the breakthrough in Quebec, northern Ontario, and northern New Brunswick in 1984 as not simply important electorally, but transformative of the party.

"Secondly, a breakthrough in the cities," he said. "We became more urban. We also became more ethnic, if you will, and I think we became more representative, strongly more representative of women. I think those were the changes, and I think the numbers are there to sustain that. I also think that as a result of that you can see the influences of some of those things on policy and on decisions."

When Mulroney ran for the leadership of the Progressive Conservative Party in 1983, he ran on two themes. One was explicitly spelled out in the terms that he reminded his caucus of on the fifth anniversary of his victory: the Conservatives could not win power without Quebec, and he could win support in Quebec. Again and again, he reminded delegates and potential delegates that there were over a hundred rid-ings in Canada with more than a 15 per cent French-speaking population. "You give Pierre Trudeau a head start of a hun-dred seats, and he's going to beat you ten times out of ten."

But, at the same time, there was a less clearly articulated theme, hinted at in jokes and cracks: "I look around this room and see a roomful of senators;" "We need people who have lived in the real problems of everyday life, who understand the agony and the pain that people go through when they're trying to run a business, when they're trying to meet a pay-roll, when they're faced with this mountain of paper work, when they knock on a bureaucrat's door and the bureaucrat has got an office bigger than your entire plant;" any bureau-crat blocking a job-creating investment would be given "a pink slip and a pair of running shoes."

Of course, the most quoted, the best-remembered line from his 1983 leadership campaign was his comment on non-partisan appointments. "I intend to appoint all sorts of Liber-als and NDP to top, sensitive jobs," he would say, and pause for a few seconds before finishing triumphantly "... after I've been prime minister for fifteen years and I can't find a living, breathing Conservative to do the job!"

Funny, earthy, shrewd, slightly titillating, Mulroney's jokes were conveying a message to the outsiders in a party of outsiders: the people who felt that Joe Clark, the establish-ment of the Conservative Party, Robert Stanfield, and all the well-bred, private-school-educated élite had been too polite, too decent, and too clumsy to win power and use it to help Tories.

Mulroney's approach was to build his base of support with the losers in the party, and convince them that they could become winners. It was a strategy with inherent risks; when he was asked about Mulroney at the leadership convention, one Clark loyalist would pull out a slip of paper, and read off Mulro-ney's supporters in caucus (a group, with the exception of the veteran George Hees, of relatively undistinguished MPs which included Robert Coates, Gordon Tower, Len Gustafson, Elmer MacKay, and Otto Jelinek, saying "Here's the Mulroney cabinet."

Yet Mulroney did not let himself be captured by his supporters. When he won the leadership, he set out to bring all the various factions and fragments in the party together. The result involved some abrupt reversals in approach in dealing with people he had been variously scornful or contemptuous of during the leadership campaign. (Privately, he would tell people during the leadership campaign how he had told Joe Clark to stop taking advice from "that fucking separatist" Arthur Tremblay, the former Quebec civil servant whom Clark had named to the Senate. Within weeks of his winning the leadership, Mulroney announced that Tremblay would be the chairman of a special advisory committee on the constitution.)

But Mulroney had learned something from his own experiences before winning the leadership. He understood a lot about the vanities and pain of political ambition. He had been there.

Martin Brian Mulroney was born on March 20, 1939, in Baie-Comeau. He was the third child of Ben Mulroney, an electrician from Sainte-Catherine-de-Portneuf near Quebec City, who had moved to the Lower North Shore mill town, first to help build and then to work at the Quebec North Shore paper plant when it opened in June 1938. (Like John Turner, Mulroney had a first-born older brother who died in infancy.)

Mulroney grew up on Champlain Street, not far from Le Manoir, but left home at fourteen to finish high school at St. Thomas College in Chatham, New Brunswick, and, in 1955, at sixteen, went to St. Francis Xavier University in Antigonish, Nova Scotia. After an unsuccessful year at Dalhousie Law School, he started at the Laval Law School in the fall of 1960.

His political career began, in some ways, at St. F.X., where he became a Conservative, and began the lifelong process of accumulating layers of friends and acquaintances, networks of relationships established long before the women's movement turned the word "network" into a verb. His political skills were developed as a process of loyalty, sentimentality and memory; more than most politicians, who like most people move through stages of their lives with shifting relationships with people, Mulroney built his career on a pyramid of long-held loyalties and friendships.

At St. F.X., he met some of the people who would be at the heart of his political career, and who would gather around to celebrate his victories: Patrick MacAdam, MacAdam's roommate Lowell Murray, Fred Doucet, Sam Wakim, Terry McCann. At Laval, he was one of the organizers of the Congrès des Affaires Canadiennes, and his fellow organizers included Peter White, Michael Meighen, and Michel Cogger; other students involved, whom he listed in his book *Where I Stand*, included Pierre de Bané, André Ouellet (later Liberal cabinet ministers), Clément Richard, Denis de Belleval, Jean Garon (later Parti Québécois cabinet ministers) and Lucien Bouchard. Along with Jean Bazin, who became engrossed in student politics, many of these men would remain profoundly bonded to Mulroney.

Throughout this period, he was also active in the Conservative Party. He had worked in the Nova Scotia provincial campaign of 1956, and was a Diefenbaker delegate at the P.C. leadership convention that same year; he took a youthful delight in the relationship he had established with John Diefenbaker, and was described by Peter C. Newman in 1963 as "one enlightened advisor [to Diefenbaker] in the province of Quebec." In the summer of 1962, he worked as an assistant to Alvin Hamilton, Diefenbaker's minister of agriculture.

At Laval, Mulroney also learned the earthy vagaries of political debate in Quebec, and French. For, while he is often considered a francophone, French is definitely a second language; he had done all of his secondary-school and undergraduate work in English before coming to law school to absorb the Quebec Civil Code. From Laval, he went to Montreal where he articled at, and then joined the long-established law firm called Howard, Cate, Ogilvy and now known as Ogilvy Renault.

Mulroney specialized in labour law; he represented the Shipping Federation of Canada before the Inquiry Commission on the St. Lawrence Ports, headed by Laurent Picard, in 1966–67. (Stanley Hartt and David Angus both represented the Stevedoring Contractors.) Mulroney quickly developed a reputation as a shrewd negotiator: skilful, sometimes theatrical, quick to see and exploit the weakness of the other side in a confrontation, but equally quick to see the underbelly of self-interest that would provide the makings of a deal. In the decade he practised law, he acquired another cohort of friends and allies: clients like Paul Desmarais of Power Corporation, who hired him to settle a bitter strike at *La Presse*, and legal colleagues like Francis Fox, Hartt, and Angus. But Mulroney's experience as a labour lawyer shaped more than his address book: it gave him experience with negotiating, and it gave him a familiarity with a much tougher, harder-edged form of confrontation and ideological debate with the toughest unions in Canada than almost any other English-Canadian politician had. While thin-skinned about personal criticism, he developed a harder shell than most when faced with demonstrators or hecklers: he had seen much harsher treatment on picket lines.

Throughout these years, he remained active in politics as the only smart Tory anyone knew in Quebec: a regular sounding board for journalists and political operators anxious to have Quebec's mysteries translated to them.

In 1974, Quebec Premier Robert Bourassa named Mulroney to a special commission investigating "the exercise of union freedom in the construction industry," after inter-union rivalries had resulted in spectacular vandalism on the construction site of the James Bay hydro-electric project. Known as the Cliche Commission after its chairman, Judge Robert Cliche, the assignment vaulted Mulroney onto the front pages in Quebec. As the investigation pursued allegations of corruption, beatings, and political collusion, the three commissioners – Cliche, Mulroney, and Guy Chevrette from the teachers' union – became household names.

On the basis of the prominence that Mulroney had achieved, and almost twenty years as a political organizer, he agreed to Michel Cogger's proposal that he run for the Conservative leadership in 1976. Relatively little known outside Quebec, Mulroney and his friends decided to run a high-profile, expensive, flashy campaign. However, many Conservatives were offended: the campaign seemed outrageously expensive, Mulroney's silky baritone seemed affected, and his allies in English Canada seemed to be predominantly handsome young men in expensive clothes who played squash and bought professional sports teams.

Asked what his impression of Mulroney was after the candidate had made a courtesy call on the then Toronto Mayor David Crombie, one Crombie aide said, "The man's a rhinestone in the rough." Resentful of the ostentation of the Mulroney campaign, organizers for Flora MacDonald had the idea of folding over Mulroney posters at the convention, so that, instead of "Mulroney," they read "Money."

Nevertheless, Mulroney was viewed as a moderate, on the so-called Red Tory side of the candidates. Mulroney came into the convention leading in the polls; he lost to Joe Clark, finishing third behind Claude Wagner. The defeat wounded Mulroney deeply, making him feel excluded and condescended to. He was angry at the party, bitter at what happened, and particularly resentful of those friends, like Lowell Murray, who supported other candidates. He saw this as the worst kind of betrayal – Murray had been an usher at his wedding only three years before, and had been one of those who brought him into the Conservative Party at St. Francis Xavier – and, with a kind of proud anger, would recount how his wife Mila had turned Murray and Richard Hatfield away, first from their table at the Beaver Club, and then from the front door as they tried to mend the breach.

His bitterness was such that he couldn't restrain himself from letting it show, not only in private, but to journalists; it finally emerged in print in an article in the *Financial Post Magazine* in the spring of 1978, where Stephen Kimber noted that talking with Mulroney about the 1976 convention was like scraping sandpaper over an exposed nerve: "With even the gentlest encouragement, the hurts tumble out."

Mulroney, then president of the Iron Ore Company of Canada, was not only bitter, but gloomy about the prospects of the Tories in Quebec under Joe Clark's leadership. "I look at the numbers, you know, and I just can't see it. God bless him if he can do it but the way I look at it, Clark is going to get wiped out in Quebec. Without Quebec, there's no way he can win the election." Ironically, a remark in the article which the authors of a biography of Mulroney, Ray Murphy, Robert Chodos, and Nick Auf der Maur, found to be the most unrealistic proved to be almost prophetic. Mulroney had claimed that Claude Ryan would have agreed to become provincial Tory leader had he won the 1976 convention. The three authors quoted the remark and commented, "The interesting element in this quote is not the implausible what-might-have-been scenario, but the notion that he could not only negotiate with Claude Ryan on the latter's decentralist constitutional position and viewpoint about the reorganization of English Canada, but also persuade the rest of the Tory party to accept Ryan and his views." The Meech Lake Accord nine years later would be proof that he could, in fact, reach just such an accommodation.

Mulroney was half right in his prediction about the next election: Clark won the 1979 election, but with only two seats in Quebec. He then lost the 1980 election after only nine months in power. When two successive conventions gave him a 67 per cent endorsement, Clark resigned, and ran as a leadership candidate at the June 11, 1983, convention.

This time, Mulroney was able to run a very different campaign. In the seven years since 1976, he had worked in the business community; while losing none of his political skills, he had developed his credentials. Though in 1976 he was viewed as part of the party's moderate wing, in 1983 he courted those who were unhappy with Clark's moderation. Mulroney managed to keep a discreet distance from the organizers who worked to defeat Clark (although bitter Clark supporters still remember seeing Michel Cogger pay for delegates' expenses in Winnipeg, peeling off the bills one by one); his organizers were able to fight Clark to a draw for delegates in Quebec; he succeeded in reaching out to the angry, disaffected right wing of the Tory party without being tied to it; he shrewdly fashioned his campaign rhetoric to have more zing than commitment. He flirted with the right, hinting at tough slashes at government programs with street-tough remarks about Crown corporations ("I'm going to put the axe to them. Just watch me do a job on them") and Petro-Canada ("Small is beautiful as far as Petro-Can goes"). "Abolish FIRA? That isn't what he said," observed Robert McKenzie in a piece that shrewdly exposed his technique of using tough phrases which didn't actually bind him to anything. "'It would be put on the back-burner for a long time.'" As McKenzie pointed out, it was hard to determine whether Mulroney would go as far as Michael Wilson, widely seen as being more moderate than he was.

On June 11, 1983, on the fourth ballot, Brian Mulroney became leader of the Progressive Conservative Party, defeating Joe Clark by 1,584 to 1,325. He had made it.

Mulroney had learned from his defeat, and cherished the lessons of his own injured pride. He reached out to the defeated candidates, to the caucus members, to the networks of Tories who greeted his arrival as leader with wary unease. To the surprise of old friends who had watched him nurse the wounds of 1976, he was conciliatory.

"Only someone who has gone through a leadership convention himself or herself can, I think really understand the emotions that come to bear when you first go through this real emotional maelstrom that occurs," Mulroney said, looking back on the event five years later. "You know, everyone by voting day believes in his or her heart that he or she is going to win. Otherwise, you'd be out to lunch. Your troops are built up, the emotions are high, the expectations are high, and when that happens, the letdown is all the more difficult. Everybody is affected by it."

He paused.

"But after a while you get on with your life and you can either learn from it or you can let it hobble you, and if you learn from it, then you want to make this your career and if you want to be the leader, then you should always remember the fundamental principles set out for me one day by my wife. She said 'Just remember, no-one drafted you for this job.'"

"If that's true of me, it's true of everybody in caucus. . . . If you hold a leadership convention and a whole bunch of people show up, their ambitions are just as legitimate as yours. They think in their own hearts that they are absolutely what the country needs. If you don't think that, why would you go through this agony and the damage that you can inflict on your financial situation, on your professional career, . . . the sorrow it can inflict on your spouse and your children? As a result of that, the fundamental responsibility of a leader after a convention is to bind up the wounds."

So he immediately set to work to bring together the different factions of the party, and to ensure that the various wings of the party had been stroked, and had a representative at the table.

Mulroney decided in June 1983 that he would take Elmer MacKay's offer of the Nova Scotia seat of Central Nova, and ran in the August 29 by-election. On Sept. 12, 1983, he entered the House of Commons as leader of the opposition. Two days later, the Liberals introduced a language resolution calling on the Manitoba government "to fulfil their constitutional obligations and protect effectively the rights of the French-Canadian minority of the province."

Manitoba's provincial Conservatives were fighting an agreement between the federal government, the Manitoba NDP government and the Société Franco-Manitobaine on extending French-language minority rights as a way of avoiding full compliance with a Supreme Court ruling on the Manitoba Act of 1870. The issue clearly had the potential of driving a wedge through the new leader's caucus.

"Now you have to be naive in the extreme to think the primary motivation for this resolution was to help Franco-

Manitobans," Mulroney said. "The primary motive for this resolution brought forward by the Liberals was to cripple my leadership on the second day that I arrived in the House of Commons, and to split the Conservative caucus right down the middle."

"You can do one of two things," Mulroney told his caucus. "You can play the Liberal games, you can split, so they can say you're divided, and therefore you can't govern the country – so they can move on with their divisive, injurious policies. Or you can resist. This is a simple proposition. Do you want to be in government, or do you want to be in opposition? If you think that I think that success in life is becoming leader of the opposition, you've got me wrong ... the office of the leader of the opposition [is] a great honour, but my success [will] depend on the rapidity with which I take leave of the office."

This would be the great symphonic theme of Mulroney's speeches to caucus: the central notion he would return to again and again. Three months before his fifth anniversary as leader, on March 16, Mulroney told his caucus he would soon be forty-nine.

"In those forty-nine years, the Liberals have been in office forty, and we have been in office nine," he said. "I don't like those odds. Those are not good numbers. And of the nine, I have supplied something already in the neighbourhood of three. That's what happens when, after a period of years and defeats, the Progressive Conservative or any party becomes opposition-minded, when a party forgets that its principal objective is to seek the election of its party, rather than to promote the interest of the group in opposition."

In 1983, it was a tougher sell; at least one member was bluntly told that if he broke with the caucus and voted against the resolution, he would be sitting as an independent. So with some difficulty, the Progressive Conservative caucus rose in unanimous support of the resolution, as it did again, after a similar exhortation, on the question of medicare a few weeks later, and again on Senate legislation that would have affected Quebec's Caisse de Dépôt.

"I can still see it," he recalled. "[The Liberals] had collective cardiac arrest on the day that I rose in the House and announced that my caucus was unanimously supporting the resolution. They couldn't believe it. And then they tried on the question of medicare. Don Johnston records in his book how flabbergasted they all were that I didn't allow the caucus to fall into the trap."

Mulroney saw this as a key event in the transformation of the Conservative Party from a group with an opposition mentality to a group that could come to grips with reality.

"We could have been crippled in the autumn of 1983," he said in retrospect. "I think they began to understand what unity was. Unity was a new perception of the country. We could only do these matters if we got to govern. We could only get to govern if we were united. We could only be united if people understood that the other guy's point of view was no less valid than his own. That was the coming of age of the Conservative caucus."

Mulroney made it clear that uniting the caucus and the party were his first priorities as leader.

"I saw my role as the leader first of all, someone who would restore the process of genuine unity in the caucus, to the party, form a majority government, and, fourthly, bring two things to the country in the process of doing that: prosperity and unity," he said. "And that's what I've tried to do."

Mulroney's account of how he brought unity to a party and a caucus "which have been historically fragile" showed how much energy he had devoted to the task, and how he perceived the role of the party leader.

"First of all, you've got to believe in it. You've got to work at it. You've got to care about people," he said, punching his words with intensity. "They have to genuinely believe that you care about them. You have to know what you're doing. You have to produce results.

"You've got to be there in the crunch. You've got to be there for the bad times, to pick up the pieces. You've got to take the hits and not bat an eye. You've got to endure the criticism. And not indicate any weakness."

He spoke each word with emphasis and precision.

"You've got to genuinely appreciate the role of a member of parliament, how tough it is for their spouses. Take the time to understand these things, and how they fit into a large apparatus that is difficult to describe."

Thus, when he took over as party leader, he set up caucus committees, caucus task forces, transition teams. Titles proliferated. Everyone had a job.

George Hees, who was then seventy-eight and had first run for Parliament in 1945 under John Bracken and served under every Tory leader since, observed that Mulroney had the knack of making everyone feel important.

"He keeps stressing the team – and makes everyone feel they're an important part of the team," Hees said, pointing out that this was not unselfishness. "Never trust a man past his own self-interest. If someone doesn't feel they're a potential leader, or at least cabinet material, they aren't very useful. People who feel they haven't got a chance – that's it. They start looking around for someone who might become the leader, and make them a cabinet minister. They start working against the leader who they feel hasn't given them a chance."

Mulroney had won the leadership because too many people had felt that way about Joe Clark. He was determined not to let the cycle repeat itself.

When John Turner called an election for September 4, 1984, the Liberals were in the lead in the polls, having surged ahead after their leadership convention. However, Mulroney was well prepared; he had taken advantage of the Liberal leadership contest to do a dry-run tour, enabling the campaign team to test people and places.

At the beginning of the campaign, he flew to Central Nova and thanked them for electing him in the by-election before flying on to Baie-Comeau to announce he would be a candidate in Manicouagan. Since the Tories had only one seat in Quebec, and the June SORECOM poll showed them with 28 per cent support in the province and the Liberals with 62 per cent, this looked like a risky strategy.

But by mid-July, it looked as if the riding was preparing to gamble that it would be electing a prime minister. "Having a prime minister in the riding is a bit like having an industry," said Jean Croteau, the owner of a hardware store in a Sept-Îles shopping centre. "It gives you an advantage over other ridings. Look at what John Diefenbaker did for Prince Albert. Who had heard of Prince Albert?"

Croteau was reflecting on the choice people in Manicouagan were facing. He considered himself a Liberal, he liked and admired the Liberal MP André Maltais, and couldn't understand why John Turner had not put Maltais in his cabinet. But he didn't think that the Lower North Shore, which had suffered layoffs, shutdowns, and closings in the iron and pulp-and-paper industries, could afford to miss the chance to have a prime minister representing it. However, he made it clear that he would be watching the polls before he voted; this would not be a sentimental decision. People in depressed areas cannot afford sentimentality, and they cannot afford to be ill-informed.

"It's a difficult decision," Croteau said, reflecting on how he would vote. "But with the polls, we will get the data from the West. If Mr. Mulroney is in trouble, we will return to Mr. Maltais."

On July 24, all that changed with the TV debate in French. Quebeckers saw that, while John Turner might have looked like a prime minister, he was awkward and unfamiliar; Brian Mulroney made a direct, almost sentimental appeal as a Quebecker. Following the debate, the crowds began to swell; as Mulroney came through Saguenay-Lac-Saint-Jean going from town to town ten days later, he was greeted with enthusiasm. In Roberval, where the Conservative candidate got 1.49 per cent of the vote in 1980, there was a packed hall; organizers joked that there were more people out to see him than had voted Conservative in the previous election.

When he arrived in Quebec City on August 3 to mainstreet down the Grande Allée, crowded with a summer long-lunch crowd, Gary Ouellet, an old friend of Mulroney's and a Tory lawyer in Quebec City, looked at the crowd and beamed. "I knew we had won the debate when Brian uttered the most beautiful words in the French language," he said. "Chez nous."

If the French debate had captured Quebec's attention and its affection, the English debate the following night managed, in a single dramatic exchange over patronage, to make Turner seem weak, vacillating, and a prisoner of the past, and Mulroney a dramatic break with the sleazy cronyism of a government too long in power.

Péquistes, provincial Liberals, Clark supporters, Mulroney supporters, former Union Nationale veterans, even former Créditistes, all worked together in Quebec while across Canada English Canadians turned away from a Liberal Party which had become tired and ineffective.

On September 3, Mulroney returned to his birthplace for the election, saying, "A boy from Baie-Comeau has made a long trip and today he's coming home" as he was met by four hundred supporters at the airport. He stayed at the Manoir Comeau, in the cottage that was once the mill manager's house; when he had come there to launch the campaign, he had joked about staying in what was once the holiest of shrines for an electrician's son. He glowed with the small-town glee of making it to the top.

When he came to the polling station the next morning, former neighbours who remembered him as a boy recalled that he had been a bundle of mischief and trouble. "We called him 'le petit malcommode' – the little troublemaker," said Donald Bouchard.

That mischievousness had been highly developed during Mulroney's career as a labour lawyer and a political organizer, both being fields that valued blunt, street-smart wit. Mulroney's smooth, often sanctimonious, public style covered up, not Nixonian nastiness, but a shrewd, vulgar, sometimes profane back-room sense of humour. At times, it would pop out in public, as it did at the beginning of the campaign, when he compared the Liberal patronage appointments to an

Edward G. Robinson movie ("The boys are in the kitchen, cuttin' up the cash") at the press conference after the writs were issued, but it is an integral part of his private style.

On September 4, 1984, Mulroney won a historic victory, winning 211 seats, 58 of them in Quebec. His challenge would be to bring the unwieldy caucus together, choose an effective cabinet, and govern.

Once elected, Mulroney acted much as he had done as leader: blessed or burdened with the largest caucus in Canadian history, he had the largest cabinet in Canadian history sworn in. The vague promises of economic growth ("I have no hesitation to inflict prosperity on Atlantic Canada") became somewhat clearer with the Wilson statement on the economy, *A New Direction for Canada: An Agenda for Economic Renewal*, tabled in the House on November 8, 1984, although its promise of spending cuts and deficit reduction became muddied when Wilson, Health and Welfare Minister Jake Epp, and Mulroney all seemed to contradict one another in December on the question of whether or not universality in social programs would be maintained.

Similarly, the woolly campaign sentiments about improving relations with the Americans became clearer with Mulroney's declaration in New York in December 1984 that "Canada is open for business again," and with the Shamrock Summit in Quebec City in March 1985, in which Mulroney and President Ronald Reagan agreed to pursue negotiations on trade, and to have a joint two-man task force look at the problem of acid rain.

Mulroney's instinct to consult, to listen to a wide variety of voices, extended beyond the cabinet and caucus to an exercise in economic consultation: the Nielsen Task Force on government expenditures, which led to a series of harsh recommendations for cutbacks in government spending and government programs, and the national conference on the economy in March 1985.

But the results were inconclusive; on the surface, despite some clear decisions that had been promised during the election (the abolition of the National Energy Program, the replacement of the Foreign Investment Review Agency with Investment Canada) the government appeared to be drifting. The attempt to end the indexation of pensions in the Wilson budget in the spring of 1985 made the worst of both worlds. On the one hand, it convinced many people that Mulroney had lied when he called universality of social programs "a sacred trust" during the election campaign. Then, when the government backed down in the face of public opposition, it appeared weak and irresolute in pursuing its object of dramatically reducing government spending.

In September 1985, the situation seemed worse than mere drifting. A series of embarrassing resignations began. Fisheries Minister John Fraser left the cabinet after it became known that he had rejected the advice of his officials that a tuna plant in New Brunswick was producing an inedible product. Defence Minister Robert Coates resigned in February 1985 after a report that he had spent the evening with a stripper in a club in Lahr, West Germany. Communications Minister Marcel Masse resigned when he learned that his election expenses were being investigated by the RCMP. (He was reinstated in the cabinet when no charges were laid.)

There were other embarrassments. Environment Minister Suzanne Blais-Grenier ineptly slashed environmental protection and research programs and was questioned about her lavish spending on a trip to Europe; although she resigned from the cabinet to protest the closing of an oil refinery in the east end of Montreal, she was widely believed to have jumped before she was pushed. After initially denying it, Minister of State for Youth Andrée Champagne admitted writing a cabinet colleague urging that government funds be used to recruit young people to the Progressive Conservative Party. And in April 1986, Sinclair Stevens resigned, after reports of conflict of interest; a judicial inquiry by Chief Justice William Parker concluded in a report issued on December 3, 1987, that

Stevens had been in conflict of interest on fourteen occasions.

Just at the point that Mulroney felt that the government was about to turn the corner and regain its popularity, he was hit by another embarrassing scandal. On January 18, 1987, he learned that there had been land flips in the industrial park in Saint-Jean, Quebec, when the arms-manufacturing company Oerlikon Aerospace Ltd. decided to build its plant there: transactions that drove up the price of land dramatically. He asked for, and received, the resignation of the minister, André Bissonnette. (Bissonnette was found not guilty on charges of fraud, conspiracy, and breach of trust; however, his friend and former campaign manager Normand Ouellet, while acquitted on similar charges of conspiracy and breach of trust, was found guilty of fraud, fined $100,000, and ordered to make restitution of $968,857, plus interest, to Oerlikon.)

In the weeks following, Mulroney showed the strain, as the opposition battered away at the government in the House. When he adjusted his tie, or moved his right hand across his chest, or ran his hand across his forehead, he gave away his discomfort to those who knew him. "He is not running his hand through his hair, he's wiping a thin line of sweat along his forehead," a friend observed. "When he does that, he wants the floor to open up and swallow him."

The Oerlikon affair triggered an avalanche of allegations and accusations of patronage, favouritism, and cronyism aimed at Mulroney and his ministers. Newspapers recalled the previous incidents, and compared the resignation with those of other ministers. Jean Bazin, who had acted for Oerlikon, was on the point of being named to the Senate; questions were raised as to whether the appointment should be reversed. Mulroney's successful trip to Africa was almost forgotten.

This was rock bottom. MPs began to speculate on the carnage that would occur in the party if, as one caucus wit put it, Mulroney turned out to be a "Pierre Cardin Diefenbaker," and led the party to what then seemed inevitable defeat. Mulroney tried to cheer up the cabinet, telling them that Margaret Thatcher had told him it didn't matter where he was in the polls two years before an election, or two months before an election; the only thing that mattered was where he was on election day. When he left the room, one cabinet minister said, "Yes, but he's not Thatcher."

In situations of stress, people who knew Mulroney well observed how much more comfortable he was in French, in Quebec, than in English in the rest of Canada; he seemed more relaxed, more self-deprecating, less given to the grasping for superlatives that made many English Canadians so uncomfortable. "When I saw the picture of him at the Canada-Russia hockey game at Rendez-Vous '87 (in Quebec City) I thought at first it was a picture from the 1983 leadership convention," said L. Ian MacDonald, who was working on contract as a speech-writer for Mulroney. "The cares had all fallen away."

But the cares didn't go far. The February public-opinion poll by Angus Reid Associates showed the Conservatives at 23 per cent, the New Democrats at 33 per cent, and the Liberal Party at 42 per cent; the February Gallup gave the Liberals 44 per cent, the NDP 32 per cent and the Tories 22 per cent. This was rock bottom. That was close to the level of support that the NDP had had in 1980 when, with 20 per cent of the vote, it won 32 seats. Of the 1,005 adults surveyed, half felt that the Oerlikon affair was a sign of "widespread corruption" in the upper levels of government; 60 per cent disapproved of Mulroney's performance as prime minister, and 58 per cent doubted that he was trying to promote fairness and honesty in government. The Conservatives were in last place in every region of Canada except Ontario, where they were only three points ahead of the NDP.

Mulroney was particularly angered at the report published by the *Globe and Mail* on April 16, 1987, detailing the renovations to 24 Sussex Drive; while the main story emphasized the fact that renovations had been paid for by the PC Canada Fund, the indelible detail that everyone remembered was the story reporting that a closet had been designed to hold eighty pairs of Gucci shoes.

Other incidents contributed to the general impression of impropriety. As public works minister, Roch LaSalle organized what Jeffrey Simpson described as a "Godfather" system whereby Quebec MPs would be responsible for contracts in ridings without Tory members. As part of that system, Michel Gravel, the MP for Gamelin in Montreal, was charged with fifty counts of influence-peddling, bribery, and abuse of public trust (and finally pleaded guilty after the election). It became known that LaSalle had two aides with criminal records. Finally, there was the case of Michel Côté, who resigned after the prime minister learned that he was heavily in debt to a Quebec City contractor and had failed to report the loan as required under the conflict-of-interest guidelines.

Mulroney responded to the broad impression that he was being badly advised by shaking up his office. Some of his closest friends moved sideways – like Bernard Roy, whose role was first diminished by the appointment of Don Mazankowski as deputy prime minister and then by the appointment of Derek Burney as chief of staff – or left. Fred Doucet, Bill Fox, Charles McMillan, Lee Richardson, Ian Anderson, Michel Gratton, and Peter White all left the Prime Minister's Office, although not all for the same reasons. However competent or incompetent they were, there was a widespread view, particularly in the Progressive Conservative caucus, that Mulroney had surrounded himself with old friends who had proved unable to do the job. The casual, collegial atmosphere that had prevailed, in which people felt free to drop in to meetings, ended abruptly. Derek Burney, who came from External Affairs, reorganized the PMO as a much more tightly structured organization.

However, despite anger and unhappiness in the caucus at the unprecedented unpopularity of the government, there was never a suggestion that Mulroney should resign. Week after week, he would pump up caucus morale: variously reading the riot act on improper conduct, pouring scorn and contempt on the Liberals, and convincing his MPs that Canadians would look at the government's whole four-year record. When John Turner was photographed wearing a "rat pack" sweatshirt, implicitly endorsing the aggressive tactics of his backbench MPs, Mulroney told his caucus "This guy's fin-

ished. This country does not, and will not, endorse the standards and ethics of the rat pack." When the party slumped in
the polls, he told his MPs: I carried you last time; you're going
to have to carry me this time. This might not have been true;
the MPs were well aware of the surveys that showed how little
the local MP counted in voters' decisions, but it was encouraging nonetheless.

At times, Mulroney would surpass himself. When he
returned from Africa in the winter of 1987, he gave a speech in
caucus responding to grumbles from right-wing MPs about
his public endorsement of left-wing African leaders, which
one of his critics in caucus acknowledged was one of the best
speeches he had ever heard. However, it was typical of the run
his luck was taking that he never gave that speech in public.

Despite the growing public impression that the government was incompetent or worse, Mulroney had been pursuing two sets of negotiations: one for a constitutional
amendment, and the other for a trade agreement with the
United States. Together, they would transform the political
landscape in Canada.

The Meech Lake Accord, signed in principle on April 30,
1987, and, after an all-night session at the Langevin Block,
confirmed as a legal document on June 3, appeared to break
the constitutional log-jam; Quebec's five points were
responded to, and Mulroney and all ten premiers signed the
agreement. All three federal party leaders endorsed the
accord: a consensus that prevented a true national debate on
the question in the House of Commons, or in the election
campaign.

But the Accord achieved only an artificial unanimity: it
brought Pierre Trudeau out of retirement to denounce it, first
in a polemic in *La Presse* and the *Toronto Star*, and subsequently in appearances before the Senate-Commons and Senate committees. Mulroney had succeeded in driving a wedge
through the heart of the Liberal Party, and in placing pressure
on Ed Broadbent on questions that had wrenched the NDP

before, in the debate over the 1981–2 Charter of Rights. The decentralist elements in the Accord fitted both the Tory agenda and the Mulroney promises; the challenge was for Turner and Broadbent to explain to their supporters and their natural constituencies that the Accord would not threaten the Charter, native people, residents of the Yukon and the North-west Territories, women, or anglophones in Quebec.

In one form or another, the debate will continue until the Accord is ratified by all of the provinces by the end of June 1990, or fails for lack of unanimity; by the summer of 1989 Manitoba and New Brunswick had still not ratified it, and a new government in Newfoundland was considering with-drawing ratification.

But, while the issue was not a formal part of what separated the parties in the 1988 election, the problem it represented would haunt both the Liberals and the New Democrats and contribute significantly to Mulroney's success.

The Free Trade Agreement also fitted neatly into the Mulroney view of the world, presented during the 1984 election campaign. Even though Mulroney had opposed the idea of free trade in the 1983 leadership campaign, he was able to claim that he had been talking about "untrammelled and unrestricted" free trade; what the critics feared most about the Free Trade Agreement were, in fact, Tory objectives. Critics objected that Canada had given away its ability to control energy prices, or introduce a National Energy Program; that the federal government had compromised its ability to launch new Crown corporations, or new social programs; that government contributions to unemployment insurance might be interpreted as a subsidy; it was hard to argue that the Conservatives saw any of these ideas as useful, or felt a need to negotiate the Free Trade Agreement in a way to protect the powers of the Canadian government to intervene in the economy.

Though polls showed about 50% percent support for the agreement, in the spring of 1988 Canadians had not decided to support the Conservatives. The Angus Reid poll in June showed the three parties in almost a dead heat: Liberals at 34 per cent, Conservatives at 33, and the NDP at 31.

But as he examined his situation on his fifth anniversary as party leader, Brian Mulroney was optimistic. Despite the low Tory voting intentions, the public view of his leadership qualities, compared to those of his opponents, was positive: more positive than the view reflected in the media. Moreover, he was convinced, as he kept telling his caucus, that voters don't examine a government's record until the writs are issued, and that when they did, they would look at record economic growth and prosperity, the success of the international summits, the child-care legislation he hoped to have approved before the election, and what he called "two cornerstones": Meech Lake and Free Trade.

"We've had a rough time," he said. "We've kept, as I say, our sense of history and our sense of humour and we've climbed slowly and surely right back up. We know we're doing well in leadership. We know that. I've never run worse than second behind Mr. Perfection [NDP Leader Ed Broadbent]. Turner always runs third, which is not bad for a guy who has to make decisions."

Mulroney paused.

"You know, there was the other poll that I noticed was in the local paper, the Reid poll. Fine, if you're asking how you are going to vote tomorrow. Well (the voter says), I'm going to vote Liberal. The next question: If free trade plays a part in the next election campaign, how are you going to vote? Conservatives first, Liberals second, NDP third. What do you think is going to be part of the next election campaign?"

He shrugged off the voting intentions, pointing out that the Liberals were doing well provincially in Manitoba, Ontario, Quebec, and New Brunswick. The public-opinion indicators he looked at much more closely involved leadership, rather than party affiliation or voting intention.

"As soon as you ask the question on policy, leadership, and orientation, bang! Up it comes. And there you had it last Saturday right in front of you in two eight-column headlines, one in *La Presse* and one in the *Citizen*. Eight-column head-lines."

On a low-level rhetorical roll, Mulroney switched into French to quote the poll question in *La Presse* from memory. "Who is most able to govern Canada? Mulroney first, Broad-bent a poor second, and then Turner who is so far behind you can't see him. And perhaps the second question we'll find over eight columns in the *Citizen*. If free trade plays a role in the next election, how will you vote? Well, I am going to vote Conservative first, Liberals second, then New Democrats a poor third. Now think about the question for a second."

Mulroney switched back to English again. "What the hell do you think is going to be part and parcel of the next election?"

CHAPTER THREE

Potlatch Politics

"You hear nothin' but politics, politics, politics, one everlastin' give, give, give."

Sam Slick
T.C. Haliburton, 1836

On June 21, the *Toronto Star* had a line on the front page that summed up the local pride which the Economic Summit had both catered to and exploited. In a small box listing the stories in the eight-page pullout section inside, one said "Maggie Thatcher just loves our Toronto." The story quoted Ron Bos, hairstylist at the King Edward Hotel, as saying that Thatcher had told him she loved the convention centre and the way Toronto was laid out.

That captured the vanity of Toronto, and the self-satisfied glow in which the city was basking during the meeting of the leaders of the seven major industrial countries. As always, the meeting represented a deadline for civil servants preparing positions for their leaders, an opportunity for public statements on a consensus of good intentions, and private discussions of collective problems. While useful as a forum for leaders to get to know each other better and share information about world issues, the events rarely lead to decisions of a binding nature.

The Toronto Summit was no exception. The leaders congratulated themselves on their record of economic growth, and predicted that their economies would continue to grow.

They agreed to denounce illegal drug trafficking (which none of their governments profited from) and to express "abhorrence of apartheid," but not to adopt stiff economic sanctions against South Africa (which would have harmed business interests that several of their governments did profit from). They agreed to allow governments to forgive sub-Saharan African debts, but not to commit any governments to doing so. Similarly, the leaders discussed but did not resolve the problem of agricultural subsidies. Mulroney conceded at the final press conference that "there was not instinctive agreement" on the issue, which had kept officials struggling until five a.m. that day to find a compromise.

Mulroney and his principal representative organizing the event, Fred Doucet, knew that the most effective way to convey the idea to Canadians and to skeptical reporters that the conference had worked well was for the leaders to feel it had been successful, and they were pleased at the results. But for Toronto, the three-day event was a triumph. With some 5,500 people involved, directly or indirectly, it served as a showcase for Canada's largest city, which was delighted with the attention. "The international recognition will enhance our bid for the 1996 Summer Olympics," said the Mayor of Toronto, Art Eggleton.

Brian Mulroney had never felt particularly comfortable in Toronto over the years; one Conservative remarked once that he lingered as long as possible at a private reception before a luncheon speech to a Toronto business audience, postponing as long as possible what he feared might be a negative reception. L. Ian MacDonald noted in his biography that Mulroney was more comfortable with people from small universities in small towns than with people from established and establishment institutions; he suspected condescension from the world of Bay Street, Albany Club Tories, and the Red Tories who came, in MacDonald's phrase, "from somewhere between Queen's University and the United Church"; he resented the complacent, unquestioned assumptions of superiority that he felt came from Toronto's and Southern Ontario's wealth and power. His staff would sometimes roll their eyes at the apparent necessity to flatter Toronto's all-too-obvious insistence on the phrase "world class."

The Summit was the ultimate flattery, and it was not chosen by accident. Early in the mandate, Mulroney's administration had planned a sequence of major events leading up to what political aides had always assumed would be an election in the fall of 1988: the Francophone Summit in Quebec and the Commonwealth Conference in Vancouver in 1987; the Winter Olympics in Calgary, the June Summit, and a fall election. One Mulroney adviser had ticked off the sequence on his fingers at the Francophone Summit in Paris in 1986. But the site for the Economic Summit had not been chosen, and the city Mulroney originally had in mind was Montreal. However, when Toronto was excluded as an International Banking Centre in favour of Vancouver and Montreal, there was considerable pressure from Michael Wilson and Barbara McDougall to name Toronto. To break the impasse, other cities were considered, but it was decided that no other city could easily hold the event. Mulroney finally decided that since the Francophone Summit had been in Quebec City and the Commonwealth Conference in Vancouver, Toronto should get the Economic Summit. He kept the option of Montreal open as he flew to Venice, but, at the 1987 Summit, he announced that the 1988 Summit would be held in Toronto.

It worked. Senator Norman Atkins, the co-chairman of the election campaign, was delighted. "I remember the magical moment at the Royal York Hotel when Mulroney introduced President Reagan," he said later. "The president got up, and there was kind of an eye exchange that not only showed the kind of affection that transpired between the two, but when the President speaks up as he did, and the way he did about Brian Mulroney, no one could ever believe that that could be manipulated."

A Gallup poll published on July 1 showed that Mulroney had made a good impression on 55 per cent of Canadians in his role at the Toronto Economic Summit. Just after it, a Liberal was taken aback to hear a Toronto cab driver say that he would vote for Mulroney for having brought the Summit to

Toronto. "Well, Trudeau hosted a Summit in Canada," the Liberal said. "I know," the cab driver said. "I would vote for him, but he's not running."

On June 20, at a working dinner in Hart House at the University of Toronto for the seven leaders and Jacques Delors of the European Community, Derek Burney came in twice to Mulroney's table to give him news of the Lac-Saint-Jean by-election. For if the Conservatives lost the by-election, the careful planning that had gone into the Summit would not have mattered much. The second time, Margaret Thatcher waited until the leader who was speaking had finished and said, "That's interesting. But, Brian, how are we doing?" "Margaret, we won," Mulroney replied. He then took the menu, and had everyone sign it as a souvenir for Lucien Bouchard. As the results came in, it looked as if the whole thing had been an easy run, and the victory a foregone conclusion. This was not the case.

In March, Mulroney and Derek Burney had met with Lucien Bouchard in a hotel room in Brussels, where they had all gathered for a NATO meeting. That evening, Mulroney laid out to Bouchard his election plan. The Conservative Party had not succeeded in sinking roots in Quebec; the government had been tarnished by the inexperience or venality of some of the Quebec members. It was necessary to rebuild the coalition of 1984, and bring together provincial Liberals, Parti Québécois members, traditional bleus, former Créditistes, and get them to vote together to support a government. Bouchard was crucial to this.

Bouchard had already played an important role in Mulroney's life. His father was a truck driver, and his grandfather had cleared the land to farm in Lac-Saint-Jean in 1900, but Bouchard and his brothers had been encouraged to seek higher education and had gone to classical college; his three younger brothers all did doctorates in Paris. Reflective, thoughtful, widely read in French literature and politics, Bouchard was much more than simply a small-town lawyer and friend from university.

Born on the family homestead near Lac-Saint-Jean, Bouchard had studied law at Laval and had returned to practise
law in Chicoutimi. He had been a Liberal in the 1960s; as a
student at Laval, he was part of the pressure for change, and
identified with the Quebec Liberal government of Jean
Lesage. In 1965, his imagination was captured by three
Quebeckers who announced that they would run in the federal election: Jean Marchand, Gérard Pelletier, and Pierre
Trudeau. "They were three of the best francophone Quebeckers of their generation, who were going to Ottawa to translate
the renaissance that had happened in Quebec," he said later.
In the 1968 election, Bouchard worked for the Liberals, and in
the Quebec provincial election of 1970, he was the campaign
manager for the Liberal who was running against the Union
Nationale cabinet minister Jean-Noël Tremblay.

But Bouchard became disillusioned with Pierre Trudeau,
and what he saw as his rigid view of federalism and his
attitude towards Quebec, which he found disdainful and
contemptuous. "I was very disappointed by Trudeau," he
said. "You're always most disappointed by the people you
admire."

Another Chicoutimi lawyer, Marc-André Bédard (later
René Lévesque's minister of justice), persuaded him to join
the Parti Québécois in 1972, when a vote for the PQ was a vote
for independence, and when joining the PQ meant a rupture
with his law firm and a substantial financial sacrifice. A year
later, Mulroney asked him to join the Cliche Commission on
labour unrest in the construction industry as senior counsel.
In 1976, Bouchard worked for the PQ in the election; he also
worked for the Yes campaign during the 1980 referendum. In
the 1982–3 negotiations with the Common Front of the public
sector, he was the chief negotiator for the PQ government: a
test of stamina and ingenuity, and proof enough that Bouchard could be tough (union members would complain with
some justice that the results were brutal) when required.

Throughout this period, Bouchard had remained close to
Mulroney despite their obvious differences politically. He
understood Mulroney's style and insecurities, and did not

take offence at his macho bluster about the PQ and Quebec nationalism when Mulroney was part of the business community in Montreal; he joined him for dinner at his home in Westmount when Mulroney made an unsuccessful attempt to bring some leading PQ members and francophone businessmen together. In 1984, during the election campaign, Bouchard moved into a hotel room in Montreal to work on speeches for Mulroney: he wrote the Sept-Îles speech, which laid out Mulroney's policy of federal-provincial flexibility and his determination to make it possible for Quebec to sign the constitutional agreement, and he worked on Mulroney's victory speech.

At about nine o'clock on the night of September 4, 1984, when Mulroney learned he would be the head of a majority government, Bouchard was sitting beside him in the suite in the guest house at Le Manoir in Baie-Comeau. "I've just achieved something I've always dreamed of," Mulroney said. "Lucien, I want you to go to Paris." The next morning, over breakfast, Mulroney insisted he had not been joking. It was an important job, and he needed Bouchard in Paris; just as Pierre Trudeau had wanted Gérard Pelletier there to protect Canada's interests after the election of the PQ, Mulroney wanted someone who could work out a new diplomacy with France based on a new relationship with Quebec.

The appointment did not happen for almost a year. But not long after the election, Mulroney asked Bouchard to work on the speech that he would give during French Prime Minister Laurent Fabius's visit to Ottawa. It was then that Mulroney said that it was legitimate for Quebec and France to have direct, privileged relations in areas of Quebec's jurisdiction. That speech began the process of compromise and conciliation that made the first Francophone Summit possible. Bouchard's appointment as ambassador was greeted with dismay. He was virtually unknown to English Canadians, and to name a Chicoutimi lawyer as ambassador to Paris was widely seen as the worst kind of patronage. In a column headed "The buddy as diplomat," Jeffrey Simpson criticized the appointment of both Bouchard and the former Ontario Attorney-

General, Roy McMurtry, who had been named high commissioner to London. "Both men are longtime friends of the Prime Minister; in Mr. Bouchard's case, the friendship runs back to Laval University days," he wrote. "But the question remains – would you hire a stockbroker to fix your roof?" He laid out the qualifications for being an ambassador, in his view: knowledge of his home government, knowledge of the country to which he is posted, demonstrated skills in international diplomacy, and an eye for trade promotion or international economics. "Mr. McMurtry and Mr. Bouchard, through no fault of their own, go zero for four." A Western newspaper even called the appointment an insult to France.

"That hurt," Bouchard said six months later. "It left wounds. I had hesitated a long time before agreeing to do the job – I had a comfortable life, I was beginning to harvest the years of effort I had put in, I was able to go to Florida and Paris every year. So when I saw the reaction, I was tempted to resign, then and there, call a press conference and blast English Canada. But I resisted."

In fact, Bouchard knew France well; it was English Canada and the federal government he was unfamiliar with. So on being named ambassador, he began by getting a thorough six-week briefing on the federal government, and went on a cross-country tour of Canada, meeting premiers and provincial officials. He then made an extremely good impression in Paris, where he succeeded in negotiating the deal that allowed Quebec to participate at the Summit in matters of its jurisdiction: a crucial agreement which allowed the event to take place. In fact, at a private dinner for the officials working on the summit, French Ambassador Jacques Leprette toasted Bouchard, saying, "I was told that he was not of the profession. But in my thirty-five years as a diplomat, he is one of the best I have met."

Part of Bouchard's success at the Francophone Summit involved reaching an agreement that the second summit should be held in Quebec. Like the first one, the Quebec summit went off almost without a hitch: together, the two events created a modest framework for aid, communications, and education for the French-speaking underdeveloped world similar to what the Commonwealth provided for the English-speaking underdeveloped world. And, while the actual discussions revolved around the tedious details of loan forgiveness and satellite communications networks to improve health resources for African hospitals, the public show was valuable for the Mulroney government.

However, Bouchard's success did not win him unanimous praise. The Quebec delegate-general when he arrived, Louise Beaudoin, cancelled his appointment to see her, and some PQ members saw his acceptance of the appointment as a form of treason. Bouchard was hurt when, in the December 1987 issue of *L'Actualité*, Jacques Parizeau accused him of betraying the PQ, saying that the Canadian embassy in Paris was destroying the Quebec delegation. Stung, Bouchard responded with a letter to *La Presse*, saying that he had made it "a point of honour and principle" to stress that Quebec's unique place in France and in France's heart should be preserved.

At the Quebec Francophone Summit, Mulroney told Bouchard to get ready: at some point, he would want him to return to Canada, and run. In Brussels, he raised the issue again. The time had come.

Bouchard agreed to come back; all that remained were the details: what cabinet portfolio, and what riding. Mulroney's principal secretary, Bernard Roy, telephoned Bouchard and told him that it had been arranged: he would become secretary of state. Bouchard had little idea of what the job involved. In fact, it had been selected, not because it was particularly appropriate, but because, with David Crombie's departure, it was vacant. Bouchard was assured that he would be able to run in Chicoutimi, his home town.

In fact, the details had not been taken care of. After a walk on Parliament Hill with André Harvey, the member for Chicoutimi, Mulroney came to the mistaken conclusion that Harvey would willingly step aside. He was mistaken. Harvey had no intention of leaving politics and began working to ensure he had strong local support. But Bouchard had no idea that this was happening. He returned to Canada, and was prepared to be sworn in to the Mulroney cabinet.

At 9:30 in the evening on March 30, the night before the swearing-in, Mulroney called Luc Lavoie, one of his staff, and told him that he was worried that the reporters would give Bouchard a rough time. Would he take care of him, and help brief him for the press conference?

Lavoie, a former TV reporter who had gone to work for Energy Mines and Resources Minister Marcel Masse in 1986, was a shrewd, hard-nosed political aide. He did not know Bouchard, and spent the rest of the evening reading the clipping file – knowing that reporters would probably do the same thing. He found, among other things, that in an interview with *Maclean's*, Bouchard had said that he wasn't sure that Quebec separation wasn't still the best solution. So, sitting at home, Lavoie banged out a briefing note on the questions Bouchard might expect, and suggested replies. Bernard Roy phoned, and told Lavoie to come over to his place the next morning for a breakfast briefing with Bouchard, who was staying with him.

At seven the next morning, Bouchard, Roy, Lavoie, and Marc Lortie gathered at Roy's house. Bouchard was extremely nervous; Mulroney had warned him that he would get very rough treatment from reporters, that he might never survive if he wasn't careful.

Early in the afternoon, the swearing-in at Rideau Hall took place. It was not a major cabinet shuffle, but a strategically organized one. Pat Carney moved from International Trade to the Treasury Board; Gerry St. Germain, whom Mulroney had often relied on for a sense of the mood of caucus, became minister of state for transport; John Crosbie became minister of international trade; Benoît Bouchard became minister of transport; and Barbara McDougall became minister of employment and immigration.

There was a pattern to the rearrangement that did not go unnoticed. "Prime Minister Brian Mulroney has fashioned a campaign cabinet that strengthens his hand in Quebec and British Columbia, but leaves Metro Toronto Tories twisting in the chill political winds," wrote Val Sears in the *Toronto Star.*

Mulroney announced, in French, that Bouchard's first task would be to make an assessment of all the party resolutions on ethics and party financing, and to make precise recommendations to cabinet. Mulroney and Bouchard had discussed this carefully beforehand, but it was not repeated in English. There were no translation facilities, and unilingual English-speaking reporters missed this aspect of Bouchard's new job.

One of the first questions Bouchard was asked was what right he had to sit at the cabinet table without being elected, when there were 208 Conservatives in the House. He didn't hear the last part of the question, and responded by saying that Quebeckers had made a historic decision in 1980 to be part of Canada, and things were not the same after that. "And I feel that since Quebeckers have decided, in a democratic way, that their future was within the federation, it is our duty ... the duty of francophones to make it work."

Asked about the need to prove himself to Canadians, he said firmly that he had proved in Paris that he could be a committed Canadian and a proud Quebecker. "I am Canadian. Who can doubt that? I was born a Canadian, and we have been Canadians since 1636 in Quebec. . . . I am very proud to be a Canadian."

When asked about entering the cabinet as "a separatist," Bouchard bristled. "I don't like the word 'separatist,'" he said. "It's a loaded word; you know it is not the reality. . . . Many people voted yes [in the 1980 referendum in Quebec] for negotiating a new deal with Canada."

Bouchard insisted that he would be running in a by-election "very soon" – but it would take a month, until April 29, for Mulroney to call a by-election. It was not an easy month for Bouchard.

First, after going back to Paris to finish packing up his things, Bouchard headed back to Chicoutimi to spend the Easter weekend with his mother. He arrived at the small airport in the fog and the rain, and there was still snow on the ground, bleak and dirty; he had a sudden sense of the risk he was taking. And, although he had been advised not to speak to the local media, he couldn't resist chatting with people he knew about his hope that he would run in a by-election in Chicoutimi. Word reached André Harvey, who was on holiday in Greece – and he began telephoning the media from Greece, making it clear that he would not, under any circumstances, step aside for Bouchard.

Then, no sooner had Bouchard come back to Ottawa than the minority-language situation in Saskatchewan exploded. To the annoyance of the federal government, Grant Devine announced that Saskatchewan was introducing legislation to extinguish the French-language rights that had been recognized by the Supreme Court, but would be introducing more French schools: most of them immersion schools aimed at English-speaking parents rather than services for the dwindling francophone minority.

As Bouchard ruefully told a press conference, he had had two months of briefings before becoming ambassador to Paris, and only two days as secretary of state before his first crisis. It was not an issue he seemed comfortable with.

In interviews, he pointed out that he had insisted that New Brunswick be present at the Francophone Summit, and that he believed that survival of French-speaking minorities outside Quebec was essential. "I've never seen what Quebec could achieve by devaluing Canadian bilingualism," he said. "I don't see why Quebec would be weakened by the fact that Canada was bilingual – on the contrary ... French-speaking Quebec has everything to gain from the extension of its majority into the rest of Canada."

But as a Quebec nationalist, his priority, and that of his political supporters, was the French language in Quebec, not outside – and he had considerable trouble relating to the English-speaking minority in Quebec. However, he denied that the Conservative Party had moved to a position of endorsing a French-speaking Quebec and an English-speaking Canada – saying that this would be a serious error, since bilingualism was a judicial guarantee – although the evidence suggested that this was the case when Quebec Tories criticized Official Languages Commissioner d'Iberville Fortier for suggesting in his annual report that it was inappropriate for French-speaking Quebec to "humiliate its adversary" with the language law, and when Grant Devine had eliminated the constitutional guarantees for French in Saskatchewan which the Supreme Court had upheld.

In addition, there was the problem of Bouchard's identification with Mulroney. "I certainly learned the English synonyms for 'friend' pretty quickly," Bouchard quipped later. "Pal, chum, crony. . . . " And there was also the problem of a seat. He was uncomfortable as an unelected cabinet minister, and he wanted a by-election as soon as possible. "It has to happen quickly."

However, the relatively positive reaction to Bouchard's initial interviews had impressed Mulroney. The criticism of his being an unelected minister had died away; some Tories, like Norman Atkins, were urging that there be no by-election at all, and that he should simply stay in the cabinet until the general election. But Bouchard was determined to run.

Other Quebec Tories began to call, wanting to meet with him, and offering their seats. Two polls had been ordered: one in Chicoutimi, and one in Montmorency-Orléans, near Quebec City. Harvey made it clear that he was determined to dig in and stay, but Jean-Pierre Blackburn, from Jonquière, was more open to discussion. However, when it was clear he wouldn't be appointed to the Senate because of the Meech Lake Accord, he lost interest. Then Bernard Roy began discussions with Clément Côté, the member for Lac-Saint-Jean, who was prepared to step aside.

Mulroney was determined that Bouchard should run in the Saguenay – Lac-Saint-Jean region, but Bouchard had no desire whatsoever to run in Lac-Saint-Jean. For while the region was viewed as one by outsiders, there was an intense rivalry and resentment between Chicoutimi and Alma. He was no more seen as a hometown boy in Alma (although he was born in the riding) than a Torontonian would be in Hamilton, or an Edmonton lawyer in Calgary.

As the situation dragged on, it was more and more awkward for Bernard Roy, caught between two old and stubborn friends, as Bouchard got more and more annoyed at the delay. Benoît Bouchard, the senior minister for the region, began to circulate the rumour that Matane would be a logical riding, since there was a tradition of electing outsiders. And Lucien Bouchard began to look for his own riding.

He decided that the best riding for him would be Verchères, south-east of Montreal. He knew the PQ member, Jean-Pierre Charbonneau, and several of his organizers; the MP, Marcel Danis, was unhappy in Ottawa as deputy speaker, and was fully qualified for a seat on the bench that was open in Quebec. So more polls were done. In the abstract, relatively unknown outside his region, Bouchard would have won Lac-Saint-Jean by six points, but would have trailed in Montmorency-Orléans by two to three points and in Verchères by four to six points. It was close enough, he thought, for a good campaign to win it.

Finally, he got angry. He was not going to run in Lac-Saint-Jean, that was final. This ultimatum led to a meeting at 24 Sussex with Mulroney, Bernard Roy, Pierre-Claude Nolin, and Bouchard. When the meeting was over, Clément Côté was resigning and Bouchard would be a candidate in Lac-Saint-Jean. The next day, April 29, Côté made his statement, and Bouchard announced that he would be a candidate in his constituency. A by-election was called for June 20.

When Bouchard headed reluctantly off to Lac-Saint-Jean to fight the by-election, he was assured that there would be an impressive organization in place. Denise Falardeau, the newly elected president of the Quebec wing of the Conservative Party, came from the riding, and there was confidence that things would be well run. Bouchard decided he would finance his campaign with donations from individuals rather than companies, and voluntarily follow the restrictions introduced provincially by the Parti Québécois, and urged on the federal party by the Tory MP for Mégantic-Compton, François Gérin. Delighted at the decision, Gérin and an aide, Jacques Bouchard (no relation), moved to the riding to help organize the fundraising.

However, Bouchard discovered that there were problems. The Côté executive had resigned en masse some time before, and the new organization had little interest in absorbing other people; the prospect of a powerful minister had attracted a variety of local hangers-on. The organizers complained that the new fundraising method was too much: they could not raise money and organize a campaign at the same time.

"When Lucien Bouchard announced he was a candidate, there wasn't much enthusiasm in the organization," said François Gérin. "For all practical purposes, there was no organization. And grass-roots fundraising has one characteristic: it is based on organization. The election was called on a Friday, we arrived on the Tuesday, and by Thursday it was clear: there was no organization. Everything had to be done – and there was no extraordinary enthusiasm. The Conservatives were low in the polls, and Lucien Bouchard was not known. But we felt we absolutely had to succeed."

Jacques Brassard, the local PQ MNA, met Bouchard privately in Quebec to tell him that he was in deep trouble: what organization there was on the ground consisted of incompetents. When Luc Lavoie, who had been acting as Bouchard's chief of staff, visited the constituency, he was appalled to discover that the campaign was a shambles: the organization was rife with conflicts, and local cliques who were not on speaking terms. On the eve of the nomination meeting, they had been unable to sell tickets to the meeting, and had to appeal to Côté to sell tickets to senior-citizen homes.

Visiting Lavoie in his motel room, Bouchard was extremely upset. He realized how bad the organization was; if something wasn't done soon, he would be defeated. His Liberal opponent Pierre Gimaïel was everywhere, and very popular; he used the campaign slogan "Fidelity," and was making the barbed remark that he was faithful to his wife, his party and his region: it slyly reminded people that Bouchard's marriage had ended, he had left the PQ to become a Conservative, and left his region to go to Paris. The New Democratic Party had a strong candidate in Jean Paradis: a junior college teacher, he was the son of Maurice Paradis, the former mayor of Alma, active on environmental issues, and both well known and well liked.

Bouchard was being treated like an outsider; he was even encountering hostility on the doorstep from teachers and other public-sector employees who remembered his role in the Common Front negotiations. He was haunted by the memory of Pierre Juneau, the friend of Pierre Trudeau's who had been named minister of communications before being elected, and was subsequently defeated in a by-election in the east end of Montreal by an unknown local Conservative.

Lavoie telephoned a skeptical Bernard Roy, and told him to commission a poll now that the Liberal candidate, Pierre Gimaïel – the former MP – was known. The results were unnerving: Bouchard trailed Gimaïel by six points; they had lost 12 points in two weeks. Back in Ottawa, it was decided that Lavoie should take his holidays and move into the riding to organize the campaign as a volunteer, so that his time would not be counted as an electoral expense. Before going to Alma at the beginning of June, Lavoie spoke to Mulroney.

"Prime Minister, I've got to tell you that there's not a great deal I can do," Lavoie recalls telling him, pointing out that there were rival cliques squabbling. "I don't know people, people in Alma are very chauvinistic and suspicious of outsiders. They call me 'the guy from Montreal' – and I've never lived in Montreal. With all that [squabbling] going on, Prime Minister, I can tell you that I can't do a lot."

"Listen carefully, mon Luc, I'll explain how politics works," Mulroney said. "You take them, and name them everywhere. Give every one of them a job. Chairman of this committee, chairman of that committee, special consultative committee of legal advisers. . . . Make sure each of them can go home to his wife and say 'I'm really important to this campaign.'"

Then, Lavoie should put together a small team that would actually run the campaign.

It was revealing advice – for it was precisely how Mulroney had organized his party after he won the leadership in 1983,

how he organized his cabinet after 1984, and how he organized the 1988 election campaign. In each case, he had distributed titles, often to former adversaries, and let committees
proliferate. All the members of each group were – and, in
some cases, still are – convinced that their group provided
the crucial strategic advice, the all-important successful element, the key factor which, with the prime minister, led to
victory. And the prime minister encouraged most of the people to cherish this belief that they were very crucial, distribut-
ing photographs to people who had been with him at any
time the official photographer was on the job, each one
signed with a personal note. Because Mulroney consulted
widely, and talked to many people over the phone outside the
official campaign structure, it was hard to argue with anyone
who insisted that one committee or another played the most
important role. However, the actual group that made the key
decisions was very small.

When Lavoie got to Alma, he found Bouchard exhausted,
pale, and shaken, feeling that he had been betrayed. The Tory
posters were stacked in the committee room while Liberal
and NDP posters were all over the riding; television time had
been bought but not used; all of the radio ads had been
bought on a single station. Lavoie spent a couple of days
looking and listening, and identified six people involved in
the campaign who seemed competent and prepared to work.

Calling them to a meeting on Saturday June 4, he showed
them the latest poll; Bouchard had slipped to eight points
behind. Lavoie, Richard Leley, a friend of his in the communications business, Conservative organizers Pierre-Claude
Nolin and Paul Langlois, and the six local people set to work
to turn the campaign around in the last two weeks, when
much of the money had already been spent.

A number of key decisions were made. For the latter part of
the campaign, they would saturate the market, but spend as
little as possible. Unused TV spots were traded for new spots
at better times; photocopied pamphlets were turned out daily
and delivered door to door by volunteer cadets. Pierre-Claude
Nolin had borrowed an idea from the presidential campaign

of François Mitterrand, who had run as "le rassembleur": the man who brought people together. So they sought endorsations from figures as varied as Robert Bourassa, the PQ House Leader (a former colleague on the Cliche Commission), Guy Chevrette, the Quebec agriculture minister Michel Page, and Corinne Côté-Lévesque, René Lévesque's widow. A former federal Liberal organizer endorsed Bouchard: he was brought along, and accompanied the candidate as he campaigned.

Bouchard had begun the campaign talking about Meech Lake and free trade; he discovered that people were much more interested in what he would do for the riding. A Liberal MP, Jean-Claude Malépart, told people in the riding that they should ask Bouchard about Lac-Saint-Jean, not about Lac Meech. So Bouchard changed tacks: he began to stress the depollution of the Rivière de la Petite Décharge, promised a wharf for Sainte-Rose, and got an acceleration of approvals so that a job-creation centre could receive $1.4 million. In addition, there were longer-term projects to be considered: the $970-million Quebec-Ottawa regional development agreement was announced during the campaign, and included $120 million for the Lac-Saint-Jean area; Bouchard committed himself to a $40,000 study to look at the possibility of over $1 million in improvements to the local airport, and vowed to get a $40-million road built to the James Bay hydroelectric project. (Mulroney publicly agreed to a feasibility study, but nothing more.)

The apparent shower of money provoked hostile comment elsewhere – the Liberal research office compiled a total of $163 million in spending, promised or committed. "If you're thinking of getting a government grant or contract, you've got five days left to apply," wrote Jeffrey Simpson, a student of patronage. "And by the way, it would distinctly help your prospects if you tied the request in some fashion to the riding of Lac-Saint-Jean, Quebec." "Come buy your fresh, hot votes," editorialized the *Vancouver Sun*; the *Financial Post* called it porkbarrel politics, and wrote that Bouchard was "papering the riding with dollars." "Brave talkers huff and hug the hope that Lac-Saint-Jean cannot be bought," the editorialist wrote.

"The people will not suffer to be bribed with their own money, they cry. Of course they will. They always have, in Quebec and across the country."

However, there was no negative reaction in the riding itself. And, back in Ottawa, Tory MPs were unconcerned. Jack Shields of Athabasca had been at two large meetings in Alberta, and the question wasn't raised. "I think people understand that we have to have good representation in the caucus from Quebec," he said. "We didn't hear anything negative from Quebec members when there were massive subsidy payments to Western farmers." "What concerns me is whether he wins," said John Bosley, from Don Valley West, who speculated that people were getting used to the fact that by-elections were expensive. "If people say 'What about Toronto?' I tell them about the federal money for the art gallery, the land for the domed stadium, the expansion of Terminal One and the construction of Terminal Three [at Pearson International Airport], and the new CBC building," said Alan Redway of York East.

A key event in the campaign was Mulroney's two-day visit: first his attendance at a ceremony marking the 150th anniversary of the arrival of the first settlers, and then a whirlwind tour of the riding. Mario Tremblay, the popular former hockey player, returned to the riding to greet Mulroney outside the brasserie that bore his name (although, in fact, he no longer owned it); and, with television cameras following, Mulroney visited the Bouchard family homestead where Lucien Bouchard had been born: a way of sending out the message that he really was from the riding, even if he had worked in Chicoutimi and Paris.

The Mulroney visit changed the mood of the campaign. On June 12, during the visit, the weekly paper *Progrès-Dimanche* published a poll showing that Bouchard was trailing. This jolted both the reporters following Mulroney and the volunteers. But there was a second question in the poll which showed that Mulroney was preferred as prime minister by a margin of 5 to 1. In that context, Mulroney's all-out campaigning during his two-day trip had a considerable impact. At every stop, Mulroney stressed the question: who did they want, Mulroney or Turner? Among other things, the tour brought dozens of national reporters into the riding. Borrowing a trick from Jean Chrétien's leadership campaign, the Bouchard organization organized a meeting for the cab drivers to meet the candidate, knowing that they would be a major source of information for visiting reporters. Luc Lavoie used the Mulroney trip to make a stylish, slow-motion television advertisement to run on local TV stations, showing Bouchard with Mulroney, who appealed, as he did during the election campaign: "Aidez-moi, aidez-moi à continuer ma tâche": help me, help me continue the job.

On the last weekend, Luc Lavoie decided to pour all of the remaining money that they could into radio ads on a single rock station. It was a warm weekend late in June, and everyone in Alma took off for the beach. At two large beaches in the riding, the same rock station was used on loudspeakers. Lavoie did a saturation buy: four ads an hour for twelve hours. And Bouchard, who had had to learn the gregariousness of campaigning, spent the weekend shaking hands from beach blanket to beach blanket, pausing only to wipe the suntan oil off his hands.

By that weekend before the by-election, the team were confident they had the election won. The decision was made to organize a huge victory show. Expenses after the polls were closed were not counted as election expenses, and the spectacle would send a strong message of victory to the rest of the country. So a series of live interviews was organized on the basis of timing to the minute. But it was a gamble.

Almost immediately after the polls closed, Derek Burney was on the phone from Hart House, inquiring about the results. It became tense: the evening had been booked up with interviews, and some of the polls were slow in reporting. Finally, about 8.30, on the basis of about ten polls in ten different sectors of the riding, the organization decided unilaterally to declare Bouchard elected, and begin the series of interviews. The show began: that night, Bouchard would appear on every national network news and public-affairs program available, in French and in English. Later, Michael Adams of the polling firm Environics would conclude that a wave had begun in Lac-Saint-Jean.

———————

On Wednesday June 22, the House of Commons took the final vote on the Meech Lake Accord, which had been sent back by the Senate. In the debate on the accord, earlier in the month, Mulroney had reaffirmed his committment to it, as had Turner and Broadbent; only seven MPs voted against it this time.

The next day, on June 23, Bernard Roy announced that he was resigning as Mulroney's principal secretary. It had been a difficult four years for him: out of personal loyalty to Mulroney, he had agreed first to run the election campaign in Quebec in 1984, and then to come to Ottawa as principal secretary. He had been the best man at Mulroney's wedding, and a steadying influence on him since law school. But he had never worked in government, and he was ill at ease in Ottawa. Lawyers at Ogilvy Renault knew that Roy had no party loyalties when he went to Ottawa, and hoped this would offset Mulroney's combative political instincts; the word went around the office a year after he had left that when a partner played tennis with him, he was astonished to find that Roy had become blindly partisan. He was cherished by Mulroney and his entourage for his fierce loyalty and his integrity, but he was often the subject of criticism because of his political and administrative inexperience.

He never became accustomed to the personal attacks that seemed to come with the job; in April 1988, he initiated a libel action after an allegation by a Montreal journalist that he had tried to persuade a Montreal judge (who had subsequently died and could not comment on the allegation) to resign and make way for a new appointee. His departure had been predicted in print periodically over the previous year or two, almost certainly guaranteeing that he would stay on. But the success in the Lac-Saint-Jean by-election enabled him to leave with dignity.

CHAPTER FOUR

John Turner
Hones the Speech

"It is of the first importance to the success of a party that it should be led by someone who inspires confidence, and whose mere name is a programme in itself."

André Siegfried
1906

On Tuesday August 16, John Turner arrived in Quebec City to meet with a group of candidates and with Premier Robert Bourassa before heading to New Brunswick and Newfoundland.

It was a meeting with a certain amount of tension built in. The previous week, Turner had told the House of Commons that the Free Trade Agreement would have an impact on measures like the Quebec Stock Savings Plan, and said that Mulroney should explain this to Bourassa; Mulroney jumped on the remark as an insult to Bourassa, and "a direct attack on his credibility."

For Bourassa, who had once been humiliated by Pierre Trudeau and never forgot, this would not go uncorrected. The Quebec Stock Savings Plan, invented by the Parti Québécois finance minister, Jacques Parizeau, in 1979 to encourage higher-income earners to reduce their tax burden by investing in Quebec companies, had stimulated a new Quebec infatuation with the stock market; if it were seen to be threatened by the Free Trade Agreement, it would reflect very badly on Bourassa's judgement in endorsing the deal.

First, he said on Friday that Turner either hadn't read the agreement, or had read it absentmindedly, if he saw a threat to Quebec programs in it.

"I understand that he has not had the time to read the thousands of articles in the agreement," Bourassa said. "Perhaps he read them, and was distracted." Then, to the annoyance of federal Liberals, Bourassa agreed on short notice to a meeting with Mulroney in Montreal on Saturday and, after a ninety-minute lunch, told reporters that Turner was wrong.

"I don't want to intervene in federal politics unless I am personally involved," he said. "Mr. Turner said two, three days ago that the free-trade treaty could affect the stock-savings plan in Quebec. If Mr. Turner had taken the time to read Chapter 16 of the treaty, and sections 1608, 1609, and 1602, he would see the stock-savings plan is protected by the free-trade treaty. We have more or less a triple guarantee for that. I don't want to intervene in the federal election. But when I am personally involved, especially to re-establish the facts, I will do it."

A reporter asked Mulroney – whom David Vienneau of the *Toronto Star* described as looking "like the cat that swallowed the canary" – if he welcomed Bourassa's rebuke to Turner on the eve of a possible federal-election campaign.

"Premier Bourassa is a very strong advocate of the Free Trade Agreement," Mulroney said. "He has said the Free Trade Agreement is absolutely vital to the economic well-being of Quebec and he is right. I am always pleased to meet with the premier and I'd like to think he is pleased to meet with me."

"Mulroney and Bourassa then turned and looked at each other with knowing grins," wrote Vienneau.

Finally, on Sunday, Bourassa spoke to a meeting of the Quebec Liberal youth wing in Sherbrooke, and said sarcastically, "I don't have any reproach to make. Everyone sometimes makes statements which aren't quite accurate." He was interrupted by a strong burst of applause, and the president of the youth wing, Marie Gendron, told the meeting, "Mr. Bourassa is intelligent enough to know what is good for Quebec."

As David Halton of the CBC said on *Sunday Report* that night, "If that's neutrality, wow!"

Intentionally or unintentionally, Bourassa had distorted what Turner had said. Turner had based his remarks on an interpretation written for the White House. When Turner went in to see Bourassa in his office and showed him the document, Bourassa looked at the paragraph and muttered, "Merde!"

After lunch, the two men met reporters in a joint press conference; Bourassa began by saying at some length that he had "very strongly appreciated" Turner's support for Meech Lake, and that this had shown Turner's courage and clarity of thought and had contributed to the accord's acceptance in eight of the ten provinces.

Both men took some pains to stress the areas they agreed on: Meech Lake, acid rain, regional policies, and the idea of having the federal government's space agency in Montreal. However, Turner conceded differences on what he called "the Reagan-Mulroney deal." "I worked hard for the distinct society of Quebec in the rest of Canada," he said. "Now I am working for the distinct society of Canada in North America."

But the awkwardness Turner felt was evident in his choice of words, and his body language. Asked about his relationship with Bourassa, he said "on a personal level, the friendship persists" – strangely difficult words implying that it was hanging on by its fingernails. When David Halton asked him if he was worried about the impression that, despite his stated neutrality, Bourassa was closer to Mulroney than to him, Turner tried to joke: "Well, I don't know how I could get any closer to the premier without being indecent." However, he was almost recoiling from him as he said it. "Grinning and often giggling, Turner sought repeated eye contact with Bourassa," Deborah McGregor noted. "The Quebec premier would meet his gaze briefly, and then drop his eyes. His cool composure was a stark contrast to Turner's oppressive friendliness. As Turner spoke in French about being friends with Bourassa for many years, 'in good times and in bad,' Bourassa merely nodded but did not smile."

The questioning poked away at Turner's position and Bourassa's position on the Free Trade Agreement and the Quebec Stock Savings Plan, and it became clear that neither one of them had budged an inch. Bourassa made it clear that, despite his commitment to neutrality, he would feel free to intervene in the election campaign if the Free Trade Agreement were being attacked. "If I feel justified to do it, I'll do it," he said.

The joint press conference was ample proof of the difficulties that the Liberals faced in Quebec. Turner felt he had won the agreement from Bourassa that no Quebec Liberal would be penalized for working for a federal Liberal, and insisted privately that this was an important message that was sent out from their meeting. However, it was equally clear that Bourassa would take no pains to avoid embarrassing Turner, and that Turner's attacks on free trade might, at any time, unleash the premier's anger.

That night, Turner flew to Moncton, where he had dinner with George Rideout, the mayor of Moncton, and his wife Zoë, a bright, outspoken woman who had supported Turner strongly at the leadership review two years before, and was the chairman of the New Brunswick Liberal election-readiness committee.

Rideout, a relaxed and amiable lawyer, was a popular mayor, and his links with the Liberal Party were lifelong. His father had been a CNR trainmaster, a Moncton alderman, and mayor, and was elected to the House of Commons in 1962 and re-elected in 1963. In 1964, when George was nineteen, his father had died of a heart attack while coming back to Moncton from Ottawa on the train. George's mother, Margaret Rideout, had been elected in the by-election in 1964, and was re-elected in 1965 before being defeated in 1968.

John Turner had campaigned for both George Rideout's parents, and he was pleased that he was going to run –

although he had not yet announced his intention, since that would have complicated his work as mayor. The riding was angry at the Conservative government: the CN Shops had closed down, ending 1,200 jobs, and people blamed the Tory MP, Dennis Cochrane. (Earlier in the year, Mila Mulroney had been roughed up by angry demonstrators during a Mulroney visit to the city.) Rideout felt that, if he announced too early, it would be more difficult for him to lobby for alternative job-creation projects for the city.

There was another issue that had hung over the constituency for twenty years: bilingualism. "Bilingualism has been an issue in Moncton for the last twenty-five or thirty years," Rideout said later. It was in part because of the bilingualism issue that Rideout's mother had lost the election of 1968. In the years that followed that election, Mayor Leonard Jones attracted national attention by his opposition to bilingualism, becoming, in George Perlin's phrase, "a national symbol of anti-French prejudice" for refusing to allow French to be used in the municipal government, and by challenging the Official Languages Act as unconstitutional in the Supreme Court. In the 1974 election, Robert Stanfield refused to accept Jones as a Conservative candidate. This, while demonstrating his own conviction, drew attention to Conservative internal conflict on the issue.

When the debate on bilingualism revived in 1987–8 with Bill C–72, Dennis Cochrane decided to intervene. On the advice of Leonard Jones, he asked to address the English-Speaking Association, and told them of his reservation about the legislation. This solidified francophone opposition to Cochrane, and helped bring Acadians back to their traditional support of the Liberal Party. "It's bad enough to go [to the English-Speaking Association]; to ask to go is another story," said Zoë Rideout. "It was a slap in the face to the francophone community, and they wrote him off."

Worse, when C–72 came to a vote in the House of Commons, Cochrane stayed away.

That night, driving from Moncton to Cocagne, Turner talked about free trade, and the Free Trade Agreement: increasingly the centre of his political preoccupation, and the key issue with which he could attack the government. A few days before, at lunch with two old friends, he had observed that in a time of prosperity it was difficult to campaign against the government, and without free trade it would have been extremely difficult. However, he felt that with the free-trade issue, he could prevent the Tories from getting their majority, form a minority government with the support of the NDP, and have a second election to get a majority.

Sitting in the car, he made the case to me that he had made to Bourassa, and would make again and again during the campaign.

"We're not a protectionist party like the NDP," he said. "We believe in freer trade. We believe we've moved very successfully under Mr. Saint-Laurent, Mr. Pearson and Mr. Trudeau through the international GATT system to 80 per cent free trade across the border. We've always done better with the United States by cutting side deals in the international negotiations – going head to head with the strongest nation in the world, ten times stronger than we are economically, is a very dangerous game. The only reason for diverting from the multilateral technique which has been so successful for Canada was exemption from the protectionist legislation. We didn't get it: [clauses] 1902 and 1904 [in the Free Trade Agreement] make it clear. That being so, all the unilateral trade remedies are still available to the president and the Congress.

"But I said that with the responsibilities of government, we will do our best, in co-operation with the United States, to continue to reinforce the dispute-mechanism system of the GATT, to enlarge its jurisdiction to include services and agriculture, to continue within the GATT to seek out further sectoral opportunities, continue to eliminate irritants as they arise; continue to maintain our defence alliances and our environmental relations with the United States – I mean, we are strong, a strong neighbour.

"But I said to him, 'Look, when I see that we didn't get what we needed to get, namely secure access, and we gave away – we gave away energy, we gave away capital markets, we gave away investment policy, we gave away supply management in agriculture, we gave away future cultural initiatives, and we subjected ourselves to a five- to seven-year negotiation on the definition of subsidy which puts into jeopardy," and his voice rose in anger, "'*any grant, any investment initiative, any equalization payment that's not open under national treatment to an American!*' And I said, 'That's the way the Americans have interpreted it, and that's the way they're going to continue to negotiate it. And we've already thrown away the cards.'"

Turner paused and said, "That having been said, that's my side of the argument, and he understands it, I think, and he knows it's genuine."

This was the heart of Turner's argument. "I'm convinced that Canadians can be persuaded to look at the contract as a bad contract for Canada, as having been badly negotiated, and having not achieved what it was supposed to achieve, and having given away too much."

But the case had been made in the House of Commons ever since the negotiations had begun, and with great intensity since the terms of the deal had been made public. Wasn't there a danger that people could get fed up with hearing about it, and that there would be a saturation point?

Turner paused. "Well then, we're talking Canada here," he said. "If people are fed up with talking Canada, then I will have fought the Last Hurrah. But I will be able to look myself in the mirror for the rest of my life. I mean, there hasn't been a more important issue in terms of the direction of Canada since the war." He numbered off the points in his case against the deal.

"First of all, we already have 80 per cent free-trade through the multilateral system. Secondly, this is not a free-trade agreement, it's selective. Thirdly, it's not limited to trade. It goes into the economy, energy, investment, capital markets, agriculture, the whole ability of the country to sponsor future cultural initiatives, the whole ability of the country to decide the level and breadth of our social programs. So it's not a trade deal! It's a bad contract!"

Turner had come through a difficult time on other issues; in April there had been a revolt in the caucus, with eight or nine members openly calling on him to quit, and a rumour that as many as twenty-two had signed letters urging him to resign (no one knew precisely how many, except Senator Pietro Rizzuto), and the Meech Lake question had torn the party apart.

"Meech Lake was a very difficult issue for me," Turner said. "I was supporting the government, it was a change in direction for the party, and my illustrious predecessor came roaring into the battle. But frankly, on the trade issue I'm very comfortable. . . . I've done my homework, it's the issue of a lifetime, it makes the return to public life eminently worthwhile for me. I never thought that I'd have a chance to fight for Canada. Frankly, one way or the other, I can live with myself for the rest of my life, you know? One way or the other."

His voice stretched with intensity. "I *couldn't believe* that the prime minister would go through with it," he continued, panting, almost laughing with excitement. "When Simon Reisman walked away from the table I said, 'Simon's smart.' He couldn't get that secure access. He knew that Congress would not yield its jurisdiction on the unilateral remedies, the Trade Act of 1930, 1974, and the Omnibus Bill. And they *didn't* yield! And [Texas Democratic Senator] Lloyd Bentsen *told* me they wouldn't yield! And the *Republican* senators told me they wouldn't yield! And the congressmen on both sides said, 'We will never yield jurisdiction over these remedies.' And without that concession in jurisdiction, without the exemption, without some secure access, there wasn't any way I'd support it. I couldn't *believe* I'd be given the issue!"

Turner was chuckling, panting with excitement, with desire to connect and be understood. But he was well aware that he faced a substantial problem. The issue was thorny, difficult, complex, and hard to convey on television. Television is a medium of emotion, and would convey the emotion he generated; it was hard to convey the lengthy argument he had developed.

"You see the difficulty of trying to communicate this through Question Period in a thirty-to-sixty-second clip," he said. "I can't do the job – although I got it down to a fifteen-minute video – but you can't get it under fifteen minutes. You can't do it under that and do justice to it. In the House of Commons, I'll be speaking for an hour and a half. And I'm not using many extra words. I'm *honing* down and *honing* it down."

When he arrived in Cocagne, Turner had an hour or so to relax before giving a speech to a hall full of Fernard Robichaud's constituents in the small town on the coast. He sat in an easy chair on the lawn in front of the motel where they had stopped to give the two reporters following him a chance to file their story, and gave George Rideout some advice. Never talk about the Free Trade Agreement, he said. Call it the Reagan-Mulroney Trade Deal.

That evening, Turner gave his speech on free trade: striding about the stage with a hand-held microphone, switching easily from English to French and back, pouring out his conviction that this was a bad deal. He had the advantage and the disadvantage of having embarked on a moral crusade. The advantage was that it gave him moral fervour, intensity, and eloquence that he had not had in the past. But there were disadvantages as well. His very intensity could betray him: it could render him obsessive, and limited; it could capture people, but it could also fail to capture them, or fail to convince them that John Turner could govern the country effectively.

Nevertheless, he was impressive: relaxed, articulate, focused. Local reporters came up to me and said, "Is he always this good? Wow!" That night, Turner flew to St. John's in a private jet loaned to him for the occasion. Satisfied after a good day, he relaxed and told political anecdotes that stretched back over more than thirty years of political experience, conveying some of the pleasure that politicians feel in understanding the motivations of their colleagues on the public stage.

John Napier Turner was born in Richmond, Surrey, England, on June 7, 1929. His brother Michael had died as an infant, and in 1933, shortly after his sister Brenda was born, his father, Leonard Turner, died. Phyllis Turner, who had interrupted a Ph.D. at Bryn Mawr to marry after getting her M.A. in economics, had nothing; it was the depths of the depression, and she returned home to Rossland, B.C., with two children under five, before gambling that she could get a job as an economist at the Tariff Board in Ottawa, and heading off with her children, without enough for the return fare. She joined the Tariff Board, where she eventually rose to be the chief economist, and the most senior woman in the public service.

She was ambitious for her only son; when he was eleven, she sent him to Ashbury College, and then, when she couldn't afford the fees, to St. Patrick's College, where he was regularly beaten up for wearing a sports jacket to school. Turner's was an upbringing full of contradictions: privilege and insecurity, success and fragility, membership and exclusion. Like many other Canadian politicians (Pierre Trudeau, René Lévesque, Gérard Pelletier, Jean Marchand, Frank Miller) he had grown up fatherless; in addition, he had a strong-willed, successful mother.

Ottawa was a small town then; civil servants, like schoolteachers or clergymen, had education and a sense of vocation, but were paid little. However, Turner's mother was well known, witty, and attractive: during his teens, some of the best minds in the country who were responsible for planning the financing of the war effort, men like C.D. Howe, Robert Fowler, and Donald Gordon, would gather in her living room.

When Turner finished high school at sixteen, his mother remarried and moved to Vancouver as the wife of Frank Ross, an industrialist who later became lieutenant governor. Turner went to the University of British Columbia, where he excelled as an athlete, wrote a sports column for the *Ubyssey* ("Chalk Talk, by Chick") and was a devoted member of the fraternity Beta Theta Pi. He won a Rhodes Scholarship to Oxford, where he studied jurisprudence and civil law at Magdalen, ran, partied, met people, and had what he would later call "the whole experience."

But a fellow-student recalled a shadow over Turner's period there. "He always seemed to be filled with some kind of terrible dread of not making it, of doing or saying the wrong thing," he said years later. "He just wouldn't say anything he figured would offend." He was already developing lists, making contacts, touching base. After preparing for bar exams in London in 1952–3, Turner spent the spring and summer of 1953 in Paris, studying international law and learning French before returning to Canada and settling in Montreal. "Frank Ross, who was a friend of mine, asked me to look this young fellow over and see if I could get him through the Quebec bar," Heward Stikeman told Jack Cahill years later. "But he wasn't sure he wanted to go into law. He'd come down from Oxford with all those degrees and he wanted to be a priest. He was really serious about it, and he talked to me about it as if I was his father. He seemed to be in need of a father figure, always did, and I guess I was one of them."

Turner joined the firm of Stikeman Elliott, and succeeded in getting a private member's bill passed by the Quebec legislature, exempting him from three years of study of the Quebec Civil Code, and from the bar exams. The bill, which he asked Daniel Johnson to sponsor, brought him into contact with Premier Maurice Duplessis, who was taken with the young lawyer from B.C. who had managed to plead his case before the Private Bills Committee in French; he would see him periodically, to discuss politics. Turner emerged with a respect and an affection for the old man: probably the first element of his profound and fundamental disagreement with Pierre Trudeau. For Turner saw Duplessis as an heir of one of the two strains of thought in Quebec: the provincial view that flowed from Honoré Mercier, who became premier of Quebec in 1887, in contrast with the pan-Canadian view espoused by George-Étienne Cartier and Wilfrid Laurier.

Turner's view of Duplessis was an unusual opinion for a young Montreal Liberal. It is revealing of Turner's political roots and reflexes that he would instinctively defend Duplessis's reputation against attacks, by Pierre Trudeau among others, which he considered unfair. Turner looked to older men for guidance; he did not take kindly to those who attacked authority.

In 1962, Liberals in Ottawa saw Turner as an asset. Paul Martin had urged him to run, and Allan MacEachen, then executive assistant to Lester Pearson, the leader of the opposition, also put pressure on him. When the election was called for June 18, 1962, Turner became a candidate in St. Lawrence – St. George: a riding held by a Conservative, but where the old Liberal machine of Brooke Claxton still existed to be activated by the right candidate.

He was thirty-three – young, outgoing, handsome, charming: apparently a natural. But some of those who knew him saw a vulnerability that was not immediately obvious. "The insecurity showed in the way he tried to please everybody," Heward Stikeman remarked years later. "It showed in the way he talked jock talk to jocks, and ordinary talk to ordinary people, whereas in fact he was a highly intellectual young man. I doubted if he would be able to take tough decisions that would displease people, as he would have to do in politics. But he eventually showed I was wrong."

Turner ran a flashy, vigorous campaign, aided by lawyer friends like Jim Robb, Kenneth Mackay, and John Claxton, and a Montreal advertising man, John deB. Payne. It attracted a large number of McGill students. "We have dozens of coeds working for us, even though the campaign is during exams," one organizer said. "And you know why? Because every damn one of them would rather be Mrs. John Turner than a B.A.!" But none of them succeeded. One of the campaign workers was a systems engineer with IBM, who was installing computers at the Bank of Montreal: Geills Kilgour, a graduate of McGill, Radcliffe, and the Harvard Business School. She introduced computers to the campaign to analyse the previous election results poll by poll.

Attractive, bright, disciplined, and sometimes abrasive, Kilgour did not endear herself to all of Turner's friends, some of whom advised him against marrying her on the grounds that he would be competing with her. They were married in Winnipeg on May 11, 1963 – less than a month after he was re-elected, increasing his 2,214 vote margin of victory over Egan Chambers to 4,756 votes.

Turner was not named to the cabinet, but joined a group of Liberal backbenchers that included Herb Gray, Richard Cashin, Pauline Jewett, Donald Macdonald, John Munro, Jean-Luc Pepin, and Maurice Sauvé. Lester Pearson felt he should serve his apprenticeship, and moved him along slowly – too slowly for Turner's liking. "I had a rough time," Turner said later. "Mr. Pearson had this sort of avuncular attitude toward me. He had known me nearly all my life and he felt I was too impatient, that I needed to understand the administrative process, to be in what he called 'the kitchen of government' for a while." So he was a backbencher, and then a parliamentary secretary.

In 1965, although originally promised Resources and Energy, Turner was made a minister without portfolio. As such, he could free-wheel, and make an impression without the burden of a ministry to manage. Then, in April 1967, he was given the minor portfolio of registrar general, and in January 1968 he became the first minister of consumer and corporate affairs. He announced that Ottawa would consider overhauling its competition legislation – a task that wasn't actually accomplished until June 1986. In the words of Martin Sullivan, Turner had the job "of sounding like the champion of the underdog in consumer and corporate affairs, without actually throwing a real scare into the big corporations." He persevered. "If Turner had been nothing more than the pretty boy the backbiters said he was, he would have buckled in the early sixties," said Senator Keith Davey in 1971. "But he didn't buckle. He learned. How to be a politician. How to roll and punch and roll again. How to be a winner."

In December 1967, Pearson announced he would be resigning, and on January 17, 1968, Turner declared his candidacy for the leadership, saying, "I'm a reformer. I think there has to be a willingness to upset apple carts." But his campaign as a young reformer from Quebec was seriously undermined by the candidacy of the minister of justice, Pierre Trudeau, who caught the imagination of the party. Turner gamely told delegates that Quebec's problems would not be solved by pure logic and intellect, "but by the heart and gut – because that is what Canada's all about." He had the bad luck to speak to the convention right after Trudeau, but uttered a line that would be repeated again and again until he left politics. "I'm not just in this race so you will remember my name at some future date," he said. "I'm not here for some next time. I'm not bidding now for your consideration at some vague convention in 1984 when I've mellowed a bit. My time is now, and now is no time for mellow men."

In one of the dramatic episodes of the convention, he stayed on to the final ballot, finishing third.

The constituency of St. Lawrence – St. George disappeared with redistribution, and Turner decided to leave Quebec and run in Ottawa-Carleton. In the 1968 election, he won his seat handily; on July 5, he was sworn in as minister of justice.

In this capacity, he continued the transformation of judicial appointments that had begun under Trudeau, naming judges from all three parties and from the best law schools, established the Law Reform Commission, and drew to Ottawa lawyers he called "young tigers, guys between twenty-five and thirty-five, who are old enough to have made their mark and young enough to still have their juice." He was justice minister when the War Measures Act was proclaimed in October 1970, and he introduced the Public Order (Temporary Measures) Act that replaced it in December. Nevertheless, in

1971 an admiring Brian Mulroney commented, "Turner's so smooth, he's never made a mistake that anybody can pin on him."

At the same time, those who came to know him could sense the insecurity, the hunger, the desire for approval. One civil servant who was impressed by him was reminded of an anxious boy trying to please adults; friends were often exasperated at his tendency to pump their hands or make speeches at them as if they were constituents, ascribing this habit to shyness rather than vanity. Again and again, over the years, the same observations about insecurity and desire to impress recur in the comments friends have made about Turner.

During the years he was justice minister, he did a lot of his most important work behind the scenes, smoothing Liberal feathers that Trudeau had ruffled, or dealing with provincial premiers and ministers who couldn't stand Trudeau or Marc Lalonde, or bilingualism. He negotiated with the provinces over the Official Languages Act and the constitutional reform that became the Victoria Charter. In doing so, he struck a deal with W.A.C. Bennett: in exchange for accepting bilingualism in the Victoria Charter, a British Columbia judge would be named to the Supreme Court. In 1973, when Trudeau reneged on the deal, Turner flew to British Columbia to break the news to Bennett, and never forgave Trudeau.

In 1972, Turner moved to the Finance Department, where he struck up a friendship with the deputy minister, Simon Reisman. In his first budget, Turner slashed the corporate tax rate from 49 per cent to 40 per cent – the basis for NDP Leader David Lewis's "corporate welfare bums" campaign in the 1972 election. The Liberals lost their majority, and Turner spent the next two years as finance minister of a minority government negotiating its existence with the NDP or the Conservatives. In February 1973, he presented a budget that deftly zigzagged between the opposition parties; by skilful manoeuvring, he kept the corporate tax cuts, and avoided a defeat of the government on the budget. Then, in May 1974, he presented a budget the New Democrats could not support, precipitating an election in which the Liberals returned with a majority.

In the fall of 1974, Turner attempted to negotiate voluntary restraints in wages and prices, but felt he failed because of lack of support from Trudeau. "I was bitterly disappointed because I thought we had an incomes-control situation, which would have started putting a cap on inflation," he said in 1984. "So I wasn't being backed up by the prime minister in that, and I wasn't being backed up by the prime minister on spending control." On March 31, 1975, frustrated that Finance was losing the battle to stop social programs being introduced, Simon Reisman resigned as deputy minister. In an unusual gesture, Turner wrote an article for the *Ottawa Citizen*, praising Reisman for his competence, his non-partisan political awareness, and his loyalty: a subtle message to Ottawa that Finance was being undermined by the advisers around Trudeau.

Less than six months later, on September 10, 1975, Turner went to see Trudeau about the conflict that was dividing Finance and the PMO, by all reports hoping that he would be asked to stay on in another portfolio. Casually, Trudeau accepted his resignation, and wondered if he wanted an appointment to the bench or the Senate. Furious, Turner left in a rage, citing personal reasons for his departure. The two men would not speak for nine years.

In 1976, Turner resigned his seat in the House of Commons and moved to Toronto, buying a house in Forest Hill for $265,000 and joining the law firm of McMillan Binch. For the next eight years, he would work as a corporate lawyer, helping negotiate deals involving the Royal Bank, the bail-out of Massey-Ferguson by the banks, and the reorganization of Sandoz Canada Inc., the Canadian subsidiary of a Swiss multinational. He was the strategist, working on the big picture. At the same time, he joined the boards of directors of companies like Canadian Pacific Ltd., Crown Life Insurance Co., Bechtel Canada Ltd., Seagram Co. Ltd., MacMillan Bloedel Ltd., and Massey-Ferguson.

His conservatism became more evident, as he criticized the government's spending, and argued for a moratorium on social programs; his differences with Pierre Trudeau on Quebec and the constitution, shrouded by cabinet solidarity for ten years, emerged after the victory of the Parti Québécois in November 1976. He told the Canadian Club in March 1977 that Canada had "a valid option – the option of decentralizing or at least rearranging our administration and even our constitution. . . . I believe we must contemplate giving more powers and responsibilities, not solely to Quebec under some form of special status, but to all the provinces." It was a remark which helps explain his later support for Meech Lake.

During the years Turner was in Toronto, a healthy myth began to develop that Turner was biding his time and waiting for Trudeau to leave. His comments criticizing the Liberal government, his reserved table at Winston's, his occasional speeches – all contributed to the impression that Turner was poised, his political reflexes and his pan-Canadian network tuned and ready. But in 1979, when Pierre Trudeau announced that he would be stepping down, although there was automatic speculation that Turner would run, those who were with him at the time immediately sensed that he would not.

"I looked at him, and I went home and I said to myself, 'This guy isn't going to run – and it's nothing to do with the intellect. There's just a body rejection; [he] just does not want to gear himself up,'" William Macdonald, his partner at McMillan Binch, said later.

The morning after the announcement that Trudeau was resigning, Turner bumped into the Montreal lawyer Stanley Hartt – who as a student had worked on Turner's campaign in 1962. They talked for an hour about it, and Turner said he would have to be asked to run; he was making big money, he enjoyed it, he was building up an estate for his children; he would have to be asked in a way that made it impossible to refuse. It would have to be said to him that it was his duty to the country, that his talents and contributions were coming together, and his leadership abilities were needed.

When the Clark government fell, Trudeau was persuaded to reverse his decision to resign; he came back and won the 1980 election. No one would say those things to John Turner for another four years. In the meantime, Turner was on a short list to succeed Ian Sinclair as chief executive officer of Canadian Pacific. However, he was not chosen.

In the winter of 1984, when Trudeau resigned a second time, the call to return to politics came. But Turner was more reluctant and less eager to run than any reporter had imagined; at one point he grumbled, "I hope you guys realize the sacrifice I'm making, and I hope the country realizes it." The contacts, the machine, and the political skills were rustier than any of his friends had realized. John Swift, a former Turner aide practising law in Vancouver, could come up with only 23 names of the vaunted 195 Club – the faithful who had voted for him on the final ballot at the 1968 leadership convention. The problem was amplified because Turner ordered his friends not to do anything to prepare for his candidacy. But little of this was visible; Turner's misgivings remained private, and his supporters continued to assume that both his candidacy and his victory were inevitable. On March 16, 1984, he declared – and the organization had to be built from scratch.

The initial organizational problems were considerable. "The general feeling after three or four weeks was that the campaign was in chaos," recalled Doug Frith, the Sudbury MP who became involved with the campaign. "In the first few weeks of April, what should have been a sure thing had become quite uncertain." So the day-to-day responsibility for running the campaign was taken away from Heather Peterson, and Bill Lee was brought in as co-chairman. "It was pretty brutal," Frith said. "The way she was removed was the beginning of a pattern that repeated itself every three weeks or so for the next four and a half years."

The pattern was unsettling. Turner seemed to have lost the capacity he had been noted for in the 1960s and 1970s, of attracting and reciprocating loyalty. To those who had known him in his golden period as a minister, he seemed less civil, less sensitive; the self-assurance had become arrogance, and the unerring human touch was gone. He was no longer surrounded with people as bright and aggressive as the aides like Irwin Cotler, Lloyd Axworthy, and Jerry Grafstein who had worked for him as a minister, or the civil servants like Simon Reisman. Time after time, Turner would either choose people who were inappropriate or choose appropriate people and then withdraw from them, listening to advice from others. (Ultimately, it didn't matter whether they had been appropriate or not; the effect was the same.)

He had also lost some important political skills, or allowed them to get rusty. He proved to be ill at ease in the thickets of microphones; he had acquired an awkward tic of clearing his throat constantly during speeches; and he had lost his political sensitivities. He had always instinctively been more sympathetic to a provincialist view of the country than Pierre Trudeau, but he was obviously unprepared for the outrage his remark provoked when he said that he agreed in principle with Quebec's language law, and that language was a provincial responsibility. Those who were not upset by the remark were upset when he backed away from it.

As a ritual of succession, the leadership convention was full of revealingly awkward moments: the palpable tension between Trudeau and Turner; the stunningly inappropriate but quite accurate characterization of Jean Chrétien as second on the ballot but "first in our hearts." Without affection or conviction, Liberals had chosen John Turner for one reason only: in a climate of public restlessness about a faded Liberal government and a growing sense that the party had run out of strong ideas and people, there was a belief that Turner, and only Turner, could keep them in power. In fact, as Turner himself knew, it was a long shot. His decision to run had been shaped by his inability to refuse to respond to the call of duty more than his opportunism. Had he been more of an opportunist, he would not have let himself get so out of touch.

Then, exhausted from the leadership campaign, Turner made a series of decisions that would transform his leadership of the party and doom his leadership of the country. For, as Jeffrey Simpson wrote, "He was dealt a bad hand and played it poorly, turning a probable loss into a massive rout. Mr. Turner erred in almost every important strategic and tactical decision he made."

He agreed to the list of appointments presented to him by Pierre Trudeau ("Turn away when I tell you this, because you're going to vomit," he told an aide after the meeting), and he reappointed the bulk of the Trudeau cabinet, failing to name more than four new faces. This gave the impression to Turner supporters that he had allowed himself to be bullied by Chrétien and Lalonde. Young MPs who had worked very hard for him, like James Peterson, Dennis Dawson, and Gilbert Parent were stunned when they were passed over, and most of the tired veterans of the Trudeau era were re-appointed.

Then he decided upon an early election rather than waiting until fall. Turner was caught by the opportunism of his colleagues; when he had announced, he was the candidate for change, and a new direction in the party and in government, and Jean Chrétien was the candidate of continuity; however, so many Trudeau cabinet ministers endorsed him as leader that he became the force of continuity, and Chrétien was transformed into a minority voice for liberal reform. As Angus Reid pointed out to him during the campaign, this became further accentuated in the election.

Then, in the campaign, the errors proliferated. While Brian Mulroney was conciliatory towards Quebec nationalism, Turner denounced the Tories for having candidates who voted yes in the referendum; while Mulroney quickly apologized for saying "there's no whore like an old whore," Turner didn't seem to understand how offended women were when he patted Iona Campagnolo's rear end, and only lamely apologized after the disapproval and mocking laughter had become deafening. In the English TV debate, his head ringing with conflicting advice, he made the grave mistake of challenging Mulroney on the question of patronage, and could only stammer when Mulroney lashed out at him in one of the most dramatic incidents of the campaign. Finally, when the internal tensions in the campaign had become overwhelming, he replaced Bill Lee as campaign director and brought back Keith Davey, the symbol of Trudeau Liberalism – the "rainmaker" Turner had insisted he would never rely on. It didn't work. It was unclear whether the voters of Vancouver Quadra had eased or added to his humiliation by electing him. The Liberals suffered the worst defeat in their history.

Politics had changed in the nine years that John Turner had been away. The House of Commons was no longer as important, and television was much more important than had been the case. However, Turner behaved as if he had been away longer than nine years. He talked about the changes as if television had not been present when Pierre Trudeau was prime minister and he was a minister, as if he had left politics, not in 1975, but in 1965. He complained that he had given major speeches in the House, and they had not been covered; that the House would be half empty for important speeches and important debates. He was discovering that the House of Commons had become a television studio, and had lost a great deal of the importance that it had had as a place of debate in itself.

But there was another aspect to Turner's nostalgia for the days when Pearson and Diefenbaker were leaders, and the House was a more important place. It was as if he so resented Pierre Trudeau that he believed that the changes that had occurred in the political environment when he was prime minister were personal aberrations and that, once he was gone, politics would return to normal.

It didn't, and it wouldn't. Question Period was no longer primarily the forum in which the opposition held the government accountable; it was the period for the opposition to get images of indignation on television. Preparation for it was now shaped almost entirely by the desire of the opposition parties to be sufficiently dramatic in their accusations of the government to get on the evening news.

Both sides of the House knew this. Government members would hustle around to fill in the empty seats behind cabinet ministers, so as to be seen in the background of the shot; opposition members would rehearse their questions to achieve the best possible impact on television. "An angry-sounding quote makes better TV," observed the Liberal Sergio Marchi, who perfected a style of outrage and indignation. Tory MPs all received some basic training in television performance; they all knew to look at the camera, beyond the opposition hecklers, rather than turn to address the Speaker as required by parliamentary tradition.

Both Turner and Mulroney responded to this new importance of television in how they hired advisers. While many other factors came into play in the changes in the Prime Minister's Office in 1987, it is worth noting that, with the exception of L. Ian MacDonald who wrote speeches, all the other people on Mulroney's staff with newspaper experience (Bill Fox, Ian Anderson, Michel Gratton) left; the people who joined the PMO with a background in the media (Bruce Phillips and Luc Lavoie) were from television. However, despite his newspaper background, Fox had grasped the crucial importance of television. He had learned from his years in Washington, watching the Reagan White House.

Similarly, Turner began to bring people in to advise him on television. The first of these was Gabor Apor, a Hungarian-born consultant who had worked with Ontario Premier David Peterson, and was credited with the transformation of Peterson's appearance from a plump, bespectacled, nondescript-looking person to a slim, sleek, confident man in a red tie. But tensions began to develop between Apor and other Turner advisers, as he would give advice on content as well as delivery, on the message as well as how to communicate it. When Turner wavered as a result, aides would say that he had been "Gabored." Apor was first joined and then replaced by Henry Comor, who advised him on television and, more generally, on public speaking and delivery.

The next major test of John Turner's leadership would be one of the high points of his career as leader of the Liberal Party. Friends often observe of John Turner that he performs best with his back against the wall; the leadership-review vote on November 1986 was one of those occasions, and he rose to the challenge.

The most direct attack on his leadership came from Marc Lalonde, his former finance minister, who sent a four-page letter to delegates on November 11 laying out his argument that John Turner had failed to win the support of the Canadian people.

"Poll after poll has conclusively demonstrated that John Turner trails not only the other two national leaders but, as well, his own party in acceptability. There are two years remaining in the present government's mandate but there exists no indicator that would allow us to conclude, or even hope, that the present situation will improve," he wrote. "I fear that under John Turner the result of the next election will once again relegate Liberals to the opposition benches."

He then went through seven arguments put forward by Turner supporters, and dismissed each one. The danger he saw most clearly was the rise of the New Democratic Party across the country and, in particular, in Quebec. "In my opinion the future of the Liberal Party is in serious question at this time," Lalonde wrote. "I am convinced that we cannot maintain the status quo, that for the sake of the party we must have a change of leadership." Or, as he put it more bluntly at a press conference in Montreal, "Loyalty doesn't mean that you have to be dumb."

However, Turner was able to rally the party behind him. He was determined to show that politics was more than good television, that experience mattered, that a party leader could come back from political reverses and bad polls to become prime minister. "I've got to prove it," he told me in an interview on November 12, just after the Lalonde letter was made public. "Otherwise, our system is not going to work. We're going to have instant politicians and disposable leaders. George Bernard Shaw used to say that politics is the only profession in which no apprenticeship is required. I happen to think it is."

So a network of Liberals across the country was established, hardnosed organizing was mobilized, and the architects of The Friends of John Turner assumed that the organization would be the basic structure for the 1988 election. However, Turner remained nervous and suspicious. Key Turner supporters in the caucus began putting great pressure on the convention organizers to allow Turner people to be present when the vote was counted: to the extent that the co-chairmen of the legal committee, Richard Mongeau and Kathy Robinson, began to consider resigning. "I went to Turner on the Wednesday before the convention and said 'John, if you think having two co-chairmen resign on this issue and go on *The Journal* is useful, I wish you good luck,'" Doug Frith, co-chairman of the convention, told me later. "He looked at me and said 'Will they steal it from me?'"

But none of that insecurity showed, as he told the National Liberal Women's Commission that he had "come a long way for a bum-patter," called for "positive patriotism," said he didn't need a poll to tell him that there was hunger on the streets and that he wanted to end the need for food banks because it was a national disgrace. As Hugh Winsor wrote, "The convention showed he could stride instead of stagger, speak instead of stutter. It provided some tangible evidence of his victory boast that he is now ready to fight the Tories."

The convention gave Turner a sweeping endorsation of 76.3 per cent. "I've waited a long time to say this to you, John, but you're first in our hearts," Frith said. Two years later, Turner would tell the Vancouver journalist Valerie Gibson that the vote, which he saw as an endorsation of a renewal process, was the most rewarding moment of his life. The public responded: in a poll taken from December 3 to 5, Angus Reid showed the Liberals at 41 per cent, the Conservatives at 31 per cent and the NDP at 28 per cent, while a Gallup poll conducted from December 3 to 6 showed the Liberals at 45 per cent – their best showing since the election – the Conservatives at 30 per cent and the NDP at 25 per cent.

But in many ways it was a Pyrrhic victory: Turner was able neither to heal the wounds nor to reward the victors of his fight for confirmation. The general impression was that, buoyed by the endorsation, he would put his own imprint on the party and make changes in the caucus. But frustrated members sensed that, after the peak of effort that Turner had reached for the leadership review, he was drifting. The caucus divided first on the issue of cruise-missile testing in March 1987, with Lloyd Axworthy, Warren Allmand, John Nunziata, and Charles Caccia voting with the NDP, and then, more substantially, on the question of the Meech Lake Accord.

For the year preceding the Meech Lake Accord, the Liberal Party had been wrestling with how to respond to Robert Bourassa's five conditions for signing the constitutional agreement. On June 13, 1986, on the eve of the Quebec Liberal Party policy conference in Sainte-Hyacinthe, Le Devoir published an interview in which Turner, in the words of the front-page news story, "breaking with the constitutional past of his party," gave a positive response to the Bourassa position: a stance that caught English-speaking advisers and members of his caucus off guard. Depending on one's view of what emerged, Turner's position either made it harder for Mulroney to engage in any hard negotiating with Bourassa, since the Liberal premier could point to Turner's support – or easier for Mulroney to strike the deal he did, knowing that Turner had moved a long way towards support.

But Turner's decision to take a position began a see-saw struggle inside the party: a resolution passed in Sainte-Hyacinthe, a scramble to mediate between that position and the previous party position, and a compromise resolution approved overwhelmingly by the November convention.

When the Meech Lake Accord was negotiated, the French-speaking Liberal MPs for Quebec embraced it as a reflection of the spirit of the Liberal Party resolution – but Donald Johnston resigned as external-affairs critic in order to be able to attack it outright: a decision that led André Ouellet to denounce him as a Westmount Rhodesian. After trying to simultaneously congratulate Mulroney for reaching an agreement and criticize the details, Turner endorsed Meech Lake; whenever challenged privately by Liberals upset about it, he would reply that he couldn't lose his Quebec caucus. In the end, eleven Liberals – more than a quarter of the caucus – broke with him and voted against the Meech Lake Accord.

The roller-coaster continued. Seven months after the triumph of the November convention, the Liberals suffered the embarrassment of seeing the New Democratic Party win all three by-elections on July 20, 1987. Turner responded by shuffling the election-planning team. However, the party president, Michel Robert, said publicly what more and more Liberals were thinking privately: if the Liberals didn't improve, there should be a further reconsideration of Turner's future.

Each crisis provoked a flurry of activity by Turner and his staff, followed by a kind of slump – which would further disenchant those who had rallied around, because the activity had raised their expectations. This became the "August crisis": Alain Tardif, an otherwise obscure Liberal backbencher, called on Turner to resign; a special meeting was called in Ottawa which brought over a hundred Liberals to town to discuss the situation; Doug Richardson resigned as principal secretary; Sharon Schollar resigned as campaign director; party finances were in bad shape. But again, the troops rallied, and senior Liberals looked for new staff for Turner.

On September 7, John Turner drove up to Meech Lake to meet Peter Connolly, who had been recommended to him as a principal secretary. Connolly, an executive with Lavalin, was a lifelong Liberal, and the son of the late Liberal Senator John Connolly. A relaxed, easy-going man with shrewd political instincts, Connolly had grown up with much of the history of the Liberal Party, and knew something of how to protect a politician, and how to do thankless jobs; he had worked on the staffs of eight ministers – most notably for Herb Gray from 1972 to 1974 and from 1982 to 1984 – and had run against Ed Broadbent in Oshawa in 1972.

Connolly had a summer cottage at Meech Lake, and came across the lake in his motorboat with his ten-year-old son, Ryan, to pick up Turner. He had talked to Herb Gray and the other members of the search committee, Gerry Schwartz and Jack Austen, and knew he would accept the job if Turner asked him to take it. But he thought, "Geez, I wish he hadn't come."

When Turner arrived, Ryan said formally, "Welcome to Meech Lake, Mr. Turner."

Turner smiled at the unintentional double-entendre and said, "What am I doing here, Ryan?"

Although he had been involved with the party in one way or another since his youth, Connolly did not, in fact, know Turner well; he had worked for ministers who were on the social-policy side when Turner was trying to cut expenditures as finance minister. But as they drove across the lake Connolly was taken with him. When they relaxed on the dock back at Connolly's cottage, the phone rang; it was Doug Kirkpatrick in Sault Sainte-Marie, where he was with David Peterson's campaign tour, calling to see if he could borrow the cottage to recover from the Ontario election. Turner answered the phone, and when he passed the phone to Connolly, Kirkpatrick – who had recognized Turner's voice – said immediately "Omigod. When do I start?"

Connolly agreed to take the job (although he had been able to make a long list of reasons why he shouldn't, and only one reason why he should) and did hire Kirkpatrick as his assistant. Connolly immediately decided that Turner's environment had to have more order to it, and began to organize how people got to see him. At the same time a national campaign committee was put together, and a policy process to prepare for the election.

While controlling access to Turner made the leader more comfortable, it made people who had been able to see him easily before very frustrated. People in his office began to talk about an "iron curtain"; senior officials in the party began to complain that they couldn't get to see him alone. The disenchantment grew again. In the fall and early winter, two things occurred that lost him the support of two people who had been strongly loyal: Doug Frith, who had been given responsibility for the campaign in Ontario, discovered only when a reporter told him that this responsibility had been removed; Jean Lapierre, who had been persuaded to take the job of campaign director for Quebec against his preference, had the job taken away and given to a former MP, Rémi Bujold.

There was a rift in the party in Quebec over Raymond Garneau's leadership, and there were rumours of more protracted grumbling when a number of Liberals got together at Senator Pietro Rizzuto's hotel in Puerto Vallarta at the New Year. On March 7, the rumours of financial trouble in the party became more concrete when Michel Robert refused to meet reporters after an executive meeting. That night, CBC-TV's *The National* presented a story with devastating images of the camera travelling down empty hallways seeking a party president who had apparently fled. The strong impression was that the Liberal Party and its leadership were penniless, furtive, and confused.

By the spring of 1988, sixteen months after the 1986 convention, most of the key people who had worked together to reconfirm Turner's leadership had either left, or become disillusioned. Terry Popovitch could not accept Turner's support of Meech Lake (and his firing from the Toronto Stock Exchange for lying on his résumé blighted his political future); Jean Lapierre was angry about the way he had been treated; Doug Richardson had resigned and gone back to Saskatchewan; Michel Robert was bitter and resentful. Doug Frith had announced that he would not be running again.

In April, Turner's mother died, after several years of slow decline from Alzheimer's. "My mother had not been actually present in life for the last five years," he said later. "I'm sure there was a certain serenity in her life during this time, but she wasn't able to communicate it. Nor were my sister and I ever convinced that the ultimate recognition . . . ever happened." Her decline into emptiness and death had been a strain on him; some friends thought that only her death would really free him.

When Turner flew out to Vancouver to bury his mother, two members of caucus came out to pay their respects: Jean-Claude Malépart and Raymond Garneau. It was a significant gesture on Garneau's part; one of the first things that Quebec Liberals had identified as a political gaffe by the former Quebec Liberal leader Claude Ryan was his failure to attend Garneau's mother's funeral. Those present were moved at

Turner's dignity and grace, standing at the door to greet everyone who came to the church, and shaking hands with everyone at the graveside.

At least one of Turner's friends had warned him that his opponents in the party would try one more time before the end of June, seeing this as the last chance to get him to step down before the election. But no one had expected that it would happen when he was still in mourning.

On Thursday evening, April 21, Turner got back to Ottawa from Vancouver. On Friday, Doug Kirkpatrick sensed there was something going on, but nothing tangible he could identify. Later, he would remember people being reluctant to look at him in the eye, shuffling their feet and looking at the floor. Something was odd, but he was too tired from the emotional trip to Vancouver to put his finger on what. On Monday, April 25, he found out.

There was something going on, aimed at the caucus. Piertro Rizzuto called Turner during dinner to see if he could see him right away. Turner wanted to wait until the next day, but Rizzuto insisted it was urgent. Turner told him to come at 8.30.

"He said he had 21 or 22 letters from members of parliament calling on me to step down," Turner recalled later. "He said 'I've got the letters.' I said 'That's an extraordinary procedure. I'll respond to you in the morning, Senator, I just want to do a little checking around.' It was a very short meeting."

Turner telephoned Doug Kirkpatrick and Scott Shepherd of his office, Herb Gray, Jean-Robert Gauthier, and Brian Tobin. (Peter Connolly's phone was out of order, and he couldn't be reached.) He made it bluntly clear that there was no way he would resign, and asked them to check around and get a reading of the situation.

He never saw the letter, a two-paragraph statement that the party could not win under his leadership. It complained about his position on Meech Lake, and the difficulties the party was having raising money, and suggested that he meet with the caucus to plan a leadership convention. The next morning, Tuesday April 26, the group sounded out the caucus to gauge the seriousness of the situation. It was immediately clear that it was more than just a threat; it was real. Rizzuto had letters, undated, on plain paper. However, Turner decided he did not want to see them, saying he did not want to put anyone in a position they could not retreat from. The decision was taken to make the caucus meeting a special session, and for Turner to see MPs individually later.

The first instinct of the group was to keep a lid on the whole affair until the caucus meeting on Wednesday morning. However, by accident, a *Globe and Mail* reporter in Montreal heard that something was afoot, and notified Toronto, who passed the news to the Ottawa bureau. The consensus of the group remained intact, but when one of the aides in Turner's office began to get phone calls from the *Globe* Ottawa bureau, the decision was made to spread the news more widely.

That night at Stornoway, phone calls began to come in, including a call from David Peterson, and from Liberals across the country offering him support. The next morning in the Wednesday caucus, a number of the dissidents spoke directly: Senators Gigantes and Watt, Russ MacLellan, David Dingwall, Charles Caccia, Alfonso Gagliano, John Nunziata, Carlo Rossi, Sergio Marchi, and Lucie Pépin.

Some like Caccia, were angry about a wide range of issues; others, like MacLellan, were upset about the rumours of Turner's personal spending; others complained Turner was inaccessible; still others simply felt that he couldn't win. The rivalries in Quebec, the party's financial crisis, and the tensions over Meech Lake were all additional factors.

During the caucus, Connolly and Kirkpatrick circulated among the waiting reporters, saying that the party would emerge stronger from this, and that exactly this kind of challenge had occurred under Pierre Trudeau's and Lester Pearson's leadership. They circulated the fact that Liberal Premiers Frank McKenna, Joe Ghiz, Robert Bourassa, and David Peterson had sent messages of support. The caucus broke for Question Period, Turner went to speak to the Canadian Federation of Labour, and the caucus returned for a continuation of the discussion on into the evening. At the end, Turner rose to address the caucus.

"This caucus is the place for this type of discussion, not letters to the leader through an intermediary," he said. "This caucus discussion should stay here, and remain here. I've never held it against a member of parliament or a senator nor will I now, for anything that's said in this room. That's what caucus is about. As a matter of fact, for those of you who got up, it took a lot of guts. I have seen no letters, nor do I want to."

"Why this challenge now?" he asked. "We have got momentum going for us. We had a tremendous convention in Windsor, a tremendous convention in Montreal."

Turner had had a long standing ovation at the Ontario convention in Windsor, and in Montreal had responded to questions in French for two hours and got another long standing ovation. He pointed this out, and pointed to the party's position in the polls, where it was doing well, at 42 per cent.

"Why now?" he asked, quoting David Peterson as having said publicly that it was political suicide. The divisions in the caucus were hurting them in the polls and hurting fundraising, and the party was incensed.

"Now, look," he continued. "I am also speaking on behalf of democratic legitimacy. I was elected at an open convention of this party, I was reconfirmed at an open convention of this party. Therefore, my mandate is from the party. And the reciprocal duty I bear is to the party. More than that, in political terms, I am the one lynch-pin holding this party together on two very divisive issues: Meech Lake, and trade. And I ask any of you to contemplate what would happen if I were driven out on either of those issues.

"The future effect of this exercise on the party is in your hands," he concluded. "I've made up my mind; you have to make up your minds. Now, before you leave this room. Because we can't afford these public divisions a moment longer."

"They know I'm staying, they know I'm leading," Turner told reporters afterwards. "I expect the caucus to follow."

After the meeting, Jean Lapierre emerged expressionless, saying there were things between him and Turner that would never become public, "I've got to collect my thoughts," said Sergio Marchi. "We'll see what happens." Charles Caccia, furious, waved his finger at Connolly and Kirkpatrick, and shouted "You bastards! This wouldn't have happened if you hadn't leaked this!"

The crisis was over; the coup attempt had failed. But it was a double failure: it had not succeeded in persuading Turner to step down, and it helped ensure he could not win.

One of the problems that the Liberals had stemmed from Turner's dramatic statement on October 26, 1987, in the debate on the Free Trade Agreement: "We did not negotiate the deal, we are not bound by the deal, we will not live with this deal, and if the deal and the final contract reflects the principles and the general terms of the agreement we have seen, we are going to tear the deal up." It was graphic, dramatic, and, for many Liberals who favoured free trade and respect for signed international agreements, highly unnerving. When Turner made the statement, Mulroney turned to Mazankowski, sitting beside him in the House, and said, "This guy is gone. He's finished. He can't win an election."

In May, coming back from a trip, Turner began to muse about how to stop the free-trade deal. "We could never ask the Senate to block this, but if we used the Senate to get an election, that would be very different," Peter Connolly recalls his saying. Turner felt that the trade issue would be a more effective theme for the election if the deal had not been ratified; moreover, if it were not ratified, he would not have to tear anything up.

Connolly took this idea to a strategy committee which he and Michael Kirby chaired, and, after a brief chat with Connolly, Kirby had a series of lengthy meetings with André Ouellet, Herb Gray, Allan MacEachen, and Lloyd Axworthy. They unanimously agreed on the strategy options, which Kirby laid out in a memo to Turner on June 9.

"Broadly speaking, there are two broad options the Liberal Party could adopt with respect to the Trade Bill," Kirby wrote. "They are:

" – OPTION ONE: To use every means possible to prevent the Trade Bill from becoming law before the public has given the government a mandate to implement the Canada-U.S. Trade Agreement.

" – OPTION TWO: To allow the Trade Bill to pass after vigorous opposition in the House and Senate and to fight a spring election with the Bill in place."

Kirby then described the details of what was involved in pursuing the first option – which had the unanimous support of all those he had consulted.

"The primary danger in this option is that the issue in the ensuing election campaign becomes the anti-democratic nature of the appointed Senate versus the legitimacy of the elected House of Commons," Kirby wrote. "If this is the issue in the election campaign, it will cause the Liberal Party enormous difficulty."

Kirby proposed a way to make the issue free trade and Turner's strong leadership rather than the Senate's abuse of power.

"Under this scenario, you would state publicly (at a date to be decided, but sometime before Labour Day), that in view of the fact that the Prime Minister stated in 1983 that he was opposed to free trade, that the government did not mention free trade in its 1984 election platform, that free trade will have a dramatic and irreversible impact on the nature of Canada and of Canadian society, and the fact that a majority of Canadians want an election on free trade before it becomes law, you have told the Liberal dominated Senate to ensure that the Bill is not passed until after an election is held," he wrote. "This scenario envisages you telling the Prime Minister point blank that you will not let him have his Trade Bill until he has a mandate for it. You would also tell the Prime Minister that, nevertheless, he can still meet his January 1st deadline by calling the election now. If he wins a majority, then the Liberals in the House and Senate will give him the Trade Bill in time for implementation by January 1st.

"Essentially you would be saying to Canadians that you will give them a chance to tear up the agreement if that is what they want done with it."

He then listed the advantages of this approach:

" – Overnight you are seen as a gutsy, strong leader; you are clearly in charge; you are calling the shots in the House *and* in the Senate;

– you are also seen as someone who is confident about winning the election and consistent in taking tough stands on issues you really believe in;

– you have set the election agenda, and in all likelihood, the timing of the election campaign; you have virtually called the election;

– you have launched a bold stroke; one which is easy to communicate; one which puts you nose-to-nose with Mulroney;

– Ed Broadbent becomes irrelevant; under this option, the issue would be a gunfight between two players, not three;

– because of the sovereignty aspects of the deal, it is likely that there will be some movement from the NDP to the Liberals during the campaign;

– for the first time, you will own the Liberal Party *emotionally*; you will have given them a *cause* to fight for;

– the trade issue is one you are extremely comfortable with; as a result, under this option, your performance in the campaign will be stronger and more convincing than under any other scenario I can foresee;

– under this option, the issues of the campaign become:
  – free trade;
  – Canadian sovereignty;
  – strong leadership;
  – your *vision* of a sovereign Canada versus all of Mulroney's weaknesses."

The disadvantages that Kirby described were the probability that the Conservatives would try to make the undemocratic Senate the issue, to which he suggested that the response be that the decision was based on the democratic idea that the people had a right to vote on the trade issue before it became law. The Conservatives would try to use what Kirby called "the politics of fear," saying that the Americans would retaliate if Canada backed out; Kirby suggested a two-fold response: first, that this shows that the agreement was negotiated out of fear, and second, that the Americans have always believed in democracy and would accept rejection of the Agreement in an election.

Kirby foresaw some objection from the caucus, but argued that this could be overcome with support from the right people. He felt the resistance would be strongest in Quebec, where many MPs believed that the deal should be allowed to pass because of its evident popularity in Quebec. But Ouellet felt that, provided Meech Lake had passed the House of Commons before the writs were issued, there would be no negative impact. Kirby agreed, and added, "it should be remembered that Quebecers, more than residents of any other province, like a strong leader, and if Option 1 is adopted it is a superb example of strong leadership."

In his description of Option 2, Kirby said that in order to soften the fear issue, Liberals could say that they would attempt to renegotiate the parts of the deal that "strike at the heart of Canadian sovereignty or autonomy," a position that they could defend because the next administration could be expected to be less ideological than the Reagan administration.

"The difficulty with proceeding in this way is that the Conservatives, and the media, will say once again that you have changed your mind and that you are not willing to follow through with your commitment to tear up the Agreement," he wrote. "Thus you will look like a weak, uncommitted leader in spite of your pledge to tear up the Agreement. *This strategy reinforces the current public perception of you.*" (Emphasis in original)

Kirby said that all those he consulted unanimously supported Option 1, and laid out the procedures for implementing it, and the likely reactions to it. He expected that Mulroney would not respond by challenging them to an immediate election, but would delay, which he said would make him look like a very weak leader. He concluded with a final thought: everyone he had consulted had an instinctive, emotional reaction in favour of Option 1.

"Herb Gray put it best when he said at the end of our meeting that he had 'an instinctive *leap of enthusiasm* in favour of Option 1,'" Kirby wrote. "The people I consulted are like the audiences you speak to who come off their chairs in reaction to the line that 'Mulroney wants to be the governor of the 51st state and you want to be Prime Minister of Canada.' Fundamentally, it is this emotional response which makes Option 1 best, and why this line of yours quoted above should be the theme of the campaign."

Turner took the memo with him, when he went on holiday to Lake of the Woods on July 1, and also the policy documents that had been prepared by Patrick Johnston and Manon Vennat from the Liberal policy conferences. When he got back, he wrote a letter asking that Robert Jackson, the Carleton political scientist who had been providing policy advice, prepare campaign documents based on the policy directions that had been laid out by Johnston and Vennat. He also had Connolly and Kirkpatrick summon a meeting of key people to discuss the Senate strategy. They invited eleven others to join them at Stornoway on Tuesday July 19 for dinner: Senator Jack Austen, Raymond Garneau, Senator Alasdair Graham, Herb Gray, Robert Jackson, Michael Kirby, André Ouellet, Allan MacEachen, Gerry Schwartz, Brian Tobin, and John Webster.

There, Turner laid out the idea that he would announce that he was asking the Senate to delay passage of the trade bill until after an election, using the theme "Let the people decide." He listened as the different people at the table put forward their reaction. After worrying the issue like a bone, a consensus emerged that it would be a good idea. The next question was timing. A similar consensus emerged that it would be a good idea to wait for a couple of weeks.

"Well, gentlemen, I've heard you all tell me this was a good idea," Turner said. "If this is such a good idea, and we can all agree, we'll do it tomorrow. Go home and get your sleep."

The next morning, on July 20, before caucus, he was going over what he intended to say with Henry Comor, who said, "I have to tell you, I think this is a stupid idea."

Taken aback, Turner told this to Connolly, who said "You've just been Gabored." Reassured, Turner went over to caucus to tell them the plan. They would, in effect, be calling the election, but the people would be deciding the trade issue. At the end of the caucus meeting, Brian Tobin summed up by saying that, as far as he could see, the reaction was unanimous. The Senate gambit had been taken. At a news conference after caucus, Turner said that when the Conservatives were campaigning in the 1984 election, Mulroney and several ministers were opposed to free trade.

"They have no mandate, the Canadian people have had no warning, and the House of Commons has been railroaded," he said.

Mulroney was unconcerned. He had already decided that the election should be called after free trade passed the House, but before it was enacted into law. In that context, he saw Turner's gambit as a bonus that played to his weaknesses.

"The fact that Mr. Turner decided to resign his leadership, to surrender in favour of Allan MacEachen, doesn't change anything," he told reporters. That afternoon, he took his son Nicolas to see *Bambi*.

But for Ed Broadbent the move posed a problem. The NDP opposed the deal, but it also opposed the Senate. Turner was using the system to try to stop the deal, and Broadbent seemed to waver. On Friday, June 22, he told reporters that Turner was acting in a "seriously anti-democratic" manner.

"We have opposed this deal from day one, but we have remained democratic," he said. "Mr. Turner has clearly decided the end does justify the means and is prepared to abandon democracy. We are not."

It was an awkward position to take, and difficult to explain. Within a week, it was clear that the Liberals had succeeded in seizing the initiative on the trade issue. In a poll for the *Toronto Star* and Southam News, released on July 29, Angus Reid found that 58 per cent of those polled supported Turner's objective, and that 69 per cent agreed that Mulroney should call an election before the end of the year. If an election were called immediately, and free trade were the issue, the Tories would receive 40 per cent of the vote, the Liberals 39 per cent, and the NDP 20 per cent. The momentum had shifted.

The move certainly laid the groundwork for making free trade the central issue in the election, and when Turner travelled to St. John's and drove on to Carbonear, it was just as clear as it had been in Moncton that this was the central theme of his personal message. But the questions from reporters in Carbonear revolved much more around whether Turner would continue support for Hibernia. (He stressed that the government had only achieved an agreement in principle.) In Carbonear, the leading candidate for the Liberal nomination was Admiral Fred Mifflin, and Turner pointed him out to the luncheon audience; one of the expectations in the riding was that the Mulroney government would announce a penitentiary to be built nearby in the hope of saving the seat, held by a popular former sealing captain, Morrissey Johnson. According to local Liberals, Johnson had received a lot of votes from people who believed that Captain Morrissey, as he was universally called, would bring back the seal hunt; there was considerable disappointment that he had been unable to do so.

A few weeks later, Allan Gregg made a strategic appraisal of what the Liberals were likely to do, and, on August 10, sent a memo to Lowell Murray, Norman Atkins, Derek Burney, John Tory, Nancy Jamieson and Tom Scott.

"Given John Turner's uniformly [in fact, Gregg spelt it uniformally] poor leadership scores, the Liberals face a major strategic challenge – namely, to ignore their leader and appeal to the Party's enduring institutional strengths: or to expose Turner at every opportunity in an attempt to exceed the exceptionally low expectations in evidence today, and thereby create momentum in their campaign through him," he wrote. "Upon reflection, the latter course, while higher risk, is probably the one they will adopt. Therefore, expect the Liberals to run a very active, Leadership oriented campaign – through news and advertising – where Turner attempts to demonstrate his assertiveness and authority."

Gregg predicted that the Liberals would position themselves as, in his words, "more practical New Democrats." He felt the Liberals had more to gain from the NDP than from the Tories, and, as he put it, "We are vulnerable on the 'softside' of the political spectrum." So he expected Liberal themes stressing nationalism, economic questions involving compassion such as illiteracy and working women, and protection questions like health and the environment.

"Implicit in this positioning will be the question 'If you're tired of this black-hearted bunch who are prepared to sell the country to business and foreign interests, we are the only practical alternatives,'" Gregg wrote. "In an even more negative sense (and especially if they start slipping in the polls) we should be expecting a very *personal* attack on the Prime Minister. This thrust would focus directly on Mulroney's integrity and trustworthiness and can also be expected to be carried through (paid) media as well as the Liberal front bench. Examples of patronage and scandal could well be 'personalized' through a focus on Mulroney's defence of the individuals involved."

On the night of August 18, Turner flew back to Ottawa for a strategy meeting with Michael Kirby, John Webster, Peter Connolly, Doug Kirkpatrick, André Ouellet, Raymond Garneau, and Martin Goldfarb. The principal purpose of the meeting was to hear Goldfarb's report on his latest polling data. Goldfarb and Kirby – who had joined Goldfarb's firm – had been pressing for a program. This was Goldfarb's evening.

Martin Goldfarb had turned fifty in the spring; he was a veteran of twenty years of being close to the Liberal Party. He had met Keith Davey at the Liberal convention of 1968 and, while he was not hired by the party until 1972, Davey had hired him as a researcher for the Senate committee on the mass media. From the beginning, Goldfarb was an activist pollster: he didn't merely give numbers, he gave advice. In 1984, Allan Gregg described the difference between Goldfarb's approach and his own as the difference between anthropology and sociology. "His approach is the anthropological one; that is, that you learn from observation. His line, and it's a fabulous one, is 'The consumer will never tell you why; he'll only give you clues why.' The creative part, the anthropological part, is to tell the client what to do, having received the clue," Gregg said. "My approach is the social-science approach; namely, that behaviour is measurable and not merely observable. It's also part of our marketing tack. No question about that. We are the counterpoint to Martin Goldfarb."

Over the previous year, Goldfarb had sensed that the sovereignty issue was on the rise. "People see a degree of sovereignty being sacrificed in the following Mulroney government concessions," Goldfarb wrote in the fall of 1987, rhyming off a series of decisions, including the dismantling of the Foreign Investment Review Agency, the end of the National Energy Program, and the decision to grant the demands of the international pharmaceutical companies. "More and more Canadians see sovereignty as the major issue in the whole free trade debate."

But in his August research, Goldfarb saw a need for the Liberals to move beyond the Free Trade issue. His numbers showed almost a dead heat: all three parties in the low 30 per cent range. But what he drew from what he called the "collective consensus" was that the public was saying "I don't know who to vote for." In his view, the public was looking for leadership.

Goldfarb presented his findings, and laid out his strategic advice based on his interpretation of the research. In his view, the research demonstrated that free trade could not carry the Liberals to victory in the election, because it did not give a clear enough indication of Turner's vision for the country.

"Free Trade should not be the central issue of the campaign," Goldfarb reported. "Free Trade should be used as a device to demonstrate that Mulroney cannot and should not be trusted. The central theme of the Liberal campaign should be that you cannot trust Mulroney. You cannot trust him on Free Trade, you cannot trust him on tax reform, you cannot trust him on patronage, and so on."

The strategy was agreed upon. Using a campaign slogan of "Don't let Mulroney deceive you again," the campaign would set out to remind Canadians of the dark side of the Mulroney government's record, and dwell on what opinion-polling analysts call "the negatives": the fact that Goldfarb's research showed that people felt that Mulroney was arrogant, was likely to say what he thought people wanted to hear, and was likelier to favour business interests than the interests of the middle class. Turner's attack on the Free Trade Agreement would be ammunition in this fight, but not the only ammunition. Then, to persuade the voters that the Liberals had a program for government, the party would present a forty-point program laying out progressive policies in housing, child care, cultural policy, and so on.

Turner agreed, but with some reservations. He had just come back from New Brunswick and Newfoundland, where his passionate speech on free trade had been very well received. He saw that Goldfarb and Kirby felt strongly about the program, and was prepared to go along with it.

"You know, the issue is trade," he said. Turner was convinced that the free-trade issue was central, and that it would be this issue which would win the election – or at least keep the Conservatives from getting a majority.

But as the meeting ended, Goldfarb felt his strategy had been agreed upon. Trade would be an important part, but only a part of the campaign; it looked as if the elements had come together for a coherent campaign. It remained to be seen if they would stay together under pressure.

CHAPTER FIVE

Ed Broadbent:
the Family Gathers

"There ariseth a little cloud . . . like a man's hand."

I Kings xviii. 44

On August 18, the same evening that Turner was meeting with strategists at Stornoway, Ed Broadbent was in a good mood. The Ottawa branch of that family firm which is the New Democratic Party gathered at the end of the afternoon in a meeting room at the Château Laurier to take wine and cheese at a book launch. It seemed to crown what had been an extraordinary eighteen months of political success, at least as measured in public-opinion polls: a biography of Broadbent by a *Globe and Mail* feature writer, Judy Steed, with a subtitle that summed up the dream that in 1984 had seemed so distant, and now seemed, at the very least, legitimate: the pursuit of power.

The key campaign strategists were there: Bill Knight, the campaign director; Robin Sears, Ontario leader Bob Rae's chief of staff, who would be deputy campaign director; Broadbent's chief of staff, George Nakitsas; his secretary Ann Carroll, who would be the campaign wagonmaster; the director of research, Arlene Wortsman; Hilarie McMurray, his speechwriter; and a variety of MPs, aides, candidates, and reporters.

When she spoke to the book launch, Judy Steed said that she hadn't known Ed Broadbent when she agreed to do the book, and joked that she learned very quickly that he was a terrifyingly fast driver, as he would drive her car to Oshawa while she sat beside him, taking notes.

There were appreciative chuckles. For, in fact, Broadbent was, in an odd way, not very well known, despite his thirteen years as leader of the NDP. He was well liked, familiar, but not well known.

In public terms, Ed Broadbent seemed like the political tortoise, slowly and steadily moving ahead of the hares of politics. It was an appealing image, which captured his earnestness, his hard work, his steady endurance, and his familiarity to voters. But, like so many images, it was incomplete and misleading. On a personal level, Broadbent's reputation as a decent plodder, and his appearance of roast-beef-and-yorkshire-pudding stolidity, missed his mischievous, playful sense of humour, his intellectual interests, and his flashes of passion.

More than that, any foreshortened view of Broadbent's Progress suggested a steady pace, which misses a central fact about the leader of the New Democratic Party. For Broadbent's political career had been a roller coaster which had careered more than once to the brink of disaster. His current success in the polls marked the first time that the NDP had not run into serious trouble between elections.

Ed Broadbent's popularity came, in part, from his old-shoe familiarity. He had been leader of his party two and a half times as long as Brian Mulroney and three times as long as John Turner. He had already weathered the crises his opponents were then suffering through. His political reflexes are pragmatic, and his natural tendency is to develop a third option to break a logjam. His leadership style is a mixture of decisiveness and consensus-building.

A politician since he scraped into Parliament by fifteen votes in 1968, and leader since 1975, he was now benefiting from what was once a liability: he had become a comfortably familiar figure.

"There is no multiple personality being that both Mulroney and Turner seem to be," said the former NDP federal secretary, Gerald Caplan. "There is no hidden side. The things he does privately everyone knows he does privately." "What you see is what he is," said Paul Fox, the retired political scientist who taught Broadbent in graduate school. "A bright, decent, affable fellow."

Married and divorced in the 1960s, he married a widow, Lucille Allen, in 1971: a charming, attractive Franco-Ontarian. He is a voracious reader, a lover of classical music, a man who enjoys cigars. A former political-science professor, he is, as his sister put it, as comfortable with diplomats as with union men.

And yet, behind the easy, affable public figure and the indignant spokesman for "ordinary Canadians" was a kind of distance, an inner inaccessibility.

"Nobody knows Ed Broadbent," said one senior New Democrat. "He's not an easy guy to get to know. He doesn't confide in a lot of people. He's a private person in important ways."

"He has a way of hunkering down when things get very difficult which infuriates people who don't know him," said Robin Sears, who had worked with Broadbent as NDP federal secretary. "He becomes less communicative, he smiles a lot, and he copes."

"Ed is a very self-sufficient kind of person," observed Bob Rae. "He likes being alone and reading and being with Lucille as much as he likes anything. He can also be very convivial and gregarious with company – but he doesn't need that sustaining a whole lot."

Now, Edward Broadbent's emergence as a major player in Canadian politics had provoked a new curiosity about this man who seemed, simultaneously, to be very familiar but little known.

Judy Steed was thus presenting the man who would be the heart of the New Democratic Party campaign: an odd mixture of distance and accessibility, an intellectual from a working-class town, a man who seemed honest and dogged, and whose tendency towards earnestness was leavened by an almost sophomoric playfulness.

Born in 1936, Ed Broadbent grew up in Oshawa, where his father worked as a clerk in an office at the GM plant, and where his grandfather had worked on the GM assembly line. He was an active boy, delivering papers, playing baseball and hockey. His older sister Velma remembers watching him box when he was only eight or nine.

But in high school he had his first brush with Parliament. He won a Rotary Club trip to Ottawa, and was given a tour of the House of Commons by his local MP, Michael Starr, a popular former mayor who was first elected for the Conservatives in 1953. More than a decade later, Ed Broadbent would defeat Michael Starr to become the riding's first NDP MP.

In high school, he was the president of the students' council and president of the boys' athletic association, and won the medal as the outstanding student. At the same time, he sang in the choir at St. George's Anglican Church: an experience that began his love of classical music.

"He's very private about that period of his life," one friend said. "But one can infer a lot. One infers that of the children, he was in some way selected for greatness. You don't come from Oshawa and end up at LSE by accident. Not just if you're smart."

But his sister Velma insists that any pressure on him to succeed was self-imposed. "He was always a good student," she said. "He loved learning for its own sake."

In her book, Steed explained one of the reasons for Broadbent's discretion about his early years; his father's alcoholism and domestic rage darkened his childhood, and seemed to drive him out of the house to succeed. She speculated that it was an experience that also helped shape his drive to seek consensus rather than conflict.

In 1955, from Oshawa Central Collegiate, Broadbent went to Trinity College at the University of Toronto on a full scholarship. "Coming from where I did, I suppose I might have been freaked out by the whole scene," he told Sandra Gwyn in an interview in 1978. "But I was lucky, I never felt any sense of inferiority. I simply fell head over heels in love with the whole ivy-covered intellectual atmosphere."

He had chosen Trinity because he was an Anglican, and remained interested in religion and theology for several years afterwards. But soon his moral concern shifted to politics. "I remember him as a serious young man worried about the future of socialism," recalled Professor Stephen Clarkson of the University of Toronto, who was in the same year at Trinity. Indeed, Broadbent recalls his complete disdain for the Model Parliament and the active socialists of the time: Gerald Caplan was prime minister, and Stephen Lewis ran his campaign.

"They had a poster of a voluptuous Swedish athlete, and a slogan 'This is what socialism did for Sweden,'" Broadbent remembered. "They swept the engineering faculty."

When he graduated, at the top of his class in honours philosophy, Broadbent returned to Oshawa to teach high school – and save enough money to go to the London School of Economics. Although he describes it as a very pleasant year, others felt he looked out of place. "He was an intellectual who seemed quite uncomfortable back in his home town," recalls Hugh Winsor, then a cub reporter at the *Oshawa Times*. "He was obviously reaching out to those relatively few people that saw beyond the assembly line."

Two of those were a couple he met at the high school: Louis Munroe and his wife Lucille. With other friends, they would often spend Friday evenings at the Tally-Ho, drinking beer and discussing ethics, religion, and philosophy.

Broadbent spent the academic year of 1962–3 in London, working under the conservative theorist Michael Oakeshott, but returned to do graduate work at the University of Toronto. Here he worked under C.B. Macpherson, the Marxist scholar who developed the theory of possessive individualism, and who became Broadbent's friend and mentor. His doctoral thesis was on John Stuart Mill.

David Crombie, who was working on his M.A. when Broadbent was working on his Ph.D., remembers a young man in British tweeds with elbow patches. "He was professorial," Crombie said. "He talked like Bill Davis: convoluted sentences, long words and many subjunctive clauses. He seemed to fit into the British connection very easily."

During this period, Broadbent married Yvonne Yamaoka, an urban planner. They were divorced in 1969.

In 1965, Broadbent went to work in the political-science department at York University, where he completed his thesis. He had become active in the New Democratic Party, and was the president of the riding association in Rosedale.

In 1968, when the Trudeau bandwagon was beginning to roll, Broadbent was asked to be the NDP candidate in the riding of Oshawa-Whitby. He was not the first choice – that was Douglas Fisher – but Clifford Pilkey, the MPP, suggested him because he'd grown up in Oshawa.

Fisher recalled that Broadbent was first described to him as a protégé of C.B. Macpherson, and speculated that since Macpherson was known as a Marxist, this probably made the party nervous. But if people in the riding were nervous about Ed Broadbent, it was not about the politics of his thesis adviser. At the nomination meeting, Abe Taylor, the president of Local 222 of the United Auto Workers, nominated Broadbent, and then listened in shock as the candidate gave a long, detailed political-science lecture.

"The speech was so awful I felt like taking the nomination back," Mr. Taylor would joke, years later. "Abe being six foot six, he couldn't find a spot big enough to crawl into!" chuckled Nester Pidwerbecki, later Broadbent's riding assistant. Afterwards, Taylor told Broadbent in no uncertain terms that he was never to give a speech like that again in Oshawa.

"Abe was right." said Lucille Broadbent. "I was there. It was a long, rambling speech; he referred to John Stuart Mill, and Marx. If you were a student of political science, you might have thought it was a great lecture, but if you were a campaign worker waiting to be fired up, you would hardly leave the room saying 'Boy, I'm really going to work for this guy.'"

Broadbent was helped in winning his seat by a strong Liberal campaign, but he kept it by understanding the dynamics of union politics, and fighting for the Auto Pact. He learned quickly that he had to keep the peace between two rival caucuses in the United Autoworkers' local 222: the Democrats and the Autoworkers.

The division, roughly between left and right, was a potential minefield for New Democrats. Broadbent learned early that he had to keep from being identified with one caucus or the other, even when his younger brother Dave became active in union politics.

"That was a very important part of my learning experience," he said. "The crucible was Local 222 politics: the toughest in the autoworkers' union. It was a good place to learn consensus-building. My experience with the union was very important in my political maturation."

(However, Jim Laxer, then involved in the beginnings of what became the left-wing nationalist group known as the Waffle, remembers Broadbent driving him somewhere and confessing that he wasn't sure he understood the autoworkers in his riding. He was driving a Volvo at the time.)

A young academic with an impish sense of humour, teasing his colleagues and sticking his tongue out in official caucus photographs, Broadbent plunged into the policy debates of the party. By August 1969, the *Toronto Star* was describing him as a potential leadership candidate. He became the chairman of the resolutions committee for the party convention, and was trying to bridge the gap between the labour unions on the one hand, and the New Left on the other, pushing for industrial democracy. But the context was clearly moderate.

"We must not succumb to the utopian temptation to create a program whose message is socialism now; nor must we yield to the impulse to play it safe," he wrote. "Ours is the unromantic middle road. A road which Canadians respect."

In June 1970, Broadbent declared his candidacy for the leadership of the party, to succeed Tommy Douglas. It was a mistake. David Lewis was furious that he was being challenged from within the caucus. And the Waffle members, who were seeking a showdown with the establishment of the party, were disdainful of the Broadbent attempt to establish a middle space of consensus.

But Broadbent had become disenchanted with the moral certitude of the academic nationalist left. The turning point was when he saw an older union activist at a meeting in Toronto.

"This young academic kid with long hair, not much younger than I was, got up and attacked him for not being a real socialist, and said that there was no place for him in the party," Broadbent said. "This guy had been on the line, building the party before this kid was born, and because he was on the more conservative wing of the party, his legitimacy was questioned."

He remembers the period as the most difficult in his years with the NDP: more difficult than the conflict over the constitution, more difficult than the dark days when the party was low in the polls.

"There was incredible acrimony in the party, and personal abuse," he said. "It was a very very unpleasant period in the party."

But why did Broadbent run for the leadership in 1971?

"Why did he run in 1971? God knows," said Sears. "What a Quixotic adventure that was!"

"That's a good question," Broadbent told me in the fall of 1987, adding that he had been urged to do so by colleagues. "But I had a totally inadequate understanding of what was required, and what would be involved. I would never advise a person in the same position I was then to get involved in something like that."

"I think he was ill-advised to run," says Lucille Broadbent flatly. "I'm not sure what motivated him. I think it was the wrong decision."

But, in fact, he learned something about one of the political principles he now cares most strongly about: loyalty and caucus solidarity.

"I smartened up a lot," he said. "I became more mature, I saw the problem of leadership, and what David was going through. During the campaign, I did a number of silly and immature things."

He paused.

"In fact, one of the few things in politics that I'm ashamed of I did during the campaign," he said. "I attacked David Lewis in British Columbia over one of the votes on the War Measures Act."

It had been a procedural vote, and Broadbent had argued that the party should vote against the government, as the Tory David MacDonald did. The caucus decision went the other way, and, during the leadership campaign, Broadbent criticized Lewis.

"I was part of the caucus," he said. "I actually felt ashamed of myself afterwards. What right had I? This was a caucus decision I was part of. When we act as a team, whoever loses a vote in caucus is still part of the team. I had engaged in moral one-upmanship, and I find it offensive."

(It was a revealing remark; caucus solidarity became something sacred for Broadbent. Two days after that conversation, when the British Columbia MP Ian Waddell broke ranks with the caucus and announced that he would be voting against the Meech Lake Accord, Broadbent was angry, and decisively stripped Waddell of his caucus responsibilities.)

At the convention, Broadbent finished fourth, behind David Lewis, Jim Laxer, and John Harney: a disappointing finish for a man who was described in the press as coming to the convention in second place. But within a surprisingly short time, he had emerged as an heir apparent.

Part of this was sheer chance. After the Trudeau government was returned with a minority in 1972, giving the NDP the balance of power, Broadbent was given new responsibilities as chairman of caucus.

"Those who had only known him as a leadership candidate saw someone with consistent and serious concern for the whole party, and the whole caucus, that went well beyond any self-interest," said Terry Grier, head of the strategy and election planning committee. "As someone who had not supported him in 1971, I was extremely impressed."

Then the 1974 Liberal majority swept away many of the members of the caucus. David Lewis was defeated, John Harney was defeated, Terry Grier was defeated, Bill Knight was defeated, and several others.

"In one simple sense, Ed survived, and continued to be an MP," said Grier. "He was the most capable and generally most attractive of the survivors."

In July 1974, Broadbent was chosen as the parliamentary leader. In January 1975, however, he stunned the NDP federal council by announcing that he would not be a candidate for the leadership because he wanted to spend more time with his family.

Two months later, after considerable pressure from the elders of the party, Broadbent relented, but told a news conference that he would take the leadership on condition that he could take weekends off "to spend time with my family, listen to Bach, or read novels."

"Some people saw my reluctance as a ploy – absolutely not," said Broadbent. "God, I'd had an intense on-the-job experience. We had a young daughter. There are other things in life! I could have gone back to the real world in the university. People had talked about Schreyer, Barrett, and Blakeney [all provincial premiers at the time]. If they had been willing to go, I would have said 'Thank you for a wonderful experience – but there are some movies I want to see, and novels I want to read.'"

"He was aware of how much more awful was the life of a leader than the life of an MP," said Robin Sears, who was then federal secretary. "Going to a caucus meeting that [previous] fall was like going to a weekly funeral. It was just awful."

Nevertheless, the "listen to Bach" remark caused some mirth.

The *Globe and Mail* columnist Geoffrey Stevens wrote a column on the eve of the convention in the form of a letter to Lucille, apologizing for being away for the weekend. "I know when I decided to run for the leadership of the New Democratic Party in March I promised you I would keep time for you and Bach and Walter Bagehot," he wrote. "But, my dearest, you have to understand I simply had to come to Winnipeg. After all, the election of the new leader is on Monday, and people might think it odd if the leading candidate did not show up."

Perhaps as a result of this apparent reluctance to accept a job that the party elders seemed to be thrusting on him, it took a surprising four ballots for Broadbent to defeat the British Columbia MPP Rosemary Brown, the Saskatchewan MP Lorne Nystrom, the former MP John Harney, and a taxi-driver, Douglas Campbell.

At thirty-nine, Ed Broadbent had, in the words of Desmond Morton, "inherited the mantle of Woodsworth, Coldwell, Douglas and Lewis." But in the eyes of many, he did not seem to have the stature to step into the shoes of his predecessors. As Bob Rae told Charlotte Gray, he was "the first mere mortal to lead the party."

"He was finding his feet," said one person who worked with him at the time. "Some days he was very good, but he was capable of being just awful."

He became leader just before the party suffered a series of provincial defeats and setbacks, losing in British Columbia in 1977, slipping back to third place in Ontario in June 1977, and losing in Manitoba in October 1977.

At the same time, Broadbent suffered from a mixture of inexperience and bad advice as Quebec began to dominate the public agenda. His own French is sometimes awkward, and there was a shortage of French-speaking staff.

In the summer of 1976, he made the mistake of opposing the demands of the Gens de l'Air, the group in Quebec seeking bilingual communication in air-traffic control: a position that ran counter to unanimous opinion in Quebec, and made the NDP seem even more foreign to Quebec than the election results had always suggested. Then, when the Parti Québécois surged to power in Quebec in November 1976, the NDP seemed irrelevant to the national debate that dominated the public agenda for the years that followed.

At the same time, Broadbent was learning the skills of leadership, and how to manage an office. There was high turnover of staff in his office between 1975 and 1983; he was hard to work for.

"Ed is a difficult person to work with unless you are entirely confident in your conduct with him," Robin Sears told Norman Snider. "Ed sometimes comes in with some brain wave in the morning that should not have left the pillow, let alone make it to the office. To the extent that you say 'That's very interesting and I'll have somebody work on it,' as opposed to 'That's nuts and we're not going to do it,' you're going to have a lot of difficulty. He operates on a lot of emotional and intellectual levels at the same time, there's a lot churning in his head, and unless you're really good at reading the cues, all of a sudden he's snapping at you and you're saying 'What the fuck did I do?' That's very complicated for a lot of people to deal with. For instance, you can't be blundering into the room raising issues when Ed's thinking he should be home listening to Bach."

Gradually, a team was put together that succeeded in working together, and with Broadbent: mute evidence that he had had a lot to learn, but that he did. Nevertheless, when crises hit, wrenching his staff and his senior party loyalists, he would still tend to withdraw. In private, he would argue that he could not abide people who claimed that a conflict-free existence was a real world; as a manager, he would shrink from dealing with conflict, and his people learned to reach a consensus among themselves before going to him. As his sister Velma put it to Judy Steed, in describing how her brother dealt with the conflict between their parents, "He has the protective veneer, many men do, that lets them shut out the things they don't want to see."

However, Broadbent proved to be most successful in dealing with the medium that the NDP had always been most wary of: television. (In his 1970 book *The Liberal Rip-Off*, Broadbent described how Pierre Trudeau had succeeded in using television to seize the attention of Canadians before the House of Commons was televised. "Instead of belabouring a point or an issue in the House, he simply presents his argument and heads as fast as possible for the television cameras," he wrote.)

Thanks to television – in paid advertisements, free-time broadcasts and televised debates – Broadbent was able to pull the party back from irrelevance during elections. With the new provisions of the Elections Act, the NDP had the resources to spend more than ever before on advertising: $1.018 million in 1979, and $1.4 million in 1980.

In the two elections, Broadbent succeeded in pulling the party up from the 16-seat caucus he had inherited in 1975 to 26 seats in 1979 and 32 in 1980. However, the apparent success of doubling the size of the caucus over two elections was a mere prelude to one of the most difficult periods for the New Democratic Party.

In the fall of 1980, Ed Broadbent endorsed Pierre Trudeau's plan to unilaterally patriate the British North America Act with a Charter of Rights. In doing so, he precipitated a crisis in his party.

"It was the most unpleasant political conflict I've seen, bar none," recalled Robin Sears, "It was a very very painful thing to go through, with family and friends divided."

Broadbent had concluded that unless someone other than Pierre Trudeau were in favour of the patriation of the constitution with a Charter of Rights, it would not happen. But NDP Saskatchewan Premier Allan Blakeney, who was working with seven other premiers to fight the proposal, was appalled. Lorne Nystrom resigned his caucus position, and the division split the party in a very personal way.

"There was nothing so bitter in the family since the Waffle," said Gerry Caplan. "Dear friends didn't speak to one another, and certainly dear friends didn't trust one another."

The conflict reached its climax at the party convention in Vancouver, where the internal squabble became a public debate, with Ed Broadbent and Allan Blakeney at the floor microphones, arguing for support from the delegates.

"It was the best debate we've had," according to Bill Knight who was Blakeney's chief of staff, and then became Broadbent's chief of staff before taking over as federal secretary and campaign director in January 1988. Broadbent won the endorsation of the party, and the issue was resolved by the agreement between Trudeau and the nine English-Canadian premiers in November 1981.

It was an important process in shaping Broadbent's experience as leader. It made everyone in the party realize the price to be paid for conflict, and laid the groundwork for the relatively smooth consensus over the Meech Lake Accord. It also taught Broadbent something of Quebec.

However, in the short term, things got no easier for Broadbent and the NDP. The constitutional crisis was followed by a recession, and despite Broadbent's years of talking about industrial strategy, Canadians did not look to the NDP to manage the economy.

This general suspicion of NDP economic policy was accentuated by a debate over the party's commitment to deficit financing, precipitated by an attempt by the research director, Jim Laxer, urging that the party change direction. In the fall of 1983, Broadbent delivered a speech in Hamilton expressing concern about the deficit, which provoked outrage from the unions, who saw the policy as a turn to the right for the party. Laxer, who had urged Broadbent to deliver the speech, was upset when he began to retreat, and responded by writing a report on NDP economic policy. The report, which was leaked to the *Globe and Mail*, described NDP economic policy as "seriously inadequate, contradictory, short-sighted and ideologically ambivalent. . . . The NDP's analysis of economic and social evolution remains locked in the 1950s and 1960s where it had its origins. . . . It is now so seriously out of keeping with the reality of the 1980s that it has become a serious impediment . . . to appropriate action rather than a guide to it."

At the same time, the public spotlight shifted to the other parties and their leadership preoccupations: first the Progressive Conservatives in 1983, and then the Liberals in 1984. The result was a steady decline in NDP popularity, from 20 per cent of the popular vote in February 1980 to a catastrophic 11 per cent in the public-opinion polls four years later.

––––––––––––––

Far from being an asset, in the spring of 1984 Ed Broadbent began to look like a liability. The Conservatives had changed leaders, the Liberals were about to change, and Broadbent looked at best stale, and at worst shrill. (This was particularly noticeable in his second or third question in Question Period, when his voice would rise in nerve-grating exasperation. Jim Laxer and Peter O'Malley put together a video cassette which spliced all of his shrillest questions together, to show Broadbent what they meant. Just as he had learned to change his tailoring and to fix the gap in his teeth, he learned to modulate his voice.)

There began to be murmurs about Broadbent's leadership. But again he was able to use the election campaign, and the media attention that it brought, to wrest the party back from the brink.

"We walked into the election campaign with very low morale, and Ed just pulled himself together in a way that was remarkable," said Gerry Caplan. "And we saved ourselves. It was a fine achievement for him. But we'd come from the depths."

In a strategy memo written shortly before the campaign began, Caplan laid out just how far into the depths he thought the party had fallen:

"1. We are very low in all the national polls.

"2. Everyone knows this.

"3. Much of the media has lost interest in us and is writing us off.

"4. Some say we are irrelevant to the present moment and there is no purpose in people voting for us.

"5. Some say we have nothing new to say, and we are fighting for a better yesterday.

"6. Whatever we do or say, some insist it is not new.

"7. When we fight to preserve medicare and pensions, or when we emphasize women's issues, we are dismissed for recycling past policies.

"8. Both other parties have new leaders, and are treated by some as if new faces are synonymous with new ideas and new directions.

"9. We are hurt by the sense that our policies over the years make us the party of big government, big bureaucracy and an outmoded belief in government intervention as a positive tool."

Despite this gloomy view ("We can avoid the apocalypse some predict for us, but it is by no means inevitable that we will") Caplan and the other top party officials succeeded in focusing the campaign on the idea that ordinary Canadians needed to be represented by New Democrats fighting for fairness. Broadbent opened the campaign identifying Mulroney and Turner as two corporate lawyers, one from Bay Street and the other from St. James Street, one a former director of the Canadian Imperial Bank of Commerce, the other a former director of Crédit Foncier, one a corporate lawyer for Canadian Pacific, the other the president of Iron Ore of Canada, and concluded "and that's where the differences stop."

Broadbent performed well in the TV debates, and managed to win back the attention and respect that Caplan had so bleakly concluded had vanished before the campaign. When the dust settled in September 1984, the party found itself with thirty seats: only ten fewer than the Liberals, and more MPs from English Canada than the Liberals.

Three years later, in the fall of 1987, after soaring to the dizzying heights of 44 per cent in the polls in the spring, the NDP had settled to a healthy 28-30 per cent. For a year and a half, Broadbent had been talking plausibly about the closest three-way race in Canadian history. The pursuit of power seemed realistic. Magazine articles and television profiles had been assigned, written, published, broadcast; people had been talking about what had previously been unthinkable: Ed Broadbent as a possible prime minister.

After the NDP won three by-elections in the summer of 1987 – St. John's East, Hamilton Mountain, and Yukon – it was possible to see deadlocks, minorities, coalitions: all adding up to unique opportunities for the NDP, but all depending on unique electoral breakthroughs.

Broadbent insisted, throughout the euphoric period, that he was approaching the party's policies no differently now from the way he did when the party was on the brink of disaster; that the NDP's strength was coming from its frankness and consistency, from saying what it meant and meaning what it said. But certainly, the new visibility brought a new strength to Broadbent's ability to modify a party policy that had always been an irritant to him: the party's unswerving determination to withdraw Canada from NATO. An April 1988 federal council meeting endorsed a report urging that this not be done in a first NDP mandate, and that it be reviewed later.

But in the mood of confidence and excitement at that August book launch there were other signs of problems that had been beneath the surface for months, unresolved.

For Éric Gourdeau had buttonholed Michael Cassidy, and was venting some of his frustrations. Gourdeau was a Quebec City consultant who had studied forest management and economics at Laval in the early 1950s before joining the Quebec civil service in 1960. He had worked with René Lévesque in the early 1960s on the nationalization of Hydro-Québec, and, when Lévesque became premier in 1976, returned to government from consulting to be his deputy minister responsible for aboriginals.

He had worked with Lévesque as a senior civil servant, and was used to being able to walk into his office unannounced. Now, he had little patience with the group organizing NPD-Québec, and succeeded in negotiating a special dispensation which would allow him to belong to the federal party without joining the provincial wing.

Cassidy, at fifty, looked ten years younger, but had been the provincial leader in Ontario. Bright, intense, but with a reputation for abrasiveness (one wit quipped that Bob Rae, who took over from him as provincial leader, was one of the few people to have replaced a robot on the job), he was one of the more bilingual members of the caucus, and had been given caucus responsibilities for Quebec.

It was a thankless and frustrating task. The caucus had, after some careful deliberation, admitted a former Tory MP, Robert Toupin, in 1987, only to have him resign a few months later, accusing the party in Quebec of being manipulated by extreme leftists. The Toupin incident was a trying one on a number of levels.

To begin with it made the federal party look silly, and incautious in ignoring some of Toupin's disturbing qualities. When he talked about the closing of the Gulf Oil refinery in the east end of Montreal, or about the two old parties, Toupin kept talking harshly about "Les Reichmann et les Bronfman." "Those two parties are at the service of high finance and the multinationals," he told a meeting in his riding in February 1987. "The Conservatives have replaced the Bronfmans with the Reichmanns, and the Liberals will exchange the Reichmanns for the Bronfmans." It sounded very like nasty, old-fashioned Créditiste anti-Semitism: the kind of thing Réal Caouette and his followers used to say.

The incident widened the gap between the federal office and the renewed provincial organization, and showed yet again how weak the party really was in Quebec.

This was certainly not new. Ever since its foundation in 1961, the NDP had had problems in Quebec. In 1968, there had been hopes for a breakthrough when Robert Cliche, a popular lawyer from the Beauce, ran for the NDP in Duvernay, a riding in the north end of Montreal. However, the Liberals had responded by nominating Eric Kierans, well known both for his career in Quebec provincial politics and for his run at the Liberal leadership. In the intervening twenty years, there had been a variety of attempts to organize a viable wing of the NDP in Quebec, but none of them had succeeded.

It was symbolic of the problems the NDP had with its organization in Quebec that the revival of the party after 1984 should occur under the leadership of a man who was seen in dramatically different terms by the party veterans in Ottawa and the newcomers attracted to the party in Quebec. The views were so radically different that it was almost as if they referred to two different people.

For the Quebeckers who had become active in the NDP, the leader of NPD-Québec after 1984 was Jean-Paul Harney, who was seen as an effective politician, a bilingual Irish-Quebecker who had built the party from almost nothing to a group with a growing membership of several thousand. He had taken nationalist positions, and drawn into the party veterans of the union movement, left-wing splinter groups, and the Parti Québécois. They saw him as hard-working, shrewd, and politically experienced.

The NDP veterans in the rest of the party, however, knew a very different man. They knew John Harney: the York University professor who was provincial secretary in Ontario in 1967 and ran for the federal leadership in 1971, finishing third behind David Lewis and James Laxer and ahead of Ed Broadbent; who was elected as the MP for Scarborough West in 1972 and defeated in 1974; who ran again for the leadership in 1975 and finished fourth behind Broadbent; and who ran against Bob Rae for the federal nomination in Broadview-Greenwood in 1978. Eyes would roll at the mention of his name in many circles of the party: he was considered to be an unreliable, unpredictable loose cannon.

In 1984, Harney ran in Lévis, where he was born in 1931. He had gone to study at Queen's and, becoming a poet and an English professor, had taught in Ontario and become active in the NDP, running for the Commons in 1962, 1963, 1965, and 1968 before being elected in 1972. In 1985, he became the leader of NPD-Québec, and began to commute from Toronto, where he taught at Atkinson College, to Sillery where he had bought a house, and to Montreal for two days' work at NDP headquarters.

Under his leadership, NPD-Québec began adopting some strongly nationalist positions on the language and constitutional questions. In January 1987, it adopted a policy calling for Quebec to have the exclusive right to legislate on language, the right to self-determination, compensation for opting out of constitutional changes that transferred provincial responsibilities to the federal government, and a veto on changes to federal institutions. The language question was a problem for the federal council of the party, and on Sunday, January 18, 1987, the council worked out a compromise. This affirmed Quebec's right to self-determination, agreed with the opting-out clause and the veto on changes to federal institutions, but avoided a decision on the prickly language question. On that issue, the Quebec committee of the federal party was to "explore new constitutional provisions whose purpose would be to protect the linguistic rights of Quebec's majority, while at the same time ensuring the preservation of minority rights as they now exist in the Constitution."

It was a compromise that papered over a fundamental difference of opinion, which would explode during the election campaign.

Six weeks later, Michel Agnaïeff successfully pushed Harney aside as the principal spokesman of the NDP in Quebec. Agnaïeff, then forty-seven, was a senior executive with the Quebec teachers' federation, the Centrale de l'enseignement du Quebec, and a hard-nosed political organizer. Born in Egypt of Russian parents, he had come to Montreal in the 1960s, and, after working as a teacher, had become active in the union movement. He brought an abstract, intellectual, European socialism to the NDP, combined with the hard experience of fifteen years with Quebec's most militant union federation. At the end of February, to Harney's angry surprise, the national council of NPD-Québec voted to have Agnaïeff, not Harney, be associate president and the party's chief federal representative in Quebec.

A few months later, Harney announced he was stepping down as leader of NPD-Québec, which precipitated a leadership race between Roland Morin, a veteran NDP activist, and Hélène Guay, a forty-five-year-old labour lawyer. To the surprise of many, Morin, who seemed to symbolize the decades of irrelevance of the NDP in Quebec, was chosen leader.

Throughout these squabbles, Michael Cassidy had been chairman of the NDP caucus committee on Quebec, and, as one of the NDP members most comfortable in French, had been travelling to the province and acting as one of the connecting links. (The other major reference point in Ottawa was George Nakitsas, who had grown up in Montreal.) It was not always a satisfying position to be in: there was little he could do to intervene and settle the seemingly endless disputes.

Some of that frustration could be seen on Cassidy's face at Judy Steed's book-launch party. Once again, he had to listen. For Éric Gourdeau was angry. He felt that the NDP campaign in Quebec was being dominated by far-left nationalists, that there was too little co-ordination, and that the squabbles were damaging the party on the eve of the election. Cassidy could only listen and sympathize before moving on to be buttonholed by Rémy Trudel, who had many of the same complaints.

More than anyone else, Trudel was the symbol of what Ed Broadbent and the people in the NDP in Ottawa hoped the NDP in Quebec would become. The president of the Université du Québec à Rouyn-Noranda, Trudel was articulate and attractive, and had no interest in the ideological skirmishes that were tearing at the party in Quebec. He had succeeded in persuading the NDP to endorse flow-through shares – a tax benefit for mining investment which was very important for the development of a mining area like Rouyn-Noranda, and he had been able to attract people from all parties in the region to support his candidacy. One of them was Donald Houle, a retired Sûreté du Québec policeman who had been the head of security at the 1976 Montreal Olympics, and during the Pope's visit in 1984. Houle, a former Liberal organizer, was drawn to the NDP by Trudel, and became the chief organizer for the party for the 1988 election. The likelihood of conflict was considerable.

There were other problems besides Quebec. Ten months before, at a council meeting Dennis Young abruptly quit as federal secretary. When he succeeded Gerry Caplan, he had reorganized the federal office, managed to move to new headquarters, and begun the introduction of direct-mail techniques. However, his role was undermined by Marion Dewar, the former mayor of Ottawa who became party president and undertook to do the job on a full-time basis. No previous federal secretary had had to make room for a full-time president, and the conflict was probably inevitable. In October 1987, when he learned that Dewar and Cassidy would be proposing a motion of non-confidence, and it appeared that Broadbent's office was not mobilizing in his support, Young resigned.

In contrast to the blood-bath in the Liberal Party, the departure was quite discreet. Nevertheless, it provoked considerable bitterness inside the party, and it required some major changes, less than a year before the election. Even those who felt that Young had shortcomings felt these should have been evaluated when he was first hired.

Bill Knight left Broadbent's office to become federal secretary; George Nakitsas succeeded Knight as chief of staff, and Arlene Wortsman succeeded Nakitsas as director of research. On the face of it, the shift looked ideal: Knight had worked for Broadbent for five years, and had previously been provincial secretary in Saskatchewan; Nakitsas knew the staff and the party as director of research; Wortsman had previously worked for Bob Rae, the Manitoba government, and the advisory council on the status of women in the federal government.

Knight was committed to winning. He said repeatedly that when he was growing up in Saskatchewan, he took the idea of an NDP government for granted. He believed in the party, and the party process; he was convinced that the NDP could meet the new challenge of coping with the pressures of running a truly national campaign for the first time, and producing policies that would meet the new scrutiny that would be applied to the NDP.

"I am a great believer that the party process is sound: debate and argument on issues," he said in December 1987, as he was preparing to take over as federal secretary. "They have to go the test, run the gauntlet. When the platform committee goes back to the election planning committee, and the election planning committee puts forward the campaign to the officers and the federal council, God, you run the gauntlet. And I think it's incredibly healthy."

As the new team took over in January 1988, some strategic thinking had been done. In a memo in April 1987, Dennis Young had pointed out that, with the NDP at its highest point ever in national opinion polls, the year ahead would be one of the most exciting and demanding in forty years.

"While presenting unique opportunities, the next year will place unprecedented demands on the Party to maintain its present standing in the polls, and to prepare to finance and run a national campaign," he wrote. "Also, it will expose the federal Party to an unprecedented degree of public scrutiny and external attack."

He proposed a clear strategic goal. "However articulated, in terms of the number of seats to win, percentage of vote etc., the strategic goal of the party should be to finish the next campaign in second place," he wrote. "This would be a dramatic rewriting of the Canadian political landscape, and would position us either to survive the run-off election if a minority House was returned, or to present ourselves as the 'natural alternative' to the party in power in any subsequent general election. It would also achieve the long-term goal of the Party to re-establish a 2 party system at the national level as our sections in the West have done provincially."

While he recognized that it was "no longer appropriate" for the party to concentrate resources on a small number of seats in Ontario, Saskatchewan, Manitoba, and British Columbia, Young clearly felt that there was a need for focusing the expansion of the party's efforts very carefully. "Even during a period of expansion, discipline is required to attain the greatest possible impact for our efforts."

Two months later, in June 1987, George Nakitsas wrote a discussion paper which subtly took a different position, arguing that the question of whether the party was running for government or opposition, who the party was running against, and whether it hoped for a minority government, should not be addressed.

"Fortunately for us, I think current circumstances provide us with an effective and credible way of avoiding answering these questions by repeating (ad nauseam if necessary) 'the 3 way race' argument," he wrote. "This argument has the double advantage of not only effectively providing an out from traditionally difficult questions but also has the benefit of being a positive message based on our polling. Needless to say it does not imply that we run for government or for official opposition or for anything but the largest number of seats in our history in every province and region of the country."

From the outside, Dennis Young's departure seemed an unfortunate but minor blip in the party's relatively smooth progress; since the musical chairs that it produced all involved people who knew one another well, it was difficult to see the change in chemistry and strategy that had occurred. Young had been an organization man, constantly reminding people of the awkward organizational realities needed to uphold strategic decisions. Bill Knight and George Nakitsas were determined to make sure that the NDP had joined the table as a national party. This meant a much greater emphasis, in terms of resources, on Quebec, and, in terms of the party's message, on leadership and the personal popularity of Ed Broadbent.

In a paper written in January 1988, analysing the latest opinion research, Nakitsas saw the emergence of a problem. Free trade was possibly emerging as a "vote-determining issue," and the Tories were trying to use free trade, along with Meech Lake and tax reform, to move public opinion away from the doubts about credibility and integrity that had dogged them for the last few years. Similarly, the Liberals were trying to use free trade to shift public attention away from their own internal divisions.

"The possible impact of these new trends poses a potential challenge to our strategic planning," he wrote. "Over the last few years, the performance of the P.C.s and the Liberals had allowed us to more easily develop and pursue our own strategy. In contrast, if these new trends continue, we will need to be much more creative and single-minded in order to keep our strategy front and centre with the electorate."

The challenge was to use the trade issue as one in a series, with taxes, patronage, and pensions, to reinforce the NDP's key messages, "not let it stand alone as a vote-determining issue," and to focus on "the last four years and on the party leaders as opposed to the upcoming year and free trade."

It was a prescient look at the emerging problem, and more foresighted than the strategy document that the secret Tory group was discussing in the January meeting at the Château Laurier, which assumed that the Liberal appeal to national feeling on free trade had failed. But the suggested solution – focusing on the past rather than the future – indicated the seriousness of the problem.

After going over some of the data on what voters expected from the NDP and how they felt about the leaders, Nakitsas found that voters "don't expect and don't want very drastic changes under a New Democratic government." There were references to "a little more" fairness and honesty in the polling and focus-group research, but no hope or expectation of radical change.

"As a result, it is very important that we use relative terms in our language and that we not overstate our case," Nakitsas warned. "To summarize, our *primary message* should and must continue to focus on *Ed Broadbent* and on *more fairness, openness and honesty for average Canadians.* This message will reinforce both our traditional vote and attempt to consolidate our new found levels of support."

The secondary messages involved what Nakitsas called "the perennial 'time for a change' message which ironically seems to be working for us and not against us this time around." (In 1984, the "time for a change" idea swung voters massively to the Progressive Conservatives.) "Even more fortunate is the specific language that is being used repeatedly in our research i.e. 'They deserve a chance' or 'Give 'em a chance.'"

In looking at the issues, Nakitsas warned that the strategic planning "must take into account the possibility of having to run in an election where the Canada-U.S. trade deal is seen at least by the media to be a key, if not *the* key, issue." That having been said, he laid out other issues that could highlight the party's message: more fairness could include regional development, jobs, taxpayers, families, environment, peace, and security; more openness would refer to consultation and access to information; more honesty would include conflict of interest, appointment procedures, contract procedures, and frankness concerning election promises.

Turning to the trade deal, he found that there was a significant gap between support for the idea of free trade and the specific Free Trade Agreement; that those opposed to free trade or the Mulroney deal outnumbered those who supported either one; that the large majority didn't know much about the Mulroney deal (80 per cent, he found in a Gallup); that a large majority (he cited 65 per cent in the August Angus Reid poll) felt that Mulroney didn't have a mandate and should call an election; that people were most concerned about jobs, the effects on farmers and small business and on Canada's ability to make decisions on its future; and, finally, that most people thought the United States got a better deal than Canada.

On the basis of those findings, Nakitsas made three recommendations on how to deal with the issue before and during the election.

"First, the less we use the words free trade the better," he said. "We should instead focus our attack on the *Mulroney deal* or on the Mulroney/Reagan *deal*."

" . . . Second, we should at every occasion relate the Mulroney deal to our key message and deal with it as the last straw in a long list of examples where Mulroney has not been open, honest or fair with average Canadians."

" . . . The third recommendation is to deal with the Mulroney deal as the *last straw*. Specifically, this would mean referring, whenever possible, to other issues where Mulroney has not been fair, open or honest when discussing the Mulroney deal or aspects of it. By doing this, we can keep the focus on the last three years and use the trade issue to reinforce our strengths and Mulroney's weaknesses."

If successful, he concluded, the party could pursue its own strategy and widen the gap between support for free trade and support for the deal. "However," he warned, "such a strategy will clearly require that we be both creative and single-minded in our treatment of the issue."

As the new team took over in January 1988, there were a number of policy issues which had to be sorted out before the election, and the party set to work to hammer out a consensus.

Everyone knew the defence policy would attract the most attention. The party leadership had been trying for years to move gradually away from the implacable pacifism and anti-militarism of the resolutions passed at every convention. In 1987, Derek Blackburn had produced a caucus defence policy which, while continuing to call for a withdrawal from NATO, urged a greater emphasis on Canadian defence. In early 1988, a special international-affairs committee headed by Tessa Hebb from Nova Scotia and the Manitoba MP William Blaikie refined this policy, and presented it to the federal council in April.

Similarly, the party worked on developing an agricultural policy acceptable to both the federal party and the Saskatchewan party. Arlene Wortsman worked on developing a policy on child-care tax credits. In these areas and a number of others, the party devoted a considerable amount of energy to reaching out to the different constituencies concerned about the issue, refining policy and reaching a consensus. The process was time-consuming, and important; it was also limited to a relatively small number of issues. But, as Bill Knight and Robin Sears would concede later, no one was prepared for what a challenge it would be to organize the resources and deal with the demands of a fully national campaign.

While strategy and policies were being hammered out, Julie Mason, the party's director of communications, was working on developing the communications strategy for the election: a strategy based on something that the NDP had not had the resources to use in the past – extensive polling and focus groups.

In May, the party did a major poll to try to find out more about the people who were indicating that they might change their votes: swing voters, or soft voters. The poll, which became known as the ACM Soft Vote Survey, reached a number of conclusions: more of the "soft voters" were Liberals (31 per cent) than Tories (24 per cent) or New Democrats (16 per cent). "The figures suggest that to bring our vote into the high 30s in the next federal election we must capture a sizeable portion of both the self-identified Liberals and Tories who comprise the bulk of these 'swing voters,'" wrote Vic Fingerhut, the American pollster who analysed the data the NDP had collected. The data suggested that this was possible: Ed Broadbent was more popular than the NDP, and preferred as the next prime minister by a 53–15 per cent margin by swing voters who described themselves as Liberals. "If we can get half of the self-identified Tories in this swing voting group, we are probably on target in terms of our overall campaign."

The "ordinary Canadian" theme tested well in the survey.

"Our populist 'ordinary Canadian' messages seem to significantly underly our strength with this group of 'swing voters' (along with the notion of it's time to give the NDP a chance)," Fingerhut wrote. "Thus, by a 65–19 per cent margin the swing voters ageed that "whatever you say about them, the New Democrats understand the needs of ordinary working families – *and that alone is a good reason to vote for them.*" (emphasis in original)

On June 1, Julie Mason produced a strategy paper for the Strategy and Election Planning Committee working group that was based in part on the soft-voter polling and previous polling by the NDP, and also on campaign themes prepared by Bill Knight and agreed to by the SEPC.

"Based on four years of polling, there are now certain 'assumptions' we can make as we prepare for the campaign," she wrote. "These assumptions are:

"1) our greatest strength remains 'Ed Broadbent and the New Democrats speak for ordinary Canadians.'

"2) our greatest asset is Ed Broadbent, still the most popular leader in Canada.

"3) our strongest argument remains the 'who speaks for whom' argument.

"4) our greatest vulnerabilities are the 'Nato' problem and the 'managing the government' problem.

"5) Canadians want a government that is fair, open and honest."

Mason went on to lay out some assumptions about the new political environment which the NDP would have to operate in: the press would be putting the NDP under a microscope, in terms both of the campaign and of the policy statements; the Tories would focus on the NDP as their enemy and would work hard "to reframe the public debate around our weaknesses"; that despite what she called "the current chaos in the Liberal Party," it was still the party most Canadians felt comfortable voting for, adding "they have the potential to pull off a good campaign"; and, finally, "the election will be decided by small numbers of voters in key ridings, so all parties must target precisely."

Mason then set out the themes of the campaign. In 1984, the NDP had used only one theme – "who speaks for you" – and, by concentrating on key ridings in key areas of support and touching a feeling of identification among voters with the idea that the NDP represented their interests, managed to come back from the precipice of possible disaster.

"Our task, throughout this campaign, is to touch the chord in people that says 'I've had it with those other two guys, Ed Broadbent is for ordinary folks like me, so this time I'm giving Ed a chance,'" she wrote. "In simple terms, the campaign looks like this: 1) who's been speaking for you, and who will speak for you? 2) This time, give Ed a chance."

The messages to convey these themes were carefully worked out: "Brian Mulroney and the Conservatives said they were for ordinary folks (older Canadians, women, working people, the family) . . . they did something (Mulroney trade deal, drug prices, regional discrimination) that showed they weren't really for ordinary folks; Ed was there to fight for ordinary folks."

Thus, the campaign would stress that, while the Conservatives said they would help senior citizens, the first thing they did was to try to cut pensions, and Ed Broadbent fought for them; Brian Mulroney said he wanted tax reform, but raised taxes for an average family by $1,000 while Ed Broadbent fought on their behalf; Mulroney said he would protect the health-care system, and instead he gave in to the demands of multinational drug companies, producing higher drug prices, while Ed Broadbent fought on behalf of ordinary people. It would identify Mulroney and Turner as being equally involved in patronage and benefits for the privileged few.

"The tone, although negative, is really more one of sorrow than anger, of acute disappointment, of frustration at not being able to get the things that ordinary folks need and want," Mason wrote. "In terms of our focus on Ed, the message here is 'Decent Ed has been there, working hard, fighting for ordinary folks.'"

Then, if everything went according to plan, the second half of the campaign would stress the need to give Ed a chance this time: a message that the time was appropriate, he deserved a chance, and he could win.

Then, Mason identified the target voters: soft voters (people who were not firm in their voting decision), undecided voters, union voters, women voters, and soft and undecided voters in families. Finally, she laid out subthemes for the campaign: the need to recognize that it would be a negative strategy to have "Trust Ed" as a slogan, since it would remind people how little they trust politicians; the need to drop the "winnability" theme if it seemed wildly implausible during the campaign, since it would undermine the campaign's credibility; the importance of stressing NDP support for the family. At the same time, she identified two potential weaknesses: the party's NATO policy, and the question in voters' minds of whether or not the NDP was competent to govern.

The strategic themes built on an analysis which the party's strategists had been developing for a long time: Ed Broadbent's decency was the party's strongest asset, but, should the trade deal emerge as the major issue, the NDP would suffer because of doubts of its ability to manage the economy and deal with economic issues. Thus, all the strategic energies were aimed at broadening the campaign beyond free trade to social issues and asking Canadians which party was best able to defend the interests of ordinary people. This analysis was only reinforced by an Angus Reid poll in June, which showed that, while 31 per cent of those polled indicated their intention of voting NDP, when respondents were asked how they would vote if the election were fought primarily on the free-trade issue, NDP support dropped dramatically to 20 per cent.

There was little talk of this at the book launch at the Château Laurier on August 18; the mood was cheerful and enthusiastic. But, as he looked around the room, Robin Sears couldn't help but feel a sense of foreboding.

CHAPTER SIX

Issuing the Writs

*"It's in politics as in racin', everything depends upon
a fair start."*

T.C. Haliburton, Sam Slick

No one, not even the Tory
insiders or senior cabinet ministers, knew exactly when
Mulroney would call the election; while he kept saying publicly that he wanted to wait until September 17, the anniversary of the swearing-in, no one wanted to be caught
unprepared; all three parties had been working on different
possibilities since 1986. Each party organization had its
strengths and its weaknesses.

The New Democrats had the fervour of the volunteer ethic,
and years of experience developing the triple canvass, with
campaigns mobilized to reach each door three times to persuade, identify support, and get out the vote. But this time,
for the first time, the party would be undertaking the rigours
of a balanced national campaign, instead of the sleight-of-
hand illusion of focusing on forty winnable ridings, and
dropping periodically into provinces where the NDP had
little chance simply to give the impression of a fully national
campaign.

The Liberals had debts, dissension, and leadership problems, but had the residual strength that came with having
been the party more Canadians felt comfortable supporting
than any other, and a base of experience in the Senate to draw

on without cost. At the same time, David Peterson's Ontario Liberals provided a group of people with fresh experience of successful political organizing.

The Tories had introduced much of the modern technology of political campaigning, and were the first to use direct mail, computers, and electronic mail. In fact, they had first automated their mail in the late 1920s, under General A.D. McRae, the chief organizer for the 1930 election. McRae established a file of 250,000 Conservatives across Canada on multigraph plates; using Addressograph machines, he was able to send out 250,000 letters or pamphlets in three days. "Copies of Liberal pamphlets and literature were in Conservative headquarters the day they were off the press," wrote Arthur Ford in his memoirs. "Answers were written the same day, and in the hands of the printers immediately afterwards. With the high-speed mailing equipment they had available the answers would be in the hands of editors and others often before the Liberal literature had left headquarters."

However, the day after the 1930 election, R.B. Bennett had the office closed down and the staff dismissed; the plates were disposed of, and the party headquarters closed. The attempt to reorganize the office in 1935 was started too late; decades would pass before the Conservatives would regain the organizational skills that they had mastered in the 1920s.

The pattern of allowing the party to wither while in power, which so hurt the Liberals in 1984, was one that the Conservatives were determined to avoid. At the same time, they were able to use the Prime Minister's Office as a central point for co-ordinating important partisan activities.

As the leader of a majority government in a parliamentary system, Brian Mulroney had a number of significant advantages in election planning: he had access to an enormous range of information from the party and the government, he controlled the government's agenda, the party's agenda, and the choice of the election date. This gave him strategic possibilities that were simply unavailable to his opponents, or, for that matter, to candidates in a congressional or presidential fixed-term situation.

In addition to the challenge of juggling the agendas of both the government and the party, Mulroney also had to deal with the fractious traditions of internecine rivalries inside the party: rivalries that he had once relished, and now had to manage. Most of his friends – several of whom were no longer working in the Prime Minister's Office but retained regular contact with him – didn't like Norman Atkins or the Big Blue Machine regulars much. They saw them as parochial Southern Ontario anglophones who thought that if they understood Southern Ontario they understood the country, logistics experts with no strategic sense; people who could read poll numbers better than they could make gut political judgements. Like Mulroney, many of these people were from small towns, and were marked by the experience of knowing what life was like for a minority. Fred Doucet was an Acadian from Cape Breton; Bill Fox, an Irish Catholic from Timmins; Gary Ouellet an Irish Catholic from Quebec City; Ian MacDonald a Scots Catholic from Montreal.

But, though Mulroney would not discourage the jokes about the Big Blue in chats with friends, he knew the value of a Norman Atkins, and the people who felt loyal to him. Mulroney was a master of the thoughtful phone call, the signed photograph; while his loyalists might be able to display a vanity wall filled with photographs of them with Mulroney – the totem of political organizers – Atkins too had his signed photograph with Mulroney, but also others: Atkins with Duff Roblin, Richard Hatfield, William Davis, Roy McMurtry, Robert Stanfield, and his mentor and former brother-in-law, Dalton Camp.

The loyalists might scorn the people they call the BBMers, and fume at the articles that appeared regularly in Toronto newspapers crediting them with winning elections; they might remark scornfully that they were great at reserving buses and planes; Mulroney might not invite them often to 24 Sussex, but he took pains not to offend them, or repulse them.

His management of the campaign would be a study in inclusiveness: Lowell Murray, the usher at his wedding who had so infuriated him when he backed Joe Clark in 1976, was there in a key role, even though Mulroney remembered that Murray had advised Clark that he could win the 1980 election. So were other Clark people: Jodie White, Clark's former chief of staff, worked on negotiating the television debate; Bill Neville, Clark's principal secretary, worked on speeches; Nancy Jamieson worked with Murray. Norman Atkins had his allies and admirers: Marjory LeBreton in the PMO, Harry Near as director of operations, George Stratton working on tour, Hugh Segal working on advertising, and, of course, Allan Gregg and Ian McKinnon of Decima working on the polling. There were also people whose primary loyalties and links to the campaign were solely Mulroney: Peter White, and, of course, Derek Burney.

However, in addition to managing tensions between the different parts of the party, Mulroney also recognized the need to overcome some of the personal resentments he felt himself. In late 1986, while John Turner was wrestling with his campaign to keep his leadership, John Tory was asked to manage the Tory polling. In part, there was a desire to have some management of the budget and execution of the political polling that would monitor the political fortunes of the Progressive Conservatives, but Tory was also chosen in order to put some kind of buffer between Brian Mulroney and Allan Gregg.

It was not a recent conflict. Tories had been suspicious of Gregg since he had first begun work for the party. With his earring and his long hair, he looked out of place to begin with. Worse, in Tory eyes, his polling firm Decima was bought by the Liberal David MacNaughton's firm PAI in 1981; the treasury committee of the party, already suspicious of Gregg's cocky style, considered firing him. The tension rose again when Gregg was the co-author of *The Contenders*, a book on the 1983 leadership race which included some very critical remarks about Mulroney, and would flash into the open whenever Gregg was quoted publicly.

"Our relationship has always been, since 1984 when he let me back, very professional," Gregg said later. "It's never been warm, until recently. There was a feeling that there was a

conflict of interest in my doing things like the year-end
Maclean's poll, or commenting publicly on current issues of
the day."

Mulroney resented Gregg's talking to reporters; Gregg was
fiercely determined to make it clear that the Conservatives
were not his only client, and that his public profile was a
major part of his business. Mulroney had a hair-trigger sensitivity to anything that even might be a breach of confidence.
When Jeffrey Simpson called Gregg to confirm what he had
heard – that Tory numbers were flat ("I can't lie! What am I
supposed to say? No comment?" complained Gregg later) –
and, without naming Gregg, wrote in a column that this was
so, Mulroney was furious, and phoned Gregg at home before
breakfast to berate him.

In that context, John Tory was the ideal intermediary. A
young Toronto lawyer in the old-established firm of Tory,
Tory, Binnington and DesLauriers, he had served as William
Davis's principal secretary and had worked for Frank Miller.
Handsome and charming in a self-effacing way, he was confi-
dent, self-assured, but very discreet.

Mulroney also established a committee shortly after he
made Norman Atkins the chairman of organization in early
1987. Every couple of weeks there would be ad hoc meetings
to prepare for election organization, chaired by Harry Near,
with Norman Atkins, William Jarvis the party president,
Jean-Carol Pelletier the national director, Marjory LeBreton of
the Prime Minister's Office, and other people as required to
deal with subjects as various as the Election Act and training
programs for MPs and for riding organizations, all geared
toward building an effective campaign team. "There was a
conscious decision not to do what the Liberals had done in
1984 – which was to run the campaign out of the Prime Minister's Office," Harry Near said later. "But a great deal of co-
ordination was required. . . . If you look at it, there were three
organizational entities: the party organization under Bill Jarvis, the campaign organization, and the Prime Minister's
Office itself under Derek Burney, with Marjorie being our
primary link. But it was critical that all those three things

were always in sync. In addition to that, you had the appa-ratus of government. It was very important from a campaign point of view that we know what was going on. So there were frequent meetings with Mazankowski."

Harry Near, an Ottawa consultant, was the director of oper-ations. A former chief of staff to Pat Carney, he had been part of the Big Blue Machine when he was with Imperial Oil in Toronto. He was Ray Hnatyshyn's chief of staff when Hna-tyshyn was minister of energy under Clark, and then had gone to work for PAI, where he became vice-president and stayed until going to work on the 1984 campaign, and then for Carney. He had worked with all the key English-speaking figures in the party for a long time.

Then, almost on a separate track, there was a crucial piece in the campaign planning as far as Mulroney was concerned: Quebec.

In the fall of 1987, Bernard Roy asked Marcel Côté to begin working on the party's Quebec strategy for the election. One of the partners of the Montreal consulting firm SECOR, Côté was part of a new political phenomenon in Quebec: rouge à Québec, bleu à Ottawa. Born in Lac-Mégantic in the Eastern Townships, he had done doctoral work at Carnegie Millen in Pittsburgh, and taught at the Université de Sherbrooke. He was one of the people who advised the Union Nationale leader Gabriel Loubier in the early 1970s, and he ran for the UN in Sherbrooke in 1973.

He then joined the Université du Québec à Montréal, and formed SECOR with another former Sherbrooke professor, Yvan Allaire. One of the firm's first projects was studying the francization policy of Robert Bourassa's language law, Bill 22. The firm became a generator of ideas for different political parties: Allaire was a Liberal, as were Pierre Lortie, Richard French, and Claude Forget, who all worked for the firm at various times; Daniel Latouche, who also did some work with SECOR, was a Péquiste, and Côté was a Conservative, who did some work for Roch LaSalle when he made his ill-fated attempt to revive the Union Nationale in 1981. However, he became involved with the Quebec Liberals in the election campaign of 1985. Shrewd, witty, and cheerful, he had a keen sense of the emergence of the new entrepreneurial class in Quebec, and worked with the businessmen who were running for the Liberals: Paul Gobeil, Pierre MacDonald, and André Vallerand.

Côté had a restless intellectual curiosity, which made him reach out to people who were not traditional conservative thinkers: authors like Jane Jacobs, or Charles Hirschman, of the Institute for Advanced Studies at Princeton. "I tease him, and say. 'Hey, they're part of our gang, not your gang,'" said Daniel Latouche, a friend and colleague who had worked for the late Quebec premier René Lévesque. "He is both very conservative, and a bit of an iconoclast. He doesn't think in terms of political ideology; it never occurs to him that someone would refuse to help him for political or ideological reasons."

In the fall of 1987, when Côte agreed to work on a Quebec strategy with Roy, the Tories were running a dismal third in Quebec, at 24 per cent; the NDP was just behind the Liberals at 37 per cent, and the Liberals were in the lead with 39 per cent. At that point, the Tories put together a team: Côté and Bernard Roy working on strategy in Montreal and Ottawa respectively, Pierre-Claude Nolin at Tory headquarters in Montreal working on organization with Mario Beaulieu and Michel Cogger, polling by the firms Createc and Sorecom, Raymond Boucher working with Côté on communications and publicity, and Beaulieu, Fernand Roberge, and Michel Cogger working on the selection of candidates.

Côté proposed three themes: free trade and the view of the economy that it represented, Meech Lake and national reconciliation, and international openness: a theme that reflected the success of the Francophone Summit. But conditions had to be created to enable the "coalition of 1984" – the phenomenon in which Liberal and PQ supporters worked together on behalf of Tory candidates – to come together again. One of the things that were agreed upon was that those questions that were perceived as "irritants," or possible obstacles to victory in Quebec, had to be eliminated: either dealt with quickly, or postponed until after the election. This was primarily Bernard Roy's responsibility. Thus, the decision to award the frigate contract to Saint John, New Brunswick, was made speedily; the Space Agency decision was postponed; and negotiations were undertaken with Quebec to renew the regional-development contract. In addition, every opportunity was taken to show how good the relations were between Mulroney and Bourassa.

At the same time, the polls showed that one of the major obstacles that the Tories faced in Quebec was the sleaze factor. The series of scandals involving André Bissonnette and Michel Gravel had disillusioned Quebeckers about the Mulroney government; focus groups showed that ordinary people felt that they were all a corrupt bunch of crooks.

To counter this, the team took two approaches. First, Roy set in place a fire-drill response in Ottawa: if another scandal occurred, the minister involved would be on the street extremely quickly. When it turned out that Michel Côté (no relation to Marcel) had not declared his huge loan on his financial statement, he was fired almost instantaneously. (Plaintively, Côté wondered if he could keep the limousine.) Mulroney, who was at the Calgary Olympics when the next public-opinion poll came out, was ecstatic at the news that the party had not dipped, but had risen to 30 per cent. ("If we're still at 30 per cent with this shit, we'll win for sure," he exulted when he got advance news of the Gallup results.)

At the same time, Nolin worked on organizing the Conservative council meeting in March, which was to set up a process of regular public meetings of delegates from riding associations across the province to debate policy and party questions. This practice had been introduced by the Parti Québécois and adopted by the Quebec Liberal Party. At this meeting, the idea of restricting fundraising to contributions from voters and eliminating contributions from corporations and unions took another step forward.

This idea became even more accepted by the party organizers when, in June, Lucien Bouchard reported that when he talked to people about it they stopped talking about the scandals. By May, when Bouchard had started campaigning in Lac-Saint-Jean, the Tories had climbed to 31 per cent in the polls in Quebec, the NDP had dropped to 27, and the Liberals were still in the lead at 40.

While this planning was going on in Quebec, Mulroney had secretly established a group to develop some plans for election strategy and timing: a key strategy group, which began meeting secretly at the Château Laurier every month or six weeks for three or four hours, starting in December 1987. It was a characteristic example of how Mulroney spread a broad net to draw in all elements of the party; the group included William Davis, Peter Lougheed, Bernard Roy, and later Peter White, Michel Cogger, John Tory, Norman Atkins, Lowell Murray, Don Mazankowski, Mario Beaulieu, Bill Jarvis, Dalton Camp, and Bob Coates. (Allan Gregg was not included because Mulroney thought he was too visible, and might lead to the group's being discovered.) It was a classic Mulroney group: every part of the party was represented, including men like Camp and Coates who had been on the opposite sides of warring factions in the Tory party for what seemed like generations.

On January 30, the group was looking at a strategy paper sketching out how the government had to overcome weaknesses in performance or record, and change negative impressions. The paper argued that "the negative appeal against free trade, and in particular that our cultural identity and other distinctive features of Canadian life are endangered, has failed." As a result, the paper speculated, the Liberals would not be able to stay on top of the polls.

"His unequivocal opposition to free trade is John Turner's big gamble, and it appears to have failed," it continued. "If this analysis is correct, could Turner's leadership be in trouble by late spring/early summer if an election has not been called?"

At that point, the options being considered included an April dissolution for a June election – although Allan Gregg thought it unlikely that the Tories would improve their standing dramatically by then – a mid-July dissolution after redistribution for a September vote, or a September dissolution for a November vote. The key question to be decided was whether the election should be called before the Free Trade Agreement passed the House of Commons, after the House and before the Senate, or after it was passed into law.

Peter Lougheed, from the beginning, was absolutely committed to the idea that the Free Trade Agreement should be passed by the House of Commons, and to hell with the Senate. He never wavered in this position. Mulroney just listened.

Before Bouchard came back to Ottawa, Mulroney had lunch with Mazankowski, and they worked out a strategy to improve the government's performance in the polls. The two men decided that they were going to sit all summer, use closure when they needed to, and tie in the results to a better leadership profile for Mulroney. The pieces of legislation they were determined to complete were language legislation, child care, literacy, land claims, and the clean-up of the St. Lawrence; it was still unclear how far they should try to get with Free Trade.

"One thing I'm sure of," Mulroney told Mazankowski. "Turner's going to take holidays, and I'm not." Mulroney was convinced that, when all was said and done, Turner was lazy.

Mulroney also had luck. He had kept back an invitation to address the American Senate; he accepted, feeling that the international exposure would be helpful, and found himself in Washington in April at the time of the Liberal caucus revolt.

In June, Mulroney was in Quebec for the signature of a federal-provincial development plan, and had dinner with Robert Bourassa afterwards at the Garrison Club, the old slate-grey building almost hidden behind the Porte Saint-Louis, only a few hundred metres from the National Assembly. As a student of politics, Mulroney asked, what did he think? No question, Bourassa replied. Pass it through the House, and pull the plug. On reflection, Mulroney agreed.

During this period, Allan Gregg kept reassuring Mulroney and the Tories in Ottawa that they shouldn't worry about the fact that they were trailing in the polls. "At that that time, I was using a fairly corny analogy, but it seemed to make people understand what was happening," he said later.

For something was happening that he had never seen before. For a year, there had been little or no movement in voting intentions: how people replied to the question "If an election were held tomorrow, which party would you vote for?" Tory support remained stagnant in the high 20s and low 30s. But at the same time, there was a steady increase in satisfaction with the government's performance, and in rating Brian Mulroney on various leadership attribute.

"They weren't moving up holus bolus as a function of an electorate that was more happy, but we saw, nonetheless, a slow, steady, absolute increase in things like who is the most competent, who has the strongest vision of where he wants to take the country, who's the best negotiator, who's prepared to do what he thinks is right if it's unpopular, all these traditional strength attributes of leadership," Gregg said. "Those, together with satisfaction with the government and the direction the country is headed in, are lead indicators of voting choice. Normally they move modestly in sync, but in tandem within a month maximum. And these numbers had moved from 10, 12, 18, in a year.

"The corny analogy I used was a river; when it gets really really frozen with ice on top of it, the water really has to move rapidly underneath before you get a break-up," he continued. "To the casual observer, nothing is changing as the water moves faster, faster and faster. I predicted somewhat wistfully – because I had never seen this before, ever – that the break-up would come, and when it did come, they would see an exponential pop-up and goosing of their popular support."

"Allan said all through the spring that the numbers weren't moving and quite honestly, in all the time I was involved in the preparation, I didn't expect the numbers to move until spring or early summer, which is exactly what happened," said Norman Atkins. "It's true, it was like a river where the ice was still there, but it was melting from underneath. And all of a sudden, it cracked. And I think it cracked with the G7 [the Toronto Summit]."

Gregg felt that the real change in public opinion did not occur until later in the summer; once the crack happened, he began to argue for an early election call. He felt the government had gained support because of a more positive outlook in the public, the sense that the government was not making mistakes, and the feeling that Free Trade illustrated Mulroney's leadership ability; he was worried about losing that if the government waited too long. Mazankowski was determined to complete as much of the agenda as possible.

"One of the things that was very important to that period was the strategy of incumbency," Atkins said, pointing out that the fact that the House sat all summer (the result of the strategy decision made by Mulroney and Mazankowski over lunch in the spring) conveyed that the government was doing things. He had always favoured a fall campaign; people felt better, there was no recent budget, and the MPs were rested from holidays. Fall felt good.

Throughout the spring and summer, there were constant speculations about when the election would be, which intensified following the two successes of the Lac-Saint-Jean by-election and the Toronto Summit: there were people arguing for a snap election, as soon as the July 14 deadline for the new boundaries passed, to ride the wave; others argued for an election call after the legislation passed the House and while it was being debated in the Senate, thereby permitting Mulroney to run against the Senate; other scenarios included an election call as soon as the Senate grudgingly approved the legislation; or an election call after January 1, 1989. By early July, the Privy Council Office had prepared a paper laying out the various constraints: the House of Commons had to be able to get back into Parliament to pass the Free Trade Agreement before the December 31 deadline. But these were speculations, often reported in the press and discussed among aides and advisers; Mulroney had already decided that the election would be in the fall, after the House passed Free Trade, and before it cleared the Senate, just as Lougheed and Bourassa had recommended.

Near the end of the day on Thursday July 14, exactly three weeks after Roy's resignation, the Prime Minister's Office announced that Peter White had been named principal secretary. White was one of a relatively short list of people who met the requirements for the job: he had had Mulroney's confidence from the time when, at Laval, the two of them and Michael Meighen had made a pact that, whichever of them was in a position to become prime minister, the other two would support him. He had worked in the Prime Minister's Office, was familiar with the operation of the federal government, he was comfortably bilingual and at ease in both French and English Canada, and knew the Progressive Conservative Party both in Quebec and in the rest of the country.

Born in São Paulo, Brazil, White studied French at a lycée in Lausanne, Switzerland, and graduated from Bishop's University in Lennoxville, Quebec, before going to Laval to study law. From that time on, his career was entwined with those of both Mulroney and the Toronto financier Conrad Black. At Laval, White presided over the famous Conference on Canadian Affairs that Mulroney helped organize, which attracted national attention. While at Laval, he met Black at a Tory convention in Ottawa. Then, after leaving law school, he worked first as an executive assistant to Liberal Forestry Minister Maurice Sauvé, and then as an aide to Union Nationale Premier Daniel Johnson – while Black wrote a biography of Union Nationale Premier Maurice Duplessis.

After Johnson's death in 1968, White persuaded Black to join him running a small newspaper in the Eastern Townships, where he has a summer home. Then, in 1970, White ran as a Union Nationale candidate in the provincial election, and lost. It was after the defeat that White suggested that the defeated Quebec Liberal leadership candidate Claude Wagner should consider entering federal politics as a Conservative – and meet with Mulroney to make the arrangements. It was an episode that shocked and ultimately embarrassed many people close to him. White then became the person who first told a reporter, during the 1976 leadership

campaign, of the $300,000 trust fund that had been orga-
nized for Wagner – a statement which would prove to be a
great embarrassment to Mulroney.

While he engaged in politics with Mulroney, playing a key
role in both the leadership campaigns of 1976 and 1983,
White did business with Black, becoming his partner when
Black took over Argus Corp. However, his position was clearly
subordinate. "I wish there was anyone who laughed as hard at
my jokes as Peter White laughs at Conrad Black's jokes,"
remarked someone who had observed the two men together.

Then, in 1983, when Mulroney became leader of the opposition, White joined his office. In 1984, he tried to win a
Conservative nomination in his home town of London, but
lost the nomination to a strong anti-abortion candidate, James
Jepson. After the election, he became a special assistant to the
prime minister, responsible for appointments: the replacement of Liberal appointees with Conservatives. He had made
a list of everyone who worked on the 1984 election campaign,
and set up a computerized system which fed out all the
vacancies on boards and commissions appointed by order-in-
council. White subsequently said in interviews that he was
also trying to overhaul the senior public service – an effort
that was interpreted as trying to politicize it. "There was
tremendous malaise [in the senior civil service]," he said in
an interview after he left in March 1986. "I made several
recommendations about it to the PM but my biggest regret is
that I left Ottawa before I could do anything about it."

In his book on patronage, Jeffrey Simpson describes him as
one of "the hard men" pushing for change. "White's imperi-
ous, dismissive attitude struck his more moderate successor
Marjory LeBreton as so distasteful that she shredded some of
White's memoranda," he wrote.

When he left to rejoin Black as president of Dominion
Stores, White would only say that bureaucratic infighting
"had something to do with it," but he left in some frustration,
having failed to keep the ear of the prime minister. After
running Dominion Stores for his partners, Black and David
Radner, White became the vice-chairman of Hollinger Inc.,

with responsibility for Unimedia, a Quebec subsidiary which owns three daily and twenty-six weekly papers, and publisher of *Saturday Night*. When he met Robert Fulford after Black bought *Saturday Night*, Fulford wrote, "He strongly reminded me of Robert Vaughn in the movies: condescending, cool, stiffly alert, a man one would never get close to."

White had become deeply involved in Black's newest publishing venture, and when Mulroney asked him to come back to Ottawa, he responded, "I wish you hadn't asked me." But he came, going through considerable contortions to comply with the conflict-of-interest requirements. However, the job that he came back to take was not the same job that Bernard Roy had when White left the Prime Minister's Office, and certainly not the same job Jim Coutts had held under Pierre Trudeau. At his first day on the job, he would discover why. For on July 15, the Priorities and Planning Committee learned the results of both Gregg's polling and Mulroney's and Mazankowski's planning over the previous few months.

July 15 was a beautiful sunny day, and considerably more reporters than usual had driven the thirty kilometres up from Ottawa to watch the ministers going in and out of the P and P Committee meeting: the inner cabinet. It was the first day that the new election boundaries came into effect and, while few people really expected he would, no one wanted to take the chance in case Mulroney did break the news that he was calling an election.

Part of the P and P Agenda on July 15 dealt with election planning. The cabinet ministers looked at a strategy memo which identified the question of prosperity as key to the campaign.

"The central message of our campaign is that the continuation of Canada's present prosperity depends on the re-election of a majority P.C. government," the memo said. "The issue of competent, successful economic management, set in the context of the recent Liberal recession and the present economic expansion, must condition and shape the debate on all other issues of voter concern. It is the issue on which all others turn."

The other key element in election planning that the P and P meeting learned about was polls. In April, when Mulroney and Mazankowski had worked out the strategy for the following few months, the Liberals were at 34 per cent, the NDP was at 31, and the Tories were at 27 – where they had been since November 1987. Mulroney told his caucus, "Let me remind you what I told you a year ago: the NDP is not going to win a seat in Quebec. You guys look after your ridings; leave Turner and Broadbent to me."

Then the strategy of visible action began to produce results: the trip to Washington, the by-election, the G–7 Summit, visits from Thatcher, Kohl, and Reagan. In July, the effect of all this could be seen: the Tories were at 39 per cent, the Liberals dropped to 27, and the NDP was at 28. In addition, the polling showed that people thought highly of Mulroney: he was chosen "most trusted" by 40 per cent, while Turner was chosen by 19 per cent and Broadbent by 35 per cent.

Gregg's data, presented to that P and P meeting on July 15, showed that the dominance of Mulroney over Turner was striking in what the polling analysts call "attitudinal" questions. (It also showed surprising strength for Broadbent, but the Tories were convinced that his strength wasn't as important as Turner's weakness; they paid little attention. Broadbent was never a factor in Mulroney's judgement.) Who makes you proud? Mulroney 38 per cent, Turner 19. Who has a vision of Canada? Mulroney 42 per cent, Turner 20, Broadbent 32. Who understands Canada? Mulroney 37 per cent, Turner 23, Broadbent 36. Who is the most trustworthy? Mulroney 26 per cent, Turner 17, Broadbent 49. Who is the best communicator? Mulroney 47 per cent, Turner 14, Broadbent 36. Who is easy to relate to? Mulroney 31 per cent, Turner 15, Broadbent 48. Who is the most careful with money? Mulroney 28 per cent, Turner 19, Broadbent 43. Who is the most caring? Mulroney 28 per cent, Turner 16, Broadbent 50. Who is the most respected by his party? Mulroney 34 per cent, Turner 10, Broadbent 53. Who admits his mistakes? Mulroney 32 per cent, Turner 26, Broadbent 36. Who understands Quebec? Mulroney 63 per cent, Turner 19, Broadbent 14.

Mulroney was first in five categories, Broadbent in six; Turner was last in all but one: he had a slight edge on Broadbent in understanding Quebec.

The first thing that struck White at the P and P meeting on July 15 was how smoothly the committee went. Since he had left two years earlier, the government had got its act together: that overused word "agenda" finally seemed to be under control: the messy business of reconciling the conflicting claims of caucus, cabinet, regional demands and translating the result into the legislation which, if not always consistent, at least pacified the disgruntled.

One of the keys to this process was a tall, amiable, bluntspoken veteran of the House of Commons, ten days away from his fifty-third birthday, Don Mazankowski. With a combination of sticks and carrots, patience, cajoling, stubbornness, listening, lazy talk and hard work, continual long hours and occasional short temper, Mazankowski had smoothed the edges of a disgruntled House of Commons, pulled Mulroney back from some of his impulsive commitments (like his claim that Air Canada was not for sale) and got a large part of what the government was determined to complete before an election through the House of Commons. "The last year leading up to the election was Maz's greatest hour," Norman Atkins said later. "Because of the personal and political relationships he had with key members of the party and the government, people trusted Maz. They respect his political judgement, and I think they knew the prime minister was counting on his advice." The success, in Atkins's view, came from the political management and the support and the control that he had in managing the situation. "That gave the prime minister the confidence he was looking for and needed."

At first glance, Don Mazankowski was an improbable figure for Brian Mulroney to turn to in order to get his government back on track. Born in Viking, Alberta, sixty kilometres southeast of Vegreville, he had finished high school at seventeen and gone to Chicago to live with his sister, and worked for a year as a dispatcher at a trucking firm. He came home a year later, and, when he was twenty, bought an Esso station at Innisfree on Highway 16 East with $3,500 he had borrowed from his family. Four years later, he and his brother Ray bought a General Motors dealership in Vegreville.

In 1968, when he was thirty-two, the MP for Vegreville, Frank Fane, was retiring and asked Mazankowski to go for the nomination. It was not an easy decision; Mazankowski and his wife Lorraine had three young sons, and the car dealership was doing well. He won the nomination on the second ballot, and was elected in June 1968 with a margin of more than 10,000 votes. When he went to Ottawa, his hair cut short and slicked back, he was named youth critic, and denounced the Company of Young Canadians, student militancy, and drugs. "The majority of Canadian youths want no part of radicalism, subversion, and mutinous activities!" he would thunder. In 1972, he became transport critic, and in 1973 caucus chairman; when Joe Clark came to power in 1979, he was named minister of transport. In his book on the Clark government, Jeffrey Simpson concluded that he was "an outstanding Minister of Transport who quickly established a reputation for competence and sensitivity in dealing with the crushing responsibilities of his department."

Despite his gratitude to Robert Stanfield, who was both a steadying and an encouraging influence, Mazankowski was in some ways a Diefenbaker Conservative: he felt that Diefenbaker had made it possible for people who were not Anglicans, Presbyterians, or United Church, and not from English or Scottish backgrounds, and had not gone to university – people who were from Polish or Ukrainian backgrounds, and got dirt and grime under their fingernails when they worked – to feel comfortable in the Conservative Party. He voted against the Official Languages Act in 1969, he was loyal to Joe Clark, and at the 1983 leadership convention had moved from Clark to John Crosbie after the second ballot in an attempt to stop Mulroney.

But he had adjusted, and grown. In 1984, he went back to Transport. But he also had Benoît Bouchard as the minister of state for transport: a down-to-earth junior-college administrator from Roberval who came to Ottawa speaking almost no English. At first, Gary Ouellet, the Quebec City lawyer and friend of Mulroney's, who had got to know Mazankowski when he was a counsel for the Dubin Inquiry on Air Safety, acted as an intermediary, helping Bouchard choose staff. But the two men developed a deep affection and an effective working relationship, with Mazankowski developing an appreciation of Bouchard's achievement in learning English and getting a grasp of issues that Maz had been following for twelve years.

In 1986, a number of issues came to a head. For a year and a half, Mulroney had been agonizing over the fact that Bernard Roy was unable to provide the kind of skills in managing the government's agenda that he needed. There had been an explosion of rage and resentment in the West over the decision to award the CF–18 contract to Canadair in Montreal, despite a lower bid from Bristol Aerospace Ltd. in Winnipeg. And Erik Nielsen had angered too many people with his abrupt, secretive style as deputy prime minister.

When he is asked about the job of deputy prime minister, Mazankowski says simply, "I help the prime minister," or if he chooses to explain a little more, he says "The role of the deputy prime minister is to fill in for the prime minister when he is away and to answer for him in the House and to sort of run the operation when he is discharging other duties." But his self-effacing description neglected to mention his skill in promoting his own priorities, his ability to assuage potential unhappiness in caucus, and his determination to get Western concerns recognized. Like his room-mate, friend, and constituency neighbour Bill McKnight, he would bristle at the continued Western complaint about the CF–18 decision, and the money going to Quebec.

"Let's talk about the money going to Quebec," he replied to an Alberta interviewer who had come down to Vegreville from Edmonton to ask him about the continued Western unhappiness about the issue, and, after spinning off a list of aid programs going to Western farmers, and the Western Diversification program, pointed out that there had been no complaint from Quebec on any of them. "You want to talk about CF–18? Let's talk about it," he continued. "Ask Northwest Industries what we're doing for them. Ask Canadian Aerospace what we're doing for them. Ask Bristol what the CF–5 contract is going to do for them. The fact of the matter is that under that balance, the West is going to end up with more in benefits for the aerospace industry that if the CF–18 contract had gone to Bristol Aerospace."

One of the key innovations that Mazankowski introduced was the "ops" (for operations) committee: a Monday morning meeting of senior ministers who established the real priorities. This was started after Michel Côté had caused a near-uprising in caucus when he announced post-office changes – a rate increase, the closing of rural post offices and the introduction of super mailboxes and the end of home delivery in new subdivisions – only three hours before the decision was announced publicly. The committee – Mazankowski, External Affairs Minister Joe Clark, Finance Minister Michael Wilson, Pat Carney in Treasury Board, Jake Epp from Health and Welfare, Robert de Cotret from Industry and Federal-Provincial Relations Minister and Senate Leader Lowell Murray – was an oral meeting with no notes or memos, at the end of which Mazankowski decided the order in which things would proceed. It was over a year before there was any public knowledge that the committee existed. Quietly, Mazankowski had introduced Holiday Inn management: no surprises.

Another key subject Mazankowski had had to deal with was bilingualism. Mulroney had probably fewer bilingual MPs than any government caucus in a long time – and for the first time in a very long time, unilingual French-speaking MPs as well as unilingual English-speaking ones. The members from Quebec were convinced that the Liberals had only paid lip service to the guarantee of services in French, while the members from parts of English Canada were equally convinced that the Liberals had been obsessed with the issue.

When Bill C-72 was brought forward, English-speaking Tories from rural areas were unnerved to see that, far from receding, as they had assumed it would, bilingualism was moving forward. The bill translated what had become practice in most departments into legislation, and brought the legislation into conformity with the Charter of Rights.

For Western MPs, the issue exploded in February, when *Western Report* and *Alberta Report* magazines had a striking cover on their February 1 issues: simply the sentence, in large letters "Si vous ne pouvez pas lire ceci, vous ne pouvez pas travailler pour le gouvernement fédéral." Below, in smaller letters: "Translation: If you can't read this, you can't work for the federal government." The story, headed "English isn't good enough," was a provocative assessment of the legislation, quoting one unnamed "long-time Tory" as calling it the "most tyrannical legislation Canada has ever presented."

Ten Western ministers signed a letter to the publication, answering the allegations, and pointing out that of the 49,000 federal jobs in Western Canada there are only three that require French only, that bilingual positions account for only 2.7 per cent of the jobs in Western Canada, and that unilingual anglophones are eligible for some 80 per cent of all positions in the federal civil service.

However, the issue had burst into the Tory party again; Mazankowski had to take on the job of conciliating the backbenchers who were worried about the legislation, or determinedly opposed to bilingualism. At the end of June, at the last moment, despite weeks and months of discussions and amendments, fifteen Tory backbenchers submitted 136 amendments to the legislation, some of which would have gutted the bill. On July 6, Mulroney came in from his holidays to speak to the caucus, making a strongly emotional appeal. He was particularly scathing about an amendment suggested by Robert Corbett of Fundy Royal, which proposed that English be the only official language of the Canadian Armed Forces.

"What do I tell [the former Tory cabinet minister] Pierre Sévigny, who left his leg on a battlefield in France?" he asked.

"What do I tell the family of [the late Quebec premier] Paul Sauvé? What about [Senate speaker] Guy Charbonneau? Is it no longer going to be possible to die in French for your country?" And, once again, he reminded the caucus of his speech to the House of Commons in October 1983, on French-language rights in Manitoba. The caucus rallied, with only a handful of dissenters making a last defiant stand in opposition to bilingualism.

At the Meech Lake P&P meeting, the decision was made to have the House of Commons continue sitting, and try to get as much as possible of the rest of the government's agenda completed: in particular the Free Trade Agreement and the child-care legislation. But the news of the day was the announcement that an agreement in principle had been reached with Newfoundland on a deal that would enable the east-coast oil development to go ahead. The deal turned out to be a $1.6-billion loan guarantee for the $5.2-billion development phase of the Hibernia oilfield off St. John's.

The government's polling showed that it was not trusted in the areas of regional development and social policy. This put pressure on it to make major announcements of energy mega-projects, and government initiatives in the social field. But the announcements did not come without some vigorous debate.

Allan Gregg had argued against big spending, and large promises. "A lot of the spending that went on I thought was to no end at all, and if anything fuelled the worst suspicions the population held about the government, namely that [they thought] the public was stupid and could be bought," he said later. "The old bread and circuses, the Lac-Saint-Jean by-election just fuelled the proponents of the 'Open-the-public-purse' [approach]. 'This is what the people want, look at the results, it's very clear.' Those who said, 'All you're doing is wasting money and potentially highlighting a vulnerability and buying nothing, absolutely nothing, zip-all' – those people lost the day."

There was also a more technical debate. In the Department of Energy, there had been two predictions over the previous few years concerning oil prices. The first was that they would rise slowly but steadily to $32 (U.S.) a barrel; the second was that, since non-OPEC production had been increasing twice as fast as world demand, the price would remain at $18. If the second theory was correct, energy mega-projects would be a mistake. At the same time, Michael Wilson had succeeded in keeping the energy depletion allowance out of his plan for tax reform. In part to compensate for this, the government invited proposals for mega-projects.

Through the winter of 1987–8, negotiations continued on the Hibernia deal. On March 5, Brian Mulroney told the priorities and planning committee's election strategy meeting that the government would proceed with Hibernia, the gas pipeline to Vancouver Island, and, as he put it, "something in Alberta": the Husky Upgrader in Lloydminster, or the OSLO (Other Six Lease Operations) oil-sands plant near Fort McMurray.

After intermittent and erratic negotiations, the key discussion on Hibernia occurred in the first week in July. Hibernia was crucial politically to the other mega-projects, since its oil was expected to be less expensive than the heavy oil in Alberta. If the government could not negotiate a deal with quite good economics in Canada's poorest province, it would be very difficult politically to justify a costlier project in one of Canada's richest provinces.

The arguments on the merits and liabilities of the Western projects, particularly the Husky Upgrader, made little impact on Mazankowski. The issue was a crucial symbol. Maz was determined to deliver. "The Lloydminster Upgrader was a natural evolutionary thing," he said, pointing out that the agreement in principle had been signed in 1984, and that progress had continued steadily. "Both the Province of Saskatchewan and the Province of Alberta wanted the project to go very badly, and we worked to find ways and means to do it," he said. "As far as Hibernia is concerned, it was the same thing. . . . Symbolically, the Lloydminster project was very helpful in terms of the fact that very clearly Western ministers, working with the Western provinces, had some clout in dealing with the federal government. It was very very important."

And so Hibernia made Lloydminster and OSLO and the Vancouver Island Gas Pipeline politically possible. They were part of a long and expensive list: $1 billion in grants and $1.6 billion in loan guarantees for Hibernia, feasibility studies for government participation in the $4-billion OSLO project, participation in the $1.27-billion Lloydminster Upgrader, and $150 million for the pipeline. This came on top of a variety of regional commitments: $800 million over fifteen years as compensation for the closing of the Newfoundland railway, the June commitment of $515 million for regional development in Quebec, $420 million in new equity for the Farm Credit Corporation, $165 million in drought relief for Western Canada in addition to a promise of as much as $1 billion in additional support, $88 million to help grape growers in Ontario and British Columbia adjust to the impact of the Free Trade Agreement and the GATT ruling that Canadian wine pricing policies were discriminatory, and $420 million for an all-terrain vehicle for the Canadian Armed Forces. Then, through August and September, there were more announcements on the social side: $110 million for cleaning up the pollution in the St. Lawrence, $110 million for a national campaign against illiteracy, $250 million over five years for the film industry, and, of course, the commitment to spend $6.4 billion over seven years on a national child-care program.

Peter White brought one particular idea with him when he joined the Prime Minister's Office in July. For some time, he had been reflecting on Margaret Thatcher's experience in the 1987 election in Britain. In that election, she had been disconcerted by the fact that her favourite advertising man from the previous election, Tim Bell, had left the Conservative Party's ad agency, Saatchi and Saatchi.

For part of the campaign, she met secretly with Bell – who had become a personal friend – sounding him out for advice without the knowledge of the main party organization. Then, at a key moment in the campaign when things looked grim, she brought him in to rework the Tory ads. Rodney Tyler wrote an intriguing insider's account of the campaign, describing this in detail. He described the tensions between Thatcher and the party chairman, Norman Tebbit, the party's (and Thatcher's) unhappiness with John Wakeham, the chief whip who was responsible for assigning ministers to television programs and gave a disastrous performance himself on TV, and the phenomenon of what he called "the isolation of a Prime Minister within the protective cocoon provided by the civil service."

"Mrs. Thatcher has fought this creeping isolation over the years," Tyler wrote. "She has a number of people whom she regards as semi-business 'friends' whom she telephones or meets from time to time. . . . She uses them because she knows it is essential to keep another perspective on her life, to get a different set of reactions to those offered as the official line."

White was intrigued. He analysed the account, underlining passages, emphasizing parallels in the margin. He proposed a similar approach: that a parallel structure be established, with a second polling company, and a second advertising agency to provide a second opinion. Thank goodness Mrs. Thatcher had other people, he argued; she had a choice.

But John Tory, who had been assigned a year earlier to be responsible for the party's polling, was strongly opposed to the idea. However, while the idea of a formal parallel system did not go anywhere, White was clearly interested in creating some source of back-channel information. So when Fred Doucet suggested setting up a telephone network, he agreed enthusiastically.

The result was the creation of a group which initially called itself the National Network Intelligence Group, but which soon became known as simply the Network. Co-ordinated in Ottawa by Fred Doucet, Gary Ouellet, and Ian Anderson – all three Mulroney confidants who had become Ottawa consultants – the key members were Frank Moores, the former premier of Newfoundland who had also become a consultant, Joe Stewart, a Nova Scotia Tory, William Davis, Walter Tedman, a communications consultant and former aide to Toronto Mayor Art Eggleton, Jamie Burns, Don Mazankowski's former chief of staff, John Bitove, a Toronto Tory, Terry McCann, the mayor of Pembroke and a former classmate of Mulroney's at St. F.X., Bernard Roy, Marcel Côté, Peter Lougheed, Richard Hatfield, and Ken Waschuk. From October 12 on, the group talked on a conference call every day, and Dean Zizzo, an assistant to Peter White, took notes. A one-page summary was sent to the Prime Minister's Office: one copy to Derek Burney, and one copy to Peter White.

The existence of the group provoked considerable annoyance among members of the campaign organization, who insisted afterwards that the Network had no impact on the campaign, and that the summary was not always sent on to Mulroney. Network members, on the other hand, asserted that the campaign organization was incapable of strategic thinking, made terrible mistakes early in the campaign, and had insufficient confidence in Mulroney himself; that the group did provide key advice to Mulroney.

The Network proved useful in a number of ways. It acted as a combination focus group and source of strategic advice. It brought a network of people into the campaign, and broadened the involvement beyond the formal organization. It also structured the thinking of key Tories across the country so that, with one phone call to Peter White, or Fred Doucet, or Gary Ouellet (people he called often) Mulroney could find out what Lougheed or Davis or others were thinking – and sometimes follow up with calls to them. At the same time, however, the group was structured so that there were several key overlapping links with the regular campaign organization: Derek Burney received the reports, Peter White attended the campaign meetings, and Marcel Côté was both a key member of the campaign organization in Quebec, and a member of the Network. Following his own advice to Luc Lavoie, Mulroney had involved a large number of people while keeping real control restricted to a small number. It was a neat formula; it worked.

John Turner's decision to announce that he was asking the Senate to withhold approval of the deal until after the election seemed to galvanize Liberal energies around the free-trade issue; however, there was a cost. In Montreal, Pierre Deniger announced to the Board of the Brewers' Association of Canada, where he worked, that he was leaving to run as a candidate. At the next meeting, two days after the Senate accouncement, he said, ''Gentlemen, at our last meeting, I told you I was a candidate; let me announce to you now that I am defeated.'' For he could feel the middle-class and business support for free trade solidify in reaction to the Turner announcement.

For the Liberals, a source of worry and speculation was Greg Weston's book on Turner: *Reign of Error*. Peter Connolly remained calmly confident that the response to the book was more important than what was in the book itself. Tories were equally full of anticipation: at least one Tory specifically included the publication of the book as part of a suggested election scenario, and Harry Near joked privately that the election wouldn't be called until the hardcover campaign literature was published.

On August 28, Mulroney gave an interview to CBC TV's Peter Mansbridge on *Sunday Report*, and said clearly that the election would be in the fall. He decided to do this because of his belief that Canadians do not focus on how they will vote until close to an election. He was convinced that the election would be on leadership, and he wanted to increase the scrutiny on Turner. Another reason came from the desire to put the election plan on the record, and not to appear to be opportunistic in taking advantage of whatever embarrassment Turner would suffer from the Weston book.

The book was excerpted in newspapers across Canada, giving the Liberals a series of unflattering headlines. Weston's unrelentingly nasty tone, flip style ("But behind the scenes, all was not well in Gritland, despite Turner's reassurances to the contrary") and heavy reliance on disillusioned former staff members provoked a negative reaction from his colleagues, and may have reduced the long-term impact of the book; however, in the short term, it added to the negative assessment of Turner's leadership. Connolly may have been right, but despite his analysis, it took Turner several days to respond to the book, during which he kept being harassed by reporters for a reaction.

Once Mulroney got to his often stated anniversary of September 17, he had other hurdles: Jewish holidays, the Olympics in Seoul, a trip to the United Nations, a desire not to have the election conflict with the Ontario municipal elections on November 14. He ultimately chose the date by picking the best time for television debates – early in the campaign – and choosing the election date accordingly. If things went badly in the debates, he wanted time to recover. But those lobbying for an early election persisted in leaking their preferred date to reporters, who would gleefully print it. After one such date came and went, and the dramatic 100-metre race was approaching, one Tory aide explained why the election had not been called, saying to a reporter, "If you had to choose between putting Ben Johnson on the front page of the *Toronto Sun* or Brian Mulroney, which would you pick?"

But when the Ben Johnson victory turned sour, some wondered whether Mulroney had waited too long.

If Allan Gregg's private numbers were showing that the ice was cracking, the publicly published numbers still showed the Tories in deep trouble, particularly in the cities. This helped provoke a feeding frenzy for Liberal nominations, as potential candidates seemed to be able to almost taste the power that they could smell in the air like bread in the oven. Publicly and privately, John Turner applauded the riding fights: sure they were untidy, sure they were sometimes undignified; but they were proof of the vitality in the Liberal Party.

Not everyone agreed. Long-time Liberals, disgusted that the rules seemed to have collapsed, withdrew. Roberta Need, shocked at what she felt were the dirty tactics that won the nomination in Mississauga East for Albina Guarnieri, left a message on her answering machine saying, "I'm out in the garden enjoying my roses. If you are calling as a member of the federal Liberal Party of Canada, please do not waste your time leaving a message. I want nothing more to do with the federal Liberal Party of Canada or its candidates, so if you're not a personal friend, please hang up."

There were accusations of membership-buying, mobilization of ethnic communities, obstructive tactics at the nomination meetings to encourage less organized supporters to go home: the worst examples of machine politics. The most notorious battles in Toronto emerged from the campaigns of four friends, each determined to seize some political turf: Joe Volpe, a forty-year-old school administrator; Tony Ianno, thirty-one, an aide to David Peterson; Armindo Silva, a forty-nine-year-old insurance broker, and Jasbir Singh, forty-five, a real-estate agent.

"It was a brilliant political attempt to put together a cross-cultural movement," observed a Liberal academic, James de Wilde. "But by 1988, it was less a cross-cultural movement than an Italian movement. Despite that effort, we still don't have an adequate representation of all the multicultural groups in the elected caucus."

Volpe took on a member of the last House, Roland de Corneille, and took the nomination in Eglinton-Lawrence away from him; Tony Ianno decided to run in Spadina, scaring away Aideen Nicholson, whose old riding was abolished with redistribution but overlapped with the new Spadina riding, and defeating former Liberal cabinet minister John Roberts in the process. Armindo Silva was defeated by Albina Guarnieri for the nomination in Mississauga East, and Jasbir Singh failed to win the nomination in Etobicoke North against a former MP and former Liberal cabinet minister, Roy MacLaren.

The conflict in Mississauga East became one of byzantine complexity: Albina Guarnieri, a short blonde woman with a deceptively soft voice, had worked for Liberal MP Robert

Kaplan, Toronto Mayor Arthur Eggleton, Ontario cabinet minister Monte Kwinter, and James Coutts; she had been a Chrétien delegate at the 1984 convention, and had voted for review of Turner's leadership in 1986. She had first tangled with the opposing group when she worked for John Roberts at the Spadina nomination against Tony Ianno, who had supported Roberts at the 1984 convention.

Guarnieri won the nomination on May 15 by 71 votes; it was challenged to arbitration on the ground of irregularities, and, after a substantial delay, a second convention was held, and she won again. But the struggle had generated insults, threats, allegations that people who had voted for Silva had also supported a Conservative at another nominating convention, investigations – all duly reported, and all contributing to the general impression of chaos.

In Montreal, several similar battles were waged. As in Toronto, some of the ethnic battles became embroiled in both local and Liberal rivalries, further complicating the already difficult situation.

In Anjou–Rivière-des-Prairies, the nomination meeting had been postponed because of all the energies which were devoted to trying to save the fundraising brunch in Montreal after the caucus revolt and the firing of Pietro Rizzuto as the chief fundraiser and organizer of the brunch, and because of the provincial by-election in the riding. This had the effect of prolonging the period of recruitment of members by would-be candidates, so that the membership grew to 9,404 members, and a series of accusations that almost 20 per cent of those members were from outside the riding. Raymond Garneau had hoped to have a woman run in the riding, which had elected Monique Bégin, but the contest quickly became an issue in the Italian community. To protest the organization of the nomination meeting, the executive of the riding association resigned, forcing the Liberal Party to put the riding under trusteeship.

However, Anjou – Rivière-des-Prairies was a fox-trot compared to what happened in Saint-Laurent. Thérèse Killens, the sitting MP, had suffered a terrible car accident during her mandate, and had decided not to run again. Raymond Garneau, whose riding was going to disappear, decided not to run in Saint-Laurent, and urged Michel Robert (who had also considered running in Rosemont) to decide if he would run there, and start selling membership cards. Robert didn't want to be parachuted into the riding, but was uneasy about plunging into the job of selling memberships, and convincing people to support him.

At the same time, there was a controversy on the municipal council, where the mayor's group had revolted against him. One of the people involved in that squabble was a councillor who became interested in the Liberal nomination, Shirley Maheu. But the most visible public presence was a dentist, William Dery. A stubborn, intense man who had engaged in a vigorous battle for the Liberal nomination in Mount Royal in 1984, which he lost in a fight to Sheila Finestone that split the Jewish community, Dery was determined to win a solid nomination this time. The fight promised to be equally bitter: local residents of Saint-Laurent, who were known as "dos blancs" (white backs) from the times when the suburban municipality was a farming village, and the farmers wore white sheepskin jackets, wanted a local candidate, while Dery was furiously mobilizing supporters.

Raymond Garneau argued in favour of announcing the nomination meeting, and letting the meeting choose the winner. However, the electoral commission of the party decided that the riding should be kept available for a prestige candidate. Garneau ended up defending the position he had argued against, causing a nationwide impression that the Liberal Party played by different rules in Quebec. Dery withdrew his candidacy, challenged the procedure, and lost; Michel Robert decided not to run after all, and Shirley Maheu won the riding. Dery remained bitter and angry, and the Liberals ended up with the worst of both worlds: national attention to the fact that ridings were being kept open for prestige candidates, and no prestige candidate.

Overall, the fights were awkward and embarrassing in a number of ways. They raised questions about the process: television items showing people waving their fists and shouting at one another conveyed yet another message of chaos and confusion in the Liberal Party, despite Turner's argument that this was proof that the Liberal Party was the one attracting this kind of energetic, muscular democracy. But more than the discomfiture of appearances, the constituency upsets were symptomatic of a deeper problem: Turner had been unable to reconcile his grass-roots Liberalism with the need for candidates whose primary loyalties were to him. Several strong candidates, who would have given Turner some of the broader strength he needed, lost to better-organized candidates who had been able to mobilize a community or an interest group: Maude Barlow, who had been advising Turner on women's issues, won the Liberal nomination in Ottawa Centre under the old boundaries, and then lost it under the new boundaries to Ottawa alderman Mac Harb. After working for ten months to recruit members in the riding, Patrick Johnston, the former director of the National Anti-Poverty Organization and co-chairman of the Liberal platform committee, lost the nomination in Scarborough West to an anti-abortion candidate, Tom Wappel, in a vicious campaign. Campaign Life had mobilized the Roman Catholic churches in the riding against Johnston, and a whispering campaign was begun, with insinuations about Johnston's private life. In other cases, people who would have been excellent candidates and good MPs looked at the new street-fight ground rules and the cost involved in running a successful nomination campaign, and declined.

On September 26, the Southam papers and the Toronto Star published an Angus Reid poll that showed the Tories at 40 per cent, the NDP at 31, and the Liberals at 26 – with 22 per cent undecided. The NDP campaign director, Bill Knight, thought Angus Reid was right; it confirmed the NDP polling, which showed the Liberals had slipped. He felt that Turner had been sliding, and that the announcement of the forty points, which was intended to kick-start the Liberal campaign after the Senate gambit, had failed to have an impact.

He argued that the government had committed itself to $22 billion in spending, and that the Liberals were now about to deliver a mass of programs which would get lost in the mix, and provoke hot pursuit by the media on how much the Liberal promises would cost.

As a New Democrat, he was delighted; as a former high-school history teacher, he wondered if the Liberals had lost their characteristic as the natural governing party. He began to think that the Tories had adjusted to power, and the discipline it required. And, from a strategic point of view, the party was precisely where he wanted it to be: at 30 per cent, with the Liberals dropping and the Tories on the brink of winning a majority. With the Conservatives having successfully driven themselves into first place, he felt that people would think about what they really wanted. "I love this going into campaign," he said. "'John Turner can't win' – that's what the last four weeks have been about."

Knight felt that this was what Mulroney had done when he told Peter Mansbridge there would be a fall election in the interview at the end of August: he pushed the electorate to think seriously about what they'd do. When they did, their conclusion was "It's not going to be John Turner." The second phase, which Knight thought would be fascinating, would be when Mulroney put the next question to the voters: "Do you think he *should* win?"

For Knight was convinced that the prospect of a majority Mulroney government helped the NDP. In the last weeks of the 1984 campaign, when it was clear Mulroney would have a majority, the NDP took off; he was sure that, if they had had another two weeks, Ed Broadbent would have been the leader of the opposition. Now, he wondered how far the Liberals could slip. What was the lowest they could go? He used to think it was 28 per cent. He didn't think that any more.

Robin Sears was finding the waiting period very frustrating. The ads were ready, the polling was done, the tour was organized, and everyone was in place. The waiting was beginning to cost money: if Mulroney waited past the end of the week, the NDP would have to start looking at where to cut back. They were at twice their regular staff complement.

Sears was in Ottawa as deputy campaign director, on loan from his job as principal secretary to the Ontario NDP leader, Bob Rae. Still in his late thirties, Sears was on the point of making the transition from boy wonder to veteran: he had been federal secretary of the party in 1975 at the age of twenty-four. The son of the *Toronto Star* reporter Val Sears and the grandson of the CCF radical Colin Cameron, Robin Sears was bright, quick, witty, and intimidatingly articulate. He had left the federal party to work in London for the Socialist International, where he had known Willy Brandt and Olaf Palme; he had returned to Toronto a few years before to reorganize Bob Rae's office, where he worked with a degree of bluntness that earned him the nicknames Boy Stalin and Vlad the Impaler. Like Knight, he was determined to make the NDP deal with the problems of playing to win: he had learned the language of marketing and polls, television advertising and election technology. Thus, when asked how different it was running a fully national campaign, as compared to the campaign focused on three and a half provinces that Gerry Caplan ran in 1984, he would say that the key elements would remain the same – the message, the marketing, feedback, and deployment of the best people – but that it was "a much larger retail operation; you're moving from fifty stores to three hundred stores." It was a vernacular of the private market which many in the NDP found foreign and offensive to the Methodist socialism of the party's tradition.

On the basis of the size of their offices and the number of people involved – they had opened offices in Montreal, Toronto, Vancouver – Sears figured that the Tories were spending twice as much as the NDP. By the end of August, he figured that the Tories had lost the advantage of surprise. He had never seen a campaign so far advanced in pre-writ readiness. But he was worried about the spending ceiling on local campaigns. He calculated that a typical campaign cost between $40,000 and $50,000. Salary for two or three senior people would eat up at least a quarter of that: $10–12,000. Communications costs – telephone, fax, electronic mail – would cost $3–4,000. Rent, $3–4,000. Polling, $5–10,000. That left almost nothing for literature or signs. In a large riding, in Edmonton or Scarborough, a leaflet would cost $15,000, not even counting postage. As a result, it was difficult to have campaign literature.

In terms of the NDP team, he was very optimistic; he had never seen such an absence of internal shoving and elbowing at the level of staff and candidates. However, he was worried about Quebec. He had been astonished when Éric Gourdeau had made some public criticisms of the party, and wondered about the political culture which underlay this sense that people were free to speak out publicly against party decisions.

On Wednesday September 28, the Liberals held a special caucus meeting to which all the candidates were invited. Turner spoke to the caucus, and impressed the new candidates enormously with his performance. The election program was presented, and was favourably received, generally.

However, there were some comments that would be remembered later. Paul Martin, the candidate in LaSalle-Émard, was concerned that the program dealt only with the distribution of wealth, and did not talk about the creation of wealth. He felt that the promises should flow from some wider vision. And another candidate expressed concern that the costs of the program were not identified. But there were assurances that this would be done during the campaign.

At the end of the meeting, reporters were ushered in, a cluster of candidates stood around Turner to show him surrounded by supporters, and the Liberal policy platform was unveiled, with the slogan "This is more than an election. It's your future."

The program consisted of forty points that laid out in brief outline the key elements of Liberal policy. The environment was given top priority: the Liberals vowed to restore the cuts to environmental programs, press for a Clean Air Treaty with the United States, and eliminate gasoline lead emissions by 1990. Other points included: rejection of the national sales tax that was proposed as stage two of Michael Wilson's tax reform; the end of the trade deal and its replacement with a trade policy aimed at reducing trade barriers around the world; a housing program aimed at people paying more than 30 per cent of their incomes on accommodation, an expansion of the pension plan to include fulltime homemakers, and partial pension for those taking early retirement at fifty-five; investment-income deductibility up to $1,000 for people over sixty-five; child care for all who needed it; equal pay for work of equal value and equal opportunities for the handicapped and visible minorities in the workplace.

In addition, there were programs promised for part-time workers and the working poor, tax breaks to encourage employee profit-sharing, help for laid-off older workers, apprenticeship training programs, a national year of service for youth, a literacy campaign, a scholarship program, more funds for universities, research, education, and hospice care for AIDS victims.

The Liberals vowed to bring back regional-development programs dropped by the Conservatives, and to establish what they called "a massive road, sewer, and watermain rebuilding program" with a $5-billion contribution. There were programs promised for the family farm, the fishing industry and forestry; a target of 50 per cent Canadian ownership of the oil and gas industry was established, and more Canadian research and development was promised.

The Pacific Rim was identified as a priority for Canadian trade, help was promised for small businesses, a National Stock Ownership Plan was announced, and a commitment was made to "a foreign policy made in Canada for Canada." The nuclear-submarine program was to be cancelled, culture was to be aided, a new national holiday in February was promised; a Department of Multiculturalism would be created, and family reunification would be made the first priority in immigration policy. Aboriginal self-government was proclaimed as a goal, as were an elected Senate, the restoration of home mail delivery, an expansion of the duty-free exemption for travellers to $1,000, and a Clean Government Act to raise the standard of ethics and eliminate patronage.

It was a long, long list, all announced at once – with a promise to flesh out the details and announce the cost of each one during the election campaign. The program was the product of the strategy that had been elaborated in August at Stornoway: Kirby, Ouellet, and Goldfarb had taken the polling data, the strategic recommendations, and the policy programs that had come out of the policy conferences, the report by Manon Vennat and Patrick Johnston, the policy co-chairs, and the policy work by Robert Jackson to produce, in effect, a policy manifesto. As Kirby observed after the meeting, there had been constant criticism that the Liberals lacked a coherent view of the country and a coherent platform.

"The purpose of today's announcement is to make clear that we have a set of policies which have a cohesion to them, which outline a clear Liberal vision of the country, and which reflect Liberal values," he said, adding that the party wanted to make people understand that the Liberals were taking an over-all approach to the role of the government rather than making piecemeal announcements during the campaign.

"The second key element is that if you look at the proposals, they are traditional Liberal areas of policy concern," Kirby continued. "They deal largely with people, and the services Canadians need from government . . . as opposed to just granting money to industry, which is essentially what the [Tory] government has done for a long time."

It remained to be seen if Turner would absorb the program, and make it his own. Nevertheless, the MPs and candidates left the caucus meeting high with excitement: things looked good. "It was a terrific morale-booster," Russ MacLellan said. "You can only go on for so long saying 'We're ready, we're ready' – this was proof. . . . Everybody left extremely happy."

On Friday, John Turner launched his campaign in Winnipeg: a symbolic gesture suggesting that, after having provoked an election with the Senate announcement in July, he would now begin the election campaign, and Brian Mulroney would follow if he dared.

On Saturday morning, October 1, a group of child-care advocates gathered in a Senate committee room to make their last arguments against the government's child-care legislation. The Senate was still considering the legislation, and at five o'clock that morning Sharon Irwin decided that she should not take any chances. As the director of a day-care centre in Cape Breton who had asked to speak to the Senate committee, she was determined to speak out against the legislation if she had the chance, and the election still had not been called. So she flew to Ottawa, and was there to make her case at ten a.m., when the committee began its hearing.

About ten minutes after the committee hearing began, Brian Mulroney emerged from Rideau Hall where he had gone to ask Governor General Jeanne Sauvé to dissolve Parliament. He had not had a formal press conference at the National Press Threatre since that gloomy Sunday afternoon in January 1987 when he announced that he had asked for André Bissonnette's resignation, and the television reporters who had been broadcasting live from outside Rideau Hall were speculating that this would be a peek-a-boo campaign, and that Mulroney might not be available to answer questions.

First in French and then in English, Mulroney read a brief statement that speechwriters had been working on for several weeks, honing it to develop the lines that would be on the news that night, the sort of lines had become dubbed "sound bites" in the American presidential campaign. He had seen the Governor General who, on his recommendation, had dissolved the Thirty-Third Parliament for an election on November 21.

With those words, the child-care legislation died; fifteen minutes later, at 10.28, Senator Orville Phillips asked, "I'd like to know under what authority the committee is operating, since the prime minister has dissolved Parliament." "Why don't you go over to the Federal Court and get a writ [to force the committee to stop]?" snapped Liberal Senator Royce Frith. "And if the [stenographers transcribing the meeting] won't get paid because Senator Phillips won't let them, I'll pay." It was an odd moment: like Wily Coyote in the Roadrunner cartoons, the committee had discovered itself in mid-air. The Thirty-Third Parliament no longer existed, they no longer had any authority to sit, and the legislation they were debating no longer existed.

But the committee decided to continue sitting informally, three more witnesses were heard, and the child-care advocates went away delighted that the legislation had died. The election campaign of 1988 had begun.

CHAPTER SEVEN

The Tories Cruise

"Mankind, as I have often told you, is more governed by appearances, than by realities; and, with regard to opinion, one had better be really rough and hard, with the appearance of gentleness and softness, than just the reverse."

Lord Chesterfield, May 6, 1751

On Saturday morning, October 1, the television networks began live programming shortly before ten o'clock, as Brian Mulroney walked from 24 Sussex across the street to Rideau Hall, and into the governor general's residence. What was about to begin was a ritual which, like the royal assent given to every piece of legislation passed by the House of Commons and the Senate, is one of the rare reminders that Canada is a monarchy. The prime minister was about to recommend to the Queen's representative in Canada that Parliament be dissolved, and the writs be issued for an election.

For a quarter of an hour, reporters milled about outside Rideau Hall, aides in the Prime Minister's Office adjusted the lectern, and television commentators speculated on whether Mulroney would answer questions or not. Then, about 10.10, Mulroney emerged.

Mulroney told the reporters, and the television viewers watching, that it was a Canadian tradition to call an election when a government had completed about four years of a mandate. "More importantly, we are at a point where the differences in our political parties require the judgement and the decisions of Canadians," he continued. "The differences are clear and substantial; the decisions Canadians face on November 21 will make a difference."

This was no exaggeration; more than in any recent previous election, Canadians faced three clear choices: three very different parties were proposing three different directions for the country.

"The key question for the electorate will be who can best manage change in the years ahead," Mulroney said, repeating what had emerged from Allan Gregg's research and had been proposed as the major theme for a front-runner's campaign in English Canada; managing change was a phrase that could reflect the voters' sense of the buoyant economy, and remind people of their unease about Turner's ability to lead and Broadbent's capacity to deal with the economy. "We intend to run on our record of the past and our plans for the future."

After repeating the comments in French (with a slightly more felicitous phrase to the effect that the key question was who should best lead the country during years of change, there being no satisfactory translation for "managing change") he continued in English.

"We intend to run on our record of the past and our plan for the future," he said. "Four years ago, we inherited a Canada scarred by economic recession and divided by mistrust of the major partners of our federation. Today we have an economy that is a world leader in growth and job creation – almost a thousand new jobs per day for every day we have served in government. Today we have a new spirit of national reconciliation, with all of our provinces full members of the Canadian Constitution. Today, Canada can speak with credibility and influence in the councils of the world. We are ready to be judged on that record."

There was a smooth, soft, unwrinkled quality to the prose, like hotel broadloom. In French, he said that the Free Trade Agreement brought the promise of new openings for producers, and better and more numerous jobs. He talked of the need for the national child-care program, and environmental action, saying that there would be "a national commitment to a pollution-free Canada," and the conclusion of an effective agreement with the United States on acid rain. "Ours is, above all, an agenda of confidence for Canada. It builds on our successes of the last four years, and the lessons and values of our history," he continued. "It is a coherent plan . . . for the future which says, first and foremost, that Canadians can shape change for their benefit and their prosperity." Then, concluding the statement, he said that he was asking Canadians to judge his record and his team of candidates.

"Prime Minister, you didn't mention free trade," called out Craig Oliver, the veteran CTV reporter who had only recently returned to Ottawa from Washington. He wondered whether Mulroney would ignore free trade, or whether it would be a centrepiece of the election.

"I mentioned free trade, Mr. Oliver, very substantially in the statement I just read," Mulroney said. He had – but only in French. During Mulroney's first mandate, reporters who didn't understand French often missed substantial elements of Mulroney's statements, particularly outside the House of Commons where no simultaneous translation was available. At times, this was accidental, but at other times Mulroney chose very carefully which language he would use, knowing that the television networks didn't like running an interpreter's voice, or subtitles.

"Will it be the centrepiece of your campaign?" Oliver persisted.

"Yeah, as I indicated in the statement I just read, it will be very much a centrepiece of our political action in the campaign," Mulroney said.

Mulroney told the reporters that the government would be judged on its record, and that Canadians would be aware that the Free Trade Agreement had passed the House of Commons and been obstructed by the Senate, as had the child-care legislation. "We have passed child care through the House of Commons, and were told publicly, the nation was told by Senator MacEachen that it would take at least another month for the Liberal senators to reflect on this, thereby killing the project," he said. "We saw yesterday a statement of some sort by Senator MacEachen – if you believe in statements like that, you still believe in the tooth fairy."

Would public morality be an issue in the campaign, he was asked in French; Mulroney replied that it was an issue in every campaign.

"Do Canadians like you personally as much now as they did four years ago?" asked Wendy Mesley of CBC.

"What do you think?" retorted Mulroney.

"What do you think?" echoed Mesley.

"Well, I'll just refer you to the various public-opinion polls that your network has been producing," Mulroney replied. "You'll get a pretty affirmative answer."

They were the terse, flick-of-the-wrist squash-shot answers that Mulroney habitually gave to scrum questions he didn't like. Some politicians respond positively to tight, skeptical questioning; Mulroney tends to be terse and uncommunicative. He would respond at greater length only when he could give the answers he wanted. Asked what the greatest strength of the government was going into the campaign, he gave a more fulsome reply.

"I think the biggest strength of the government is a record of accomplishment, particularly in the area of economic growth and prosperity, national unity, and a very credible contribution to a moderate, effective and modern role for Canada internationally," he said. "I think there are specific achievements that merit underlining, for example the Free Trade Agreement with the United States of America, which has been cited by the leaders of the G7 countries as a model for the world, as a catalyst for the multilateral round of trading in the GATT. This is a historic initiative, as is the Meech Lake Accord, as are undertakings such as child care, a major social advance on behalf of Canadian families and Canadian women. So. These are the kinds of things, Mr. Oliver, that I hope Canadians will want to consider and I hope will regard favourably."

Despite Mulroney's occasional chippiness at questions he didn't like, the campaign was launched with a certain air of serenity and decorum. He answered questions for fifteen minutes or so, making it clear that he would go to Sept-Îles and Baie-Comeau the following week to announce where he would be running, and that he would be addressing the question of Sinclair Stevens's candidacy the next day, and then left. That afternoon, he went off to Montreal with his family: Mila Mulroney's brother was getting married.

On Sunday, Mulroney gave reporters a tour of the Tory campaign headquarters, and announced that Sinclair Stevens would not be a Conservative candidate. This cleared the deck of embarrassing questions: for some weeks, the Tory organization in Quebec had been working to ensure that André Bissonnette and Michel Côté would not run again, and were pleased that they both announced during the same week. As a bonus, without planning or co-ordination, Michel Gravel, who was still facing court charges, announced he would not be running again. But there had been no word from Stevens, who was a nominated candidate, and seemed blithely unaware of what a liability to the party he had become. Quebeckers were beginning to mutter that there was a double standard at work, and that it would be extremely unfair if Bissonnette (who, had, after all, been found not guilty by a jury) were forced to step down and Stevens (who had been found by Chief Justice Parker to have made fourteen breaches of the conflict of interest guidelines) were allowed to remain a Tory candidate.

The campaign had begun.

The beginning of the campaign meant the beginning of the prime minister's tour: an activity which had become the hallmark of Conservative election campaigns, and was known in Tory jargon as simply "Tour."

The professionalization of the prime minister's – or the leader's – tour was not an original Conservative innovation. Colin Kenny had brought the same almost military concern for advance work and tour logistics to the Liberals in the early 1970s: skills he had developed by studying *The Advance Man*, a book by Jerry Bruno, chief advance man for

the Kennedys, and Jeff Greenfield. But these were also preoccupations of Norman Atkins and the Big Blue Machine.

One Big Blue Machine trademark was a smooth tour operation, guided by a daily itinerary which averaged between
sixty and sixty-five pages. Pointing proudly to George Stratton, the tour chairman, and his assistant Joan Peters, Atkins
described Tour as "a profession . . . a profession in itself."

The profession was virtually invented by Jerry Bruno. In *The
Advance Man*, he describes the essence of the job, which an
angry John Kennedy laid out to him in late 1959, when the hall
in Superior High School in Superior, Wisconsin, was only
one-third full because a football game had been rescheduled.

"Whenever you plan any appearances, make absolutely
sure of the details," he said. "Don't ever, ever schedule
another appearance until you know all the facts and make
sure every detail's been completed."

This principle, adopted by Colin Kenny in the Trudeau
office, was elevated into gospel by the Mulroney PMO. Bill
Fox, who had watched the Reagan White House as a reporter
before coming to work for Mulroney in early 1984, understood the mandate: he had to make events work, and did not
hesitate to speak harshly to local dignitaries, volunteers, or
diplomats who were slow to appreciate the importance of a
good television shot. Similarly, in spite of his background in
External Affairs, Derek Burney endorsed the idea of a Tour
official that when Mulroney spoke to the General Assembly
of the United Nations in September the Canadian diplomats
should get on the phone to diplomats from countries receiving Canadian aid to make sure that there were as many people
as possible in attendance. It didn't matter if the diplomats
were unhappy at taking instructions from a political advance
man; Burney made it clear that the prime minister wanted it
done. A good crowd has always been a crucial test of good
advance work; good TV pictures are now equally important.

Atkins paused. "The key is the people on the plane, and
the relationship they have with the leader, and the confidence the leader has in the whole process: the ability to put

together the physical elements of a tour: the right kind of a plane, the right buses. All of that, while it may look overdone, is very very important to the success of Tour. Then it isn't by gosh and by golly."

The selection of people to go on the plane was jealously fought over; the final result was a group that blended effectively with Mulroney, and with each other. John Tory was Mulroney's chief aide, who received messages from the ground; Art Lyon, who had worked on three previous campaign tours, was the wagonmaster, and Paul Troop, who had worked with him on the Pope's visit, was his assistant; L. Ian MacDonald wrote speeches on the plane; Marc Lortie was the press secretary, Luc Lavoie supervised the television aspects of the tour, and Richard Rémillard worked with reporters.

But while Atkins and Stratton contributed substantially to the elite culture surrounding Tour, a crucial element was provided by a bland-looking young man in horn-rimmed glasses and short hair, who faded inconspicuously into the background: Stuart Murray. Confidants of Mulroney said that he would visibly relax when he saw that Murray was present.

Stuart Murray had worked on the movements of Mulroney as prime minister. He had been spotted by Bill Fox during the 1984 election campaign as a volunteer advance man in Southern Ontario. As Mulroney left London, Ontario, to go to Kenora and then back to Quebec and Baie-Comeau in the last week of the campaign, he took a few steps up the back steps of the 737, and then came back down and said to Murray, who was standing on the tarmac, "We're going to give you a call!" and flashed him a thumbs up before heading up into the plane.

Murray glowed with pleasure at the acknowledgement; the next thing he knew, he was working in Ottawa in the Prime Minister's Tour Office. Originally from Saskatchewan, Murray had lived in Toronto for some time, working in the music business. He was a road manager: the person who organized two- and three-month tours for groups like Blood Sweat and Tears and Rush, and for Murray McLauchlan and Bruce Cockburn. He had also done some work with Bruce Springsteen.

His responsibility had been to make sure the tours ran smoothly, that everyone got paid, and that everything looked right: the stage, the lights, the backdrop.

It was ideal training for a Prime Minister's Office in the television age, for the jobs were very similar. Murray came to the PMO with a sense of what made a road show work, how to put the performer at ease and enable him to deliver his show. He knew that, regardless of the speech Mulroney was going to make, if it was a visual failure, the message would not be delivered. People absorbed their information from television.

In his office in the Langevin Block, Murray kept the famous photograph that Andy Clark, later to be Mulroney's official photographer, had taken when he was with Canadian Press during the 1984 election campaign, of John Turner with the forks on a plaque behind him appearing to come out of his head. It was a constant reminder of what was to be avoided; Murray would wince at the thought of the Tory brush with the same kind of thing: a photograph of Mulroney taken in Napanee, Ontario, where an eagle on a mural behind him seemed to be swooping down on him.

As a result of his professional experience, Martin Schram's book *The Great American Video Game* (which one of Murray's counterparts at the White House had recommended to him) just confirmed what he already knew: if the events were organized in a way that produced good pictures, and the pictures made the leader look good, the networks would have no choice but to use them. And Murray had spent his years organizing rock tours developing the visual impact of a show, so that when the lights went up, people would say, "Wow, this is fabulous!"

Over the summer, Murray and the other tour organizers ran a series of nation-wide tour schools. Over the years of the mandate, the Tour Office had developed a network of 400 volunteers across Canada, and had used Mulroney's travels to develop their skills, and to strengthen their loyalty to Mulroney. Even if a trip could get by with one volunteer in a specific town for a visit, three would be used: two to accompany

Mulroney, and one to accompany his wife. This shared the training, and spread the net a little wider: each one would get a personal thank-you note. On occasion, as on the Mulroney trip to the United Nations, key volunteers would be invited to join the advance team.

At the tour schools, the organizers would go through what they wanted to achieve, and distribute the tour manual and tour check list that they had developed so that volunteers would feel comfortable. Then, as a final preparation, two key people from each province were flown to Ottawa for a final run-through on how itineraries should look, and what images they were looking for. The key element that they stressed was that Mulroney was to look like a leader and a statesman at all times: no footballs, no funny hats, no potentially embarrassing situations. No risks. No disruptions of the basic message.

As the campaign began, Mulroney headed to Southern Ontario. The campaign days had been planned so that in the morning there would be an event to illustrate the theme of the day (called, at least in the early days of the campaign, the "process event"); at noon, a speech before a non-partisan but sympathetic audience, and at night a speech to a Tory rally. Interspersed with this were interviews with evening-news television hosts, and visits to riding headquarters.

It was a smooth, well-controlled operation. Three buses were available for the reporters: a smoking bus, a non-smoking bus, and, for those who were writing and didn't want to listen to music on the stereo system, a working bus. Each one was equipped with refrigerators and microwave ovens; campaign staff would have popcorn waiting for reporters after events. But reporters were annoyed by the decision to use ropes or plastic chains to keep the crowd of reporters, cameramen, and soundmen at a distance from the Mulroney party.

At times, the efforts of the advance crew were extraordinary. "On the middle of the Prairies outside Dundurn, Sask., with not another farm as far as the eye could see and only a herd of Black Angus cattle on the horizon, the Mulroneys followed a meticulous little route behind ropes, while Conservative farming families watched from a respectful distance," Linda Diebel caustically noted. In Toronto on October 12, when Mulroney spoke to a Rotary Club meeting at the Boulevard Club, zealous advance people kept Tory supporters several hundred yards away; one volunteer came up to the police officers waiting in the club's hallway and said earnestly, "You'll come to attention when the prime minister comes in."

Members of the press began writing about "the bubble," and "the cocoon," much to the annoyance of members of the Mulroney entourage, who insisted that the measures had been introduced for two reasons: to ensure that no one would accidentally get trampled, and to give clean shots for both the television cameras and the cameras shooting for Tory advertisements.

In fact, there was some disagreement among campaign strategists about running a smooth, passive front-runner's campaign. Allan Gregg saw the need to distinguish the Tories from the other two parties in the very early stages, making it clear that there was a very real difference: that the Tories had a plan, and the others didn't, that the future was too uncertain not to have a clear plan, and that the Tories were more competent.

One of the things that had struck Gregg in his data was that there was a feeling that there was no great difference among the three parties. In focus groups, people would be asked what they thought of John Turner, and, after they had said negative things, they were asked if the country would be worse off under him. No, people said, he would learn. Similarly, people felt that, while the stock market might drop and the dollar might lose value with an NDP victory, it would only last a month or so, and the NDP would then do the same things as everyone else.

"That really scared us," Gregg recalled. "That was my major goal in the early part of the election: to drive those numbers up. We got them up to 60 per cent saying there were major differences between the three parties. Then that worked to our disadvantage when everybody got worked up about free trade, and everything focused on that."

Gregg felt that, despite a general sense of comfort and happiness, Canadians had a vague, unfocused anxiety that change was imminent, and that these were immutable forces that government could not deal with. As a result, he argued, people wanted a government that recognized that change was coming, and had some plan to cope with those uncertainties, and the competence to implement it.

"We'd do focus groups in Burnaby, B.C., and blue-collar workers would slam their hands on the table and say, 'You know what governments have got to do? They've got to get a strategic plan!'" he said. "They were saying you can't fix today's problems; you can manage them. That's what we set out to do."

This was the source of the "managing change" theme, the visits to high-tech factories gearing up for free trade, and the television ads quoting newspapers suggesting that Mulroney led an effective team with a vision. "[We were] establishing that there was a choice to be made, and that there was a risk in voting for the other guys," Gregg said. "Our concern was that something would happen, and it would be 'throw the rascals out'; if there was no risk or threat associated with voting for the other guys, the electorate thought they could do that with impunity. Then you would see our support slide very very very quickly. When you start from the lead – very few people understand this – you start from the assumption 'I don't want one more vote. All that I want to do is add some conviction to what is now an inclination to support my guy. I've just got to build some roots, that's all I've got to do.' And so you do run a relatively uninspired campaign. You've got to be active, there has to be some juice going, you have to capture the agenda, but having said that, you don't have to say 'And if you elect us, we'll do . . . fill in the blank.' The Quebec guys were saying, 'We want a clean sweep.' I was saying, "That's chasing the last dollar in the marketplace; you go bankrupt.' They were saying, 'How do we reach blue-collar, east-end allophones?' I was saying 'Forget 'em.'"

Marcel Côté, the SECOR consultant who had been working on the preparations for the Tory campaign for almost a year, took different soundings of public opinion in Quebec, and, while the findings were similar to Decima's, he drew different conclusions, disagreeing with Decima's strategy in terms of Quebec.

"Election campaigns are about switching voting intentions and consolidating soft voting intentions," he wrote in early September. "Thus, at any given time, two segments are of key interest to us: potential (likely) switchers to PC and soft PC voters."

Labelling the soft voters as PC1s and the potential switchers as PC2s, he found that the two groups constituted 40 per cent of the electorate in French-speaking Quebec.

"From that vantage point, our own research says that the PC1s and PC2s are relatively satisfied with life, with the economy, with the government, and with Mulroney," he continued. "The sleaze factor explains much of their softness (PC1) and reluctance (PC2)."

His recommendation was that Mulroney emphasize the environment, which he called "the only operational issue that cut across most PC1s and PC2s," and that, on the tour, he make commitments on the environment, day care, the economy, pensions, good management, taxes, and the deficit; and that he reduce anxiety on free trade.

On the basis of that analysis, Côté felt that having Mulroney tour high-tech plants asking if people were ready for the changes that free trade would bring, and talking about "managing change," would do little to attract the soft, or reluctant voter; rather, it would provoke anxieties about what change might do. "Mulroney was putting too much emphasis on free trade as change," he said later. "People wanted security."

Certainly, Mulroney did not expect that the front-runner's campaign would last long.

At a meeting with senior advisers, shortly before the election was called, he predicted what he thought would happen.

"Well, somewhere along the road, maybe during the debate, Turner is going to say something that is going to have a dramatic impact," he said. "This is because he is starting from so far back, there are such low expectations of him, and the media will be looking for something to inject some excitement into the race, All these things are going to be combined and exaggerated beyond their importance."

Similarly, on that first day on the road on October 3, as he got back into his bus heading from Georgetown to Lambeth, after Marc Lortie had turned down requests for a scrum on the favourable polls published that morning, Mulroney said to Lortie, "Marc, don't trust the polls at the beginning. We're going to have a campaign that will be tight. We'll be strong at the beginning, but there will be a drop at some point. It will be part of the dynamic of the campaign. We'll have a drop, we'll have a tight struggle, and I think we'll have a fine fight (une belle lutte) right up to the moment of the vote."

"M. le Premier Ministre, I told them that you wouldn't comment on the polls, because we have nothing to say," Lortie replied. In Georgetown, visiting the Mold Masters Inc. plant, which produces equipment for the plastic injection moulding industry, Mulroney said, speaking of the Free Trade Agreement, "It may not be perfect, but the option is tearing it up. For those who say they're going to tear it up, I ask you to ask them what they're going to do after they've torn it up. A policy of tearing up a sovereign treaty in 1988 is not good enough as a fundamental policy for the people and workers of Canada."

Then, after speaking in London, and a day of visiting six ridings in central and southwestern Ontario, the campaign plane took off for Calgary.

In London-Middlesex, Conservative MP Terry Clifford knew that he had a particular problem with free trade. John Wise, the very popular minister of agriculture who had been MP for the adjoining riding, was not running again, and Clifford knew that there was anxiety in the farming community in his riding about the impact of free trade.

Early in the campaign, he asked Don Mazankowski to visit a group of farmers in the riding. It was very early in the morning; Mazankowski arrived about seven, and the farmers from the area had gathered after they had finished milking. Mazankowski began by saying that he and his brother ran a wheat farm – and Clifford could see faces relax as the men standing in the cold barnyard realized that the new minister of agriculture was also a farmer.

While the Mulroney plane was flying from London to Calgary, Marc Lortie noticed that many of the reporters were reading the *Time* magazine cover story on the Bush and Dukakis campaign managers. As more and more stories began to be written about "the bubble," he concluded that the increasing American interest in the "handlers" of the candidates was shaping the approach that Canadian reporters were taking. However, despite the Tory sensitivity to the complaints of reporters about the "Papal Tour" phase of the campaign, with plastic chains to prevent reporters from getting in the way of the cameras or asking hard questions, and bland speeches about prosperity, growth, job creation and the challenge of changing times, it was clear that there was a substantial effort being expended to keep the tour as wrinkle-free as possible. This was one area in which Marcel Côté agreed with the front-runner's style of campaign that Allan Gregg had recommended. "My reading of the present campaign is that too much emphasis is put on formal speeches and on answering journalists' questions," he wrote to Tory and Near. "I would prefer that we identify daily thematic objectives – say, demonstrating a commitment on cleaning our rivers – and then build scenarios to achieve them. The focus, in terms of performance, should be the nightly 45 seconds on TV news, and the morning headlines, front-page photos and lead-in paragraph. This is 90 per cent of what reach the PC1 and PC2s and this is what we should be concerned about. The rest is mostly for political junkies, who had made their mind [up] anyway."

He enclosed an underlined and annotated copy of a September 16 piece in the *Wall Street Journal* on the U.S. presidential campaign, entitled "As Campaign Becomes a 'Made
for TV' Race, A Picture a Day Obviates Thousands of Words."
The Tour organizers did not need the advice; they had been
operating on that principle for quite some time.

That night in Calgary, Lee Richardson dropped around to
chat with Mulroney in his hotel room about midnight.
Richardson had worked in Mulroney's office from the time he
became leader of the opposition until December 1986, and
then, in 1988, decided he would run in the new riding of
Calgary Southeast. Richardson was forty but looked at least
ten years younger, with the cherubic good looks of a well-
dressed student.

They were both feeling good about the campaign and the
mood of the country, and spent part of the chat talking about
tolerance: the theme of Mulroney's speech the following
night. Richardson was able to tell him about his campaign,
which he had been working on all summer, and which had
begun when, to the surprise of some local observers, he had
won the nomination in April. It had been a hard-fought nomination, with Rod Love, Ralph Klein's assistant, Hari Sohol,
and Richardson all waging vigorous fights. It showed that
multicultural battles were not restricted to Toronto and Montreal: there is a fairly large Sikh community in the riding,
substantial Hindu and Moslem communities (Gujarati and
Ismaili), Lebanese, Vietnamese, and Filipino communities.

Although Richardson had been living in Ottawa for almost
five years, he was a veteran of Western Tory politics: he had
worked for Peter Lougheed in 1966–7, when he was a university student, and helped him get elected in Calgary West; he
had worked on the 1968 federal campaign writing speeches,
he worked for Fred Peacock, a businessman who subsequently became a minister in the Lougheed government, and
for another Tory businessman, Peter Bawden. He went to

Ottawa when Bawden was elected to Parliament in 1972, and ended up working as John Diefenbaker's executive assistant. In 1974, he returned to Alberta to work as Peacock's executive assistant in the Department of Industry and Commerce; from 1977 to 1979 he was Lougheed's executive secretary, and from 1979 to 1983 he ran Lougheed's Southern Alberta Office, functioning as his eyes and ears in Calgary and his liaison with the business community. In 1983, when Brian Mulroney won the leadership, Richardson went back to Ottawa as his deputy chief of staff. The one embarrassment in his political past involved a bank loan with the Bank of Montreal. While working as Mulroney's deputy chief of staff he struck an agreement on a $410,000 debt by giving up stocks and agreeing to pay a flat $50,000 a year, interest-free, in monthly instalments over nine years.

They established a warm relationship: on New Year's Eve 1987, Richardson, Gary Ouellet, Frank Moores, Bill Fox, and Charles McMillan and their wives were invited over to welcome in the New Year with the Mulroneys.

That night in Calgary, when they chatted at the hotel, everything looked rosy. However, the next day, Richardson discovered that Ed Broadbent had given a speech in Edmonton that night, in which he told an audience at the Kiwanis Lodge senior citizens' home that the trade deal meant that Canada's health-care system could be threatened by the introduction of American-style profit-making health centres, "operated for profit rather than to service human needs.' (He also promised that an NDP government would repeal the drug-patent legislation, and reintroduce the policy favouring generic drugs in competition with brand-name drugs.)

Richardson felt the impact immediately. "Here was Ed in Edmonton, on his knee talking to some poor old senior, telling her she was going to lose her medicare," he said later. "Bingo! The next day! I was shocked. The next afternoon. You've got to think . . . who's at home in the afternoons? You've got essentially senior citizens, people out of work, people not otherwise employed outside the home. So it's a

different constituency, clearly, but just the same, very concerned. It stunned me! When I saw the thing on television the
night before, I thought 'Broadbent! How can you stoop so
low? What a lot of nonsense this is! People are not going to
believe this stuff! You really are hitting below the belt, scaring
senior citizens! This is despicable!' I was really irate about it
that the guy would stoop to this level, but I thought, 'No-one's
going to buy it.'

"But the very next day, it's a sunny afternoon, and I'm
skipping along, door-knocking, and at door after door, I'd run
into seniors particularly, who would say 'You've done a good
job, we've always voted Conservative, we think this free trade
could be helpful – but what about our pensions? What about
our medical care?'"

Most afternoons, Richardson was able to knock on 250 doors.
That afternoon, in the Fairview neighbourhood, he barely got to
a hundred, because he had to stop at every one and give his
defence of the free-trade deal and social programs.

On October 13, Brian Mulroney flew to Newfoundland for a
rally in St. John's East, where Ross Reid was the candidate.
Like Lee Richardson, Reid was a veteran political aide. He
had been John Crosbie's executive assistant during the Clark
government, and, after the Clark government fell, had gone to
St. John's to open a branch of the consulting firm PAI. When
Clark stepped down and the leadership race was on, he
worked on Crosbie's leadership campaign. Bright, charming,
Reid was adept at cushioning the blows of Crosbie's brutal
frankness. When Crosbie lost, he travelled: two months in
Europe, six months in Africa, through the Soviet Union to
China. In the 1984 election, he worked on the Mulroney campaign, dealing with reporters with sardonic good humour,
but returned to PAI. He quit again in June 1986, and travelled
through Canada before going to Eritrea and Sudan to work for
one of the aid agencies before going to Nepal and Tibet,
Burma and Thailand.

On his return, he went to work in Ottawa: first in Michael Wilson's office, and then in the Prime Minister's Office as a troubleshooter, dealing with issues as various as free trade and poisoned mussels. In the spring of 1988, he decided that he was prepared to make a ten-year commitment to politics: he was going to run in St. John's East. He had considered the idea in the summer of 1987 when there was a by-election, but he didn't feel ready. This time, he was ready. "Are you going to be content knowing that you can't just bugger off to China, or go back to Burma, or Ethiopia?" was the focus of discussion he had with a number of people; he decided that he could, resigned at the end of July, and spent the next six weeks preparing for the nomination.

Reid's adversary was Jim Morgan, a populist provincial politician in his late forties, who had first been elected in 1972, and had been named minister of transportation and communications by Frank Moores in 1975; he had been re-elected with one of the largest pluralities in the province in 1982. On September 10, some 2500 people showed up, and Reid won with a superb organization.

But there was one cloud on the horizon. During the nomination campaign, people began to telephone phone-in programs to ask whether – or suggest that – Ross Reid was a homosexual. This was potentially devastating for a particular reason: the first of what would be a series of arrests had been made of priests charged with the sexual abuse of altar boys. In that context, a widespread questioning of why Ross Reid was not married and the corresponding nudges and grimaces could be very damaging. It was a conservative riding, between 60 and 65 per cent Roman Catholic.

On October 13, the prime minister's tour came to St. John's, and after the meeting Reid was questioned by three reporters about the rumours. Reid said that the question was preposterous. "If I answer that question, I give it a credibility it doesn't deserve," he said.

This led to a CBC interview the next day, where he continued to refuse to answer the question. After the interview, he talked to his campaign manager, and said "I can take this; I don't know if I want to put my family through this. Because it's not going to get any better. I've got to go and discuss it with my family."

The final date for submitting formal nomination papers had not yet come; he could still withdraw. So Reid went home and sat down with his sister and his parents, and spent the evening discussing it. "I want two things out of this: my self-respect and my family," he said. "You know what politics is like; it may not get any better."

But the family wouldn't hear of his withdrawing. You've never quit anything before, they said. We all knew that this sort of thing might be coming, particularly after some of the stuff that went on during the nomination. What do you want to do?

Reid didn't want to quit, but he didn't want his family to be dragged into a sordid, sleazy campaign. But they didn't flinch. So Reid headed back to tell his official agent and campaign manager: he was staying in.

A few nights later, there was a meeting of Ross Reid's campaign workers. His staff were determined to rally support. John Crosbie was there, Senator Doody was there, John Lundrigan was there, Brian Peckford was there with almost all of his staff and almost all of his cabinet, and almost all the the Tory MHAs.

A second priest was charged, the head of the St. John's swimming pools was charged, and there were reports that two other priests were being investigated. But the issue was never raised at a public meeting, and never raised at the doors (except by people telling him they applauded the position he was taking, and not to pay any attention). But the Canadian Press story had gone across the country (with the inaccurate implication that Reid was pointing the finger at his NDP rival, Jack Harris – the only note of the coverage of the issue that annoyed Reid), and Reid received phone calls, notes and fax messages from across the country, from party organizers, cabinet ministers, reporters, old friends, and people he had never heard of – all telling him to hang tough, and applauding his stand.

On October 12, a group of Tories had got together in Ottawa to discuss the campaign: Fred Doucet, Gary Ouellet, Ian Anderson, Frank Moores, Mulroney's director of communications Bruce Phillips, and Dean Zizzo, an assistant to Peter White. Most of them were the core of the Network.

They were concerned that the Tories were not getting enough attention when Mulroney took the day off, and suggested that senior ministers like Wilson and Mazankowski should be used in Ottawa to take advantage of the fact that the national press corps would be there that day. They were also worried that Broadbent, rather than Turner, had become the main opponent, and wondered who would tackle him on controversial issues like NATO, bank nationalization, and regional-development programs.

In a full telephone conference call, the whole Network discussed the idea of a forward-looking environmental policy; it became clear that Eastern and Central Canadian Tories saw it as a more important issue than Western Tories, who were worried that it might appear to mean more money for Quebec and Ontario. Like the core group, the full Network wrestled with the question of what appeared to be the rising fortunes of the NDP: should Broadbent be attacked? If so, who should do it? On free trade, there was discussion about how to deal with the criticisms. One Tory put forward the idea that the Free Trade Agreement should be emphasized as protection, saving existing jobs, as opposed to creating new jobs.

The Network sent on a summary of its reflections to Derek Burney, Peter White, and Norman Atkins; while the people involved were not necessarily shaping strategy and policy, they served as a useful sounding board, a uniquely experienced focus group. It was also a classic Mulroney gesture of reaching out to bring in people who might otherwise have felt neglected or ignored: a problem that both the other campaigns had, as senior Liberals and senior New Democrats across the country felt that they had not been consulted on strategies and plans.

On October 14, the Mulroney campaign came to Halifax. About six days before, Fred Dixon, the senior Nova Scotia Tory organizer, and Paul Murphy, the Nova Scotia tour co-ordinator – both lawyers with the firm Patterson Kitz – were phoned by George Stratton and told that the tour was coming for the day, and that the theme that day would be the environment. The organizers had to decide what other region of the province the plane would go to that day (they chose Sydney rather than Yarmouth, in part because the recent provincial campaign had produced a very good crowd in Sydney and there were some problems with the question of lobster licences in Yarmouth), and the advance team had to decide on what Mulroney would do, and where he would do it.

It was decided that he would meet with a group of scientists and Environment Minister Tom McMillan: a group that would be pulled together by Robert Fournier, an oceanography professor at Dalhousie who was on a federal environmental panel.

The organizers and the advance people worked out the following event: Mulroney would come in from Dartmouth, the tour would proceed to the Ferry Terminal where Mulroney would be met by the local MP, Michael Forrestall, Halifax West MP Howard Crosby, and Halifax MP – and Public Works Minister – Stewart McInnes. Forrestall, a veteran backbencher, was in a fight to keep his seat from a bright young Liberal candidate, and McInnes was being challenged by two high-profile opponents: Liberal Mary Clancy, an outspoken feminist lawyer who was very active in the party, and New Democrat Ray Larkin, a lawyer. (Interestingly, Larkin was at the same firm as Dixon and Murphy, Patterson Kitz.)

Mulroney would meet them, go onto the ferry, and head across the harbour as he met with the scientists. Then, at lunch at the Museum of the Atlantic, he would speak about the environment.

At the ferry dock, one of the advance men saw that there were some demonstrators from the trucking division of CN, where 2,700 had lost their jobs when the division was sold. They were reasonable and articulate in the interviews they were giving, and the advance man passed on the message that Mulroney might want to stop and speak to them. But the campaign was still working to its tight, no-risks schedule; Mulroney strode past the demonstrators, and onto the ferry. ("I said 'hello' going by," he told a reporter who asked why he hadn't talked to them.)

When he saw that the boat was relatively small, and the reporters and cameramen were squeezed fairly tightly, Marc Lortie became upset: there wasn't enough space, and there was too much noise. However, the event turned out to be a success, in Tour terms: there was a photograph of a wind-blown Mulroney on the front page of the *Globe and Mail* and in papers across the country, and of Mulroney speaking at the lunch on the front page of the *Halifax Chronicle-Herald* the next day.

However, Mulroney's remarks on the environment – he said that his government would rigorously enforce environmental protection laws, submit all new federal projects to full environmental-impact studies, and conclude an acid-rain treaty with the United States – were overshadowed by another issue. That afternoon, in an interview with the Atlantic Television System, Mulroney was pressed by Steve Murphy to promise that he wouldn't tamper with the social programs that he had called a "sacred trust" in 1984.

"Can you guarantee that we're all going to be alive and well tomorrow?" asked Mulroney. "I hope that there will be more programs, I'm almost absolutely certain that there will be."

Murphy pushed for a short answer, and a guarantee that he wouldn't cut social programs.

"Oh, that's [a] when-did-you-stop-beating-your-wife question," said Mulroney, in irritation, saying that to answer the question would be to dignify it, and that he had no intention of cutting programs.

"So, no guarantees?" persisted Murphy.

"I don't think you, in fairness, want me to comment on any possibility that may or may not come up in the next ten or twenty years."

Reporters' ears prick up and pencils scribble furiously during exchanges like that; the Mulroney staff on the plane twitched nervously at the problems that might emerge from Mulroney's equivocation. John Tory became really worried about the possible impact. An hour later, on the flight to Sydney, he wrote a paragraph to go into Mulroney's speech that would make it definitively clear that social programs would not be affected, but Mulroney was reluctant to do it. Calmly, but firmly, Tory insisted: it had to be done.

It took several versions of the paragraph; several times, Tory indicated that the statement was not strong enough. Finally, Mulroney and Tory were both satisfied. That night, to a large crowd in Sydney, he spelled it out. "As long as I am prime minister, social benefits, especially benefits for the elderly, will be improved, not diminished, by this government," he said. "Some of our opponents attempt to sow fear among groups in society, particularly the elderly. Let me say a special word to senior citizens I see here tonight. In the future Canada will be doing more and not less for all of you."

That night, on *The National*, Wendy Mesley summarized the day, showed the exchange with Steve Murphy, and said that Mulroney's advisers had said they were afraid there could be more negative reactions to the comment. Then, after showing Mulroney making the remark, she gave her "standup": the TV reporter's closing statement.

"The opposition has already accused Mulroney of having a hidden agenda," she said. "There's nothing they'd like better than raising doubts about what Mulroney would do with social programs, if given a second term. That's why he moved so quickly tonight to try to put the issue behind him."

The next day, the big red headline in the *Halifax Chronicle-Herald* read NO SOCIAL PROGRAM CUTS – PM. The staff on the plane were relieved: they had met a challenge, a potential problem, and they had dealt with it quickly and decisively.

In Montreal, on October 20, the Mulroney campaign came to an evening meeting in the east end of Montreal: a church basement on Sherbrooke Street, not far from the Olympic Stadium. The room was packed, the music (a theme song that Marcel Côté had taken from a Toronto ad man, Tom Scott; John Crosbie had been violently critical of it some months before) boomed out, and the Tory supporters chanted, cheered and clapped to the words, the Tory slogan in Quebec, "Continuons dans le bons sens" (a pun meaning both "keep going in the right direction," and "carry on with good sense.")

He was in good form, making fun of the NDP ("I learned that the NDP bus stopped twelve times in a single day in Quebec last week – two campaign stops, and ten stops to ask directions") glorying in the progress the Tories had made in Quebec ("When I got to Montreal twenty-five years ago, the members of the Progressive Conservative party didn't have to bother a parish priest to find a room for a meeting; a table at Butch Bouchard's restaurant worked just fine!"), and basking in the support that the Meech Lake Accord and the Free Trade Agreement had achieved in Quebec.

With point after point – Meech Lake, a place for Quebec in the constitution, Quebec participation in the Francophone Summit, the creation of jobs – Mulroney repeated the phrase "We promised that – and we kept our word!" and won strong applause.

In English – the English television and radio clip for the night – he said, "I can't imagine a constitution without Quebec, any more than a constitution without the approval of the people of Ontario. Let me tell you this: Canada without Ontario is not my kind of Canada, and a Canadian constitution without Quebec is no constitution at all."

The Meech Lake Accord, he said, was about tolerance, about living together in a pluralistic society, and about a fundamental recognition of one fact of our citizenship: we were all Canadians, irrespective of background, colour, and creed. "This is one Canada, for fairness, honesty, integrity, equality of opportunity for all," he shouted. "That's what this government believes in, one Canada . . ." and his riff on national virtues and abstract nouns was drowned out in the applause and the chanting "Brian! Brian!"

He was home and having fun, talking about prosperity and jobs and federal-provincial conciliation, shouting "The time is over when the prime minister of Canada calls the premier of Quebec a hot-dog eater! C'est fini!" Montreal was growing and prosperous, the years of uncertainty were over, and things would get even better with the Free Trade Agreement: "the richest market in the world is now only an hour away." They had listened to the young generation in Quebec, Mulroney said, who wanted to compete in the American market, and had negotiated the Free Trade Agreement; the Liberal policy was to tear up the treaty, and that was unacceptable to the youth of Quebec.

"Robert Bourassa supports free trade! Jacques Parizeau supports free trade! and Brian Mulroney supports free trade!" Those were his aces in Quebec: he could stand beside both provincial leaders, the business community, the new heroes of the Quebec middle class, and present that most reassuring nationalist ideal in Quebec: a Common Front.

After the meeting, getting onto the bus, assistant wagon-master Paul Troop remarked how meetings in Quebec were different, there was an energy and enthusiasm unlike the meetings anywhere else in the country, and Mulroney responded to it.

CHAPTER EIGHT

Stumbles

"A faulty position, a single false march may be decisive in its consequences."

Von Clausewitz

When the campaign was launched on Saturday morning, the Liberals had gambled that they could get live coverage of their campaign opening on the road. They managed it, and had what was probably the most successful launch of the three parties – but it was a close thing; the networks barely managed to make the right links for a live broadcast.

In the morning, Turner was campaigning in Kensington Market, and then he drove up to the Liberal headquarters in a Willowdale shopping centre. The room was packed and hot, but full of chanting, cheering candidates and their supporters, giving the campaign the cheery, upbeat note it needed.

"For two months, I have been asking the prime minister to let the people decide; today he finally agreed," Turner began. "The Liberal Party is ready, our people are in place, we're set to go."

It was true; even after the campaign was over, candidates and organizers agreed that the party had never been readier, even when the Liberals were in government and could control the timing of the election. "We intend to run an active, upbeat, positive campaign; we intend to present Canadians with a clear choice, and we intend to win," Turner continued, saying that he was ready to meet the other two leaders in a debate.

"This election is primarily about two things," he said. "An independent and sovereign Canada, which has never been so threatened as it is by the Mulroney trade deal, and fairness, particularly for low- and middle-income Canadians who have been hit by Tory tax increases over the last four years. That is why we are going to be saying to Canadians: this is more than an election, this is your future."

Right on! someone shouted. Bravo! And the crowd clapped furiously.

"This campaign is about equality for women, it is about rights for our minorities, it is about secure pensions for our grandparents, it is about decent high-quality child care for our children, it's about preserving our priceless environment, it's about creating opportunities in all parts of Canada. It's about honesty in government, it's about integrity in government, it's about forthright, clean government, and a cleansing of our public process."

It would be a referendum on Brian Mulroney and his government, Turner said, and attacked him for raising taxes when he promised not to while he gave tax breaks to the rich, and promised to uphold social programs as a sacred trust, but tried to de-index old-age pensions. Patronage, scandals, abuse of public office for political gain: it looked as if Turner would be campaigning against Mulroney as Goldfarb had urged, six weeks before.

"A prime minister who signed over the sovereignty and independence of our nation, that will make us nothing more than a junior partner and even a colony of the United States of America!" Turner said to applause. "A trade deal which will fundamentally alter our way of life, our way of doing things, and the way we make choices as Canadians. A trade deal which endangers our social programs, endangers our regional-development programs, sacrifices our farmers, our wine-makers, our grape-growers, our fishermen, our textile workers, our lumber workers, our autoworkers, our furniture workers – all to satisfy Brian Mulroney's unholy desire to fulfil the American Dream. A trade deal which ignores our history, and denies us the right as Canadians to choose an independent Canadian future. That is what Mr. Mulroney has to answer for, and I believe that the judgement of Canadians will be absolutely decisive."

That, in a nutshell, would emerge as the heart and soul of the Liberal campaign. For Turner would not be fighting a referendum on Brian Mulroney's government, as he said he would and as his strategists advised him to, but on the Free Trade Agreement: the one element of Liberal policy he felt totally comfortable with.

For Turner achieved a grace when he talked about the country, its history, and its geographical challenge. It was a speech that rang true to the patrician nature of the man, his love of canoeing, his awkward, old-fashioned qualities that sometimes made him seem hopelessly out of date. When Turner had left politics and moved to the business community, he had lost a great deal; but he had not lost his patriotism. The shock for him was the discovery that his business friends did not share his commitment to the country. Lloyd Axworthy could pinpoint the day Turner acquired a sense of genuine outrage about the trade deal. It was on January 1, 1988: the day that the deal was initialled by Mulroney and Reagan. Turner had just come back from a holiday with a group of Toronto business friends, and he was stunned by their reaction to the trade deal. He conveyed this to Axworthy, as they met for a press conference to respond to the signing of the deal. "Jesus, Lloyd – I've just come back from Collingwood," Turner said. "They don't believe in Canada any more!"

Whatever the strategists said, whatever the plan called for, Turner was already campaigning primarily on his visceral attack on the Free Trade Agreement.

On Monday morning, October 3, John Turner's campaign headed out to a suburban Ottawa high school for the first of many freewheeling question-and-answer sessions with students. It was an approach not without risks.

One student put it bluntly. "Hi," she said. "I'm wondering: where do you stand on abortion?"

"Where do I stand on abortion?" Turner asked, as the students applauded the question. "When, uh, I was minister of justice, which was some time ago, I had the responsibility in 1968 and 1969, of bringing in an abortion law under our criminal code which allowed a therapeutic abortion, or an abortion for therapeutic reasons, if the life or health of the woman was in danger. OK? That was what I believed at the time was a reflection of what judges and juries were doing in Canada in any event and also was a reasonable accommodation – I didn't say compromise – a reasonable accommodation between that point of view that felt that a woman ought to be able to terminate a pregnancy on consultation with her doctor, and the other point of view that believes that abortion is the murder of the unborn. Now there's no way that philosophically, or theologically, you can reconcile those two points of view. They are irreconcilable in terms of logic, and in terms of philosophy and in terms of theology."

He then pointed out that, although his accommodation had worked for twenty years, it had been struck down by the Supreme Court as incompatible with the Charter of Rights and Freedoms, since it offended a woman's right to security of her person. Turner then criticized Mulroney for presenting the House of Commons with a multiple-choice resolution, instead of legislation.

"He failed to provide leadership," he said. "Parliament is now dissolved. There is now no abortion law. We are now faced with a Supreme Court of Canada decision, and without a law, which means that despite Mr. Mulroney's professed personal opinion, we now have abortion on demand in Canada. That's what the situation is."

It was a carefully constructed preface, after which Turner said his job was to examine the Supreme Court decision to see how, under the new circumstances, a new accommodation could be reached between the rights of the woman to choose and the rights of the fetus. But he gave no hint as to what that accommodation might be – although he stressed that Liberal candidates and MPs would be free to vote according to their conscience in a free vote "because of the deep moral implications."

"I think you should let the babies live," the girl replied, to applause.

"Another question," a second girl said, wearing a Mickey Mouse sweatshirt and speaking with the lilting interrogatives of adolescence. "OK, you have a daughter? Let's say she was pregnant? And asked for your advice? To have the baby, or not to have the baby – what would you say?"

"I would, uh – that is such a personal question that that would be between me and my daughter," Turner said. "So help me, that is too personal."

Again, he was applauded, but the directness of the questioning and the evasiveness of the response were an indication of how the abortion issue had entered the Canadian political scene in a way that politicians in both the Liberal and the Progressive Conservative party found very difficult to deal with.

After the high school, he visited the headquarters of John Manley, the Liberal candidate in Ottawa South. As he came into the office, Turner's face lit up when he saw Yvonne Kerr: a woman who had been on his riding executive when he had been the MP for Ottawa-Carleton from 1968 to 1975. She introduced him to the small crowd of Liberals and reporters, and talked about Turner's integrity and his concern for people. Mrs. Kerr had first become involved in the Liberal Party in 1940, when George McIlraith was first elected, and, with a mixture of sadness and pride, she told a group of reporters later of the changes she had seen in politics, and of her knowledge of Turner.

"Now you have to be a media star in order to be a success. I think it's very, very unfortunate that your ratings have to be almost like the Nielsen ratings in order to be a success," she said. "But I wasn't talking through my hat. . . . You have to work with a person at close range for a long time to realize the modesty, and integrity, and the concern that he has for the little people."

She told how she had spent three months with her husband in Rochester, when he was being treated at the Mayo Clinic, and that Turner had phoned her every week to see how things were going. She blamed the rise of television for Turner's difficulty in projecting his human qualities.

"How do you project that?" she asked. "How do you project kindness and thoughtfulness? People today live by slogans. What is the attention span of the average person? Commercials aren't sixty seconds for nothing, you know. You don't give people too much time to dwell on things."

Mrs. Kerr had put her finger on a problem that Turner, his friends and his advisers and members of caucus had been wrestling with ever since his return to politics. Some of those Liberals who had known him as a minister sensed that he was faintly suspicious of them, and more comfortable with the friends he had made in business; old friends knew that he was unhappy when given blunt appraisals, or bad news. Some felt he had become lazy, while others argued that he had always been lazy – but had surrounded himself with strong people who would push him. He seemed to have lost the sensitive touch he had been known for as a minister. Instead of strong people who would push him, he seemed to prefer the soothing company of aides who would encourage and protect him. Members of caucus were frustrated by the degree to which he could rise to meet crises, and then relax, and revert to what one MP called "jock mode: punching shoulders and mouthing inane comments."

At the same time, however, he had learned a great deal about television. First Gabor Apor, the ad man who had coached David Peterson, had worked with him, and then Henry Comor. Comor had taught Turner something of what an intimate medium television is: how Turner had to be relaxed and comfortable to be able to put the viewer at ease, and how he had to reveal something of himself.

Monday went relatively well, and on Tuesday the campaign flew to Toronto, where Turner had a successful day. There was some awkwardness in the morning – Turner appeared on a CFRB phone-in show with Andy Barry, and had to deal with Sam Shephard, the president of the Liberal riding association in Etobicoke-Lakeshore, who phoned in to challenge Turner's assertion that the party had come together, and that there were good candidates, and Barry pushed him hard on his refusal to reveal the details of the housing policy he would be announcing that afternoon. (Before he went to the interview, Comor had told Turner that Barry was a former student of his; that evening, Turner growled, "How many more of your former students am I going to run into?")

But the most important element of the day was the announcement of the Liberal housing policy: an ambitious plan to reintroduce a homeownership savings plan, and $1.3 billion in tax credits for homeowners and tenants paying over 30 per cent of their income for rent or mortgage payments.

The campaign plan called for Turner to announce two major social-policy programs on two major issues, housing and child care, in Canada's two largest cities, Toronto and Montreal, on two successive days. It was a tall order.

On October 5, the Turner campaign had a disastrous day. At 11.15 in the morning, John Turner emerged from a meeting with the editorial board of Le Devoir to a crowd of reporters.

"Mr. Turner, Keith Penner said he is quitting because he doesn't think the Liberals can win," said Carl Hanlon of Global. "How do you feel?"

That morning, the Globe and Mail had published a story based on an interview with Penner, a twenty-year veteran, widely respected for his work on aboriginal issues, who said that he was not running again because he did not want to spend another four years in opposition.

"I had a telephone conversation with Keith two or three days ago, and he told me the reasons he was not running again," Turner said. "It was deeply personal reasons. Nothing to do with the policy of the party. I'll leave it at that."

The questions that followed were equally pointed: the poll published that morning must have been demoralizing for the troops; what was his reaction to the fact that the party's campaign launch had been disrupted by William Dery, who wanted the nomination in Saint-Laurent, and was furious that the riding was being kept for some star candidate?

Turner was determinedly cheerful, repeating his stock lines ("the future of the country is at stake – this is more than an election, it's our future, and I'm very very encouraged by the way things are going"), and saying that the question of keeping seats open for candidates was a prerogative of the Quebec wing of the party. But the atmosphere of skeptical provocation continued among the reporters as the campaign visited a day-care centre.

Like both the other campaigns, the Liberals planned, as best they could, to organize a scene that would enable the television reports to illustrate the subject of the day. The Liberal child-care announcement was coming that afternoon, so the tour, accompanied by a group of Liberal candidates in Montreal, visited the Garderie Papillon, and a crush of reporters, candidates, photographers, and aides milled about in the corridor as Turner was given a tour.

"It's a total mess [une pagaille] – with Dery, with Penner," commented *Le Devoir* correspondent Michel Vastel.

"We're still at the very beginning of the campaign," replied Marcel Prud'homme, the veteran MP running in his ninth election.

"Marcel has more experience than I do – we'll talk about it in fifty days," said Paul Martin, the president of Canada Steamship Lines, viewed as a possible successor to John Turner.

"It looks like Frank Miller's campaign in Ontario," Vastel said, referring to the disastrous campaign by the Ontario premier which resulted in the end of the provincial Conservative hegemony in the province in 1985.

"Or perhaps the 1984 campaign, when we were the ones ahead, and we lost our way," Martin retorted. "That's what's going to happen with Mulroney. It will be the party policies that will be decisive, things like today's announcement. Child care – the Conservatives have abandoned a good proportion of our children. Tax reform – our tax reform compared to the Tory tax reform. The complete abandonment of the environment for three years by the Mulroney government: our environmental program as compared to theirs. That's what will decide it."

"Rather than the leader?" said Vastel.

"I'm proud of our leader – he's going to be the next prime minister," replied Martin stoutly.

At forty-nine, Paul Martin was the same age as Brian Mulroney, and, in superficial ways, had a number of similarities in background. Like Mulroney, he was a lawyer who had spent most of his adult life in the corporate world in Montreal. Like Mulroney, he was an anglophone comfortable in French (although not as comfortable as Mulroney). And, like Mulroney, he had been much closer to politics than his election début suggested.

But while the private Mulroney was shrewd, hard-edged, colloquial, and street-smart, friends described the private Paul Martin as thoughtful, affable, decent, and reasonable. This produced occasional bursts of disarming frankness. In an interview given after he announced his candidacy in August 1987, he responded to a question on whether or not he was being coached for television by saying "I guess if I had really learned my coaching, I'd know how to fudge the answer to this. But since I haven't, the answer is yes, I'm being coached."

But the affability and self-deprecation hid a reflectiveness and a business judgement that had produced an intriguing mixture of wealth and progressive liberal instincts. He took over Canada Steamship Lines in 1981 with a $180-million loan, and expanded it into an international concern. "We are the quintessential Canadian company, but in the last five years we have expanded down the Atlantic east coast into South America; we're going into Europe and, within the next year, we will have moved into Asia," he said in an interview in August 1987. "In my opinion, the political process in Canada is far behind what is really happening economically. That is why I say that international or global competitiveness has got to be the second main thrust of the Liberal vision for the nineties."

Similarly, he could speak knowledgeably and with intensity about the environment, Third World debt, the need for worker retraining, and the problems of native people. Since his days as a law student, he had been drawn to the idea of working in the Third World, and this gave him a breadth that was unusual for corporate presidents.

But he was both blessed and haunted by heredity. He had grown up with both the excitement and the pain of politics. His father, Paul Martin, had been a candidate for the Liberal leadership in 1948, 1958, and 1968 – losing each time to future Prime Ministers Louis Saint-Laurent, Lester Pearson, and Pierre Trudeau. His father had shifted, in the public's mind, from a young left-Liberal reformer to an aged caricature of a non-committal politician, full of small vanities and orotund turns of phrase. He was crushed when his father's record of service produced so little support that he failed to survive the first ballot at the 1968 leadership convention, and when his father went from the Senate to be High Commissioner in London, Paul would still wince when journalists would describe the old man working a room, still asking, "Is there anyone here from Windsor?"

Martin insists that, while his father's experience might have angered him about malicious journalism, it neither pressured nor clouded his decision to enter politics. "I always felt that my father had one of the great public careers," he said in an interview. "He had the opportunity to shape the basic welfare structure in this country. I have never felt sorry for my father." But he did conclude that politics was not a career; that his father's longevity, exceptional then, would be impossible now. So he concluded that there was a ten-to-fifteen-year window for political life in a person's career. The only other shaping force he will concede that his father's career represented to him is his deep conviction that public life represents the most important service someone can give the country.

"That I feel so strongly has got to be the way I grew up, and whose son I am," he said. Now, twenty years after his father's departure from the House of Commons, Paul Martin was running for the first time. He was well enough known to be surrounded by a throng of reporters once the crowd emerged from the child-care centre. He was being vigorously optimistic.

"The NDP has just disappeared, and we're picking up the bulk of their vote," he said. "I can tell you the polls we are taking with the ridings coupled with the door-to-door work make me very comfortable about this election. I think we'll come out of Quebec with more seats than the Tories, and I think the NDP will come out with no seats at all."

"You're going to have to be pretty far off what the polls are reading now to come even close to that," said CBC radio reporter Dick Gordon.

"Well, I tell ya, not our own internal polls," Martin said. "Come door to door with me, and then we'll have this discussion."

"What are those polls saying?" Gordon asked.

"Those polls are saying we are by far the majority party on the Island of Montreal, and that it is nip and tuck off the Island of Montreal," he said, using the time-honoured euphemism for "trailing badly." "I think the social issues are really the Tories' Achilles heel. The environment, number one, the fact that they haven't done anything; their day-care program – to abandon 70 per cent of Canadian children is simply morally wrong; their fiscal program is a regressive program. The squeeze on the middle class is really being very heavily felt. That's going to be reflected in the election results. Or at least, it sure as heck is being reflected when you go door to door."

None of the reporters were convinced; as the scrum ended, and Martin was walking away, a reporter called out that Keith Penner had said it would take a miracle for the Liberals to win. What did he think?

"I believe in miracles," Martin called back – and was embarrassed when that line proved to be almost the only comment of his quoted the next day. However, before the day was out, it seemed that only a miracle would save the Liberal campaign from itself.

As the reporters got on the bus and were driven back to the press room at the hotel, they were handed a thirteen-page background paper on the Liberal child-care policy, and a copy of the text Turner was to deliver at another child-care centre that afternoon.

The policy committed a Liberal government to creating 400,000 new child-care spaces in seven years, encouraging provinces to establish child care in school facilities, and giving a capital-cost write-off of over 100 per cent to employers establishing child care in the workplace, enriching parental-leave benefits, and improving child-care tax measures.

It was this last promise that proved troublesome. The statement read, "Make child-care tax measures more equitable and recognize those women who do not work outside the home: convert existing child-care expense deduction into credit, and make the married credit both transferable and refundable – in effect, create a refundable homemaker's credit."

Several reporters in the press room simply did not know what this meant. In trying to explain it, the Turner aides added to the confusion.

First, David Lockhart, a policy adviser, was sent to the press room to explain the policy, and, while he clarified it for those reporters who did their own tax returns, he left those who used accountants still baffled – and he could not explain how much the program would cost. Then Turner's chief of staff, Peter Connolly, came into the press room to explain it.

"For the amount of money that the government has dedicated to create 200,000 spaces, we will create a great deal more than that through a more efficient delivery system: somewhere over 300,000. But the commitment is to at least 400,000 – triple the present amount, and double the proposal of the government. That is a commitment. At $4 billion plus."

Someone asked exactly how many spaces would be created.

"It will be somewhere over 300,000," he said. "But what is important is the commitment, and the commitment is to 400,000, and no child shall go in need of day care. No child."

And the cost? he was asked again.

"Four billion plus," Connolly replied. "But you are not able to adequately forecast the demand that far forward. That's not a cop-out."

The CTV reporter Alan Fryer asked whether this meant that the cost could be $6 billion, or $8 billion.

"Whatever," said Connolly, a word that would haunt him. "There's a commitment. Realistically, the commitment is to 400,000 spaces for seven years."

"I still don't understand the $4 billion," said Fryer. "You're taking existing deductions – the $2,000 deduction, and turning it into a $2,000 child-tax credit. Right? Which, as I work it out, is going to be roughly the same cost as the Tory deduction."

"Correct," said Connolly.

"So let's say that equals out," said Fryer. "So you're saying you're going to create twice as many spaces as the Tories would for less money?"

"I didn't say that," said Connolly. "We're committed – but we don't know how much it's going to cost. No one can. We know we can create well over 300,000 for the $4 billion, through a more efficient delivery system."

"How is that?" Fryer asked.

"Because it is going to be delivered on a tripartite basis by the parents, governments, and child-care organizations rather than by a straight private-sector system," Connolly said.

"It's going to be well over $4 billion," said Fryer.

"You are more certain than we are, that's all I can say," said Connolly. "There is a further commitment that no child in need of day care will go without. But you cannot adequately project the effect of the tax system on the cost to the treasury."

"You've already admitted it could be $8 billion," said Fryer.

"I didn't admit anything," replied Connolly. "You said $8 billion, and I said sure."

He then said it was not his place to answer for the leader before he had made the announcement, but that Mr. Turner was aware of the concern the journalists had about cost.

So, a few minutes later, the reporters and aides piled on to a bus and headed for another child-care centre in the east end of Montreal where, after another visit to the centre accompanied by television cameras, Turner made his announcement – flanked by Montreal MPs, with others standing behind him.

He delivered it well, ad libbing from the text when he talked about the need for after-school care: a particular concern of Lucie Pépin, the tall aristocratic-looking MP for Outremont who had worked on the Liberal policy, and had represented the party at the parliamentary committee discussing the government's child-care legislation.

"Latchkey children we call them, with a latchkey around their neck; a key to their apartment or their home. In school, but without any parental supervision after school," he said. "It's becoming a major problem in Canada. Many of these children have no other choice but to hang out on the streets where they are exposed to street gangs, to violence, drugs. My fear is that many of these children will end up among the dispossessed, the abandoned, the disadvantaged, the homeless of the next generation."

Whatever concerns his advisers might have had about parents taking offence at such apocalyptic language was washed away in the questions that followed. For it became clear that no one could answer the most basic questions: how much the program would cost, and how much recipients would receive.

Alan Fryer asked him the question he had been asking Peter Connolly.

"Your tax proposal and the Tories' tax proposal will roughly cancel each other out," Fryer said. "If that's the case, and I'm assuming it is, you're telling us you're going to create twice as many day-care spaces as the Conservatives for less money."

Paul Martin, standing behind Turner, figured out what Fryer was saying, and leaned over to Raymond Garneau and whispered, "You're the finance minister – it's going to cost twice as much," assuming that this would be the reply to Fryer's question. But it wasn't.

"No, no," said Turner. "We're saying we can do it with the same amount of money in terms of the money that's going to be available for the program by use of the tax system, by using a better delivery system and by using CAP."

He was referring to the Canada Assistance Plan, the program that subsidizes the cost of child care for low-income families.

Lucie Pépin chimed in to explain that the Conservatives had money in their child-care program for research, and that CAP funds were being cut, while the Liberals would be using all the designated money for child care, including the money targeted for research, and keeping the CAP funding.

"It will be more expensive, we won't do the 400,000 spaces with the same amount of money," she said.

Then Turner weighed in, presumably to correct the impression that it would be more expensive.

"In other words, Alan, if you use the funds we've redirected from CAP, if you use the extra funds available from converting the child-care deduction into a tax credit, if you use the delivery system we contemplate against the existing budget allocated, the $4 billion plus the funds from CAP plus the extra funds through the tax system will deliver the result without an extra burden on the tax system."

Now, some reporters were more confused than ever. Standing behind Turner, Raymond Garneau looked as if he were feeling intense physical pain.

David Vienneau of the *Toronto Star* got to his feet to point out that there were a lot of people with small children who would be very interested in the proposal, who would want to know two things: how much the system would cost, and how much they would receive.

As he was asking his question, Turner turned to Lucie Pépin and asked "We can't get more precise than that?" Sotto voce, but audibly through the microphone, she repeated that the Tories were giving a $2000 tax deduction, and that the

Liberals would change that to a credit instead of a deduction.

"I, uh, unless Mme Pépin can, I can't give you in exact dollar terms what people are going to receive," Turner said weakly. And, as the press conference ended, reporters bolted after MPs to see if they could explain the policy any better. Raymond Garneau's temper finally cracked when he was questioned about it by the CBC television reporter Keith Boag, and he snapped, "I don't know what game you're playing, but I'm not playing your game!" and bolted off.

For the Turner campaign, the day had been a disaster. David Vienneau's story in the *Toronto Star* the next day was headlined "Confusion reigns as Turner unveils child-care plan" and began, "One of the bright spots of the Liberal election platform – a national day-care policy – turned into a publicity nightmare for party leader John Turner, who could not explain how it would work, or what it would cost."

But it was more than just a bad day. The images of confusion and irritation reminded people of the internal problems in the Liberal Party; as Michael Kirby would write later, it "rekindled the image that Turner lacked competence." The longer-term effects were even worse: it undermined Turner's confidence in the strategy of announcing policies, and widened the gap between the staff members on the plane, and the strategists on the ground.

After everyone had filed their stories from rooms at the Dorval Hilton, the reporters and aides climbed onto a bus again to drive out onto the tarmac. Patrick Gossage asked Keith Boag if he had edited his piece at the CBC offices in Montreal. Boag replied that he had done it at the hotel.

"Did it work?" asked Gossage.

"I don't know," shrugged Boag.

"Gee, I'd be really upset if a technical glitch meant that item didn't get on the air," said Gossage deadpan.

Then Alan Fryer looked out the bus window and quipped, "Isn't that Keith Davey getting on the plane?"

There was an explosion of laughter, as everyone remembered the disastrous Turner campaign of 1984, when Senator

214

Keith Davey had replaced Bill Lee as campaign chairman in the middle of the campaign.

The next day, in Surrey, B.C., while Turner gave a speech on the Liberal housing policy before throwing away his text and ending on his free-trade speech, vowing to fight for the Canadian way of life, Peter Connolly was still trying to explain the problems with the child-care announcement.

"It won't happen again, and if it does, you'll be talking to someone else next time," he said. "How could I hold my head up if it happened again?"

Working to turn their liabilities into assets, the Turner campaign avoided large crowds – which were difficult to find and hard to organize – and sought out captive audiences: a high school in Ottawa West, a small committee room in Ottawa South, a phone-in show in Toronto, a windblown group of reporters and supporters at the foot of an apartment tower in Toronto's Parkdale – High Park for the housing announcement.

But while they avoided the risks of small crowds of supporters, they ran other high risks of trouble in one form or another: embarrassing questions, and awkward replies. But Turner could claim, rightly, that he was stepping out and taking the cut and thrust of public questioning. As each day went by, he challenged Mulroney each day to "Come out of his cage! Come out and debate!"

He particularly wanted a debate on free trade – for he knew the issue, and was completely comfortable with it. Whenever he got the chance, as he did on radio on Friday morning October 7 in Vancouver, he would hammer away at his argument that the Americans had struck it lucky with Brian Mulroney, that they had found someone stupid enough to give them what they had always wanted.

"The Americans were clever enough, in articles 1902 and 1904, to preserve the complete jurisdiction of American protectionist law, the ability to apply all the remedies they've used in the past: countervail, surtax, quotas, or anti-dumping," he said. "We didn't get the secure access. . . . We surrendered our energy, we surrendered our capital markets, we surrendered our investment policy, we surrendered the supply management of agriculture. I think, and believe sincerely, that we've surrendered the economic levers of this country, that political servitude is inevitable as a colony of the United States."

After the radio show, Turner strode out to the microphone outside the station. Not only had the show gone well, he was fuelled by the mixture of private delight and public indignation that the perfect political opportunity inspires in a politician. That morning, the *Toronto Star* had quoted Housing Minister John McDermid as saying that there were enough shelters for the homeless, and that a lot of them did not want permanent homes.

"We have a new minister of homelessness," he said. "I'm shocked, as I'm sure everybody else is," and held up a facsimile of the front page of the paper, and read it aloud: "The homeless have shelter in Canada. They can always get off the street and find a warm place to sleep and be taken care of on a temporary basis."

"How's that?" Turner asked. "That is a reflection of the Tory philosophy, the Mulroney philosophy of how we take care of those in Canada who are not able, through no fault of their own, to take care of themselves. We see it in the tax system, we see it in their child-care proposal, and now we couldn't get better evidence than from the new minister of homelessness as to how we're going to treat people who can't meet shelter costs."

It was an ideal coincidence for Turner. Earlier in the week, he had announced the Liberal housing policy, which promised a tax credit for homeowners and tenants who paid more than 30 per cent of their income on housing – some 1.2 million people. That same morning, while the *Star* was reporting McDermid's remarks (which McDermid insisted were taken wildly out of context), the *Globe* reported that Don Blenkarn, chairman of the finance committee in the last House, said that tax reform could result in Canadians paying as much as $10 billion a year more in sales taxes under the universal sales tax being proposed by the Mulroney government. For Turner, at the end of a difficult week, the remarks were gifts.

"You've got to admire their frankness," Turner said. "Prime Minister Mulroney is still in his golden cage, being carried by his handlers from city to city and town to town. Apparently, some of his senior Conservatives are getting a little frustrated and want to speak out on their own."

In a kaleidoscopic beginning to the campaign, Turner had begun well – but had been hobbled by poor staff work, and his failure to answer the most basic questions in public life: how much will it cost, and how much will people get? That night, Peter Connolly lost his temper in a bar, and swore at reporters.

The next day, the campaign had a boost from a banal photo opportunity at the Armenian Cultural Centre in suburban North York. After singing some Armenian folk songs, a children's choir in traditional costume sang "O Canada," and, after singing it in English, then, without missing a beat, sang it in French. Even observers cynical about events staged for television were impressed, even moved. The event was to illustrate the Liberals' multiculturalism policy. Tucked inside the policy document was a note to the effect that the Liberals would work to do away with the "notwithstanding" clause in the Charter of Rights: the clause that enabled provinces, or the federal government, to exempt a piece of legislation from the application of the Charter. When they learned that this had been voted on as part of Liberal policy months before, most reporters decided not to bother mentioning it. Almost as an afterthought, the Presse Canadienne reporter wrote a story noting the fact. When Lucien Bouchard denounced this as an attack on Quebec, the question suddenly became an issue in Quebec.

Late that afternoon, in Ottawa, as the campaign week ended, the policy co-chairman, Patrick Johnston, had to tell reporters that the child-care package would cost, not $4 billion, or $6 billion, or $8 billion – but $10.1 billion over seven years. Some Liberals quietly noted the irony that Johnston, who had been defeated for a nomination by a pro-life campaign, had emerged to help the campaign as best he could on the issue of child care – an issue on which the pro-life people had always been strangely silent.

The episode was a disaster in several ways. It not only anchored the impression of Liberal confusion and squabbling in the minds of the voters, it undermined the Liberal strategy and Turner's confidence in the strategy. "The press never gave us a shot at putting other policies out; they didn't trust Turner to know what he was talking about," Martin Goldfarb said later. "Turner never had the confidence to put another policy out. As a result, we kind of danced around our program and never really used it."

The child-care incident was the first major incident to shake the relationship of confidence between the Liberals on the plane and the Liberals on the ground. But the second incident, a week later, was much more serious.

While the first weeks of the Liberal campaign had been marred by problems, the New Democrat campaign fairly hummed along. Broadbent was alone at the National Press Theatre for his response to the election call on Saturday morning, October 1: sitting at the table, delivering his statement, in front of dark blue curtains. He had touches of eloquence, but at times seemed a little stiff and awkward. The symbolism was clear: if Mulroney had chosen the silent authority of the Georgian stones of Rideau Hall to frame his announcement, and Turner the shrill, gaudy enthusiasm of shouting candidates, supporters and bright Liberal signs, Broadbent conveyed a solitary solemnity there alone.

"The election is about a fair deal for families, for women, for young people, for our parents, for our grandparents," he said. "It's about fairness in taxes, in housing, in job opportunities throughout the country. It is about protecting medicare. It is about talking about cleaning up pollution, and actually doing it. It's about having a government in Canada that we can all be proud of. It's about Canadians making their own decisions about their own future in their own country."

It was characteristic of the New Democratic Party and the labour movement in Canada that each theme and message had to contain all the messages. "Fairness" was an ideal message in this all-inclusive tradition: fairness could include every interest, and every concern in the NDP, from pay equity to native land claims, from lower interest rates to peace, from better pensions to medicare.

The statement faithfully reflected the strategy that had evolved over the last year: broaden the campaign, and try to prevent it from becoming a single-issue, free-trade election. It had referred to free trade in code when Broadbent said that the election was about "Canadians making decisions about their own future in their own country": an oblique reference to the anxiety about Canadian sovereignty. Otherwise, the trade deal was not mentioned; Broadbent spent most of his time attacking (but, as the Julie Mason strategy paper of June 1 had suggested, more in sorrow than in anger) the government's record on scandals.

"A great many Canadians are seriously disillusioned with Mr. Mulroney and the Conservative Party," he said. "They simply lost the trust of men and women from one part of the country to another."

He went on to quote Mulroney as saying in 1984 that he would not play the old Liberal game of saying one thing before the election and another thing after, adding "Well, as Canadians know very well, Mr. Mulroney played that old Liberal game. He did it to ordinary taxpayers, he did it to seniors, he did it on our environment, and about the very future of our country. He promised fairness, and he did the opposite. He promised openness, and produced more patronage. Brian Mulroney, simply stated, has let an awful lot of Canadians down."

Broadbent then turned to the Liberals. "Having said that about Mr. Mulroney, I know that Canadians who are disappointed with the performance of himself and his government for the past four years, have no intention of turning to John Turner and the Liberal Party. The truth is that John Turner says one thing on Monday, another thing on Tuesday, and as often as not, a third thing on Wednesday. I believe Canadians want consistency in their political parties. They want to know where, on a continuing basis, we stand on the great issues that confront them as a people.

"Canadians don't expect miracles," he continued. "They don't expect perfection. I know that. But Canadians do expect, and what they desire from their politicians is honesty, and a great commitment to fairness. Not from time to time, but throughout the life of a government. I'm convinced, then, that on election day, thinking of fairness, thinking of the future of their families and their country, Canadians are going to be saying No! to Mr. Mulroney and the Conservatives and this time, Yes! to the New Democratic Party."

It was a carefully crafted statement which struck all the strategic notes which had been designed so carefully by the strategy committee. After answering questions, as if to offset the austerity of that presentation, he headed out to the Byward Market to shake hands.

But the statement never actually used the words "free trade." Taken aback at this omission, the British Columbia NDP decided to correct the flaw, and called a press conference for Monday morning at the Hotel Vancouver to denounce the deal, and make this explicitly the theme of the NDP campaign in British Columbia.

The NDP campaign team was smaller than the others: George Nakitsas, Broadbent's chief of staff, was the tour director, Ann Carroll the wagonmaster, Rob Mingay the events producer (an innovation for the NDP), Hilarie McMurray the speechwriter and policy adviser, Bill Gillies and Christine Dyck the two press attachés. By dint of considerable effort, the research director, Arlene Wortsman, had produced a range of policy documents, enabling Broadbent to announce policy statements, what they would cost, and how they would be paid for. Even by the time the writs had been issued, the campaign staff was feeling stretched under the new demands – from candidates and media – as the NDP tried to run its first truly national campaign.

And yet, despite the pressures, they were hopeful. Bill Knight still felt that there was a good chance that Broadbent could take off during the campaign; Julie Mason felt that he could succeed in touching the emotions with his emphasis on nitty-gritty, human issues that affected families. "Ed will be talking a lot about the pressures on family life, about working mothers, about pensions, day care and equality," she told Hugh Winsor of the *Globe and Mail*. "When the election is fought on these grounds, we win."

Broadbent formally launched the NDP campaign from the front steps of the Boucherville City Hall, not far from the warehouse in Saint-Basile-le-Grand, where a warehouse containing toxic PCBs had burned in early September, forcing the evacuation of some 3,500 people. He accused the Mulroney government of hypocrisy in the field of the environment, and, at the local campaign headquarters, charged it with breaking its promise to the people who had been evacuated.

The election, he said, was about fairness in taxes, in housing, in job opportunities; echoing his remarks on Saturday, he criticized Mulroney for losing the trust of Canadians, and Turner for being "a profoundly conservative man."

The riding of Chambly was held by a Conservative, Richard Grisé, who had won in 1984 by defeating the Liberal former MP, Bernard Loiselle. The NDP candidate was Phil Edmonston, the American-born consumer advocate who had founded the Automobile Protection Association, and was a weekly resource person on a Radio-Canada radio program on problems people were having with their cars. His slogan "Votez sans vous faire rouler!" (Vote without getting taken advantage of) was an echo of his best-selling book on the best cars to buy, and the best way to negotiate guarantees: *Roulez sans vous faire rouler!* (Drive without getting taken advantage of.)

Edmonston was one of the NDP candidates believed to have a solid chance; Broadbent had been in the riding time and again over the past six months, and the Saint-Basile-le-Grand disaster had brought him back once before. A loner and not a modest man, Edmonston made it clear to people in the NDP that he felt he was the party's major asset in Quebec; by the time the election was called, staff members in Broadbent's office (and other candidates in Quebec) were already irritated by his attitude. The Tory MP, Richard Grisé, was not a strong member, although Edmonston was worried that he might win on Mulroney's coattails.

At his nomination meeting, Bernard Loiselle was confident that a strong showing by Edmonston would help his chances rather than hurt them. The riding included strong Parti Québécois support (it was in part of the provincial riding in which Jean-Guy Parent, the former mayor of Boucherville, had defeated Robert Bourassa in the Quebec election of 1985), and Loiselle felt that Edmonston could draw some of the PQ support away from Grisé and give him a better chance at winning the seat.

The party's hopes in Quebec were further bolstered on Monday, when Louis Laberge, president of the Quebec Federation of Labour, told a crowd of over six hundred that he was "fully engaged" in the NDP campaign. There was a sense that, if Laberge were committed so strongly so early in the campaign, the NDP's popularity might be translated into a dream come true for Broadbent: a breakthrough in Quebec.

The next day, October 4, Broadbent had a similar success in Edmonton, where he was greeted by an enthusiastic crowd, and sixteen members of the Alberta legislature. And, at the Kiwanis Lodge, he told senior citizens that the Free Trade Agreement would mean that Canada's health-care system could be threatened by the introduction of corporate hospitals functioning for profit, on the American model.

The first part of the Broadbent tour went very smoothly. In contrast with the Liberals, the NDP announced the cost of their promises, which they had gone to considerable pains to calculate, with every announcement, and, in addition, explained how they would pay for them.

Thus, with the environmental announcement the following day in Steveston, B.C., Broadbent promised to bring in a new Clean Water Act, saying "We want a country that is both prosperous and clean, that will nourish – not threaten – the lives of our children."

In addition, Broadbent's staff issued a seven-page paper, which began by detailing the cuts in Environment Canada by the Mulroney government. "With 432 positions wiped out in the department, the work of many internationally respected researchers was halted, stopping progress on renewable energy, PCBs and recycling," the paper said. "The Canadian Wildlife Service was cut by 23 per cent; the Great Lakes pollution-monitoring program was eliminated; wildlife interpretation centres and a toxicology research centre were closed. The damage done by these cuts continues. Then this past August, the Mulroney cabinet cut $35 million from the energy conservation budget."

Then the document laid out the details of the commitment that Broadbent had announced: a new Environmental Protection Act, the inclusion of crimes against the environment in the Criminal Code, greater public participation, an additional $120 million a year for Environment Canada, the naming of the minister of the environment to the Priorities and Planning Committee of cabinet, the creation of an environmental clean-up fund, the establishment of an inventory of toxic and hazardous waste, the banning of oil and gas exploration in environmentally sensitive northern and Pacific coastal waters, a reassessment of pesticide use, the clean-up of the Canadian sources of pollution of the Great Lakes, and better compensation for the victims of environmental damage.

In addition to this full, detailed program, Broadbent announced that the proposed programs would cost $580 million a year with over a third of this ($200 million) coming from taxes on the corporate sector, and some $250 million coming from closing the tax loophole allowing investors unrestricted interest deductibility over income in any given year.

It was solid, responsible, and the result of long, time-consuming research and production work. It is unclear whether, in the final analysis, it had any impact at all on the voters.

On Tuesday October 11, Broadbent travelled through Southern Ontario, visiting Mohawk College to attack the Conservatives for cutting job-training programs. "The government took the decision to give subsidies directly to the private sector, even for McDonald's hamburgers or Burger King," he said. "The government wants to suggest that the program even at McDonald's is sophisticated. This is ridiculous."

Some confusion arose when one college official contradicted Broadbent (who had been briefed by another official) when he said that the college had been cut back $1 million. Briefly, some reporters pounced on the discrepancy; it appeared to some as if this were the equivalent to the Liberals' problems with the child-care announcement, and the Broadbent aides were peppered with questions, and responded by peppering the NDP research office in Ottawa with fax messages. It was a classic example of what Martin Cohn of the *Toronto Star* later called "nit-raking."

However, the issue faded away after Broadbent appeared on Tom Charrington's interview show on CHCH-TV, Hamilton. The conversation turned to the difficulties that the Liberal Party was having, and Charrington asked Broadbent if the campaign would witness the death of the Liberal Party.

"It would be healthy for Canada to evolve the way other countries have with one party that's left of centre – like us – and a conservative party," Broadbent replied. "Some may say [the end of the Liberal Party] is wishful thinking, some may think it's highly desirable, and, as unbiased as I'm not, I would like to see it that way."

Broadbent insisted later that he had no regrets about making the remark, although many New Democrats across the country winced when they heard that he had said it.

In Northern Ontario, John Rodriguez had been campaigning for re-election as the NDP member for Nickel Belt. There were some people, traditional Liberals, who had not put signs on their lawn this election, and who had indicated that this time they were thinking of voting NDP. But on his second canvass, one of these houses had a Liberal sign up.

"What happened?" Rodriguez asked at the door.

"Your leader said my party's disappearing," he was told. "I don't want my party to disappear."

And an elderly Franco-Ontarian woman who had told Rodriguez she would support him said "Mr. Rodriguez, they say the party is going to die – I have to vote Liberal."

However, in Kamloops, in the interior of British Columbia, Nelson Riis found that Broadbent's comment had little or no impact. What he was describing had already happened there, and no one seemed to find the comment unusual.

While perhaps politically foolish, the remark had one quality that made it easy for Broadbent to say it: he believed it, and always had. It was a common belief among many in the NDP: Terence Morley wrote after the 1984 election that it explained some of the delight that followed the results, since many social-democratic activists were convinced that the Liberals, in his phrase, "reduced to a scanty forty seats, would conveniently disappear, leaving the opposition field to the New Democratic Party battalions."

It was, he argued, always a fond hope of English Canadian socialists in a party that had traditionally had upper-middle-class Canadians educated at Oxford, Cambridge or other British universities in the leadership and working-class British immigrants in the membership. "The hope and expectation that the NDP will one day become one of the two rivals for power in the land (as indeed it has in three western provinces) is central to the party's sense of itself as a genuinely important player in the political game, and central to its ability to sustain the morale of the membership given the harsh reality of third-place finishes and exclusions from power," he wrote.

Natural or unnatural, central or marginal, a public expression of the belief was unwise in the middle of an election campaign. There were a lot more Canadians who had voted Liberal than had ever voted NDP; to suggest that their party was dying was almost an open invitation to give the Liberal Party artificial respiration. However, the belief that the Liberal Party was dying was not restricted to Ed Broadbent. The party's campaign strategists were carrying on in a way that suggested that the Liberals were in their death throes.

CHAPTER NINE

A Very Canadian Coup

"A prince ought to reckon conspiracies of little account when his people hold him in esteem. But when it is hostile to him and bears hatred towards him, he ought to fear everything and everybody."

Machiavelli

At the end of the first week of the election campaign, things were disastrous for the Liberals. The incident in the bar at the Royal York on Friday night, in which Peter Connolly had screamed and sworn at reporters, was filtering into notebook columns in the weekend papers; the day-care fiasco had dragged on for several days; Turner's strong performances were undermined by the devastating television clips that showed him to be either too emotional, too extreme, or limping and in pain. There was despair in the party, and among the senior campaign strategists. Turner's unpopularity was being reinforced, and all the accumulated negative feelings about his leadership began to coalesce.

All this began to be reflected in the opinion polls, which showed the Liberals lower than they had ever been before. Seeing these, Liberal strategists, organizers, and candidates began to feel even more desperate, frantically trying to come up with some way of fending off disaster. There was discussion among the senior strategists of doing some specialized polling on leadership in order to try to develop a strategy for recovery.

The Environics poll, conducted between October 2 and October 10 and published in the *Globe and Mail* on October 12, showed the Tories with 42 per cent, the NDP at 29 per cent and the Liberals at 25 per cent. The next day, October 13, the *Globe* published the Environics data on leadership: asked who they would like to see as prime minister, 40 per cent said Mulroney, 29 per cent said Broadbent, and 15 per cent said Turner. The Liberals had not been able to afford their own national poll, and depended on their own analysis of published polling. However, they were polling twelve "bellwether" ridings: constituencies won by the Conservatives in 1984 in which the Liberals ought to have a chance, and therefore worth sampling: Halifax, Moncton, Charlesbourg, Beauce, Saint-Jean, Rosemont, St. Paul's, Don Valley North, Sudbury, Windsor – Lake St. Clair, St. Boniface, and Vancouver Centre. The results there were disastrous: they were behind in eleven of the twelve, trailing in Beauce by 40 points, and ahead by only 1 per cent in St. Boniface. Crudely putting the results together with the Environics data, they concluded that, if those results held steady, the Tories would win 205 seats, the NDP 61, and the Liberals 29.

Those results began to circulate among the senior strategists over the Thanksgiving weekend. As the Liberal candidates began, first, to hear about those results and then to read the Environics figures in the middle of the week, they realized the terrible gravity of the situation. A kind of frenzied panic began to set in.

It is important to understand that context of desperation, and the quite real prospect that the Liberals might sink to third place, before trying to sift out the extraordinary events that took place in the two weeks before the television debates. Senior Liberals, elected and unelected, felt they were looking disaster in the face: the Liberal Party of Canada seemed to be on the point of sliding to third place, and undergoing the same fate as the British Liberal Party.

It is also important to realize that there remain quite contradictory versions of what took place: a complete and totally accurate reconstruction of what took place is probably impossible. Too many people have too much at stake to concede their involvement in what one veteran Liberal delicately called "a contingency plan": the dramatic, but always implausible possibility that, in the middle of an election campaign, John Turner might step down and Jean Chrétien might take over as leader. Yet the question was considered, the option was developed and prepared; more astonishing, both the other campaigns were aware that some of this was happening.

Liberals in key campaign positions are still weighing contradictory versions of events and important conversations, which they have been given by other, equally important Liberals. As one of them said, after talking to two colleagues in an attempt to piece together the story and make sense of it, "Who do you believe? Someone who lies strategically, or someone who lies pathologically?"

What remains important is that, at a critical moment in the campaign, the Liberal Leader was convinced that his senior campaign advisers were trying to force him to step down. In addition, senior MPs were seriously discussing whether or not he should continue as leader, and wondering whether the only way the Liberal Party might survive would be if he agreed to step down. That fact, and the fact that the CBC broadcast a story reporting some of what had been happening, confirmed some of the public impressions of chaos in the Liberal Party, and made the continuation of the campaign strategy much more difficult.

On Wednesday October 12 at noon, the campaign was in Hamilton at a knitting mill, where the owner had invested $10 million and feared he would lose it because of free trade. While Turner was performing, Connolly got a call from Kirby on his cellular phone, saying he had something important to discuss.

So Connolly went into the manager's office for a little privacy and phoned Kirby on a regular phone. The people on the campaign bus were nervous that their conversations might be picked up if they used cellular phones. (In the 1987 British election campaign, a team of reporters from the *News of the World* had trailed Margaret Thatcher's bus, recording a number of the radio-telephone calls to and from the bus, forcing the Conservatives to install scramblers.)

"Well, the data's in," Kirby said. "And it's very clear the message is being well received by those who have received it. But the messenger is going nowhere. The numbers have fallen off a cliff."

Kirby was deeply concerned about Turner's health, and wondered whether he could carry on. He was also worried about a Gallup poll which showed Turner at 8 per cent, trailing the hypothetical choices of Trudeau and Chrétien. When he raised this, Connolly became convinced that Kirby was planning to run a poll looking at the question of the leadership. Connolly remembers his saying that he wanted to ask people about Turner's popularity compared with that of other Liberals, like Chrétien, MacEachen, Martin, and Lalonde.

"Well, Mike," said Connolly, "we expected this. You expected this. We've had nothing but a hammer job since we started, combined with child care. A campaign lasts fifty-one days – we've got six, seven weeks to go. We know he's performing well. This is nuts – I think we should be designing some questions to find out how to get out of this box. Although it may be just steady as you go."

"Well, we'll talk on Saturday," said Kirby.

While the reporters were filing at a campaign headquarters, Turner and his staff went over to the Sheraton Hotel in Hamilton for a sandwich. After they arrived, Martin Goldfarb called to say he had talked with Kirby. Connolly and Goldfarb agreed that the best approach was to try to develop a plan to deal with the problem, and they said they would see each other at the Saturday strategy meeting.

That night, Turner spoke at the Confederation Dinner in Toronto: a huge dinner, which drew some 4,200 people. From the political professionals and veterans, there was a mixture of respect and sympathy and, at the same time, a feeling of near-pity for Turner who, clearly in pain from his back, was making a valiant campaign. But it was not a partisan crowd. Dennis Mills and Frank Stronach had organized the dinner, and the tables were filled with salesmen and secretaries from companies in the auto-parts industry that dealt with Stronach's firm, Magna International.

Turner threw away his written text and made a passionate plea to the audience on the free-trade issue. "I know that opinion on the trade issue is divided in this room," he said. "The business of business is money and the bottom line – that I respect. The business of politics is people. This debate goes farther than the economy.

"Any country that is willing to surrender economic levers inevitably yields levers politically and surrenders a large chunk of its ability to remain a sovereign nation. I don't believe our future depends on our yielding those economic levers of sovereignty to become a junior partner in Fortress North America to the United States."

For the pros in the room, the situation looked disastrous. Martin Goldfarb remarked, as he got off the escalator, that he felt sorry for Turner. "Good speech," remarked one Liberal businessman as he headed for the washroom. "I don't agree with it, but it was a good speech." "Liberals are working to rule," observed another Liberal veteran.

John Webster, Tom Axworthy, and Martin Goldfarb were sitting at the same table, as was Henry Comor. At one point, Webster said to Axworthy, "How would we do if we replaced Turner with Chrétien?"

"Well, you'd win Toronto," Axworthy replied.

Webster asked how the Liberals would do in Quebec, where Axworthy, a former principal secretary to Pierre Trudeau and Lloyd Axworthy's brother, was then living.

"You'd do better in Quebec," Axworthy said.

Comor got up from the table in annoyance, saying "I don't want to be part of this conversation," and sought out a senior strategist. He found Senator Al Graham in the bar with his son and, horrified, told him what he had heard. Graham said very little. (Neither he nor Webster recalls this incident.)

That night, to the fury of Liberals, *The National* ran a clip of Turner stumbling over the phrase "birth right" and saying "birth rate." "For two weeks, Turner performed very very well – and got awful, awful, awful, awful coverage," Connolly observed later, saying he had overheard TV people saying "He's limping! He's limping! Shoot that!" "TV was just brutal. But he just continued to perform well. He did things, and you'd look at the television that night and say, 'Jesus Christ, was I there?'"

The next morning, the news was that Martin Goldfarb and Tom Axworthy had published a book criticizing Turner. The book was an essay on polling, and an argument that, far from being identical centrist parties, the two major parties were very different, and becoming increasingly more so as the Conservatives became more conservative, and the Liberals more liberal: they were, in the words of the book's title, marching to a different drummer.

After analysing the two parties' fundamental beliefs, they found that the logic of both free trade and Meech Lake were central to the ideas of the Conservative Party: the former being that "the market should reign supreme and not be distorted by tariffs, regional industrial grants or cultural protection," and the latter that the power of the federal government should be reduced.

"Because antipathy to government forms the core of the Conservative party's value system, it should not come as a surprise that the Mulroney government has championed two policies that seek to embed this anti-government bias deep into the Canadian fabric," Goldfarb and Axworthy wrote. "Whether one agrees or disagrees with this Conservative perspective, there can be little doubt that it reflects the ideological world view of Conservative activists."

But if Mulroney was keeping the faith with free trade and Meech Lake, Turner's support for Meech Lake was, in their view, a virtual betrayal of the party's history. They stressed that the Liberals saw government as a partner, not an opponent: "Conservatives may place their faith in self-regulatory private markets, but Liberals still dream of a Just Society," they wrote.

"Given this Liberal value structure, the Meech Lake Accord strikes at the heart of Liberal belief," Goldfarb and Axworthy continued. "Brian Mulroney moved in tandem with his party's deepest beliefs in forging a deal with the provinces; John Turner's endorsement of the pact repudiated his party's intrinsic heritage. Liberals would not have negotiated the Meech Lake pact."

This was the theme that was picked up by the press. Edison Stewart of Canadian Press wrote a story that began, "Liberal pollster Martin Goldfarb says in a new book that the party may be on the road to political oblivion and leader John Turner is out of touch with party values."

"Imagine! Their own . . . pollster!" Mulroney said in amazement to an aide on the plane. Mulroney would fly into a rage when he saw unattributed references to Conservative polls in columns; a book critical of the leader by the party's pollster was incomprehensible to him.

Lamely, Goldfarb told the *Star* that the recent election promises (which he had had a hand in developing) showed Turner was moving in the right direction. "He's come a long way. And that's what the book argues as well," he said. "This isn't meant to criticize Turner or any one Liberal. It's about two parties."

Turner was in the embarrassing position of having to defend keeping Goldfarb as the party's pollster, and said he saw no reason to dismiss Goldfarb from the campaign team. "I don't expect Mr. Goldfarb or Mr. Axworthy or anybody else – and I haven't read the book – to reflect my opinion on everything," Turner told reporters in Winnipeg. "We retained Mr. Goldfarb for his expertise."

Peter Connolly had read the book – and he was furious at the interpretation that the Canadian Press story gave it. He felt the book was a useful delineation of the two parties, and a reminder of what the Liberal Party stood for, and he was angry that the impression was being created that Axworthy and

Goldfarb were bailing out on Turner, and that somehow he was a klutz, more of a klutz than even Greg Weston suggested. Later, both he and Michael Kirby would use the same terse euphemism: the book "wasn't useful".

The key figures in the Liberal campaign team were very different in approach and in style; they came to the jobs they held with different backgrounds, different loyalties, and different sensibilities. As events turned out, almost all of them would feel wounded in some important part of themselves.

One of the two campaign co-chairmen was Senator Alasdair Graham. The son of a Nova Scotia doctor, Graham, at fifty-nine, had a reputation as a cheerleader and party loyalist. He was a former journalist and broadcasting executive who had gone to work for Allan MacEachen between 1964 and 1966. Like MacEachen, he came from the Scottish Catholic stock of Cape Breton, and had been educated at St. Francis Xavier University, the home of Father Coady and the co-operative movement. Appointed to the Senate in 1972, he became president of the Liberal Party of Canada in 1975 and held the post until 1980. He had been asked by Turner to be co-chairman in late summer 1987, after the party upheavals in August. Amiable, easy-going, friendly, he prided himself on his loyalty to the party and the leader; he had been selected for the job because he was viewed as someone who knew everyone, and was a positive, upbeat enthusiast.

The other co-chairman was André Ouellet. Of all the Liberals who had survived the Tory tidal wave in Quebec, Ouellet was the one who was most closely identified with the backroom politics of the Trudeau Liberal Party. If Graham was viewed as a cheerleader, Ouellet was seen as a schemer, the man who had done Marc Lalonde's dirty work in laying down the law to the Quebec caucus. He was forty-nine, a month younger than Mulroney, and had known him in university – which didn't prevent Mulroney from making Ouellet his principal rhetorical target during the 1984 election campaign. Once close friends, he and Jean Chrétien had had a rift over Ouellet's decision to support Turner in 1984. Experienced, blunt, occasionally hot-tempered, Ouellet had a reputation for toughness, political judgement, and an ability to absorb the effects of hard political decisions without flinching.

The chairman of the strategy committee was Michael Kirby, forty-seven, senator, mathematician, game theorist, and former adviser to Pierre Trudeau. As a civil servant, he had supervised the preparation of the 1980 strategy paper that became known as the Kirby Memo: a hard-nosed, blunt assessment of how the provinces would deal with the constitutional talks, and how the federal government could play them off against one another. Short, good-looking, with a direct style of speech, Kirby had acquired some public profile as the Liberal analyst on Canada AM, the CTV morning show, where he appeared every Thursday morning with the Tory Hugh Segal and the New Democrat Gerry Caplan.

Michael Robinson, the director of finances, had been a consultant for ten years with Public Affairs International, David MacNaughton's consulting firm. Before that he had been a notably effective executive assistant to Judd Buchanan in the mid-seventies. He had been brought in to rescue the Liberal Party's dismal financial situation after John Turner removed the responsibility for party finances from Michel Robert.

Finally, the campaign director was John Webster. At thirty, Webster was the most junior of the team in terms of experience. He had met John Turner as an articling law student at McMillan Binch, and had worked on his leadership campaign and on his preparations for the 1986 leadership review, where he had worked with Ouellet at dealing with the more intense and excitable co-chairmen of the Friends of John Turner, Jean Lapierre and Terry Popovitch. After working for some provincial cabinet ministers and helping on the 1987 Ontario election, Webster had agreed to come to Ottawa to become the campaign director: an extraordinary experience for one so young. Blond, heavy-lidded, and handsome, Webster was considered by many to be competent and hardworking, but suspected of indiscretion because of his inexperience in functioning under so much pressure.

Each one of the strategists had a reputation he was proud of: Graham as a loyalist, Ouellet as a shrewd political operator, Kirby as a tough-minded strategist, Robinson as a careful financial organizer, and Webster as a political whiz-kid. Every one of them would emerge with his reputation diminished, with some Liberals convinced that, on a crucial issue, they had been stupid, disloyal, or duplicitous.

On Thursday, October 13, David MacNaughton, Al Graham, and Michael Robinson had lunch, and agreed that Robinson should go to the meeting in Ottawa on Friday and oppose what they saw as a plan to force Turner to step down.

On Friday afternoon, Kirby, Graham, Robinson, Ouellet, and Webster met at Liberal headquarters. The mood was bleak: Goldfarb had polled thirty key ridings, and the results were disastrous. Turner was the preferred leader of 8 per cent of those polled, and the day-care disaster had further stained the image of competence the Liberals had tried to project. There was some discussion of whether Turner should be told how bad the situation was, since this might further dishearten him, and it was agreed that he should be told. But the question remained: the polls were disastrous, the campaign was looking bad, and Turner was obviously in physical pain. What was to be done?

Early in the meeting, the question was raised. One person asked whether they should ask Turner to step down; the others vehemently argued that this would be really stupid, and should not even be considered. Aside from everything else, it would be counter-productive: he would be less likely to step down if he were asked. Nevertheless, he seemed in such pain, and so low in the polls, that some people at the meeting felt that a fall-back position should be developed in case he did step down.

Either way, the party was in desperate shape: in third place and dropping. What should be done?

Ouellet had been arguing since the beginning of the campaign that the only way to counter the overwhelming consensus in favour of free trade in Quebec was a massive show of unity: Turner, Trudeau, and Chrétien on the same stage, attacking the free-trade deal. Was his interest in getting Chrétien's participation a matter of solidifying support for Turner, or undermining it?

"What if, [one strategist] said, the leader decided that he could not carry on, that he was just not well enough to finish the campaign. Turner was visibly suffering every time he took a step, and this possibility was not considered far-fetched," Michael Kirby wrote in *Election*. " . . . In effect, there was a brief discussion of the possibility that Turner might decide that for the good of the country and to ensure the defeat of the trade deal, he would offer to step down if that would increase the probability of a Liberal election win."

Another participant remembers people stressing that they would not discuss such a thing, and as a result, in not discussing it, they discussed it. But much more of the meeting was spent discussing whether or not Turner should be told how bad the situation was. While some believed that in the interests of morale he should not be told, brutal realism prevailed, and the memo was written, laying out the numbers.

After the meeting, as he did every week, Kirby wrote a memo summarizing the discussion. The memo began by saying how well Turner was performing, and then described the media coverage.

"Media coverage appears to be less generous, or less tolerant, towards Liberal mistakes than it is to the mistakes of other parties," Kirby wrote. "The TV clips being used of Turner are generally unfavourable, even at events which have gone well." He was advised to calm down, since he "looks like he is yelling at Canadians rather than talking to them; looks far too emotional, too passionate, rather than calm, rational and low-key like Mulroney or Broadbent. . . . This television image is made worse by Turner's limp which . . . is helping destroy the image of Turner as a strong leader."

On Friday night, the plane arrived back in Ottawa; Kirkpatrick drove with Turner to Stornoway, because he'd left his car there. When Turner got to Stornoway, the memo was waiting for him. It was stark in its description of the situation.

The analysis of the numbers was blunt. "The leadership situation is getting worse," Kirby wrote. "Three-quarters of this week's sample in Montreal and Toronto say that Turner is losing momentum. Since leadership is the single most important motivator of voting behaviour, the data suggest we may not have bottomed out."

May not have bottomed out? With only 15 per cent saying that they preferred Turner as prime minister? With the Liberal share of the vote at 25 per cent? With the party leading in just one of the twelve key ridings? The assessment was brutal. After that, any profession of loyalty, or obligation on the part of strategists to present the cold truth must have seemed gratuitous.

Turner opened it, and read it. He found it a dismal memo reporting dismal poll results – and showed it to Kirkpatrick, who phoned Connolly and told him about the memo, and summarized it.

"Well, that's pretty well what he told me on the phone," Connolly said. Speaking to Turner, Connolly got him to agree that he was performing well. Turner didn't feel he was getting balanced coverage, and was encouraged by the reaction of the crowd. He remained convinced he would break through.

"Sure, and everybody thinks so." Connolly said. "We expected this. How do you think we're going to be looking, with everything that's happening in the media? The next poll is going to be worse. The Axworthy-Goldfarb thing maybe, or maybe with the debate coming that will be forgotten."

Connolly was convinced that Turner knew he was doing well, that he was getting a good reaction from crowds, and that the media coverage would change. On Saturday, October 15, Turner spent the day relaxing with his family, while the campaign committee went to their regular meeting.

It was a meeting for giving out marching orders: summarizing briefly the events of the previous week, and laying out the themes and locations for the tour for the following week: Turner was heading to rural Quebec on Sunday, where he would be talking about the environment, to Vancouver on Wednesday where he would be making a speech on foreign policy, and coming back to Ottawa to prepare for the debate.

But there was no mention or discussion of the memo, or of the idea of Turner stepping down. Goldfarb wanted the meeting to end early because he had to give a speech, and Connolly kidded him, wondering if he was speaking to the Book-of-the-Month Club.

According to Connolly, André Ouellet asked him if they could talk for a minute. The two men stepped into an empty office. Ouellet closed the door and said "Well, Peter, you have to go over to Stornoway and tell him how serious this is. And you're going to have to tell him to go."

He gave Connolly the reasons: that Turner was endangering the party's chances, that the Liberals were in third place and falling, and Turner was pulling them down. He didn't say so explicitly, but Connolly assumed that he was speaking on behalf of the top strategists.

"André, it's the way his performance is being perceived, or being communicated, that's dragging us down," Connolly said. "That may change."

Ouellet said no, the perception was too solidly implanted.

Connolly then asked what he was proposing to do.

Ouellet said that they would call all the candidates in to Ottawa on Monday, name Chrétien as the new leader, and spend the rest of the week preparing him for the debate. When Connolly asked him how this would be received, Ouellet said that there would be an enthusiastic reaction: they had a poll showing 44 per cent support for Chrétien. Connolly remembers replying that there were polls that showed 77 per cent support for Turner when he was not yet leader of the Liberal Party.

But Connolly said he was prepared to deliver the message to Turner, but on only one condition: that Ouellet would agree in advance to stay on and devote his full energies to the rest of the campaign if Turner gave the reply Connolly expected. Ouellet agreed. Throughout the conversation, Ouellet had never said he represented the campaign committee, but he left that impression with Connolly; Connolly left the Liberal headquarters believing that Ouellet had been speaking on behalf of all the people who were at the meeting on Friday. To Liberals trying to sort out what happened afterwards, Ouellet insisted he did no such thing.

Saturday evening, Connolly phoned Turner at Stornoway, saying he had been asked to pass on a message, which did not carry a recommendation from him: he had been told that Turner ought to step down in view of the way the campaign was going.

"They're nuts," Turner recalls saying. "Tell whoever it is 'no way.'" Turner thought it was the most ridiculous thing he had ever heard; he couldn't believe it.

The next morning, Henry Comor came to Stornoway early in the morning to deliver a memo; he and Turner had a cup of coffee, and before Turner left, he said to Comor "They want to get rid of me."

"You're not going to take any notice of it, are you?" Comor asked. "No," Turner replied.

After Turner drove off, Comor asked Connolly what he had been referring to, and Connolly said "Well, they came to get him." But when Comor asked Kirby about it later, he said "It wasn't a group – I just came around and gave him the polling figures."

Later in the day, André Ouellet reached Turner by phone. He was vague, and put no proposition. "He went around the mulberry bush; he put no proposition, no request, no conclusion," Turner said later. "It was a conversation without purpose: he asked 'You got the memo, what did you think?' I said 'Hell, that's the way it is.' I was vague too; there was no proposition or request made to me, and I wasn't going to make it easier for him."

Turner told Ouellet that the memo gave a very sad picture, that it was a terrible presentation: what did it mean?

"We're going to be beaten, that's what it means," Ouellet replied, and added that everything now depended upon the debate. They discussed the situation for about fifteen minutes.

In the confusion that subsequently surrounded the events of that weekend, a few things are clear: the strategists met on Friday, they discussed the possibility that Turner might step down, Turner received a hardnosed assessment of the desperate situation that the party was in on Friday night and, before twenty-four hours had passed, became convinced that there was a serious attempt to force him to resign.

That morning, the debate preparation team was meeting in Toronto. Hershell Ezrin, Raymond Heard, Henry Comor, and Patrick Gossage all met in Gossage's office in a nondescript building on Richmond Street West, in Toronto's warehouse and clothing district. They developed a fall-back strategy for Turner during the debate: if Turner were losing the debate in the early period and the abortion issue came up, he could grab attention and headlines by announcing an abortion policy: a variation of the Canadian Medical Association policy. This was sent off to the plane as a strategy option.

The next morning, to their horror, they saw a version of the proposal in the paper. In Asbestos, Quebec, while Turner was inside doing a radio interview in French, Peter Connolly had been chatting with English-speaking reporters outside. In Monday's *Toronto Star*, David Vienneau wrote that Turner was ready to call for a Criminal Code amendment that would allow a woman to have an abortion up to the twenty-second week of pregnancy, and quoted Connolly as saying that Turner was deciding whether to unveil the policy during the week, or during the debate. Vienneau pointed out that the Law Reform Commission had recommended access to abortion in the first twenty-two weeks of pregnancy, while the Canadian Medical Association had said it would sanction abortion after twenty weeks only in extreme circumstances.

Connolly was very angry; he insisted he had never said this to Vienneau, but had simply led him through the options the party faced. The debate strategists were doubly furious. To begin with, they had urged the CMA position, not the Law Reform Commission position, and it had been confused. But they were even more astounded that the day after they had made their recommendation it was in the *Toronto Star*. For the senior members of caucus, this was an outrage. The Liberals were down at rock-bottom support in the polls: the bedrock base of ethnic, Roman Catholic Canada. With this policy, the party would be taking an axe to the only base it had left.

In Windsor, Herb Gray was particularly upset. Several of the Windsor-area Liberal candidates – particularly Shaughnessy Cohen – were active pro-life campaigners, and the Roman Catholic diocese was actively involved in the anti-abortion campaign. That morning, he got a call from his wife: Shaughnessy Cohen had been trying to reach him; other candidates were also phoning him at his campaign office. The abortion issue was one of the issues in Windsor that the Liberals were using to distinguish themselves from the NDP; there was a group purporting to be former New Democrats, who called themselves New Democrats for Life (and, when the NDP threatened them with court action, Now Democrats for Life), and anti-abortion constituents were telling Liberals that they liked the fact that the Liberals were not imposing a party policy on their members.

The *Toronto Star* story left the impression that Turner would be announcing a party policy that everyone would have to endorse: a significant change from the previous position of calling for a free vote in Parliament to vote on a government policy. So Gray started trying to get through to the campaign headquarters in Ottawa, to find out what was happening.

Gray had already been worried about the situation. He, Lloyd Axworthy, Robert Kaplan, and André Ouellet had been discussing the dreadful straits the party was in. The four of them began to discuss whether or not Turner should continue. All though the discussions, there was a consensus that the idea should not be pursued unless they all agreed – and they didn't – but the option was wrestled with. Should they replace the leader? Could they? Two conditions were necessary: there had to be agreement among themselves that it was a good idea, and Turner had to agree. Ultimately, they never agreed, which enabled them to cling to their denials when the CBC story went on the air. As far as they were concerned, nothing had happened, and they could deny the suggestion that something had.

The abortion story only worsened their mood. Lloyd Axworthy was in a rage; he thought the idea showed bad political judgement, and was stupid. Gray and Brian Tobin called Axworthy; other people called around.

One of the things discussed was the idea that the senior caucus members should get together with Turner to discuss how bad the situation was. Inside the party, there were rumours circulating of how angry the MPs were; one senior Liberal had received a call from Western Canada on his car phone as he was driving home from a meeting, and his caller told him he had hot news: that Herb Gray and Lloyd Axworthy were going to try to catch up with Turner in Edmonton when he was there on Tuesday October 18, and talk to him about possibly stepping down. When he passed this on to Michael Kirby, Kirby said briskly "Oh, I know I know I know – I'll talk to you about it later." An angry meeting between Turner and his front-bench MPs could have been much more devastating than the concerns raised by the strategists, particularly since one of them had considered threatening to refuse to file his nomination papers. Herb Gray was particularly critical: he was the ultimate loyalist, but his principal loyalty was to the party. If he decided that Turner had to step down for the good of the party, it would be a devastating blow.

Also on Monday, André Ouellet and Raymond Garneau met for a bite to eat in Montreal, before they went off to their respective campaign offices. Ouellet was profoundly discouraged, but they discussed the possibility of a mass rally of all the Liberal forces, including Trudeau and Chrétien. Later that day, Garneau told a confidant that Ouellet had raised the possibility of Turner's stepping down, and that Garneau had cut him off immediately, and wouldn't hear of it.

On Monday night, Al Graham flew to Quebec City to see Turner, and ask him to phone Chrétien to ask him to participate in the campaign. (The day before, Turner had told Francis Fox flatly that he would not appear on the same stage as Chrétien.) Turner said that Chrétien was welcome to campaign, but that he would not telephone him to ask him to do so. (Connolly, at that point, was convinced that Graham's real purpose was to deliver another message to Turner that he should step down – and that he didn't have the nerve to do so.)

On Tuesday, the Liberal campaign made an unscheduled trip to Hamilton for the funeral of Vic Copps, the former Mayor of Hamilton and Sheila Copps's father. Fluent in French, comfortable in Italian, and strongly, sometimes harshly partisan, Copps had endeared herself to Turner by her vigorous and unswerving loyalty. The plane then headed west, where Turner announced a plan for a $211-million program to help entrepreneurs and encourage profit-sharing and staff ownership. In addition, he said that a Liberal government would appoint an ombudsman to defend the interests of small business in government administration.

However, the announcement was not given much attention. Senator Al Graham had been in touch with Senator Pietro Rizzuto, begging him to do what he could to help. In Montreal, Le Devoir reported that Rizzuto was prepared to help candidates who asked, and that Jean Chrétien would be speaking on Saturday night at the nomination meeting in Shawinigan. Francis Fox told Le Devoir that, when he had met with Turner in Quebec City the previous Sunday, Turner had asked him to make an appeal for unity.

On Wednesday, October 19, Turner was in Vancouver: first flipping hamburgers in a McDonald's, as Liberal candidates did across Canada, and then appearing before University of British Columbia students. Heckled by Tory students shouting "Brian, Brian" and "Trade Turner, Free Canada," he taunted them about Mulroney's refusal to go before similar meetings.

"I would love to have the other side represented here! I would love to have Brian Mulroney standing on the other side of the podium. I would love to give him equal time so we could satisfy some of the people here, but he won't come out of the glass bubble. He won't come out of the cage!" Turner shouted. It was one of his favourite themes: Mulroney's smooth, risk-free campaign compared to his own open, high-wire performance.

Mulroney, he said, didn't have the guts to defend his own agreement. "He refuses to debate, to meet students, to go on hotline shows," Turner said. "He is not here. . . . Either he has no guts, he doesn't understand the agreement, or he is not willing to stand in front of a public audience like this and defend it!" The Liberals in the audience gave him a strong ovation, chanting "No guts! No guts!"

By this time Brian Mulroney had learned, through his own personal sources, that there was discussion going on inside the Liberal Party of Turner's stepping down. He didn't mention it to anyone until later, but he began to wonder whether he would be facing John Turner or Jean Chrétien in the debates the following week. Had he found himself facing Chrétien, he was prepared to challenge the legitimacy of his being there, and accuse him of being an assassin.

The idea of a party leader being challenged by his party was far from unusual: it had happened to a whole series of leaders of both the Conservative and the Liberal Party. But for a leader to step down, or be pressured to step down, or even to have his stepping down seriously contemplated in the middle of an election campaign was extraordinary. However, the prospect of Chrétien's entering the race, while dramatic and unprecedented, was far from a certain asset for the Liberals. Chrétien was a strong opponent of both free trade and Meech Lake, both of which were extremely popular in Quebec; it was clear that, if Chrétien entered the race, Robert Bourassa would do everything he could to block him from winning Quebec.

Mulroney saw the continuing unhappiness with Turner's leadership in the Liberal Party as a confirmation of his view that the primary, if not the only, job of an opposition leader was to establish party unity and bring everyone together into the tent. He had told his caucus that Turner had made a fatal error when he put on a Rat Pack T-shirt; this gut reaction developed into a fuller analysis of Turner's problems, which he told friends and advisers.

In his view, Turner had become party leader with the determination to reorganize the party, develop new policies and themes, attract new candidates, raise a lot of money, and challenge Mulroney on the basis of leadership and competence. However, Mulroney felt he had made a critical error in allowing the Rat Pack's personal attacks on the government to continue unabated, and was first frustrated and then reconciled to the fact that his lengthy speeches in the House of Commons got no attention at all in the media, while the shrill assaults of the Liberal backbenchers got front-page treatment. Mulroney came to believe that a symbiotic relationship developed between the Liberal Rat Pack and the Press Gallery, dominated by reporters he called "knee-cappers": Claire Hoy and Derek Hodgson of the Toronto Sun, and Robert Fife and Tim Naumetz, initially at Canadian Press, and later going to the Sun after Hoy and Hodgson were forced to leave the paper. Mulroney told friends that the Rat Pack and the Press Gallery had developed common assumptions: that Mulroney was a goddamn thug running a bunch of thieves, he engaged in hyperbole, he was shallow, his wife was an airhead, and the kids were probably rented.

As a result, Mulroney concluded, Turner had made the false assumption that the country shared this view, and had stopped working at keeping the party together. When Chrétien quit, a critical element of the party had lost an idol, and dissent was legitimated. (Mulroney also concluded that the Press Gallery was out to get him, and, from the day he announced that he had asked and received André Bissonnette's resignation in January 1987, did not give a formal press conference in the National Press Theatre, limiting himself to brief remarks to the thicket of microphones on the stairs up to his office from the House of Commons, to comments at Rideau Hall, or the occasional interview. One of the effects of this approach was to further divide and restrict his coverage, since there was no translation available for his remarks in French, and a significant number of the English-speaking reporters couldn't understand him when he spoke French.)

Both Mulroney and his election planners and the key Liberal strategists knew – as the Liberal backbenchers did not – that Mulroney's leadership qualities were much more highly rated by the voters than were Turner's, and that an election campaign that focused on leadership would be to the Tories' advantage, rather than to their detriment. On the other hand, a change of leaders in the middle of the campaign could be equally destabilizing.

As a result, Mulroney heard with satisfaction the almost unbelievable reports of pressure on Turner to step down.

Similarly, Robin Sears, the NDP deputy campaign director, became aware of the machinations in the Liberal Party; he had been taken aback by some of the contemptuous, disloyal remarks about Turner that he had heard from Liberal campaign people, and had learned that there had been a threat conveyed to Turner that senior caucus colleagues in Quebec would make it clear that they did not support the abortion policy if it were announced. While pleased as a partisan, he was stunned at the disloyalty.

On Friday September 30, Elly Alboim was sitting in his small office on the eighth floor of the National Press Building at 150 Wellington, and Peter Mansbridge was sitting on the window ledge with his feet on Alboim's desk. At forty, Mansbridge was the nearest thing to a star in Canadian TV journalism: a few months before, he had caused a dramatic stir in the country when he turned down an offer from CBS to join their morning show and, as part of the effort to keep him, Knowlton Nash had agreed to make room for him as the anchorman on The National. He was handsome, poised, and an experienced reporter: he had covered Joe Clark from 1977 to 1979, and worked as the anchor on leadership conventions and elections.

Elly Alboim, the Ottawa bureau chief, at forty-one, was even more of a veteran of political coverage. He had graduated from McGill in 1968 where he had worked on the *McGill Daily*, and then had gone to Columbia for a journalism degree. He joined CBC-TV in Montreal the week of the October Crisis in 1970, and, after a few years there, and some time in Toronto, came to Ottawa in 1978, just as the House of Commons began to be televised. In that time, he had been responsible for every first ministers' conference on the Constitution from 1977 to Meech Lake, some twenty-three other federal-provincial conferences, and the coverage of every election, federal and provincial. His beard, turning to salt and pepper, and his thickening at the waist gave him an added air of almost Talmudic authority; his sudden sucks at cigarettes were signs of his intensity and impatience. He was intolerant of stupidity, and angered by duplicity.

Over his twelve years in the Ottawa bureau, Alboim had acquired a reputation and an influence both with his reporters and with his sources, many of whom were awed by his intelligence and his information. In the bureau, he gathered information, challenged reporters, coached and directed them, and acted as Devil's advocate, providing an intellectual rigour that is rare in journalism.

That afternoon, Mansbridge and Alboim were chatting about the campaign launch that was then expected the next morning when one of them noticed that Charlotte Gray, the Ottawa editor of *Saturday Night*, was on the local CBC supper-hour television show. As part of her weekly chat about politics, she reported that there were rumours in the Liberal Party that senior Liberal MPs had approached Turner before the election and asked him to step down. It caught their attention, and they decided to look into it, and monitor the situation inside the Liberal campaign.

For some years, Mansbridge had worked on what he called "re-creation" pieces: fairly lengthy pieces of television reporting in which he reconstructed complex events. He had done it to tell the story of how Canadians had helped American hostages in Iran escape, how Joe Clark had agreed to adopt the policy of moving the embassy from Tel Aviv to

Jerusalem, and, in his longest TV news item, a twelve-minute piece, how the deal had been struck on the patriation of the Constitution in 1981. In each case, he had used unnamed sources, and various graphic visual techniques to illustrate things which, by their nature, had not taken place in front of TV cameras.

Stimulated by Charlotte Gray's piece, Mansbridge and Alboim did some checking, and they learned that Michael Kirby had met Turner before the announcement of the Liberal forty-point program and told him that the Tories would probably win a majority government, and that leadership was a problem. They filed this away for the reconstruction of the Liberal campaign that they expected Mansbridge would do after the election. Then they began to pick up some indication of trouble at the time of the child-care announcement.

When the polls began to be published, some of the high anxiety at Liberal headquarters began to leak out. At about that point, at the beginning of the second week in the campaign, Alboim – who had moved to Toronto to supervise the election coverage – and Mansbridge began actively checking into the rumours they were picking up, and started filing what they were learning. On Thursday October 13, they learned that there were senior strategy meetings going on, and began following the story intensely through the weekend.

On Friday, Mansbridge had a lunch date with Michael Kirby, which Kirby confirmed at 9.40 that morning. Mansbridge caught the next flight to Ottawa, and walked into the lobby of Hy's, where a woman who was waiting for him apologized. "Things are crazy at the office," she said. "He can't make it." This further confirmed his feeling that something odd was happening, and further encouraged him to check out the situation.

On Saturday October 15, the first public indication of unrest in the Liberal Party came in Le Devoir, with a front-page story by Michel Vastel entitled "Les libéraux s'attendent au pire – Les rumeurs d'un putsch refont surface" (The Liberals expect the worst: Rumours of a coup emerge again).

In the story, Vastel wrote that Liberals who had predicted that there were only thirteen safe seats in Quebec now felt that there were only five, and that, in the worst of scenarios, they would end up with fewer seats than they had won in 1984.

After summarizing the controversy over the Goldfarb and Axworthy book, Vastel wrote that there had been a meeting of strategists planned to discuss a poll that had asked people if Turner's resignation would encourage them to vote Liberal and had also asked them which interim leader, Herb Gray, Allan MacEachen, Marc Lalonde, or Paul Martin would have the best chance of leading the Liberal Party to power. According to Vastel, David Peterson's entourage denied the existence of an organized plot but conceded that Keith Davey, Tom Axworthy, and Michael Kirby were playing with the idea of some spectacular event in the middle of the campaign.

Alboim and Mansbridge worked through the weekend on the story; on Monday, Mansbridge was driving to the airport when he got a call from Alboim telling him of an unbelievable development; in addition to what they were working on, a source had heard a conversation that told them the depth of unhappiness the MPs were feeling about the impending abortion announcement, and that they were pushing for a meeting with Turner to have a showdown. At that point, the CBC reporter Don Newman was brought in on the story to work on that angle.

The reporters were tracking the MPs' concerns so closely that sometimes they were phoning to inquire about conversations only minutes after they had taken place. Until then, Mansbridge and Alboim had both felt they were compiling information for a reconstruction story later. However, they began to feel that they were dealing with something more substantial, that needed to be reported during the campaign. A series of meetings with senior editors began, as they debated whether they should hold the story or run it.

Over the weekend, Pietro Rizzuto was getting calls from desperate Liberals. "People were calling me who were very upset, who were afraid they were losing," he recalled. "I had the impression that some of them thought that I could do something. . . . When it became public that some people thought that Turner should step down, I said publicly that it was no longer the time. You can't ask a leader to step down in the middle of an election campaign. That was what I told those people. The time to do it was in the spring of 1988. But it was total panic for some people. Total discouragement."

During this period, the debate continued on whether or not the story should be broadcast or not. Alboim's style was to play Devil's advocate; to challenge a story, or an argument, and make sure that it would stand up. His intuitive sense was that the story should not be broadcast. Nothing had happened, the discussion was in the past, it was in the back room, it involved strategists and not elected officials. Mansbridge was convinced that, whatever happened, Turner would not step down, and the manoeuvrings were preposterous. Since nothing was going to come of it, was it a story?

But gradually, the group came to the conclusion that there were real discussions by real people in the campaign that ran totally contrary to their public role, and showed that there was serious turmoil at the most senior levels of the Liberal campaign. More than that, they concluded that if they didn't tell the story, they would be participating in a fraud by carrying on the TV coverage of the Turner campaign.

But what was given relatively little discussion was whether or not it was appropriate for Mansbridge to do the story himself. He would not entertain the idea of anyone else's doing it; he felt he was bringing reporting skills to the anchor job, he resented the picture of TV anchors presented in the film *Broadcast News* and had written a critical review of the film for the *Toronto Star* (ironically, Mansbridge bears a considerable resemblance to William Hurt, the actor who played the airhead anchor in the movie), and he was determined to do the story, which he felt was his.

With the information they had amassed, Mansbridge started writing the story, and ended up rewriting it a dozen times. On Tuesday night, the item was ready to roll, but at the last minute, about 8.50 – ten minutes before it was to be broadcast to the Maritimes – it was pulled. There was a loose end that still had to be checked.

However, producers for *The Journal* had seen the little preview of the item prepared for the beginning of *The National*; the next day, they began to make phone calls, and politicians and campaign organizers started calling the CBC television newsroom to find out what they had. The producers decided that, if they were going to run the item, they would have to do it that night.

At the same time that Alboim, Mansbridge, and Newman were running down the last details of the story, a special unit was working on ways to make the images visually compatible with what Mansbridge would be saying. Half an hour before broadcast, they were still arguing over the script; when the agreement was settled, Alboim phoned the Turner campaign and read Peter Connolly the script over the phone to prepare him to react afterwards.

That night, *The National* was broadcast at 9 p.m. in Central Canada, because the Los Angeles Kings were playing in Edmonton for the first time since Wayne Gretzky had left the Oilers. At 9.08, after the first three items, Sheldon Turcott introduced the item, saying that the Liberals' division on abortion – described in Keith Boag's report from Vancouver – was part of a much larger problem.

"For the last several days there has been some astonishing manoeuvring at the highest levels of the party," he said. "Some of the most senior people thought the unthinkable. Deep into this election campaign, they thought about putting pressure on John Turner to quit. But CBC News has learned they've pulled back, and are now prepared to work to salvage the campaign. Our chief correspondent, Peter Mansbridge, has the story of a party in crisis."

Mansbridge then began describing the meeting that the strategists had held, but made two mistakes: he identified the meeting as taking place on Thursday rather than Friday, and he named only four of those present – as photographs of

Kirby, Webster, Graham, and Ouellet flashed onto the screen – leaving out Michael Robinson. He then said that all four men had signed documents that outlined the desperate situation the party was in – whereas, in fact, the document was the weekly memo written by Kirby.

At that point, a graphic image of a memo flashed on the screen – and, watching it, Mansbridge and Alboim both swore under their breath. The picture insinuated that they had a copy of the memo, and they did not.

"At Stornoway, Turner read the briefing, but remained resolute, convinced the campaign was still winnable, even if he had to do it alone," Mansbridge said. "He refused to meet the strategists. The next day, Saturday, Turner talked to some of them by phone, leaving them convinced he would not step down. The strategists decided a leadership change was not an option any longer, and others impressed upon them that the campaign must go on, that dissent must end."

Then, Mansbridge said, the CBC's poll came out on Sunday night, showing Turner "ranked dead last on every one of ten different qualities." This prompted what he called "a frenzied series of cross-country phone calls" by strategists and senior Liberal candidates. He said that five of the candidates, all of the front bench – Herb Gray, Lloyd Axworthy, Robert Kaplan, André Ouellet, and Raymond Garneau – had expressed a desire for a meeting with Turner, that Gray had put in the request late Monday, and that this had been blocked by Peter Connolly.

In fact, Garneau had not been part of these discussions, and Connolly had agreed to schedule a meeting with Turner on Friday, and Gray had decided against it.

"It's not clear yet what the five MPs wanted to tell Turner, but it is known that asking Turner to step aside had been discussed by some of the group," Mansbridge said. "But some also felt that if Turner was forced out the party could be left in ruins by a very public bloodbath."

Mansbridge went on to describe the meeting between Kirby and Turner ten days before the election campaign began, in which Kirby laid out the situation, and another meeting in which Garneau and Turner raised their voices at each other, and, according to Mansbridge, Garneau told Turner he must quit.

"And while all this was going on, Turner was in agonizing physical pain," Mansbridge said. "He'd pinched a nerve in his back, could barely walk, could barely stand up for speeches."

He ended by saying that the strategists and the MPs had pulled back, that Liberals seemed to realize "that they were heading towards a major confrontation, and the party, in the process, was only destroying itself." There had been an agreement on a meeting between the strategists on Friday, he said, and the candidates had backed off on their request for a meeting.

"But they're not happy," he concluded. "They're not happy with the treatment they've been getting. They're not happy with the lack of consultation on major new policies like abortion, but mostly they're not happy with the performance of their party or their leader, now almost halfway through the election campaign. Peter Mansbridge, CBC News, Toronto."

The members of the crew who had not been involved in the story were very excited; there were cheers and applause in the studio when the item was finished. But Mansbridge and Alboim were tense and uneasy about the projection of the impression that they had a copy of the memo; Mansbridge didn't sleep that night.

In Vancouver, Turner was about to go in to deliver the speech when he was told that the item would be broadcast; he took a tremendously deep breath, and said "Well, we've got a speech to make."

As the news was being delivered, John Webster was on the phone to Connolly, holding the phone to the television loudspeaker; unaware that Connolly had had an advance reading of the script, he was taken aback when Connolly seemed to be denying things before they had been said. Meanwhile, outside the dinner where Turner was speaking, the press corps was waiting for a reaction to the story. Connolly called it "preposterous"; Turner called it "the craziest thing I've heard in the last four years"; both carefully chosen phrases that implied that they were a comment on the story, when in fact they were a comment on what the story had reported.

At Liberal headquarters in Ottawa, the reaction was shock. The story had, inadvertently, struck at the identity of all those strategists named, making them appear to be disloyal, naive, and stupid. Alasdair Graham prided himself above all on his loyalty; it was put in question. Michael Kirby prided himself on his ability to look unflinchingly at all the options, and he felt this had unfairly criticized him for doing this.

Others, like Robinson and Webster, felt that, while struggling to keep the party from flying apart and working to keep warring clans working together, they had been unfairly involved in a story about something that had, in fact, not happened. Robinson had the additional difficulty that, because he was not identified, some automatically assumed that he was the major source. In a strange way, the person whose reputation seemed less affected than the others was André Ouellet: since he had had a reputation as a sinister, manipulative back-room politician, covering every angle was almost expected of him, and he had learned to be thicker-skinned than the others. Kirby, for all his high tenor swagger and apparent pleasure in being seen as a Machiavellian strategist, and shocking people by the bluntness of his analysis, had a bundle of insecurities about his role which his Senate tenure could not assuage.

That night and the next morning, Graham, Ouellet, Webster, and Kirby set to work to craft a statement that would deny the insinuation and innuendo that they felt was in the story, rather than challenge the story fact by fact. Graham was all for a blanket, flat-out denial, but the consensus was that they should tread carefully. "The four of us meet weekly, as we have for many months, to discuss the state of the campaign and to review what the strategy should be for the remainder of the campaign," the statement said. "As usual, the results of this meeting were communicated to the leader in a memorandum. It is preposterous to conclude that because we meet we are plotting against the leader. In fact, we are plotting with the leader to win the election."

And in Toronto, Michael Robinson categorically denied that he and David MacNaughton had been approached by the MPs, as the *Globe* story had mistakenly suggested.

When the item was broadcast, a number of us who were covering the campaign for the *Globe and Mail* had immediately set to work trying to confirm the story. Within half an hour, I reached a veteran Liberal who had already talked to one of the strategists at party headquarters. The source said that the story was true, and added some details about the degree to which the abortion issue had outraged caucus members. However, although the source had been in touch with headquarters, there was a sufficient degree of misunderstanding and distrust among all the senior players in the Liberal campaign that some of the errors in the CBC story were perpetuated, and new ones were added. The source knew that Michael Robinson had been at a meeting, but got the meeting wrong: the *Globe* story reported that he had met with the MPs. Similarly, Raymond Garneau – whose loyalty to Turner had angered some of the Quebec federal Liberals who felt that Turner was dragging them down – continued to be identified as part of a group that had wanted Turner to quit.

Garneau had been in Sherbrooke at a meeting, and was at the home of the Liberal candidate Dennis Wood when local reporters began asking him about the story that had been broadcast. The next day, he rushed back to Montreal and, distraught, called a press conference, where he called the report "an insulting and false piece of news," and denied categorically that he had participated in any discussion of forcing Turner to resign. "If there is any Liberal who has proven his loyalty to John Turner and the Liberal Party, it is me," he said.

Questioned by reporters, he said that he had talked with André Ouellet on Monday of that week, but that they had discussed the possibility of a rally opposed to the Free Trade Agreement, bringing together people like Pierre Trudeau in a

similar fashion to the rallies that brought Jean Lesage to speak
on behalf of the No campaign in the 1980 referendum.

Asked about reports that Senator Graham wanted Marc
Lalonde and Jean Chrétien to campaign, he said "We never
closed the door to anyone. If they want to help, the door is
open. Marc was saying he would campaign for Lucie Pépin -
good. Jean is going to Grand-mère – so much the better. We are
an open party."

He described the election as "almost a referendum" on the
free-trade issue, and said that every single person who shared
the Liberal Party's objectives in trying to defeat the trade
agreement was welcome.

"But you yourself, as chief here in Quebec, will you yourself go out and solicit the aid of Mr. Trudeau and Mr. Chrétien?" a reporter persisted.

"I've said it publicly time and again; it's not the first time
it's been reported in the press," Garneau said. "We are in the
middle of an election campaign; each one is fighting. If they
want to help - and I'm asking them to help, not because we are
in a mess, but because we are dealing with the future of the
country; not because we can't run the campaign – we've organized the campaign – but it's a very important issue, and I
think it should go beyond personal friction . . . if they want to
come, they are welcome."

He then said it was particularly important that people work
and campaign on the riding level.

"Outside Quebec too?" the reporter asked.

"You started your question saying I was the boss of Quebec," Garneau said. "I'm not sure I'm such a great boss, but I
will certainly not talk for the other provinces."

It was a sad appeal, and a sad admission from a man who
had sacrificed a great deal over the previous four years to go to
Ottawa, having been the president of a bank. He had succeeded in helping John Turner make a significant change in
Liberal constitutional policy, bringing it back to what he considered the real traditions of the Liberal Party under Wilfrid
Laurier and Mackenzie King: a more provincialist approach
to federal-provincial relations, as shown in Turner's support

for Meech Lake. But he had failed to create a party in Quebec that could work together, had failed to win the neutrality, let alone the support, of his former boss Robert Bourassa, and had failed to impose himself on the warring factions of the party.

Astonishingly, despite the impact of the Mansbridge story, the question of Turner's leadership being challenged was not dead. On Thursday October 21, the day after the CBC story was on the air, John Webster learned that there had been serious discussions in Quebec of Liberal candidates running as Independent Liberals, and effectively dissociating themselves from Turner's leadership. Similarly, Robert Kaplan got a phone call from a Quebec MP saying the same thing: the MP was thinking of running as an independent Liberal, and publicly dissociating the campaign from Turner.

That day, Jean Lapierre phoned Pierre Deniger. The polling in Quebec showed the Liberals with between five and eight seats – some said as low as four – and Lapierre was now very worried he was going to lose his own seat. Thin and intense, Lapierre had been the co-chairman of the Friends of John Turner during the 1986 leadership review, and had worked very hard. However, he had become angry and disillusioned with Turner when, after only reluctantly agreeing to accept the position of director of the Quebec organization, he had had the job taken away abruptly and given to Rémi Bujold in the fall of 1987. He had been very disheartened by the way the April caucus revolt had turned out, and had been convinced then that his career was blighted by his involvement.

Now, with support for the Liberals dropping like a stone in Quebec, he felt that the only solution was to get rid of Turner and replace him with Chrétien. Deniger said no, it made no sense. Personally, Deniger was in the odd position that his own chances seemed to improve when it was clear that the Liberals were doing badly. In addition to feeling that changing leaders in the middle of a campaign was a disastrous idea, he was finding that, if it looked as if the Liberals might form a government and defeat free trade, Quebec voters would close ranks behind the Tories.

But Lapierre was convinced that getting rid of Turner was the party's only chance for survival. "We have to; we will all be beaten," he said. So Deniger met with his campaign organization in Laprairie to sound them out. They agreed it made no sense, and Deniger told Lapierre again that he would not get involved. Lapierre said that he had talked to Tobin and Dingwall, and was proceeding.

Friday morning, there was a meeting of the Quebec political commission at the library room of the Château Champlain: a meeting that included Rémi Bujold, Richard Mongeau, Jean Lapierre, André Morrow, Alfonso Gagliano (the Quebec caucus chairman) and Raymond Garneau, who came later. (Ouellet was not present.) It was almost a wake: everyone had always assumed that the Liberals could win between twenty-five and thirty seats; on Monday October 10, it looked as if they were down to Finestone, Allmand, Prud'homme, Jean Lapierre, Shirley Maheu in Saint-Laurent, David Berger in Westmount, and the two Outaouais ridings of Hull and Gatineau – Le Lièvre. Now, on Friday, the total number of Quebec seats was dropping to three, on the way to a total wipeout.

Lapierre had spoken to Axworthy and Kaplan to see what the situation was elsewhere. The conclusion of the meeting was that they owed it to Turner to give him a true description of the situation. Richard Mongeau was going up to Ottawa that afternoon to accompany Turner on visits in Hull, and he left at lunchtime for Ottawa with the direction to talk to him.

That afternoon, back at the Peel Street headquarters, Garneau agreed that, instead of having Mongeau tell Turner what the situation was like, it was his job to tell him the situation the next day in Ottawa. So Mongeau was phoned, and told not to discuss how things were going in Quebec with Turner. Garneau and Fox were going to go to Ottawa the next day. Some of those in the party organization were convinced that the message would be not simply how badly things were going, but that he should step down – a rumour that infuriated Garneau even more than the speculation earlier in the week.

However, by the end of Friday, after conversations with Kaplan, Herb Gray, Axworthy, and Del Zotto, the conclusion was that he should not be told to step down, but that they should await the outcome of the debate, and they should do everything they could to ensure he performed as well as he could. That virtually settled it: the deadline for nominations was 2 p.m. Monday, October 24. After the debate was over, it would be too late for anyone who was not already a candidate to step in.

To the annoyance of some, Garneau never deviated: he could have seen the party go to zero seats and still have been loyal to Turner, one Liberal complained.

On Friday afternoon, Michel Gratton, the former press secretary to Brian Mulroney who was writing a column in the Montreal *Daily News*, phoned Jean Lapierre in his car as he was driving back to the Eastern Townships. Gratton had learned that a group of Liberal candidates, many of them from Quebec, had been trying to persuade Chrétien to prepare to step in, should Turner agree to step down. Lapierre denied involvement, and called the report of a request to Chrétien to lead the party "pure fabrication from start to finish."

But Gratton and his colleagues working on the story, Bernard St-Laurent and Peter Black, were sure of their source.

"The conspirators, many of them from Quebec, believed Turner could be convinced to resign after being presented with a list of Liberal candidates who would withdraw from the campaign if he stayed on," they wrote. "The master plan pre-supposed that Turner's Quebec lieutenant, Raymond Garneau, would already have resigned because of his opposition to the putsch. Garneau remains staunchly loyal to Turner."

According to the story, the hope was that Chrétien would accept the challenge that night in Grand-mère, in his former riding of Shawinigan. However, he refused.

"'He turned it down because it is not his agenda, the candidates are not his choices, the party has no money, and he doesn't want to destroy himself,' the source said. Even yesterday, two days after the CBC broke the broad outlines of the frontal assault on John Turner's tenuous leadership, the same Liberal strategists were still trying to convince Chrétien to change his mind and accept the incredible task."

The publication of the story helped kill whatever attempt there might have been to deliver yet another message to Turner on Saturday. However, after the election, Chrétien told acquaintances that he had been approached, and told to prepare for the debate, in case Turner should step down; he might be hit by a bus. If he were hit by a bus, the party would elect the bus driver, Chrétien said that he replied.

If he were asked technical questions, Chrétien said that he had been advised to reply that, unlike the other two leaders, he didn't pretend to have all the answers, just common sense. He was in an extremely awkward position: on the one hand, if he had encouraged people in their efforts to persuade Turner to step down, he might have further weakened the party; on the other hand, if Turner had voluntarily stepped down, he might have been obliged to step in. But the contingency planning dissolved with the weekend, as Turner plunged into his last preparations for the debate.

It had been a disastrous week for the national Liberal campaign. As a result of the memo, and the television item, the Liberals had yet another bad period. The level of tension and distrust inside the campaign rose. (However, Peter Connolly insists that, despite all the suggestions to the contrary, the confidence that Turner, Connolly, and Kirkpatrick on the plane had in Ouellet, Graham, Kirby, and the other strategists on the ground was unshaken.) There was a widespread consensus that, if Turner did not perform extremely well in the television debate, the campaign would collapse.

It was an extraordinary episode, which still leaves an enormous number of questions unanswered. Is Kirby to be believed when he writes that "there was a brief discussion of

the *possibility* that Turner *might* decide that for the good of
the country and to ensure the defeat of the trade deal, he
would *offer* to step down *if* that would increase the probability of a Liberal election win?" (emphasis added). The sentence is suspiciously dense with conditionals. Reading that,
many political veterans assumed that this description of
events was so implausible that Kirby did not care whether he
was believed or not. Turner remained suspicious: other Liberal campaign people were struck by the fact that, at a dinner
at Stornoway in March 1989, Turner graciously thanked all of
the key people in the campaign – except Kirby.

For many Liberals, the whole episode was like a bad dream:
an intense embarrassment that is best forgotten. Nevertheless,
questions remain: questions that even the participants still
ask themselves. Was Connolly hasty in the interpretation he
drew from his conversation with Ouellet? Was Turner draw-
ing conclusions from a misinterpretation of the situation?
Who were the sources for the CBC story? Should the CBC
have run the story? Had the story not been broadcast, would
the situation have turned out differently?

Journalists are still debating other questions. William
Johnson dissected the CBC report phrase by phrase, noting
that Mansbridge said that "some of the most senior people in
the party thought the unspeakable." "Did they also speak the
unspeakable?" he wondered. "And they also 'thought about
putting pressure on John Turner to quit.' Did they translate
those thoughts into words or actions? I don't know how journalism can deal with thoughts. And I mistrust any 'news
report' that reports on other people's thoughts." Johnson
argued that the report was "television at its most allusive,
most impressionistic, least precise, and most irresponsible."

Alboim and Mansbridge argue, equally eloquently, that it
would have been much more irresponsible to continue covering the Liberal campaign without reporting what they knew
to be true: that there was desperate dissension in the ranks,
and that senior MPs and strategists were independently wondering whether Turner should step down. In retrospect, they

wonder about the capacity of television as a medium to convey a story as complicated and as full of nuance as the story reported on October 19.

Whatever the answers to these questions – many of which will never be answered – it remains clear that, as the debates drew near, the stakes were extremely high for John Turner.

CHAPTER TEN

The TV Debates

"Television has replaced the political party."

Arthur Schlesinger Jr.

When Brian Mulroney chose the election date, he did so with the date of the television debates in mind. He remembered very clearly how the 1984 election campaign had been disrupted by the debates; he wanted to be sure that there would be time for him to recover, should there be a similar event in the 1988 campaign. Once the campaign was under way, the first job that had to be done was to negotiate the dates and the format for the debates. Mulroney's preference, and his direction to the Tory negotiating team, was to have them held very early: on October 16 and 17. (The World Series later forced the debates to be moved ahead.)

A group of Conservatives had begun meeting to discuss the television debate in June to discuss strategy: Norman Atkins, Finlay Macdonald, Jean Bazin, Jodie White, Marjory LeBreton, and, in considering the idea of whether or not to have a debate on women's issues as had happened in 1984, there were discussions with Barbara McDougall. The Tories were not at all happy with the women's debate in 1984 – production values were poor, there was a live audience, which reacted strongly, and which the Conservatives saw as pro-NDP, and the forum was controlled by a special interest – and they expected another request from the National Action Committee on the Status of Women. On the one hand, they didn't want a repeat, but on the other hand, they did not want to be seen as killing a discussion of women's issues. So when NAC asked for a debate, they responded by saying that they wanted one, but only if the networks sponsored it.

The day the writs were issued, on Saturday October 1, the networks sent a telegram inviting the parties to a meeting which was held on the following Thursday, and, in preparation for that, there was an informal meeting over a drink early in the week between representatives of the three parties: Jean Bazin and Jodie White for the Conservatives, Henry Comor and Ray Heard for the Liberals, and Robin Sears for the NDP. The Tory starting position was four debates: one on the major issues and one on women's issues, in French and in English. The Liberals wanted six debates: general issues, free trade and women's issues, while the NDP wanted at least four, and were ready to take as many as they could.

The networks, on the other hand, wanted as few debates as possible. Fall was ratings time, and they were determined to lose as little money as possible. Their firmness in this regard worried the opposition parties, who began to fear that the fix was in between the government and the networks to restrict the debates as much as possible, knowing that, if negotiations broke down and there were no debates at all, the government would gain.

On Thursday October 6, the networks met with the parties, and Tim Kotcheff of CTV opened the meeting with the networks' proposal: two debates of two hours each, one in English, one in French. The discussions became so tense, and the NDP so annoyed, that some participants wondered if Sears would show up at the last meeting. In previous elections, the party leading in the polls – such as the Liberals in 1980 - simply negotiated in such a way that a meeting could not be held, but Tories felt that because of the commitment Mulroney had made in the past to a debate, and the criticisms about Mulroney's inaccessibility, they could not afford not to have a debate, or not to show up.

What finally emerged was a compromise that was widely viewed as a format that would guarantee a small number of viewers: two three-hour debates, back to back: the French debate on Monday October 24, and the English debate on Tuesday October 25, with one hour in each debate to be devoted to women's issues. The marathon format was widely considered to be too long to attract viewer attention, and the fact that the French debate was to be held first was felt to guarantee Mulroney's advantage. Both these assumptions turned out to be false.

Over the weekend before the debate, Mulroney had a briefing book and interrogations from key people. On Sunday night at Harrington Lake, there was a briefing and interrogation that was attended by Derek Burney, Stanley Hartt, Pierre Blais, Lucien Bouchard, Michel Cogger, Hugh Segal, and Lowell Murray. It was not done in the form of role-playing, but Mulroney was drilled with questions about the government's record, free trade, child care, and the other issues that they expected would be raised. In the early evening before the English debate, Murray, Segal, and Burney went over the questions and issues with him.

Everyone was aware that the debate was a burden that was heavier on government than on opposition: Mulroney was constrained by his record, and by the weight of the office. In retrospect, one of those advising him said that they were also affected by the experience from Question Period: if Mulroney emerged without being damaged, this would be seen as a victory.

Mulroney was also very conscious of the advantage that John Turner had of coming into the debate with very low public expectations about his performance. He had always been very aware of the expectations game, of the degree to which Turner could win an audience by showing up. For months, Mulroney's friends and advisers had been saying to anyone who would listen that they were afraid that if Turner managed to make it through the debate without falling over, he would be declared the winner – to the extent that strategists in the other parties began to point out that this was part of the Tory strategy of trying to counter the expectation game.

That weekend, Pierre Blais – a lawyer from Berthier-sur-Mer, downriver from Lévis, who had served as Mulroney's parliamentary secretary before being named minister of state for agriculture in 1987 – was delighted to see that the Quebec City radio station CHRC had done a poll in Eastern Quebec which showed that only 7 per cent thought that Turner was competent to be prime minister. When he showed it to Mulroney, he was told he had it wrong way around.

"If this guy shows up and makes a nice presentation, he's going to be canonized," Mulroney said.

Like Mulroney, Ed Broadbent did not engage in any elaborate role-playing exercise. There were two meetings of strategists and aides the previous week to go over strategy, responses, and possible one-liners. John McInnes, an Alberta New Democrat, prepared the briefing book, and a briefing book was available in French. Broadbent had his French teacher spend some time with him before the French debate to make sure he had the terminology he wanted to use very clear; George Nakitsas, Christine Dyck, his French-language press secretary, and Hilarie McMurray spent part of the day with him going over questions on the trade deal, and constitutional questions in French.

"I was tired, but feeling reasonably confident," Broadbent said later. "The campaign had gone reasonably well. I knew the arguments I wanted to make."

If both Mulroney and Broadbent were feeling confident, the situation was very different on the Liberal side. There, the debate represented a question of survival.

On Monday October 10 – Thanksgiving Monday – Michael Kirby met in Toronto with Martin Goldfarb, Patrick Gossage, Hershell Ezrin, and Ray Heard to discuss how John Turner should prepare for the debate. That afternoon, John Webster sent Kirby's memo summarizing the discussions out on the Zoomit Network to the participants, with copies to Peter Connolly, Bob Jackson and Henry Comor (who had not been present at the meeting because of a bout of flu).

Inadvertently, someone left a copy behind somewhere – and the person who found it gave it to me. When a detailed description of the memo appeared in the *Globe and Mail* on November 19 (coincidentally the same day that the CBC story ran), Kirby and the other senior strategists were furious, and convinced that there was a saboteur in their midst.

"Clearly, at least one person and possibly several were, for reasons of their own, deliberately leaking significant documents to the media, either to help their own image or because they wanted to destroy the campaign in some way," Kirby wrote later. "Inevitably, there was considerable finger-pointing and plenty of accusations tossed around, but no one had any proof. That, in turn, led to the expected increase in tension and acrimony among the group of people with access to the information seeping out. So much was getting out that one person observed that the Liberal party no longer had a leak; it had a fire hose."

Kirby laid out the primary strategic objective as follows:

"[The] primary objective is to cause the press to rethink their conclusion that the election is already over," he wrote. "To do this, we must surprise viewers and our opponents with Turner's performance; he must be much better than anticipated. [The] secondary objectives include rallying our own troops (this will be accomplished in large part by the quality of Turner's performance) and obtaining video clips which we can use in a TV ad."

Kirby then set out the assumptions that the approach to the debate should be based on. "No one who is an uncommitted voter will watch the whole debate, so the key output will be the 30 second clip (e.g. as in the U.S. vice-presidential debate and the line about 'You're no Jack Kennedy')," he wrote. "This means that we must give the leader a set of one-liners which we can fit into his answers."

The memo said that the key to the success of the debate would be the quality of Turner's presentation. "It must be reasoned; it must show deep conviction; it must not be strident or excessively accusatory," Kirby continued. "The use of specific, detailed examples is essential if we are to illustrate the major points of our platform and if Turner is to show real compassion; these examples will be in the briefing material."

Kirby pointed out that post-debate polls would affect public opinion, adding, "We will be ready with our own."

The final point in his list of assumptions was, "We can predict most of the attacks on us which our opponents will make; the briefing material will outline these and give suggested responses to them."

The briefing book was to be built around four themes: the preservation of national identity, including trade and the environment; women's issues such as child care, abortion, and equality for women in the workplace; fairness for the middle class, including tax reform, housing, and programs for senior citizens; integrity in government, which would include the Liberals' clean-government package.

Potential attacks from Mulroney were predicted to be Liberal incompetence, party disunity, the allegation that the party was turning the clock back, was too far to the left, and was spending too much. No likely NDP attacks were spelled out, but the memo identified one likely question from reporters: why did the Liberals support the Meech Lake constitutional accord? In addition, the Liberals would be preparing a series of explanations described as "spin lines" to be used by those people dealing with the press before and after the debate, in order to put the most positive light possible on the event.

The memo concluded with a schedule of meetings for the debate-preparation team, and the rehearsal times for Turner.

On Friday October 21, while the Quebec strategy committee was having its emotional meeting at the Château Champlain in Montreal, John Turner was engaging in his rehearsal for the English debate. He was the only leader to engage in a full-scale rehearsal: an exercise which had become routine in the American preparations for the TV debate, but which was being tried for the first time in Canada.

Scott Shepherd, who had been a discreet but crucial adviser to Turner since 1984, played Mulroney; Hershell Ezrin, David Peterson's former chief of staff, played Broadbent; Patrick Gossage was the moderator, and Ray Heard, Turner's director of communications, was the reporter.

"I did not take the debates lightly," Turner said later. "They were the most important single events in the election."

In retrospect, he remembers feeling confident: confident he had an excellent chance of winning. He had been speaking well for two, two and half years, he felt he had been winning the head-to-head confrontations with Mulroney and Broadbent in the House of Commons, he had learned a great deal about television since the humiliations of 1984, he was confident that he had been performing well, and he was determined to correct the public memory left by that encounter.

However, he was exhausted, he was in physical pain, he had spent the last three weeks flying across the country, and he was under the additional pressure of no longer knowing whom he could trust in his campaign team. In at least one important way, his confidence was shaken: he believed that the strategists were no longer loyal, and the debate-strategy memo had been leaked – suggesting that possibly one of that group was untrustworthy. Much of Turner's success or failure in the debate would depend upon the skills and advice of two men: Henry Comor and André Morrow.

Comor was a white-haired middle-aged man who had been hired by Ray Heard over a year earlier to help Turner work on his preparation for television. Heard, the director of communications, was a former television executive with Global who had worked with Comor, and seen how he had trained television reporters, teaching them some of the techniques of their trade.

Trained in medicine in England, Comor became an actor and director in London's West End, and worked in British television before coming to Canada in 1956 where, after working in radio and television, he became the president of the Alliance of Canadian Television and Radio Artists (ACTRA). Subsequently, Comor worked as a consultant to Canadian and U.S. television networks, and also as a playwright, an adviser to U.S. politicians, and host of the CBC-TV program *The Medicine Show*.

"Henry Comor was the first person who taught me that television is a medium of emotion rather than words and pictures," said Doug Small, of Global News. "He shows you how to let your voice drop at the right time, and to let your eyes break at the right time. I assume he is doing the same thing for John Turner."

Comor had carefully studied questions of eye contact, communication, body language and reflexive motions: the fact, for example, that when one is asked a question that requires thought or reflection, one's eyes move; instinctively, someone who replies to a question without any pause or eye movement appears less thoughtful or reflective.

Much of what he had done over the previous year involved looking very closely at Turner, and playing television clips of his questions in the House or his scrums outside it over and over again, and showing him what he had noticed: involuntary reactions, facial expressions, and physical tics that often contradicted the emotion and thought behind what he was saying.

One of his early observations was that Turner was not breathing properly. As he became wound up in a speech or a question, he would not inhale, and, as he ran out of breath, his voice would become irregular, forced, and awkward, and his eyes would bulge. Then, apparently to make a point, he would wave his arms – in fact, unconsciously raising them so that his lungs could expand. Showing Turner this in slow motion, and explaining what was happening, Comor gave him the kind of breathing instructions that any trained actor or singer absorbs.

In addition, Comor would push Turner to think, not only of the words he was using, but of the hidden message he wanted to convey.

"What I try to do is help people be themselves as much as possible," Comor said in an interview in early 1988. "One of the secrets is relaxation."

On the flight back from Vancouver, Turner asked Comor if André Morrow, the media consultant in Montreal who had worked on the French commercials and was slated to help prepare Turner for the debates, could be trusted. Uneasily, Comor realized that Turner's views of people who would be crucial to his performance in the debates were being undermined by other staff members who were planting seeds of doubt in his mind.

On Friday, Turner went to a studio that had been rented to do his rehearsal for the debate.

"I felt that rehearsals were absolutely necessary," Turner said later. "I wanted mock debates, just as before any trial, I used to have mock examinations and cross-examinations of my witnesses. I'd hammer the hell out of my witnesses. If I were defending you in a libel case, I would put you in a room and say, 'OK, this is our case, but you're going to take now what I believe that Julian Porter on the other side is going to put to you. I think I can put it tougher and better than Julian, so by the time you get in there. . . .' I'd have you grilled for two or three hours until the sweat was coming down your face. And then you'd feel confident that nothing Porter could do to you could be any worse than what your own lawyer had done."

Turner wanted the same thing done to him. In addition to Shepherd and Ezrin, Henry Comor was in the control room, literally calling the shots. Since he wanted Turner to learn as much as possible from the tape, he had the television camera focus on him more than it would in the real debate, so that Turner could see the importance of remaining focused and self-aware all the time. Much as Turner would have done in rehearsing a witness, Comor had ensured that the questions and the attacks would be brutal: worse than they could be on the night of the real debate. He felt that Turner had to realize how difficult a challenge lay ahead. Shepherd had been preparing Turner for Question Period, and had studied Mulroney's style, while Ezrin had watched and studied Bob Rae, the Ontario NDP leader, whom he had known since university, and felt very comfortable adopting the NDP themes to go after Turner. The result was, in the word used by several of those who saw the rehearsal, brutal.

"Hershell and Scott were fantastic; they'd really done their homework," Turner said. "They won! But they were throwing curves all over the place – beanballs. Really."

Turner finished his rehearsal and went off to an event in Hull, telling Comor that he was too tired to go over the tapes that night, and he would do it in the morning. So Comor spent the evening reviewing the tape, and making notes. About midnight, he got a call from Raymond Garneau, almost in tears, with terrible news. In an attempt to settle the growing anxiety about the debate in French, Garneau had offered to publicly take responsibility for the preparations, and assume the blame for what more and more people thought might be a disaster, but to no avail. André Morrow was not going to be coming for the French rehearsal. Comor phoned Morrow at home, and learned that he had indeed decided not to come. Morrow had been shocked and appalled by what he had seen at the meeting of Quebec Liberals that day, and by rumours he had heard from the advertising industry that Turner had lost confidence in him. He had concluded that Michèle Tremblay, one of Turner's advisers – whom he had never met – had turned the leader against him, that his professional reputation was being denigrated, and he had decided that he would not be involved if she was going to be present. Comor understood that bitterness; Turner had suspected him earlier that day of leaking things to the press.

At nine o'clock, after only a few hours' sleep, Comor showed up at Stornoway to try to repair the situation. He told Turner how angry and distressed he was at being suspected of disloyalty, and being accused of leaking things to the press. Turner assured him that there was no problem. Then, Comor told him that Morrow would not be coming, because his reputation was being undermined by the unjustified suspicions that had been allowed to develop.

When it was clear that Comor would not continue unless Morrow changed his mind, several phone calls were made to Morrow in Montreal; finally, Turner spoke to Morrow personally.

"André, I need you, you have to come," he said. "I have total trust in you."

With that assurance, Morrow jumped in the car and drove to Ottawa to set up the studio for the Sunday rehearsal. Mean-

while, Comor went over the English rehearsal with Turner –
who was shocked at how bad he had appeared, because he
thought he had done all right.

That afternoon, Francis Fox, Raymond Garneau, Rémi
Bujold, and André Morrow arrived.

The next day, on Sunday, the French rehearsal was held,
with Francis Fox playing Mulroney and Serge Joyal playing
Broadbent. Both stand-ins knew their role models well. Fox
was a friend of Mulroney's; when Fox had resigned from the
Trudeau cabinet after forging a signature in arranging for a
woman to have an abortion, Mulroney had been supportive.
Similarly, during the same period, Joyal had talked regularly
with Broadbent, and seriously considered crossing the floor
to join the NDP.

"In both cases [French and English], I got a working-over
like you wouldn't believe," Turner said later. "The French
rehearsal was a disaster. I got creamed. I think some of the
people watching were thinking 'Holy God!'" He was right:
Comor and Morrow were devastated. They didn't know what
to tell Turner, and felt very nervous about the result.

"The reason it was a disaster was that I hadn't yet come out
of the campaign mode into the debate mode," Turner said
later. "The reason we'd set aside Friday and Saturday and
Sunday and Monday was not only to prepare, but to convert
from a campaign mode, when you're out on the hustings,
reaching out, to a debate mode when you're on television: two
people in bilateral exchanges."

Turner had wanted no distractions in his preparations,
which was why he had not wanted to meet with Herb Gray on
Friday, and agreed with André Morrow's plan that he should
make the final preparations for the debate with the kind of
rigour and discipline associated with a prize fight. Morrow
cut off access to Turner, controlled his diet, cut out coffee and
alcohol, and made him work and work on the preparations
for the first debate. Morrow's principle was that one person
had to be in charge, and so had Connolly and Kirkpatrick
throw everyone out of Stornoway, cut off the phone, and leave
them alone.

At thirty-nine, André Morrow had a solid reputation in the Montreal advertising community. From Quebec City, he had studied communications under the two authorities in Quebec: the cerebral Claude Cossette, author of a dense, academic study of communications theory, and the intuitive Jacques Bouchard, the man celebrated as the father of Quebec advertising, who had worked on most of the Trudeau campaigns in Quebec and had first developed the approach of persuading Canadian companies to hire Quebec firms to do their French advertising. Morrow had worked for Bouchard's firm BCP, had worked in theatre, had been the creative director and a copywriter in different agencies, and had written and directed television shows. He was close to the Quebec film scene, and his friends included the film-makers Denys Arcand and Yves Simoneau.

In addition, he had grown up with a taste for politics, and had been fascinated by political rhetoric: collecting video tapes of political leaders, and watching how politicians as different as Kennedy, de Gaulle, Lévesque, Reagan, and Gorbachev all used television to their best advantage.

Morrow began working with Turner in the spring of 1988, before he spoke to a Liberal meeting in Montreal, and felt that, until recently, Turner had been told a lot of contradictory and confusing things about television by the people advising him before Comor arrived. "Henry had done a superb job," Morrow said later. "If I have been able to do what I did, a big part was due to the work Henry did in the previous year and a half with John Turner."

Both men agreed that while cosmetic aspects – having suits that fitted properly, for example – were important, it was much more important to be relaxed enough for emotions to show through as well as rational arguments. In talking to Turner before his speech in Montreal in the spring, Morrow saw that it was natural to him to pace around. He persuaded him to try using a hand-held microphone – which Turner instinctively found more comfortable. When he made the speech, he started on the podium, and then picked up the hand-held microphone and walked around the stage. People were struck by how much more relaxed and sure of himself he seemed, which calmed down everyone in the room.

To prepare Turner for the French debate, Morrow ensured that he had food that was easy to digest, and that he got some rest; he then began to psych him up to be as aggressive as necessary, and as focused as possible.

In order to psych out Mulroney, Comor had already used the debate negotiations as a ruse. He had loudly insisted that the candidates had to know at all times which camera was on – implying that Turner would be advised to look at the camera. On the contrary, he was advised to stare at Mulroney as malevolently as possible, at all times, so that whenever Mulroney glanced over at him, he would see Turner glaring at him.

In addition, Turner was told not to sit down in the studio; to remain standing, to give himself an air of authority. These were all small ways of destabilizing Mulroney and Broadbent.

However, for all the advice and coaching, there were only three men who would be in front of the cameras for the two debates; whatever their preparation, they would have to do the job alone.

––––––––––

At six o'clock on Monday, the leaders arrived at the CJOH studio in suburban Ottawa, to be greeted by crowds of supporters and demonstrators. Once inside, the three men posed for pictures in the studio – and, once again, Ed Broadbent showed some of his sense of mischief or feeling of discomfort. While Mulroney and Turner smiled distractedly or warily at the camera, Broadbent flashed up his hands and formed binoculars to gaze back: a bizarre gesture of mugging at the camera that was part of Broadbent's refusal to accept the formalities and rituals of public events.

After an introduction by the moderator, the Acadian novelist Antonine Maillet, Turner had the floor first, and he started by saying that he wanted to discuss what was at stake in the election.

"The Mulroney-Reagan deal leaves threats hanging over our economy, our agriculture, our environment," he said. "Beyond the election, we have to decide on our future as an independent country."

Then, addressing head-on what he expected Mulroney would raise, Turner said, "This evening, Mr. Mulroney and Mr. Broadbent are going to talk to you about leadership. They are going to talk about the leadership of the head of a party when they should be talking about the leadership of a country. What is at stake is not the popularity of a leader, but the future of our country."

"That caused panic in the Conservative Party," said André Morrow later. "Two guys left the studio very quickly. The second Turner said that, Mulroney turned his head, and tried to find people in the room. In the opening statement, Turner started the fight."

The Turner tactic was to throw Mulroney off balance, and, whenever Mulroney was on the set, to keep the tempo of the debate very rapid. However, when Broadbent was the opponent, the tactic was to let him talk as much as possible, and for Turner to talk much less, since the quality of Broadbent's French would lose him support in Quebec.

Mulroney began by saying that he would avoid personal attacks. "But in fact, this is not an ordinary election. What is at stake next November 21 is, in fact, leadership. I say indeed, the leadership of Canada."

He went on to talk about the four priorities of 1984 – national reconciliation, economic renewal, social justice, and constructive internationalism – and briefly summarized the record: Meech Lake, job creation, increased pensions and a proposed child-care program, and the Francophone Summit. For the future, he pointed to the Free Trade Agreement, which he claimed would bring prosperity while respecting social programs and the environment.

Watching the debate in his riding office in Montreal, Marcel Prud'homme commented, "Mulroney wants to play statesman. He'll lose doing that, because he is good when he throws himself into the fight."

Broadbent began with simplicity, if not necessarily clarity. "Bonsoir," he said. "The priority for me in this election is our families, our children, our parents, our grandparents. Those are our real needs. That should always be the priority, in the past and in the future, in a democracy."

In the opening session, Mulroney flatly contradicted Broadbent's arguments against the Free Trade Agreement, saying that there was nothing in the deal that threatened Canada's social programs. "It is profoundly unfair and unfortunate for a political leader to make such a wounding claim for the elderly, and those concerned about regional development," he said.

"It is clear that Mr. Mulroney has not read the agreement," retorted Broadbent, who argued that the only subsidies specifically referred to in the agreement were for energy, and that businessmen had complained of the pressures to have Canada's social programs harmonized with American programs.

Mulroney vowed that the agreement would not affect social programs. "We are going to maintain all our social programs," he said. "We are going to do even more."

By dint of considerable effort, Broadbent's French had improved since 1984, but French-language journalists would still compare it to fingernails on a blackboard. The unfair reality was that the standard of French expected of a political leader had also been raised; what had been benevolently considered an indication of good faith in the past was no longer good enough. Having the French debate first, and having it last three hours, was a serious handicap for Broadbent.

This proved to be a particular problem in his first exchange with Mulroney, when Broadbent was arguing that François Mitterrand had been opposed to the Free Trade Agreement. There was a case to be made in this area: there had been some frantic negotiating at the G-7 Economic Summit in Toronto to find a formulation that all the leaders could agree on, and there were indications at the time that Mitterrand had objected to a full endorsement. But when Mulroney jumped all over Broadbent, the NDP leader was simply not fluent enough to defend himself effectively.

Mulroney, in contrast, had the advantage of being a Quebecker, and went out of his way to underline his roots, talking about himself as a son of the North Shore and, three times in one answer, using the phrase "chez nous," as he had so effectively in 1984.

Facing Turner, Broadbent said that he would close polluting companies if necessary, while the Liberal leader argued that using injunctions and making pollution an offence in the Criminal Code would be more effective.

In the session between Mulroney and Turner, there was an aggressive exchange on the impact of the Free Trade Agreement, as the two men ignored the moderator and engaged in vehement, fingerpointing argument. Turner said that since the Conservative government did not get the exemption from U.S. trade laws that it had been after, Canada should have withdrawn from the trade talks.

"That would have shown courage, Mr. Mulroney," Turner said.

"Perhaps that's what you would have done," retorted Mulroney, adding that eight of ten provincial premiers, including some Liberals, supported the deal, and that it would create 250,000 jobs.

"Over ten years, over ten years," replied Turner.

"Are you against that?" Mulroney shot back.

"Marginal," Turner said derisively.

"You think 250,000 jobs is marginal?" asked Mulroney, his voice rising in indignation. It was a point he would use again and again during the campaign – that John Turner thought 250,000 jobs were marginal, but families in whatever town he was speaking in certainly didn't think they were marginal.

"No, marginal over ten years in our economy," Turner said before the argument degenerated, with both men talking simultaneously until Maillet called a halt to the exchange. The depth of animosity between the two was thinly disguised in their other exchanges, on the federal deficit, spending on social programs, and the dismissal of André Bissonnette from the cabinet.

At the end of the second hour, which was designated for women's issues, Mulroney was reminded that he had tried to de-index pensions, and was asked if he was prepared to commit himself to maintaining pension levels. He replied that he had already acknowledged that this was a mistake, and that his government had increased pensions by 36 per cent and was committing itself to "maintaining and respecting" pensions.

"He's almost making an act of contrition," Turner joked, pointing out that in a recent interview with Deborah MacGregor of the *Financial Times*, Mulroney had said that he would examine the question after the election.

"How can the elderly trust you?" he asked.

Mulroney replied by blaming Turner for the Liberal campaign in 1974 against the Conservative proposal of wage and price controls, adding that he had already made a commitment that closed the door to cuts in pension benefits.

"I have a problem," Turner said. "You said that social programs were a sacred trust – and then you tried to de-index pensions and you did de-index family allowances. That's a social program. You said you wouldn't raise income taxes, and you've raised them by 62 per cent." He concluded by pointing out that Mulroney had said he would never stand for free trade with the United States, and a year later had begun negotiations on the issue.

Mulroney replied by quoting the late Premier of Quebec, René Lévesque, as saying that only imbeciles never changed their minds, and added that he had been influenced by the report by the former Liberal finance minister Donald Macdonald.

"These are the fine words of a salesman with a weak product," scoffed Turner.

"A leader who can't lead his party can't lead the country," snapped Mulroney.

"You're an expert in that," Turner replied before Maillet called them to order.

One of the difficult moments for both Turner and Mulroney came when Hélène Fouquet of the network Quatre Saisons asked them why, when they insisted on respecting the conscience of their MPs in allowing a free vote in the House of Commons, they would not allow women to choose according to their conscience. Both danced around the question of abortion; only the NDP had a clear position, that abortion should be a matter between a woman and her doctor, and only Broadbent was clear on the subject.

"Broadbent just lost points," observed Prud'homme, the veteran politician, watching in his office with Gérald LeBlanc of La Presse. "One must never be as open as that in statements about abortion; it's too explosive."

In the exchange between Broadbent and Mulroney in the third hour, Broadbent ridiculed the government's record on the environment, suggesting the Tories only discovered the issue after the PCB fire at Saint-Basile-le-Grand in the summer. "The law to protect the environment is a farce," he said.

Mulroney countered that his government had set aside money for the clean-up of the St. Lawrence River and the harbours in Hamilton and Halifax, and had repeatedly, on the campaign trail, called for a national commitment to the environment involving individual citizens and all levels of government.

As his candidates in Quebec had hoped he would, Broadbent endorsed the notion of the distinct society, and stressed his acceptance of the "notwithstanding" clause in the Constitution. But he was not particularly effective in defending himself when Turner attacked the NDP's NATO policy.

While the debate was going on, reporters were watching on television monitors in an adjacent studio, sitting in the gallery of a game-show set, while all three parties sent in representatives to put the most positive light possible on their leaders' performance: spin doctors.

Thus, Jean Bazin, Bernard Roy, Bruce Phillips, and Luc Lavoie all mingled among the reporters for the Tories; some reporters noted wryly that they seemed particularly visible during the hour that women's issues were being debated, and wondered if this was timed intentionally.

The Liberal MPs Jean Lapierre, André Ouellet, and Don Boudria, the media consultant Michèle Tremblay, and the Liberal Party secretary-general Marie-Andrée Bastien all wandered about the room, telling anyone who would listen how good Turner's French was, and how well he was doing – to the extent that one French-speaking reporter asked Boudria when they could expect Turner to be named to the Académie Française. The "spin doctors" knew that they could be particularly influential during the French debates, since many English-language reporters didn't understand French, and, even if they did, radio reporters needed "clips": edited interviews that they could broadcast as part of their reports.

The Ontario NDP leader, Bob Rae, came in just as Broadbent was having difficulty explaining his claim that Mitterrand had opposed the free-trade deal and, spotting a reporter he knew who had written an advance story on spin doctors, mimed a pitcher throwing a curve ball. He was immediately surrounded by English-language reporters seeking comment; Broadbent's problem went unnoticed.

At ten p.m. Michèle Tremblay withdrew to watch *The National* and, a few minutes later, burst into the room to announce loudly that David Halton had said that Turner was just great, and was winning the debate.

Several reporters were sitting nearby with laptop computers on their laps; it was just the point when many of them would have to declare a winner. "Did Halton really say Turner is winning?" one asked. Tories and New Democrats winced, and grabbed their walkie-talkies or cellular phones to find out if it was true. Although Halton had said that Turner was doing very well, he hadn't actually said he was winning; in fact, many reporters that night were hesitant to call winners. Turner had done well, better than many expected; Broadbent's handicap in French was obvious; Mulroney was significantly more comfortable in French than the others, and seemed sure of himself. All three had done a creditable job, although Turner had gained an advantage because of the expectations game. But reporters in Ottawa had seen the three men perform many times before; while Turner seemed to have done well, they were reluctant to call winners. (The next day, *Le Devoir* concluded that Turner had won, *La Presse*'s headline suggested that Mulroney had held his opponents to a draw, and the *La Presse* columnist Lysiane Gagnon felt that Mulroney had won.)

After the debate was over, John Turner said to André Morrow – who had been in the trailer with Turner and Serge Joyal between rounds – "I don't know how you did that, but you're a genius. Will you please stay with me tomorrow night?"

Morrow said that he thought Henry Comor was coaching Turner in English. Turner said that he wanted Morrow there too, but Morrow insisted that there couldn't be two coaches. Later, Webster and Ouellet both asked him to repeat the coaching job the following night. So, to Comor's intense disappointment, he was excluded from the climax of his work with Turner. Knowing that his absence from the trailer would provoke comment, he stayed at home, watching on television, and taking phone calls from the station.

Though Morrow had urged Turner to set a rapid pace at the beginning of the French debate, he recommended a change of approach for the English debate: to begin slowly, and to keep his energy in reserve for the final hour. Turner was exhausted from the night before, and his back was in great pain. So, as the debate began, Turner held back a bit. At one point, watching in the studio, Morrow thought he saw Mulroney turn and smile, as if to say "We're going to win this one; he can't do it two nights in a row."

In fact, shortly after the moderator, Rosalie Abella, introduced the debate, it became quite scrappy. Ed Broadbent, the first leader to speak, used his opening statement to attack the Free Trade Agreement.

"This election is about the future of our country," he said. "It is about maintaining our independence and using that independence for fairness for ordinary Canadians." Then, after saying that Mulroney had completely failed to answer the criticisms of the trade deal and its threat to families, the environment, medicare, pensions, regional development, and farm programs, Broadbent sharpened his attack.

"The truth is that Mr. Mulroney signed a trade deal that goes away beyond the exchange of commodities between Canada and the United States. It affects virtually every aspect of Canadian life," he said. "And the truth is also that, time after time, Mr. Mulroney gave the Americans what they wanted but failed to get what Canadians wanted. Mr. Mulroney's deal permits subsidies in our energy sector because that is what the Americans wanted. It does not permit [Canada] to use subsidies to stop polluters, to encourage and to foster development in the arts, and that is what Canadians wanted.

"Mr. Mulroney's deal will permit the United States to have a say in what is to be included in our regional-development policy, instead of making it clear that decisions in such a crucial area affecting Canadians should be made only by Canadians. Mr. Mulroney's deal threatens our medicare and pension plans. As businessmen are already saying, benefits in Canada must be reduced to meet U.S. standards, a country where you find 36 million without any form of health insurance whatsoever."

It was punchy, it was direct, and ironically – given the criticism Broadbent received later for supposedly ignoring the free-trade issue – it got almost no public attention.

Mulroney, in his opening statement, argued that the Free Trade Agreement was central to Canada's future. "I know that Canada can compete and I know that Canadians can excel in the markets of the world and strengthen our identity as Canadians in the process," he said, adding that his government had chosen growth. "My opponents tonight have a duty not only to criticize, but to explain to you their alternative. They would tear up the Free Trade Agreement. And then what? They offer you nothing but the poverty of protectionism. That is the real threat to our social programs and our environment. And just because you sell someone your products, as we all know, doesn't mean you have to buy his values."

Saying that free trade was supported by eight premiers, small and large business, agricultural producers, consumers and public policy analysts, Mulroney said "I ask you very directly: do they all love Canada less because they want to trade more?"

As he had in the French debate, Turner began by addressing the leadership question directly, saying that Canada was more important than any single person. "This election is not a popularity contest," he said. "The issue is the future of Canada." He went on to accuse Mulroney of having a hidden agenda of turning Canada into a pale replica of the United States, and to accuse Broadbent of hiding his party program. Then, after mentioning Mulroney's plan for a national sales tax which he called "a $10-billion hidden sales tax on everything," and the Liberal promises of affordable child care and shelter and environmental protection, Turner brought up the issue of scandals.

"My personal commitment is that I will give you an honest and ethical government. My cabinet ministers will spend their time in the cabinet room defending Canadians; not in the courtroom defending themselves," he said. "Above all, we will never, never sign a deal which surrenders our control and ability to manage our economy, or our social and regional equality programs, or our destiny as a people. Mr. Mulroney's trade deal does just that."

David Halton picked up the ethics issue, and in his first question to Mulroney, reminded him of the "electrifying moment" during the debate in 1984 when Mulroney confronted Turner on patronage, and his promise to clean it up. Instead, he suggested, Mulroney had appointed hundreds of Tories.

"Sure, you also appointed some very high-profile Canadians from other parties. We know the list," Halton said. "But, surely, you have misled Canadians in promising them a new political morality in Canada and practising very much the old one."

Mulroney acknowledged that he had not done as well as he should have in moving to de-politicize the appointment process, but gave a lengthy answer detailing the proportion of women who had been named to judicial positions, and members of other parties. But the opening enabled Turner to come back to the subject, and hammer away at Mulroney on the issue, as if to avenge his own embarrassment during the debate in 1984.

"You promised to clean it up and you did not clean it up," he said. "You made it an issue throughout the whole [1984] election campaign, and then, for the first three years afterwards until you saw another election on the horizon, you campaigned and ran a government as if nothing had changed, as if this was the opportunity, once in power, to take advantage of it."

In their first one-on-one session, Broadbent and Turner began with a question on free trade. Broadbent quoted Laurent Thibault, president of the Canadian Manufacturers' Association, as saying that Canadians were obviously forced to create the same conditions in Canada that exist in the United States in terms of unemployment insurance, workmen's compensation, or the cost of government. (Later, he was roundly criticized for the fact that the comment was made in 1980; it was small comfort that, after the election, Thibault repeated precisely the same idea.) Broadbent went on to say that, as a result, free trade would affect social programs, regional development, and unemployment insurance "to radically change Canadian life."

He also showed some of his annoyance at the way Turner seemed to be taking over the free-trade issue, pointing out that Turner had been absent for two of the three votes on the question.

"Now, it is one thing to make a big deal of this in an election campaign when your party was in third place, and you say 'We will start waving the flag, and we will pretend we are saving our country, and maybe that will get us back elected,'" he said. "I want to know, when it counted in the House of Commons, why you were not there."

Turner responded by asking why Broadbent never mentioned the trade deal in his statement when the election was called. "Obviously, it did not have pride of place."

"Let's really have a go on this one," retorted Broadbent. "Right from the word go, I said we would, from the very day they announced it, be totally opposed to this deal. You and your caucus were still trying to make up your mind. Then you finally, after an alleged interesting caucus discussion, said – well, you tried to one-up the NDP, so you would come out and tear it up."

The CTV panelist Pamela Wallin said that both parties were opposed to free trade and supported Meech Lake, and she would like each leader to give a short statement as to why the voters should pick one of them rather than the other.

Turner said that when Canadians looked at the two parties, they would see that the NDP was "beholden to organized labour with all those protectionist instincts still there," while the Liberal Party was independent of any economic group. "We are not beholden to big business, we are not beholden to big labour, we are not beholden to any particular interest group in the country," he said. "Second issue, we are . . . outward-looking in trade and have always been international. . . . We are also outward-looking in our defence alliances. And we are committed to NATO, we are committed to our European and American friends and the defence alliance, and we are committed to our North American Defence Pact.

"The New Democratic Party has on its books a resolution that is binding on the party, binding on Mr. Broadbent as leader, calling upon the party, if it ever forms a government, to pull Canada out of our defence alliances," he continued, going on to list the other points in the NDP program that he claimed Broadbent was trying to hide: nationalizing a bank, and nationalizing 50 per cent of the resource industry.

"You, Mr. Turner, get over 50 per cent of your money, your party, from banks, from big corporations that have no democratic vote whatsoever; they don't consult their customers, they don't consult their shareholders," responded Broadbent, who said that he was proud that the NDP got 25 per cent of its money democratically voted by the members of the labour movement. And, on the question of why people should vote for the NDP, he stressed consistency.

"Unlike Mr. Turner, we don't favour the cruise-missile testing one day and oppose it the next," he said, "We don't say yes, we have to deal with polluters one day and oppose it the next."

However, his major argument was that Turner had been prime minister, and should be judged on his record.

"You talk about the environment. You were part of a government that did virtually nothing about it. You criticize the prime minister on patronage," he continued. "But you, sir, were prime minister, and you made a whole list of patronage appointees, every bit as bad as any precedent in the past. You brought in tax loopholes for the rich. You don't now favour a minimum corporate tax. Sixty thousand profitable corporations in this country pay no tax whatsoever. Even Ronald Reagan, when he discovered his secretary paid more in taxes than large corporations, . . . brought in a minimum corporate tax."

It was a vigorous exchange which Mulroney, in the next section of the debate, sardonically referred to as "a lovers' quarrel." On the free-trade question, Mulroney responded as he had the night before, saying that there was "not a word [in the agreement] that would justify what you have been doing, going around trying to scare senior citizens in saying that there is something in the Free Trade Agreement that would justify or suggest or empower the government of Canada, as a result of the Free Trade Agreement, to affect pensions, to affect our capacity for regional development. There is nothing [like that] in that agreement in the slightest, sir."

During the second hour, when women's issues were being discussed and Mulroney was saying that he didn't feel he had to consult women's groups on day-care because he could consult the six women in his cabinet, a number of reporters missed the exchange; it was during that period that Michael Wilson and Flora MacDonald came into the press room to tell reporters how well Mulroney had done defending free trade in the first hour.

In the trailer, shortly before the beginning of the third hour, John Turner was getting clear advice. Henry Comor was on the phone with Scott Shepherd, who was in the trailer with André Morrow. "You can tell him he's lost," Comor said. "He's got nothing to lose. He's got to be relaxed, and fire with all his guns. Nothing terrible can happen any more; this is the end of it."

That was precisely Morrow's feeling as well. Any energy that Turner had left, any strength, should be hurled at Mulroney. "Now, GO!" he said to him.

A few minutes earlier, among the network representatives in the CJOH boardroom, Laszlo Bastyovansky of Global said that he felt there had not been enough on free trade. His colleagues agreed, and the point was made to Cameron Graham, who relayed it to the panel. Pamela Wallin raised the subject again.

The ensuing exchange became the moment that everyone would recall: the argument that wiped out the impact of the debate between Turner and Mulroney on patronage, or Broadbent's questioning of Mulroney, or the vigorous exchanges between Broadbent and Turner. Fairly or unfairly, it would become "the clip."

Wallin began by asking what rules the two men would envisage to ensure that jobs in which women are largely vulnerable would stay in Canada if the Free Trade Agreement went ahead. This opened the door for Turner to make his arguments about how much Canada had given away in the deal: energy, investment, supply management in agriculture, all of which left thousands of workers vulnerable. Mulroney responded by quoting the Economic Council of Canada forecast that 250,000 jobs would be created, and by saying that "to make absolutely certain that we have done more," he had created a commission headed by Jean de Grandpré to look into the adjustment measures that would be required.

Turner then started in on Mulroney's refusal to have a debate exclusively on the trade deal. "I think the Canadian people have a right to know why, when your primary objective was to get unfettered and secure access into the American market, we did not get it; why you did not put clauses in to protect our social programs in this negotiation that we will have on the definition of subsidies, where the heavy weight of the American republic will be put in against us," he said. "Why did that not happen?"

The questions continued, until Mulroney retorted that Turner was standing two feet away, that he had been with him for six hours, and responded to everything he had to say. Then, Turner increased the intensity of his attack.

"I think the issues happen to be so important for the future of Canada. I happen to believe you have sold us out," Turner said.

"You do not have a monopoly on patriotism!" interrupted Mulroney angrily. "I resent the fact of your implication that only you are a Canadian. I want to tell you that I come from a Canadian family and I love Canada and that's why I did it, to promote prosperity, and don't you impugn my motives!"

As Turner was delivering his critique, Mulroney was snapping back; in the parties' respective holding rooms, both groups were wildly cheering their men on.

"Once a country yields its economic levers," interjected Turner. "Once a country yields its investment, once a country yields its energy . . ."

"We have not done it!" Mulroney shot back.

"Once a country yields its agriculture . . ." Turner continued.

"Wrong again," interrupted Mulroney.

"Once a country opens itself up to a subsidy war with the United States in terms of definitions . . ." said Turner. "Wrong again," repeated Mulroney.

"Then the political ability of this country to sustain the influence of the United States, to remain as an independent nation – that has gone forever, and that is the issue of this election," Turner finished.

Mulroney responded that over the past 120 years, his family and many other immigrants had helped build Canada.

"Mr. Turner, I today, sir, as a Canadian believe genuinely in what I am doing," he said. "I believe it is right for Canada, I believe that in my own modest way I am nation-building because I believe this benefits Canada, and I love Canada," Mulroney said.

Turner came back, saying that he admired what Mulroney's father had done, and that his own mother was a miner's daughter in British Columbia.

"We are just as Canadian as you are, Mr. Mulroney, but I will tell you this: you mentioned 120 years of history. We built a country east and west and north. We built it on an infra-structure that deliberately resisted the continental pressure of the United States," he continued. "For 120 years, we have done it. With one signature of a pen, you've reversed that, thrown us into the north-south influence of the United States, and will reduce us, will reduce us I am sure, to a colony of the United States, because when the economic levers go, the political independence is sure to follow."

By that time, the Liberals in the holding room were cheering, jumping up and down and hugging one another.

"Mr. Turner, it was a document that is cancellable on six months' notice," Mulroney retorted. "Be serious. Be serious."

Nose to nose, they went at it, each interjection overlapping the other in a counterpoint of indignation.

"Cancellable?" repeated Turner. "You're talking about our relationship with the United States."

". . . A commercial document that's cancellable on six months' notice," Mulroney echoed.

"Commercial document? You're talking about . . ."

"That document is a commercial treaty . . ." Mulroney continued.

"It relates to every facet of our life, it is far more important than . . ."

"Mr. Turner, be serious," Mulroney said.

"Well, I'm serious, and I've never been more serious in my life!" Turner concluded.

When the exchange was completed, and the Global panel-ist Doug Small was called on for the next question, he said, "I'd be quite happy to let them keep on rolling on that if they've got anything more to say." It was the climactic moment of the debate. Turner had given, in its most dramatic form, the essence of the attack on free trade which he had been making for months, distilled by practice, adrenaline, and the drama of the moment. Mulroney had responded using a piece of advice he had been given by the Network: if things got very heavy on the free-trade question, point out that it was cancellable. However, at least one senior Liberal felt that Mulroney had made a serious tactical error: he was saying, in effect, "Hey, I can tear up the deal too!"

In the rest of the hour, Turner pushed Broadbent hard on the NDP NATO policy, and Broadbent criticized Mulroney's handling of aboriginal rights. The three men made their closing statements – Mulroney saying that his opponents had very little in the way of plans of their own and would leave Canada "frozen in the headlights of progress as the world passes us by" and reiterating that the issue of the election was which party and leader was competent to lead the country into the 1990s; Turner summarizing his criticisms of the Free Trade Agreement; and Broadbent arguing that it was time to make fairness for the average family a priority – and the six-hour marathon was over.

Turner came back into the trailer and asked Pat Gossage how he had done. Gossage was upbeat and enthusiastic.

"I thought it was great," he said. "I thought the clips were terrific."

"Oh, Gossage, don't bullshit me," Turner said skeptically. "Don't flatter me, how was it?"

Just then, the clip of the Turner-Mulroney confrontation came on the news. Turner stopped, watched it, and smiled. "Hey! Not bad, eh?"

Many New Democrats were pleased at the way Broadbent had performed, and felt he had succeeded in regaining the ground he had lost on Monday night. But when Hilarie McMurray came into one of the rooms the party had been allotted, she found Robin Sears slumped in a chair. He had just seen the Turner-Mulroney clip on the news, and he knew that it would be the memorable moment of the debate, the clip that would be played and replayed until it was the only thing anyone remembered of the three hours. And Ed Broadbent wasn't in it.

Mulroney was satisfied. He felt he had done well, that they hadn't laid a glove on him, and, when he returned to 24 Sussex and got on the phone, checking with Tory friends across the country, he didn't find anyone who thought he had been hurt by the debate. At 1.30 a.m., he talked to the last friend, who said "Well, you can sleep easy tonight – you won."

CHAPTER ELEVEN

The Ground Moves

"Government, in the last analysis, is organized opinion."

W.L. Mackenzie King

Liberals began to feel the impact of the television debate almost immediately. During both debates, Paul Martin dropped into his campaign headquarters, and was greeted by enthusiastic volunteers who shouted "We're doing wonderfully!" His wife Sheila kept on canvassing door to door during the debates, and was greeted by people who had been watching, and were saying "Your leader is in the process of clobbering those guys."

But Conservatives, like Mulroney himself, were equally confident that Mulroney had done well.

John Gormley, the Conservative MP for The Battlefords – Meadow Lake, had driven to Meadow Lake on Tuesday. Stopped for speeding by an RCMP officer who spoke French, he chatted briefly with him about the debate; while he was annoyed about the ticket, Gormley was relieved to hear that the officer thought Mulroney had won. He had been asked to comment on the debate for *As It Happens* that night, and went out of his way to say that John Turner had done well, thinking that this might encourage anti-free-trade voters to support the Liberals rather than the NDP. He had been worried about the debate, but had found Broadbent to be chippy.

That night, sitting in a family room with George McLeod, the local provincial member and minister of health in the

Saskatchewan government, Gormley watched the English debate. The consensus was generally that Mulroney had done pretty well, that Turner had helped to distance himself from his reputation for weakness, and that Broadbent had not been a factor. They were not prepared for the dramatic change that ensued.

"In our campaign, it was the most radical turn I've ever witnessed in politics," Gormley said later. "The campaign, until that point, was one of the dullest I'd ever been involved in. Literally, in one night . . . it was the most dramatic turn I've ever seen."

The next morning, he could feel the campaign change. It wasn't John Turner, it wasn't the Liberals; rather, it was the whole question of whether, by undertaking free trade, the country would be selling its social trust, and would be selling part of Canada. "For the next twenty-five days, it was free trade at every single stop."

Also in Meadow Lake, Len Taylor, the NDP candidate, watched the debate with some satisfaction, sitting in a room in the Empire Motel. He felt that Turner had performed well and solidified the anti-free-trade vote, but also felt that his success would drive votes to him, since the Liberal Party was so marginal on the Prairies and Neil Currie, the Liberal candidate in The Battlefords – Meadow Lake, was running third. The only place that anti-free-trade votes could go was to the NDP.

In Kamloops, Nelson Riis could not see the debate having much impact; people in his committee room kept on working, and did not pay much attention.

The next day, candidates across the country could feel the effect of the debates. In St. John's East, Ross Reid began feeling the impact of the arguments on free trade, as the Liberal candidates in Newfoundland began telling people that unemployment insurance might be affected.

In Humber – St. Barbe – Baie Verte, Brian Tobin was in Pasadena, a bedroom community of Corner Brook. He had watched the debate the night before, having told the people there that John Turner would surprise them, and he did. The next day, canvassing door to door, he got an incredibly positive response to Turner; people wanted to talk about him at every door. His fear was that the Liberal campaign would lose its emphasis on non-partisan patriotism, and that the television images would show Turner with his hands in the air, looking like a politician on a roll.

Mary Clancy, the Liberal candidate in Halifax, had taken a taxi home from a friend's during the last half-hour of the debate, and thought that it felt like New Year's Eve, the streets were so deserted. Everyone was at home watching the debate. The next morning at 6.30, at Tim Horton Donuts, she was struck by the enthusiasm of the people she was canvassing.

In Moncton, George Rideout had been formally a candidate for only a week. On October 17, Paul Martin had come to speak to his nomination meeting and had told him that things looked bleak in Quebec. A couple of days later, on *Canada AM*, a commentator had said the Liberals were going to get only twenty-six seats and finish third. Rideout was shaving when he heard this, and said to his wife "I wonder who the other twenty-five are?"

But the next morning, the mood at his campaign headquarters was transformed, and Rideout felt as if a black cloud had been lifted. For the first time, his volunteers began to feel they were working to form a government. In Montreal, Paul Martin felt the difference shaking hands at the Métro station.

Paradoxically, the change in mood was fatal for Pierre Deniger. When the Liberals had been sinking, he felt he might win back his seat on the basis of his own personal popularity. But the middle-class francophones in La Prairie, one of the Montreal south-shore ridings, were fervent supporters of free trade. When Turner surged upwards because of his opposition to free trade, Deniger could feel his support evaporate. Even personal friends began saying apologetically, "Pierre, I just can't."

For the campaign had suddenly, intensely, focused on the free-trade issue almost exclusively. In Toronto, John Bosley was canvassing the commuters getting off the buses at Eglinton subway station. He had watched the debate with about twenty people in his campaign headquarters the night before, and everyone felt that Mulroney had done fine. "No one came out feeling the roof had caved in, but it had," he said later. "We knew within forty-eight hours. I could tell at the bus stops the next morning. At the doors that night, the questions started. 'What about social programs?'" Similarly, the Liberal candidate in Scarborough East, Betty Fevreau, could sense the change in attitude when she was shaking hands at the GO commuter-train station in the morning. Overnight, the mood had changed.

In Broadview-Greenwood, Lynn McDonald of the NDP could feel the difference at the door, as support began to shift to the Liberal Dennis Mills. Voters began thanking her for all the work she had done in the last House, as if she were resigning.

Terry Clifford, the defending Tory in London-Middlesex, could feel his campaign drop like a stone from the reaction he was getting the next day, and the urgency of the questioning about free trade. Over the past few months, he had knocked on twenty thousand doors; he suddenly felt that he had to figure out some way to reach those people all over again.

In Vancouver Centre, the Tory candidate Kim Campbell had been campaigning for only a week, having been nominated on October 18. Interestingly, the debate also generated a lot of Tory volunteers; people who supported free trade, and had been jolted by Turner's performance. Her Liberal opponent, Tex Enemark, had voters honking their horns as they drove past him the next morning, giving him the thumbs-up sign.

Although the candidates were picking up a spontaneous public reaction to the debates early enough to indicate that people were not simply being influenced by the verdict in the media, that verdict tended to indicate that Turner had done very well. The headline in the *Vancouver Sun* was "Tenacious Turner riles PM to cite patriotism"; the *Winnipeg Sun*: "Turner on Points"; the *Winnipeg Free Press*: "A scrappy Turner outstrips foes"; the *Globe and Mail*: "Turner, PM turn trade deal into scrap over patriotism"; the *Toronto Star*: "Turner jabs on patronage put Mulroney on defensive"; the *Gazette*: "Debate turns into shouting match," and, over another front-page story, "Turner steals show with crisp encounters"; the *St. John's Evening Telegram*: "Turner revives flagging campaign."

On the other hand, *La Presse* called it a draw. Pierre Gravel and Gilbert Lavoie wrote that Mulroney had pulled his chestnuts out of the fire effectively when faced by the joint assault from Turner and Broadbent, and that he had "repeated his excellent performance of Monday night while his New Democrat rival regained, along with his mother tongue, all the ease and aggressiveness necessary to claim to be a serious candidate for leader of the opposition." Similarly, Lysiane Gagnon wrote that for the second night in a row, but with more vigour, Mulroney had defended himself well against the attacks of his adversaries. And the *Toronto Sun* called Mulroney a big winner.

Two days after the debate, in the riding of Lac-Saint-Jean, Lucien Bouchard was speaking to a senior citizens' home. They listened to him very politely, and, although a few asked him questions about the free-trade deal, the audience was quite reserved. But after the meeting, one woman came up to Bouchard and pulled his sleeve.

"I knew your grandfather Joseph," she said. "A fine man. What I don't understand is this: why is his grandson trying to take away my old-age pension?"

At that point, Bouchard realized he had a serious problem on his hands.

All three leaders had good days on Wednesday October 26. Mulroney travelled to Sherbrooke and Weedon-Centre, where he was greeted by huge crowds. Broadbent campaigned in Toronto and, that evening, spoke to the largest NDP rally of the campaign in London, Ontario. John Turner campaigned in Cornwall, and, at a rally in the evening in Ottawa, told the partisan crowd that if he had had a little more time, Mulroney would have fallen apart. He specifically mocked Mulroney's argument that the Free Trade Agreement was just a commercial arrangement, cancellable with six months' notice.

"When you're leading a nation, you're playing for keeps," he said. "You don't mess around to see how it's going to turn out."

The phrase was revealing; all three leaders were playing for keeps in the campaign. Their visions of the country, their reputations, and their political careers were at stake. Only the winner would survive as leader of his party.

The initial reaction of the Tory strategy meeting after the debate was positive. Every morning, in the boardroom on the second floor of the Langevin Block, looking over Parliament Hill, the key Tory campaign people would meet. Lowell Murray would sit at one end of the table, with Nancy Jamieson on his right and Bill Neville on his left. Beside Neville sat Norman Atkins, and, beside Atkins, whoever was joining the group that morning: Dalton Camp, or Allan Gregg, or John Tory, or Marcel Côté, or Hugh Segal. At the opposite end of the table from Murray sat Harry Near: on his right sat Derek Burney, on his left Marjory LeBreton. Beside her sat Michel Cogger, and beside him sat Peter White.

Hugh Segal had flown back to Toronto on Tuesday, and watched the English debate with his wife. (He had been at the studio on Monday night for the French debate.) Halfway through the English debate, he began to think that the Tories were in very, very deep trouble. He flew back to Ottawa for the Thursday morning meeting, where he was one of the few people to express concern.

Similarly, the Network began to feel that Turner and Broadbent had made the Free Trade Agreement, sovereignty, and social programs the issue, and that this had not been dealt with decisively. Mulroney was urged to say that Canada could afford more social programs with the agreement, and that jobs would be protected. In addition, the Network began to express concern about the advertisements. They urged that the Tories had to deal with the Free Trade Agreement in a positive, aggressive manner; otherwise, they would be in trouble.

But by then, Allan Gregg had got some of the first overnight polling indications that the situation was changing dramatically, and communicated this to Mulroney and John Tory on the plane. A text for the speech that day to the ethno-cultural conference on small business at the Villa Colombo in Toronto had been sent from Ottawa, and it was in the same bland style as the speeches before the debate. Instinctively, Mulroney and Tory felt that this was no longer appropriate. So Mulroney, Tory, and Ian MacDonald wrote a new speech to produce something more aggressive.

For the first half of the speech, Mulroney gave the bland litany of support for free trade and the prosperity that it would bring which had characterized the first three weeks of the campaign. But then, he began to raise the intensity, accusing the opposition of trying to raise fears among the elderly about their pensions, among producers about their farms and among Canadians about their social, cultural, and regional-development programs.

"At its worst, the tactics of Mr. Turner and Mr. Broadbent are shameful and dishonest," he said. "At the least, they are an attempt to hide the fact they offer Canadians no realistic alternatives, no plan of their own to sustain and expand the economic momentum we have built these past four years. It is classic negative politics – if you shout long enough and loud enough about what you are against, perhaps people won't notice there is nothing you are for."

He was interrupted by applause, and then repeated the paragraph in French for French television and radio before extemporizing an appeal that it didn't matter how long one had been here, or what one's background or religion was: "We all love Canada" – to more applause – before renewing his attack on Turner and Broadbent.

"Our opponents would have you believe that they have a monopoly on patriotism, that our sovereignty, system of social programs and capacity to develop regional-development programs have been put at risk in the Free Trade Agreement," he continued. "I think that they have impugned the motives of many Canadians. They have insulted the intelligence of the Canadian voters. And they have resorted to the most shameful kind of scare tactics, telling Canadians, as the NDP have in their television advertising that is going on now, that the trade agreement jeopardizes medicare, telling senior Canadians, as the NDP has, that their pensions are in danger."

He went on to repeat that nothing – "I repeat nothing" – in the Free Trade agreement compromises social programs in any way, and to list some of the announcements of government interventions since the FTA had been signed: the $1-billion Atlantic Canada Opportunities Agency, the $1.2-billion Western Canada Diversification Office, $2.6-billion in federal funding for Hibernia, and $6.4-billion committed to child care.

It was the beginning of a new, punchy, passionate defence of free trade. However, the strategy committee was by no means unanimous that this approach was the right one. In fact, some of the people on the plane were quite deflated by the negative reaction. Uncertainty was beginning to plague the people at the centre of the Tory campaign, uncertainty fed by the unease created by the growing indications that things were going wrong, unease which, in some cases, bordered on panic.

Norman Atkins's recipe for political organization was to choose the best people for each job, and then never second-guess or interfere. Even his greatest admirers in the party pointed out that he provided almost no strategic advice, or advertising strategy: he left that to the people whose job it was. But, as the fear began to increase, and people became more nervous and fidgety, the rule began to break down. Backbiting started: people would complain that Allan Gregg had been wrong about the Catholic schools question in the Ontario election, or that Norman really didn't understand strategy, or that Lowell Murray was an autocratic, aloof son-of-a-bitch, or that they were all Clark loyalists anyway.

As the strategists at headquarters were still groping to understand what was happening, Mulroney was carrying on, on his own. "After the debate, the Prime Minister literally carried the campaign on his back for four or five days," Harry

Near said later. For Mulroney picked up intensity, delivered a new, aggressive style of campaign, and conveyed to the volunteers and candidates that he was not flinching. On Saturday, he bused from Toronto to Kingston, stopping again and again along the way, at Pickering, Bowmanville, and Port Hope, trying to pump up enthusiasm, and revive flagging energies. But reporters on the bus noticed a coolness in the crowds, a lack of enthusiasm; Tories on the leader's tour remember it as one of the most difficult days of the campaign.

In Kingston that night, Mulroney paid tribute to Flora Mac-Donald, on the eve of her sixteenth anniversary as an MP. He knew that she was afraid that she was going down, and paused to praise her in the florid tones that he often used for someone with whom he had had an uneven relationship. "When the history of the long struggle for equality is written, when the story of the fight for fairness is written, the contribution of Flora MacDonald will be written in big bold letters," Mulroney said, to cheers from the crowd, and chants of Flora! Flora! Flora!

She was being challenged by a forty-two-year-old lawyer, Peter Milliken, running for the Liberals, and by a retired general running for the NDP, Leonard Johnson. In addition, there were a Christian Heritage Party candidate, Terry Marshall, and a Libertarian, John Hayes.

MacDonald was right to be uneasy. Milliken had started his canvassing in the rural areas of the riding, and had managed to reach every farm and every village before the writs were issued. Farmers in eastern Ontario were worried about the impact of free trade on farm marketing boards, and he was working hard on the issue. In addition, there were other groups in the riding who were annoyed at the government. Prison guards in the numerous penal institutions were angry that she had voted against capital punishment. Military personnel at the various units – the Royal Canadian Electrical and Mechanical Engineers, the Canadian Signal Corps, the Royal Military College, and the National Defence College – were all angry that, while she had been minister of employment and immigration, Michael Wilson had changed the rules so that on retirement they would no longer be able to draw unemployment insurance in addition to their pensions. In addition to the general civil-service resentment of the government, some observers thought that there was also a feeling that perhaps Flora was tired, and perhaps it was time for a change.

MacDonald was afraid that she might be the victim of an organized campaign by the Public Service Alliance of Canada, which had targeted twenty-five ridings across the country, including hers. Forty per cent of the labour force in Kingston and the Islands was employed in the public sector; she was a prime target, and she knew it.

On Thursday and Friday, the public-opinion polls were published on the English debate. On Wednesday, CTV broadcast a poll done by Insight Canada, which found that 59 per cent declared Turner the winner, 16 per cent picked Mulroney and 11 per cent Broadbent. On Thursday, the *Toronto Star* published a Gallup poll which found that 72 per cent of those who picked a winner chose Turner, 17 per cent Mulroney, and 11 per cent Broadbent. But 63 per cent said that the debate hadn't changed their mind. Nevertheless, 15 per cent said that they were more likely to vote Liberal, 7 per cent said they were more likely to vote Conservative, and 4 per cent said they were more likely to vote NDP. And on Friday, the *Globe and Mail* published an Environics poll which found that 46 per cent of anglophones felt Turner had done best, 19 per cent picked Mulroney, and 10 per cent picked Broadbent. Among francophones, the result was much closer, with 35 per cent picking Turner, 31 per cent Mulroney; only 4 per cent picked Broadbent.

For the first time, it looked as if Turner might turn things around. Suddenly, he began to be treated like Cinderella at the ball. Jean Chrétien seemed to be rallying to his support, speaking in Ottawa at Algonquin College and congratulating Turner on his performance, appearing at a rally for Lucie Pépin in Outremont, and campaigning for David Berger in Saint-Henri-Westmount.

In Halifax, Turner's day was a triumph. It began with the release of a regional-development plan for the Atlantic Provinces, entitled the Atlantic Charter: a proposal including a $200-million income-stabilization plan for fishermen, a "significant contribution" to the Trans-Canada Highway improvements sought by New Brunswick, and access to $2.43 billion in regional-development funds. Mary Clancy, the Liberal candidate in Halifax, had been present at the meeting when the candidates were briefed on the package the day before, and, while feeling it was worthwhile, didn't think it would be a determinant in the campaign. "That's not going to change what's on the doorstep," she remarked to her campaign manager, Dan Campbell. "Free trade is on the doorstep."

That afternoon, Clancy arrived at the St. Mary's University campus about five minutes before the Turner tour, expecting to see some young Liberals, organized to provide an enthusiastic welcome, and a classroom full of students. She was astounded to see the place jammed with the largest crowd that she had seen in Halifax since the glory days of Pierre Trudeau: the classroom packed with people standing six deep at the back, six hundred people outside, crowds lining the entrance way, cheering and wanting to get close to him.

Turner was obviously buoyed, but comfortable. At one point, when questioned by a student on student loans, he misheard the question, and began answering it in a way that showed he hadn't understood. His daughter Elizabeth stood up in the front row and called out "Dad, that wasn't what he asked."

Grasping the question, Turner answered it, and, while there were still tough questions about his leadership and his ability to hold the party together (Turner responded by saying that the Liberals were open enough to allow dissension over issues, adding, "Or do you want a party with ministerial resignations, conflict of interest, and police investigations?") Clancy thought she could feel the sympathy of the audience swing in his favour, partly because of his daughter's intervention.

Mary Clancy, a robust feminist lawyer, had been an active Liberal for years, and had become well known in the Halifax area for her work on women's and social issues. She was a regular panelist on CBC Radio, and felt that the time had come for her to run. It looked like a difficult assignment: the sitting member was Stewart McInnes, the minister of public works, and the New Democrat was Ray Larkin – also a lawyer, and her fellow-panelist. With her profile, and the work that she had done in different neighbourhoods in the riding, she felt that she had a strong chance of unseating McInnes; she also reflected later that, had it not been for Turner's performance in the debate, none of it would have mattered.

"You've got to say I'm a survivor," Turner told the students. "I guess in terms of the two competitors for the job we're seeking I've had more experience in government. You don't have to compare me to the Almighty. You've just got to compare me against the alternatives."

Later, in a television interview, Turner showed some of his new-found confidence. "The next time I'm back here I'll be prime minister," he told a television interviewer. "I think we've got great momentum."

That triumphalism was precisely what Brian Tobin had predicted and feared: having risen to the challenge of the debates, Turner was reminding people of the old Liberal Party assumption that it had a right to govern.

Martin Goldfarb had felt since his analysis of his polling in the summer that the Liberals could not win on free trade alone. What was required now was to move beyond free trade to other issues; Liberal candidates and strategists began to feel that Turner would have to change his focus. But there were a number of problems. Turner's confidence in both the strategists and the strategy had been shaken. He was comfortable with the free trade issue, which had won him the debate.

However, there was another problem. When he tried to talk about other things, audiences' eyes glazed over, and the reporters failed to give these things the same prominence as his attacks on free trade.

In the NDP campaign, the strategists could sense within forty-eight hours that they were in trouble. Their own polling showed it, and they could see the massive coverage of the

Turner-Mulroney clip on television. Their worst fear – of polarization around a single issue – was coming to pass.

"Our polling showed the shift back to partisanship," Bill Knight said later. "What we tried to do was figure out a niche in the marketplace."

As public opinion shifted, and the published polls reflected the same changes that the parties' private polling was finding, there began to be a strange dissonance to the Broadbent tour.

On the one hand, he was campaigning well: consistently addressing the largest crowds ever attracted to hear the NDP in a number of cities: loud, enthusiastic crowds. But at the same time, he and his candidates began to face flurries of microphones from reporters questioning them, not about the meeting, the speech, or the policies that had been discussed – but about the polls, and about Broadbent's use of an eight-year old comment by Laurent Thibault during the debate.

In St. John's on Thursday night, October 27, Broadbent spoke to a large crowd of six hundred supporters, and defiantly responded to Thibault's complaint that his comment had been taken out of context.

"I got a message from Mr. Thibault and he said – listen to this – his thinking has evolved," Broadbent said, to laughter from the crowd, going on to compare the president of the Canadian Manufacturers' Association to the Conservatives who had previously opposed free trade. "Well, like Mr. Mulroney and Joe Clark and Michael Wilson and David Crombie, Mr. Thibault certainly has the right to change his mind, especially in an election campaign."

His voice was shaking when he talked about it. The next day, on Saturday morning, Broadbent suggested that Thibault might have got a phone call from Mulroney. The whole incident angered Broadbent: it made him look as if he had been unfairly using old quotations, and he was clearly unused to being criticized, or having his integrity questioned. He started snapping at reporters in annoyance.

It also became clear that the NDP had to change its approach, and deal with the resurgent Liberals. On Saturday, an Angus Reid poll showed the Liberals and the Conservatives tied at 35 per cent, with the NDP at 28 per cent.

"Starting out a couple of weeks ago, everyone was saying that the Liberals ... were totally finished," he told a news conference on October 29. "I think it was a mistake to say that. ... No one ever said that with any historical perspective in my memory."

It was true that Broadbent hadn't actually said that himself; he had said that he thought it would be a good idea. And it was clear that his careless remark had contributed to the problems the NDP was facing once the campaign began to polarize.

There was another shadow on the NDP campaign which both New Democrats and reporters were beginning to notice. Broadbent was beginning to seem isolated, and cut off. The people who had attended meetings the week before the debates to discuss strategies, responses, and one-liners were shocked that none of their material had been used, and began to wonder if he had seen it. Union members were annoyed that, in London and in Halifax, Broadbent had made no reference to bitter strikes being fought in the area, and wondered if he had been told about them. And reporters began to sense that he seemed cool and distant from some of the crowds.

One reporter noticed him eating alone with an aide after a meeting in Vancouver, rather than spending time with candidates who had gathered from across the province for the rally; another wondered why he had not paused to shake hands with party members when the time seemed right to do so at a meeting in Peterborough. A third noticed how he had gone straight back to the bus after a meeting in Lewisporte, Nfld., without stopping to shake hands with school children who had wanted to meet him. Broadbent was feeling the pressure, and it showed.

CHAPTER TWELVE

Bombing the Bridges

"Every carefully combined attack requires time for its preparation, and if a counterstroke by the enemy intervenes, our whole design may be upset."

Von Clausewitz

The people around Mulroney had been very influenced by the Reagan presidency and its approach to television, and had learned that everything had to be planned in terms of what was seen on television. Bill Fox, Mulroney's first press secretary, had covered Washington for the *Toronto Star*, and seen the care and effort that went in to the presentation of the President. As Martin Schram explained in his book *The Great American Video Game*, and Hedrick Smith described and analysed in *The Power Game: How Washington Works*, the care was enormous and the effort unceasing.

Both Schram and Smith recount the story that opened the eyes of many print and television reporters about the Reagan presidency's view of the medium. On October 4, 1984, Lesley Stahl of CBS did a long, four-and-a-half-minute piece describing how Reagan used television, presenting carefully chosen pictures to "erase the negatives" and project the impression his advisers wanted, and either to lull people into forgetting or to overtly contradict Reagan policies.

"Mr. Reagan tries to counter the memory of an unpopular issue with a carefully chosen backdrop that actually contra-

dicts the President's policy," she said. "Look at the handi-
capped Olympics, or the opening ceremony of an old-age
home. No hint that he tried to cut the budgets for the disabled
and for federally subsidized housing for the elderly."

The piece was illustrated with many of the images that
proved her point: Reagan participating in staged events,
which had been chosen to project positive images and ignore
negative ones. Stahl thought it was the single toughest item
she had ever done on Reagan and the Reagan presidency, and
was braced for negative reaction from the White House. She
was stunned when a White House official phoned to say
"great piece."

Astounded, she asked if they had listened to what she said.

"Lesley, when you're showing four and a half minutes of
great pictures of Ronald Reagan, no one listens to what you
say," the official replied. "Don't you know that the pictures are
overriding your message because they conflict with your message? The public sees those pictures and they block your
message. They didn't even hear what you said. So, in our
minds, it was a four-and-a-half-minute free ad for the Ronald
Reagan campaign for re-election."

Thus, Michael Deaver, who described himself as "the vicar
of visuals," had spent $20,000 backlighting the window in
the Oval Office from the garden outside, because he felt it
made Reagan look ten years younger, and hired consultants to
design the chair, the lectern, and the podium at the Republican Convention in 1984 with no sharp corners but curves
everywhere, in reassuring tones of beige and brown.

Fox brought an awareness of this with him to the Prime
Minister's Office, as did Stuart Murray, and the subsequent
media advisers like Luc Lavoie and Bruce Phillips, both of
whom came from television. As one of his last jobs in the
PMO, Fox had done the advance work for Mulroney's trip to
Africa during the winter of 1987, walking every step of every
route with the constant thought of what television pictures
would emerge. When the trip actually occurred, he was in
Ottawa, and amused himself by watching the news programs

with a friend, predicting each shot as the item went on the air.

While these truths were relatively new to political management, they were almost a sacred text in advertising, first articulated twenty-five years earlier by David Ogilvy.

"In the early days of television, I made the mistake of relying on words to do the selling; I had been accustomed to radio, where there are no pictures," Ogilvy wrote in *Confessions of an Advertising Man* in 1963. "I now know that in television you must make your pictures tell the story; what you show is more important than what you say. Words and pictures must march together, reinforcing each other. The only function of the words is to explain what the pictures are showing.

"Dr. Gallup reports that if you say something which you don't also illustrate, the viewer immediately forgets it. I conclude that if you don't show it, there's no point in saying it. Try running your commercial with the sound off; if it doesn't sell without sound, it's useless."

Innovative ideas in 1963, these were taken for granted by 1988 – although the nature of the parliamentary system, the fact that politicians had to be able to campaign in two languages, and the relative diversity and multiplicity of television channels in Canada as compared to the United States made it somewhat more difficult for politicians and their managers to exert such absolute control over the television pictures as the Reagan advisers had been able to do. The nature of the television debates – much more demanding and free-wheeling than the American presidential and vice-presidential television debates that had occurred that fall – had created an element of unpredictability. Because the debate might produce an unforeseeable event Mulroney's campaign must be ready to respond with new, forceful, negative television advertisements.

For the Tory campaign had been jolted, not only by Turner's performance in the debate, but also by the Liberal television ads.

The Tories were taken aback at the impact of the initial Liberal ads, particularly the commercial which became known as "the map ad" – the most dramatic television ad of the 1988 election campaign.

As the commercial began, the camera panned through the doorway into a well-lighted, high-ceilinged room, where two men were sitting at a table; an American and a Canadian flag could be seen in the background. "Since we're talking about the Free Trade Agreement, there is one line I would like to change," a voice is saying.

There is a quick shot of a young man, with carefully combed dark hair, wearing horn-rimmed glasses. He looks young, earnest.

"Which line is that?"

There is then a very close shot of part of the face of an older man: his nose, eyes and part of his forehead are visible; he has blond eyebrows, and he looks older, with slightly battered features.

"This line here. It's just getting in the way."

The camera then shows a hand with a pencil eraser, starting to rub out a red line on a map: the Canada-U.S. boundary, starting at the Great Lakes.

A third voice says firmly "Just how much are we giving away in the Mulroney free-trade deal? Our water? Our health care? Our culture?"

During this phrase, an overhead camera pulls back, and the shot shows the young man erasing the line on the map, on the table, and sweeping away the bits of eraser with his hand as the older man looks on impassively, watching carefully, with only the hint of a smile.

"The line has been drawn – which side do you stand on?" the voice continues, and a shot shows the younger man looking back. Done. What's next?

Finally, the voice says "Don't let Mulroney deceive you again – this is more than an election, this is your future. On November 21, vote Liberal."

Only thirty seconds long, the ad was extraordinarily powerful. The natural lighting in the shot made the room look as if it might be the White House, or Camp David: some gracious environment for negotiations. (In fact, it was shot at Casa Loma in Toronto.) The older Canadian and the younger American were a faint echo of Simon Reisman and Peter Murphy, but done subtly enough that one could easily have mistaken the older, more experienced figure at the table for the American, and the younger man for the Canadian. It was the most memorable ad of the campaign, and had been produced by the Liberal advertising team put together for every English-language Liberal advertising campaign, Red Leaf Communications.

On Sunday night, October 23, the CBC program *Sunday Report* put together a "focus group" similar to those used to test commercials, and the people who watched the ad were very impressed. "In terms of impact, I have one word: Pow!" said one man. "It hits you right in the eye."

The man in charge of Red Leaf was the forty-four-year-old vice-president of marketing for Quaker Oats, David Morton. A cheerful, unpretentious man who had been living in Peterborough since he joined Quaker Oats; in the spring of 1987, Michael Kirby – who knew Morton because he was on the board of directors of Quaker Oats – asked him if he would take over Red Leaf Communications. Somewhat intimidated, Morton turned the job down twice before finally accepting in the early summer of 1987.

Beginning at that point, Morton attended strategy meetings to put together an election advertising strategy. He heard Martin Goldfarb say that all campaigns were run on either love or fear. With a great leader, a party could run on what he called "love issues"; without one, they couldn't. "In this case, we ain't got a leader who is loved, so we have to play fear," Goldfarb said.

In January 1988, the Red Leaf team began meeting: a group that included people from Maclaren's, and others from Vickers and Benson. Three themes were devised for the ad campaign, and the campaign itself: integrity, or Mulroney's lack of it; fear of the free-trade deal; and fear of the government's proposed sales tax. On that basis, over seventy ads were developed and tested; from the reaction of focus groups to the sketches laid out on storyboards, five commercials were produced.

In the course of the elaboration of the ad strategy, there was one major debate: whether John Turner should be used, or avoided in the Liberal commercials. Some vigorously argued that he would only hurt the party, while others – including Morton – argued that effective advertising could help overcome the public antipathy to Turner's leadership. At the focus groups during the summer, people said that they didn't want to see Turner much, but they wanted to see Mulroney. "Oh, show me more of Brian," said one woman in a focus group. "I love to hate him."

On the free trade issue, the creative group decided to focus on the question of cultural sovereignty, and began to bounce ideas around of how to visualize the differences, and symbolize what might be lost through free trade. In the brainstorming, there was talk of Anne of Green Gables and Rambo, Canadian flags and stars and stripes, beavers and eagles. But gradually, the idea began to be focused on the negotiations themselves.

"It seemed we were going to lose out on any level of a meeting, almost like the Yalta conference," said Donald Murphy, the fifty-two-year-old creative director at Vickers and Benson who worked on the Red Leaf team. In August, the creative group drew up a storyboard, showing the negotiators face to face at the table. This was sent off to focus groups for testing with a substantial number of other drafts for commercials in early September, and after it received a positive reaction, they had to wait until the writs were issued, because they didn't have any money to produce it.

Originally, the American negotiator was described in the script as "obviously an American" – perhaps with a Southern accent.

"But we said 'hey, hey – hold it guys, this is pushing it too far,'" Morton said later. "What we wanted to be clear – and it was not easy – was that it was the soft, concerned Canadian negotiating with the tough, more how-the-West-was-won American. But we didn't want to get into accents. And when we saw the casting, we were ecstatic. Because the Canadian guy looked very serious, very good, but a little bit 'Oh, geez, am I getting taken to the cleaners here?" Whereas the American looks much more sure of himself, and we did this with no voice things, they were both decent people, and we didn't make one seem like the ugly American. We wanted to be very pro-Canada, but we didn't want to be anti-American. But it's really tough – it's a tough, tough balance."

Morton was in a particularly delicate position in this regard, because he worked for the Canadian subsidiary of an American multinational. As it was, executives at Quaker Oats' head office in Chicago saw a glimpse of the ad because a TV item was done on the Canadian election campaign, and they inquired why Morton was working on an anti-American ad campaign. Morton replied that it wasn't anti-American, but pro-Canadian.

The actors were drawn from a standard casting call: the Canadian was intended to be what Terry O'Malley later described as "a normal kind of Canadian-looking guy, and a friend; the American was not unlike the Peter Murphy character [the American free-trade negotiator]." Donald Murphy thought of the Canadian as experienced, not a wimp, going a little bald, and the American as a young, stylish, Harvard-educated official.

Morton wanted the Liberal ads not to look like political ads – and while some of the other ads had a clumsier feel to them, the map ad had some of the production values of much more expensive advertising.

The ad was shot in about four hours at Toronto's Casa Loma, to convey the sense of formality of a negotiating session. (The same day, the crew also shot a commercial with an actor portraying Brian Mulroney kicking a soccer ball labelled "middle class." The model bore a considerable resemblance to Mulroney, and during the shoot, a woman came up to

Donald Murphy and asked him if he could get her Mulroney's autograph. When he explained that it wasn't Mulroney but an actor, she said "I'm here with my husband – he won't know. Get him to sign anyway.")

For Terry O'Malley, the key element of the map ad was the erasing of the line: the pure symbolism of the gesture struck at the heart of people's fears about what the Free Trade Agreement might involve.

"[It] visually just captured it in a very concise way – it really got people thinking about it," David Morton said later. "I think it really did a superb job for five or six or seven days of making people think 'Gee, I wonder. . .' at exactly the time [John Turner] performed well in the debate."

The ad jolted the two other parties. Hilarie McMurray, who had written a line for one of Ed Broadbent's speeches to the effect that the agreement rubbed out the boundary between our two countries, was upset when she saw that idea portrayed so vividly by the Liberals.

But the Conservatives were particularly taken aback. Later, Hugh Segal would tell David Morton that it was the best ad of the campaign, and that it scared the hell out of them. Segal had been worried that if the Liberals had stuck to the map ad for the remainder of the campaign, it could have done the Conservatives much more damage. Allan Gregg showed the commercial to a focus group: the first time they saw it, they laughed; the second time, they were eerily silent.

"They said 'You know, it's obvious that they're exaggerating; the border's not going to go away, and we're not going to become Americans, and we'll never become Americans,'" Gregg recalled. "'But it tells us that we're going to lose something in free trade, and that really worries me; I wonder if the risk is worth it.'"

Gregg knew that this could be dangerous; his favourite question in public-opinion research asks people, if someone told you something was safe and someone else told you it was unsafe, whom would you believe – and 66 per cent reply that they would believe the person saying it was unsafe, 14 per cent say they would believe the person saying it was safe, and the remainder say that it depends on the person doing the saying.

The impact of the Liberal map ad helped consolidate and solidify the unhappiness that existed in some circles about the first Conservative ads: an element of considerable tension between the Mulroney people and the Big Blue Machine people. For, in contrast with their unease about the possible impact of the Liberal commercial, many Tories were extremely unhappy with the first batch of Conservative ads. (However, Gregg defended them, as he did the bubble stage of the Mulroney campaign.)

On the question of advertising, the tension involved not simply clashing loyalties, but differences in style, approach, and preparation. Mulroney was a harder sell outside Quebec, as was free trade. But there were also differences in approach.

The main creative person on the Tory advertising side was Tom Scott, a veteran of the William Davis ad campaign in 1971, the Stanfield campaign in 1972, the Davis campaign in 1981, and the Mulroney campaign in 1984. He felt strongly that it was a mistake to make any commitments to advertising approaches too early.

The early Conservative ads were developed with the aim of reassuring Canadians about Mulroney. They were relatively static commercials, quoting positive comments about Mulroney and the Mulroney government from newspapers across Canada.

The first image was a head and shoulders colour photograph of Mulroney, in his office or the cabinet room: oak panelling was visible in the background, as was a Canadian flag.

"The *Kingston Whig Standard* calls him a national leader of purpose and courage," the voice-over said, and the quotation was flashed on the screen with the date of the article, June 25, 1988.

Then the background photograph changed to a shot of Mulroney at his desk, with people in his office. "The *Toronto*

Star praises his strong team of ministers and advisers," the voice said, as "... strong team..." was on the screen.

"His ability to get people working together is 'truly world class...' says the Montreal *Gazette*," the voice continued, over a photograph of Mulroney at the Toronto Summit with the six other leaders.

Over another photograph, of Mulroney with Chancellor Kohl, the voice said "The *Winnipeg Free Press* calls the party he leads 'the party of change and modernization.'"

Finally, over a photograph of Mulroney in profile, addressing an audience, the voice said "Prime Minister Brian Mulroney: 'The initiator of (Canada's) great new era'" while the quotation on the screen identified the *Windsor Star* as the source.

Tory strategists like Allan Gregg and Hugh Segal argued that the ad played the same role as the early stage of the tour: confirming the idea of Mulroney as prime minister, building that identification so that, if and when the free-trade issue became more controversial, it would have been established.

But many people close to Mulroney, including people who consulted through Fred Doucet's telephone network, hated the ad, and sent furious messages to the campaign headquarters to get it off the air. Those people could only have been further annoyed by the analysis given on *Sunday Report* on October 23.

"I think it was a very classy ad," said a man in a green sweater who was part of the CBC's "focus group" that discussed the ads. "It shows Mulroney in his typical surroundings, in front of a board room, with bank managers and that. His typical position, where he likes to be. He doesn't like to be down. . . . He's not an earthy person."

If there could be a comment likelier to drive Mulroney and his personal friends into a rage, it is hard to think of it. The pressure on the advertising team began to increase dramatically. Then, on Nov. 3, Jamie Portman's story was published in various Southam papers, calling the Tory campaign "the most astonishing so far" of all the parties. "It is pompous, boring, pretentious and monstrously repetitive," he wrote. "The Conservatives are hard at work producing new ads. They need them – and quickly."

On the other hand, David Morton breathed a great sigh of relief: the map commercial had whipped the other two spots. Martin Goldfarb would conclude that the changes in the daily polls at the beginning of the week were due almost entirely to the map ad, which had been playing even before the debate. The New Democrats were pleased; their commercial had also stimulated positive comments.

The New Democrats had only been using television advertising for less than a decade, thanks, in large part, to the election-financing legislation. But the whole issue of advertising had been foreign to the party, and its social-democratic, anti-capitalist, Methodist traditions. There continued to be elements in the party that felt that J.S. Woodsworth would have spun in his grave at the idea of his political heirs hiring ad agencies.

However, as the election approached, the party interviewed four agencies, three in English Canada and one in Quebec, and decided on Michael Morgan and Associates in Vancouver, and Nouvelle Société, a group formed with creative people who had worked on advertising and communications for the teachers' federation.

The most memorable ads in the NDP's campaign in English Canada were two: one on the environment, and one on free trade and medicare.

At the end of the first week of the campaign, Julie Mason flew to Vancouver, and discovered that the situation was in chaos. However, with producer Stan Olson and a good crew, they pulled things together and began to shoot commercials at the end of week two and the beginning of week three.

The environment ad was shot in the early morning on a lake in the interior of British Columbia: it was a beautiful morning, the mist was still on the lake, and a young boy and his grandfather were walking by the shore. It was a striking scene: the grandfather was a long-time NDPer, and the child a natural performer. What had been intended as a minor, low-key commercial became one of the central NDP ads of the campaign, and was dubbed "the On Golden Pond ad" by the press.

The ad began with a shot of a beach, and the camera rose to show a white-haired man with a small boy, about five or six, on a dock.

"Your Dad and I swam in this lake when he was a boy," an older man's voice says.

"Why can't we swim in it now, Grampa?"

"The lake is ruined by pollution."

Then, the old man can be seen holding the boy's hand as he skips along a log on the beach.

"Can we fix it?"

"First we need a leader who isn't afraid to stand up to the big corporations."

The boy, who is a strikingly good-looking child, looks up at the old man.

"Brian Mulroney promised that, but he let us down, just like the Liberals."

As the grandfather looks fondly on, the small boy chucks some pebbles in the lake.

"What are you going to do, Grampa?"

"This time, I'm voting for Ed Broadbent."

"Can I vote for Ed Broadbent too, Grampa?"

Seeing it, Tory ad man Hugh Segal was relieved that it had focused on a subject like the environment; had the old man said that he had gone overseas to fight for Canada because he believed Canada was special, and that he didn't want to see the Canada he had fought for lose what made it special because of free trade, Segal feared it could have done terrible damage. But the NDP's research, in polling and focus groups, indicated that had they done that, it would have simply encouraged people to vote Liberal, since they trusted the Liberals more than the NDP on issues like trade and international affairs.

"The environment ad was pretty squishy," Julie Mason said later. "It was nominally about the environment; in fact, it was about trusting Ed. It implied that Grampa had never voted that way before, and he was coming to a difficult decision because of an issue he cared about, and because he trusted Ed Broadbent."

As a result of conversations with journalists who had interviewed Liberals, Julie Mason knew that the Liberals were preparing a map ad on free trade as she was involved in shooting the NDP commercials. But, while she later thought that it was a masterly ad, there was no question of the NDP's trying that kind of commercial, which played to Liberal strengths and NDP weaknesses. On the trade issue, the NDP strategists felt that the only area in which the party had any credibility was social programs, and in particular medicare. That led to the nurses' ad.

Mason felt strongly that NDP ads should show ordinary people, and reflect the jobs they did. She had been struck by a documentary on *The Journal* which focused on a scrub nurse, the effective boss of the operating room: a strong, warm, caring, capable person. She was determined to project that feeling into an ad about the impact of free trade on medicare. In Vancouver, an actress had come forward to volunteer for NDP ads, and wanted to do this one; her mother was a nurse. It was shot in a Roman Catholic hospital – several other hospitals, fearing reprisals from the Vander Zalm government, refused to allow the NDP to use their facilities – because the director of the hospital said that he felt so strongly about the possible impact of free trade on medicare that he wanted them to do it in his hospital. The only time they could get space in the hospital was at night, so, about eleven p.m. coached by a nurse who worked as a scrub nurse, they shot the ad, with every line of the text drawn from Vic Fingerhut's polling research.

When the ad was completed, Julie Mason and the other NDP strategists were scared about it, worrying that it was too strident. In central Canada, it had relatively little impact. But in the West, where there had been cutbacks felt in social services, the impact was powerful. "When that ad ran in Saskatchewan, the phone didn't stop ringing," Julie Mason said later. Bill Knight agreed. "That wasn't a national ad, it was a Saskatchewan ad – and it did extremely well."

On Sunday, October 30, at Harrington Lake, Mulroney was shooting some commercials, after having got back into Ottawa at two a.m. the night before from Kingston. Tom Scott was quite pessimistic, and John Tory was struck by the gloomy mood. That afternoon, after getting a call from Tory, Lowell Murray pulled together a meeting at the Langevin Block at five p.m. of all the senior people who could be reached on short notice: a group that included Derek Burney, Allan Gregg, Tom Scott, his associate Rich Willis, Hugh Segal (all in town for the shooting of the commercial), Marjory LeBreton, Bill Neville, and Dalton Camp.

That afternoon, and again at the large weekly meeting on Monday morning, Allan Gregg laid out how the situation had changed: information he had been giving Mulroney piece by piece in daily conversations since the debates.

He told them that the belief in John Turner had really gone up, and that the correlation between how people would vote and how they felt about each party's position on free trade had changed dramatically. At the beginning of the campaign, free trade and party preference was what Gregg called "a fifth-order variable": it was number five in a list of forty or fifty positions which overlapped that of the party people were intending to support. After the debate, free trade shot to the top of the list.

"We're into a single-issue campaign," Gregg told them. "The bridge which joins the growing fear of free trade, with its roots in social programs, and the growing support for the Liberal Party, is the credibility of John Turner. People feel he really believes what he's saying."

About two days before, Decima had begun asking people whether they believed that John Turner was attacking free trade because he genuinely believed that it would be a disaster for Canada, or because his leadership was in trouble, and he was just trying to keep his job. By a two-to-one margin, they believed that Turner was sincere, and genuinely believed what he was saying.

"That's the number," Gregg said. "That's the number we've got to move."

If John Turner's credibility was the bridge between Liberal support and opposition to free trade, the strategic response would be to bomb the bridge, and destroy Turner's credibility.

It is worth noting that the language of marketing, polling, and product sales had sufficiently taken over the senior levels of all three parties that all the strategists, regardless of the party affiliation, talked about the marketplace, market niche, and moving numbers; at times, it sounded as if the election process of choosing policies on the basis of their merits had been privatized.

At the Sunday meeting, everyone knew that the ads that were on the air were not right, that the situation had changed, and that something more aggressive was called for. At that meeting, Scott began thinking out loud about the impact that the Liberal map ad was having.

"You know how to neutralize the map ad," he said, taking a piece of paper. "You put the line back – just draw it back: here's where we draw the line on free trade."

That night, Scott, Willis, and Segal returned to their rooms at the Four Seasons, and worked until four a.m. developing new commercials. By the time the full campaign committee met on Monday morning, Scott – who doesn't fly – was back at his desk in Toronto, having left the hotel before dawn to drive back, as Segal was ready to brief the committee on what he called the "eviscerative" concepts of the new campaign: a campaign intended to eviscerate John Turner.

On Monday mornings, there was a larger meeting than the regular morning meeting: a broader group of people came once a week to what one weekly participant called "the cattle call." Gregg saw that the mood was bleak.

"It was dire, it was black," he said later. "The election was on the route to being lost."

He laid out the situation – Turner's credibility had risen, along with the support for the Liberal Party – and the strategic response, some of which had already begun: Bomb the bridge.

From that point, the assault began. The Tory map ad was produced as quickly as possible, and put on the air as often as possible – in order to create an image in the viewer's mind of the line being drawn back when it was rubbed out. Hugh Segal later concluded that this led the Liberals to pull their map ad off the air. "Had they run that ad consistently right to the end of the campaign, it would have done us much more intense damage than it did," he said later. "They never should have pulled that ad. Our ad got them to pull it early."

The Tory response began to come together. At the strategy meeting on Thursday, it had been decided that since Mulroney did not campaign on Mondays, Michael Wilson should make an aggressive speech on Monday while the national press corps was in Ottawa. With Derek Burney, Lowell Murray, and William Neville, Tom Trbovich, Wilson's chief of staff – who was responsible for co-ordinating with the campaigns in Ontario and Manitoba – worked on the speech.

After the Monday meeting, various people began phoning reporters to tell them that they shouldn't miss the Wilson speech. The speech was tough: Wilson accused the Liberals and NDP of lying.

"Taking this lie into our senior citizens' homes is the cruellest form of campaigning I've seen in ten years in politics," Wilson told the luncheon crowd. "When politicians feel that they have to prey upon the fears and emotions of some of the most defenceless people in our society today, I say that is despicable. . . . Programs which are generally available such as medicare, pensions, old-age security aren't trade-distorting subsidies and are not subject to trade laws. Not even the most rabid protectionist in the United States will state otherwise."

However, Wilson did not shrink from a little scare-mongering himself.

"Maybe Donald Macdonald had it right when he said consider this scenario," he said. "Mr. Broadbent or Mr. Turner goes down to the White House and says 'Mr. President, we've just ripped up the Free Trade Agreement.' The President looks back at Mr. Broadbent or Mr. Turner and says 'That's a coincidence, because we've just ripped up the Auto Pact."

When reporters asked him how he could reconcile those remarks with his accusation that the opposition was scare-mongering, he replied that twelve governors from auto-producing states had asked for talks with the U.S. administration to discuss changes in the Auto Pact; when asked what possible changes worried him, he retreated, saying that the idea was hypothetical.

Broadbent was shaking hands with General Motors plant workers arriving for a shift change in Oshawa that afternoon, and when he was asked about Wilson's remarks, said they showed how desperate the Conservatives were getting.

"They know, the whole country – well, except for some Conservatives – knows that there is pressure for harmonization," Broadbent said, referring to making Canadian social programs similar to American programs.

The new attack had begun. In an interview with the French-language radio network Nouvelles Télé-Radio, Mulroney made the same point as Wilson. "You know very well that to sow fear and peddle lies is much easier than to build a country," he said. "That's why Mr. Broadbent and Mr. Turner were throwing out charges, because it's easy to sow uncertainty."

While Tom Scott, Hugh Segal, and Rich Willis were scrambling to get new ads produced and on the air, Harry Near, Marcel Côté, the trade lawyer James McIlroy, and William Neville were working together to produce a tabloid entitled "Ten Big Lies."

"All that stuff was done very quickly," Harry Near said. "But it still took us five days to get it all turned around and ready to roll. While that was going on, obviously the campaign didn't shut down while the Tories got their act together. The only guy we had to deal with it was the PM, by himself. It was unbelievable. I cannot tell you the pressure on the man. But he did it."

On Tuesday November 1, the published polls confirmed what the Tories knew from Allan Gregg: the Liberals had risen dramatically. The Environics poll, published in the *Globe and Mail*, showed that the Liberals had moved into a six-point lead, with 37 per cent of decided voters, with the Conservatives at 31 per cent and the NDP at 26. The feeling, which was stimulated even more a week later with the publication of a Gallup poll, provoked in the business community that endorsed free trade something of the same response that the initial Decima polling had stimulated at the centre of the Tory campaign: confusion, followed by a determination to retaliate.

The result was an overwhelming avalanche of advertising and propaganda: full-page newspaper advertisements, folders, brochures, speeches by executives in the lunch-room, employee "information sessions," letters to workers in pay envelopes – a tidal wave of frenetic activity by the corporate community that has been estimated to have cost anywhere from $2 to $3 million (the Liberal estimate – and almost as much as the entire Liberal advertising budget) to $10 million (the thumbnail estimate current in the labour movement) to a whopping $56 million calculated by Nick Fillmore in *This Magazine*, which includes the federal government's promotions, the Tory election spending, campaigns by provincial governments and the Canadian Alliance for Trade and Job Opportunities, its member organizations and additional corporate donors over the previous two years.

Ingenuously, Hugh Segal would claim that the onslaught of third-party advertising was not helpful, that no one read it, and that it had little impact. This was comparable to a duellist complaining that an AK-47 was inelegant. Inelegant the corporate swarm may have been by the standards of the advertising community; its sheer tonnage was astonishing – 800,000 copies of a four-page brochure on free trade, and full-page advertisements in Sunday newspapers, the day before the election – and they were completely outside the controls and restrictions of the provisions of the Canada Elections Act.

Thus, Crown Life Insurance organized a meeting for four hundred employees, which purported to be an open discussion of the agreement, and consisted of a lecture by a vice-president who was an advocate of the agreement. The Canadian Alliance for Trade and Job Opportunities acknowledged that it had encouraged its 150 member companies to set up employee programs. James Richardson and Sons of Winnipeg distributed the newspaper advertising supplement on free trade to its three thousand employees, as did Canfor Corp., a Vancouver forest-products company.

In Toronto, Enfield Corp., a finance and management company, distributed ten thousand copies of a free-trade paper to employees and shareholders. The supermarket chain Loblaws inserted a letter endorsing the Free Trade Agreement in the pay envelopes of its employees throughout Ontario. In Sault Ste Marie, the president of Algoma Steel, Peter Nixon, went on television to say that the defeat of the Free Trade Agreement would cost $1 million in jobs. Similarly, Stelco endorsed free trade in a message inserted in employees' pay envelopes, saying that the deal was crucial for the future of the steel industry.

In smaller companies, the pitch was more direct and more brutal. In his study of the business campaign on behalf of the deal, Nick Fillmore recounts how the president of Valley City Manufacturing, a wood-working company employing 150 people in Dundas, Ont., called a special meeting and told his employees that many of them might lose their jobs if the deal did not go through.

Individuals who had not been involved in public life before became heavily involved. Jack Fraser, the president and chief executive officer of Federal Industries in Winnipeg, became the driving force behind the Manitoba free-trade group. David Culver, the president of Alcan, became active in both the Business Council on National Issues and the Alliance for Trade and Job Opportunities. As one Tory put it later, "There are a lot of business people who got heavily involved – and really enjoyed it. They may not go away now." It was an extraordinary closing of corporate ranks, which created a kind of schism between business and labour, rich and poor, affluent region and poor region, such as the country had rarely, if ever, seen before. But veterans of the NDP, who had either lived through or learned the history of the party, remembered the 1940s. In his memoirs, David Lewis recounts how the Canadian Chamber of Commerce had developed plans to "combat the menace of the CCF" in 1943, and how the Canada Life Assurance Co. sent instructions to their branch managers on how to bring the CCF threat to the attention of customers.

In addition, free-enterprise organizations were established in order to finance crusaders like Gladstone Murray, who waged a constant campaign against the CCF with a $100,000 fund provided for him by many of the same firms (Algoma Steel, Stelco and many others) which, forty-five years later, were funding the Business Council on National Issues, the Canadian Alliance for Trade and Job Opportunities, and the avalanche of pro-free-trade advertising.

"You may vote CCF against my advice as this is your privilege," said J. H. Andrews of Lyman House, in a letter to employees during the 1945 election which was remarkably similar in tone to the messages conveyed to thousands of employees by their corporate employers in 1988. "I cannot, however, accept the responsibility of maintaining employment for you and the other members of our organization for any length of time under a CCF-controlled government."

Forty-three years later, the tone of the attacks had changed; no-one accused the opponents of free trade of being Communists or Nazis, a common charge by the coalition of business interests that threw itself into the battle in 1945. But the mobilization of resources by the business community was remarkably similar.

CHAPTER THIRTEEN

The Parting of the Ways

"Canada . . . is at the parting of the ways."

President William Howard Taft, 1911

On November 2, Brian Mulroney was in Victoria. In the morning, the campaign headed out to the University of Victoria to watch a scene from Molière's *Tartuffe* – a choice of play which, since Tartuffe is almost a synonym for hypocrisy, raised a few eyebrows among francophone reporters and aides. ("The character Tartuffe is an impostor, a religious impostor," said Linda Hardy, the director, to reporters who asked her about it. "Whether it has any particular application to anyone at all . . . is not for me to say." However, she had no hesitation in saying that, personally, she was opposed to the Free Trade Agreement. "I . . . wonder about questions with regard to our medical system, our social system," she said. "I lived in the States for a time. I had some very horrendous experiences with the American medical system.")

The event had been chosen to illustrate comments on culture that Mulroney was to make at a Chamber of Commerce luncheon speech, but it soon became irrelevant. For Mulroney used the speech to make an impassioned defence of the trade deal, and to counter the criticisms that had been made of its effect on social programs.

"I know that many Canadians, especially seniors, are concerned, and in some cases even confused, about the impact of the Free Trade Agreement on social programs, particularly medicare and pensions," he said. "I don't wonder that people are concerned after the reprehensible tactics of the opposition parties in telling Canadians that social programs, specifically pensions and medicare, are at risk. Newspaper editorials – forget the politicians – newspaper editorials from coast to coast have denounced that statement for exactly what it is: a lie. From the *Vancouver Province* to the *Winnipeg Free Press*, from the Toronto *Globe and Mail* to the *Kingston Whig Standard*, from *La Presse* in Montreal to the *Halifax Chronicle-Herald*, the country's leading opinion-makers have called on the opposition leaders to stop their campaign of fear among senior citizens.

"And yet, the NDP continues to run a television ad in which an actress, portraying a hospital worker, states that medicare is in danger. And Mr. Turner, in our debate last week, stated that I, as prime minister, and I quote, '. . . agreed to let the Americans have a say in the future of our social programs, such as unemployment insurance and medicare.' Unquote."

Mulroney paused for effect.

"Well, I ask you, in your own lives, and with your own families, and in your own careers in your own regions – how do you fight a lie? Except with the truth. The simple, unvarnished truth is that medicare, pensions, and social programs are not at risk in the Free Trade Agreement; they have never even been mentioned in the Free Trade Agreement. Ambassador Simon Reisman, Finance Minister Michael Wilson, and Trade Minister Pat Carney were in Washington, and they signed the deal. They stipulated clearly that medicare and pensions and social programs were never negotiated, they are not mentioned in the agreement, and they are not at risk. That is the simple truth."

"But they are not protected!" shouted John Wilcox, from the audience. A farmer who had toured the country as Johnny Canuck attacking the deal, Wilcox was one of a number of members of the Council of Canadians who had come to the lunch to challenge Mulroney.

"Oh, I see there's somebody here from the NDP," retorted Mulroney. "If you hear me out, I'll hear you out. If you let me speak, I'll let you speak."

"Explain where they're protected!" called out Dave Szollosy, a church worker, and a member of the Coalition against Free Trade.

"Just give me a chance, just give me a chance to speak, and I will," Mulroney said. "Then, I tell you what, if you disagree, you can speak."

When the applause subsided, he continued. "Simon Reisman, for example, is a loyal and devoted Canadian – as you are, sir, as we all are. Earlier today, he made it very clear. He stated that never once in two years of negotiations with the Americans did the subject of social programs ever come up. Not once. And why? Because genuine social programs have no relevance to trade. All developed countries have that, in one form or another, and never have they been deemed to be unfair trade-distorting subsidies: not by United States law, not by Canadian law, or not by any international trade law. Any suggestion to the contrary is without foundation. There is no other term for it. So I would hope that our opponents would get off the backs of senior citizens and address this agreement on the basis of fact, and not distortion."

Then Mulroney reached for the dramatic personal example, in the kind of sentimental way he did when provoked.

"Let me tell you this – my mother is a senior citizen who receives medicare, and receives a pension," he said. "If Mr. Broadbent did what he did in Edmonton, and walked into her senior citizens' home and said that her pension and medicare were being challenged, or were being affected, I want to tell you, quite properly, she'd be on the phone to me right away saying, 'Hey, Brian – son, I love you dearly, but I love my pension too.'"

There was some laughter and applause, and Mulroney continued.

"Slowly but surely, Canadians are beginning to realize that the Liberals and the NDP have abused their trust. Let's personalize it. We all have parents, grandparents, mothers and fathers. I just referred to the case of my own mother. She receives medicare, she receives the old-age pension, she receives the universal programs to which she is entitled. Why would I, as her son, as prime minister of Canada, pledged to defend and maintain the integrity of this nation, to strengthen its independence, which is what I have done and to what I have committed my life, why would I do anything other than ensure that my mother, and all the mothers of this country, get the programs to which they are entitled and which they richly deserve? That's what the Free Trade Agreement does!"

When the applause subsided, and one of the hecklers had shouted a bit, and Mulroney had asked again to have a chance to say a few words, and to ask a few questions, he went on.

"Slowly but surely, Canadians are beginning to realize, I think, that the Liberals and the NDP have abused their trust. The opposition parties thought they could get through an election campaign, propagating deception and distortion and deceit. I think that the opposition parties believed that a lie that goes unchallenged for twenty-four hours would automatically become a truth. Well, they underestimated the intelligence and the integrity of Canadians. Here are the questions, sir, that I put. Not complicated; I don't think they are difficult, and I think they are straightforward. . . . Mr. Broadbent and Mr. Turner, where in the Free Trade Agreement is mention made of pensions or medicare? What article in the Free Trade Agreement allows you to say that pensions and medicare are affected? The opposition leaders are now honour-bound to answer these simple, straightforward questions in a simple, straightforward way."

Hearing a shouted answer from John Wilcox, Mulroney repeated it. "1807-9," he snapped, and the words tumbled out excitedly. "This is exactly the response the NDP deputy campaign chairman threw out in the Mansbridge show on Sunday night, and it was false then and it's false today!"

Mulroney went on to finish his speech, which included a summary of the government's commitment to Canadian culture – originally the theme for the day. But that was overshadowed by Mulroney's attacks on the opposition, and by the event that would follow the speech.

For when Wilcox shouted out a number from the agreement, Marc Lortie decided that Mulroney should face the hecklers directly. He had agreed to let them speak, to hear their views – but there was no commitment to do so in public. When the speech was concluded and everyone began eating lunch, Lortie came over to Mulroney's table, and urged him to meet with the hecklers in front of the TV cameras.

He felt that if he didn't deal with the issue decisively, hecklers would be shouting numbers at him for the rest of the campaign. Mulroney agreed – and Luc Lavoie headed into the crowd to tell the three hecklers that Mulroney would meet with them afterwards.

The cameras were set up in the upstairs lounge of the St. Michael's University Racquet Club, where the lunch had been held, and the three hecklers – John Wilcox, Dave Szollosy, and John Lewis Orr, a retired civil servant, waited nervously for Mulroney to arrive.

He came in just as Szollosy was saying to reporters "Why lie to the Canadian people?" – and it was a revealing sign of the natural courtesy of the country that Szollosy immediately stood up, turned and shook hands with Mulroney. Saying that he didn't have as long as he wanted, Mulroney sat down, and, clarifying that Wilcox had been talking about clause 1807, section 9, said "1807 deals with the [dispute] panel procedures, right?"

"That's right," said Wilcox, who argued that the procedures would enable the Americans to use countervail measures against Canadian social programs, since the binational panel procedure would withdraw the dispute from GATT.

Mulroney took the agreement, and read the clause aloud. It stated that, if the commission had not reached a decision within thirty days, either country, if it felt its rights would be impaired by the issue, could suspend the benefits of equivalent effect until the matter was settled.

"This, sir, if I may say respectfully, hasn't the slightest thing, directly or indirectly, to do with medicare, old-age security of any kind," Mulroney said, adding that Wilcox's remark had been "absolutely misleading" in suggesting medicare and pensions would be affected.

"No, it's not," said Szollosy. "What happened with this is that they can force us into a corner where our businesses have to face so much flack in terms of becoming competitive that we will be forced to cut these programs. They're not protected in this deal."

This was the key issue, in many ways: not whether or not clause 1807 directly affected medicare or pensions, but whether Canada, through the Free Trade Agreement, was moving towards a more competitive free-market environment where Canadian businesses would clamour for reduced social programs to lessen their tax burden.

"What you are giving me, and I'm not quarrelling with it, what you're giving me is your interpretation of what might happen," Mulroney said. "Do you also agree with me that there is nothing in the agreement at all that deals with medicare or social security?"

"That's one of the problems with the deal," Szollosy replied. "We haven't maintained our ability to protect these programs. They're up for grabs."

"You made your point, I tried to respond to it," Mulroney answered.

Wilcox returned to the question of clause 1807 and the panel procedures, saying, "All the objectives in the agreement are undermined by this weakness. This is the germ that will infect the whole thing and destroy it."

"I take note of your argument," Mulroney said, turning to John Lewis Orr, who argued that the problem with the agreement was that it left out the whole question of defining a subsidy, deferring that contentious issue to negotiations over the next five to seven years.

Then Wilcox returned to his argument that a bilateral mechanism meant that any dispute would be settled outside the rules of GATT.

Stabbing his finger on the table, Mulroney said "Medical care, social programs, regional development, are not part of the agreement!"

"They can be made part of the agreement!" Wilcox persisted.

"They cannot, neither under the GATT, nor under international law."

Wilcox retorted that pressure could be brought to bear in a countervail when a dispute was not settled.

"What you are saying is that your interpretation of what might happen is that," Mulroney said.

"Yes," replied Wilcox.

"That's your interpretation," Mulroney continued. "It's not in the agreement, agreed?"

"It certainly is a possibility," replied Wilcox. "Do you not agree with that?"

"Look, anything's a possibility, but it's not in the agreement," Mulroney insisted. "It has nothing to do with the issue that has been raised."

"It does!"

"It may be . . . it's a possibility in your mind. It's not a possibility in mine," Mulroney said. "Fair ball?"

"You just said that anything is possible," Wilcox retorted. "I'm saying if they had a dispute over anything you want to name . . . then they want to countervail because they won't be able to resolve the dispute, because the arbitrator hasn't implemented the result of the dispute in thirty days, [so] they can countervail."

Finally, Orr argued that any benefits that were included in the deal could be wiped out by a rise in the Canadian dollar: that 370,000 Canadian jobs could be lost by a rising dollar.

"The basic carrot of the Free Trade Agreement is to protect the two million jobs now that depend on access to the United States market, that are not protected," Mulroney said. This was a point that Allan Gregg had been urging on him: Canadians had to see that there was a risk in not having the Free Trade Agreement, and as this crucial week in the campaign began, it was a theme that Mulroney would repeat again and again.

As the discussion ended, Orr said crustily that Mulroney should pay attention to what they had said.

"May I ask you this," retorted Mulroney. "When is the last time, sir, that a prime minister has sat down and listened to you?"

"OK, that's fine, I'm delighted," rumbled Orr – and Mulroney, Szollosy, aides, and reporters all burst out laughing.

Neither side conceded any points, no one was persuaded of anything, and it is unlikely that anyone who watched the exchange that night on television was really illuminated about clause 1807, section 9, of the agreement. But everyone had made their arguments well. The risks had been very high for all concerned, particularly Mulroney: it could have turned nasty, it could have been awkward, and it wasn't. The reporters were excited; as they scrambled for the bus, and headed back to the hotel where they were staying, some began writing furiously on laptop computers, since the time difference on the West Coast meant they were perilously close to deadline, and television reporters got on the cellular phone to their offices to argue for additional time.

Alan Fryer of CTV News was on the phone from the bus, arguing that he needed four minutes; that he had just come from the most exciting event of the campaign. He succeeded in getting three minutes and twenty-four seconds on the news that night, running a long excerpt of the debate: his longest item in the campaign.

The next day, Doug Small of Global kidded him about it as the bus headed for the airport. "I remember when we were in Africa, and you said I was remaking Ben Hur," he said, chuckling. "We've got more than one movie-maker on the plane."

Back in Ottawa, Tories were delighted. The television clips showed Mulroney's passionate, and sentimental argument about his mother in the speech, and the debate with the hecklers. In the cold eye of the camera, the hecklers looked earnest, tweedy, a bit eccentric; the room looked relaxed, with brown clubby colours; the exchange was polite and good humoured; Mulroney looked calm and sure of himself. The argument over free trade, which had become an intense evocation of the future of the country during the leaders' debate, became a technical but civilized argument over subsections of clauses, and the possible ramifications of a deadlock on an as-yet-to-be-established commission examining apparently hypothetical disputes. Mulroney had succeeded in making the question appear to be something on which people could agree to disagree, and, at the same time, a question he felt very strongly about.

"I think it was a turnaround point," Harry Near said later. "Mulroney was saying, in effect, 'I believe in this thing. I know this thing. I'll debate this thing.'"

And, instead of facing John Turner and Ed Broadbent, he had been able to do it to a farmer in a tweed jacket, a retired engineer with a walrus moustache, and a bearded church-worker in a fisherman's sweater. While the reporters had all been impressed by the poise shown by the free-trade critics, and newspaper reports may have conveyed the impression of a stand-off in the argument, the television pictures inevitably conveyed unspoken impressions: Mulroney seeming calm and sure of himself, while the critics of the deal appeared somewhat eccentric.

On November 3, in Penticton, Mulroney gave one of the few indications of his campaign that there might be a dark side to the Free Trade Agreement.

"The world is changing dramatically," he said. "We have a responsibility, as the government of Canada, as the people of Canada, to accommodate that change, but to make sure people don't suffer from that change, to cushion the blows when they occur. . . . I believe that if we bring in those adjustment programs, which we are going to, they are going to be among the most generous brought forward anywhere . . . to help individuals cushion the blow."

Cushion the blows? He made it clear that he was talking about BC wine producers, whose blows would come from the Europeans and from GATT rather than the Free Trade Agreement, but nevertheless, it was a sombre tone which he didn't adopt often. He moved quickly to the partisan attack.

"Mr. Turner says that he's on a crusade," he said. "It's degenerated into a destructive mission which is anti-trade, anti-growth, anti-investment, anti-expansion, and anti-American. His reckless actions and statements are hurting Canada." The attack was completed with a gibe that Allan Gregg had drawn out of his research and focus groups: "It's pretty clear that the only job Mr. Turner is interested in protecting is his own."

That afternoon, in Castlegar, B.C., three people in the audience gave their very different interpretations of what the deal might mean.

Norm Le May and Neil MacKay were two Alberta students, who were in British Columbia studying Japanese at the immersion school in Nelson. They were planning to return to Banff to open an adventure-tour company, aimed at Japanese tourists, and they were convinced that Japan was watching the outcome of the Free Trade Agreement like a hawk. They were concerned that the world was forming into trade blocs ("The world is going to the corners," Neil MacKay said) and that Canada needed the deal, and the millions of dollars of Japanese investment they were convinced it would bring.

At the same meeting was a heckler, who was thrown out of the meeting, and prevented from approaching Mulroney: Derek Todd, an employee of the local school board. "What about the dispute-settlement mechanism and its inadequacies?" he asked reporters, who gathered around to interview him. "What good is a dispute-settlement mechanism that just interprets American law? I haven't heard the answer to that question. .... If you want economic union, come out and say so."

He was frustrated about his treatment at the meeting.

"One day, Mr. Mulroney's arresting people; the next day, he's inviting them to his room; the next day we're back to being arrested again," he said. "I'd like him to come clean about the criticisms of the Free Trade Agreement. I'm tired of him telling me this person endorses it and that person endorses it; I'd like him to address the criticisms of the dispute-settlement mechanism. I'd like him to address the question of how, exactly, social programs won't be definitely considered subsidies. I don't think he's considered that question."

In a strange way, the contrast between the two views at that meeting in Castlegar was an illustration of the gulf that existed between the two sides. For if each had been asked about the concern of the other, it is probable that Derek Todd would have been prepared to see the loss of Japanese investment as a reasonable cost for killing the Free Trade Agreement, while Norm LeMay and Neil MacKay would probably have been prepared to see a reduction of social programs as part of the process of making the Canadian economy more competitive internationally.

For what was at issue in the election was less a decision on what the details of each clause might mean than a vote on a direction for the country. In that sense, the Free Trade Agreement was a symbolic turning point: the most dramatic economic choice for the country since 1911.

On January 26, 1911, Sir Wilfrid Laurier's finance minister, William S. Fielding, announced to the House of Commons the terms of a reciprocity treaty that had been negotiated with the United States: free trade in natural products from poultry to asbestos, identical lower duties on food, farm implements, and cars, and special customs rates on aluminum and iron ore: a sweeping agreement.

"If the government benches were jubilant, the Opposition was stunned. The bargain was better than they had imagined possible," wrote Laurier's biographer (and reciprocity supporter) O.D. Skelton. "Western Conservative members could not be restrained from applauding. Outside the House, Conservative newspapers like the *Toronto News* and the *Ottawa Journal* expressed approval."

But after some initial hesitation, the leader of the opposition, Robert Borden, decided to attack the treaty – although the Conservatives were dismayed by having to fight it, and the Western members were convinced that they would lose their seats if they did. "The agreement would be challenged, but the full assault would be on its inner meaning, its apparent threat to nationhood and the imperial connection," wrote Borden's biographer, Craig Brown. "The appeal would be to loyalty, to patriotism, and to support from an indignant business community."

On the same day that Fielding spoke to the House of Commons, President William Howard Taft delivered a message to the House of Representatives. Canada, he said, "has greatly prospered. It has an active, aggressive, intelligent people. They are coming to the parting of the ways. They must soon decide whether they are to regard themselves as isolated permanently from our markets by a perpetual wall or whether we are to be commercial friends."

As Lawrence Martin noted in his book *The Presidents and the Prime Ministers*, Taft would use the phrase "parting of the ways" again and again as he spoke on the reciprocity agreement. "Now is the accepted time," he said later. "Now Canada is in the mood. She is at the parting of the ways."

What Taft said subtly, the speaker of the House Champ Clark said much more bluntly – to Taft's horror – uttering what Martin described as "the most damaging words of support that any Canada-U.S. legislation has ever received." On February 14, 1911, he declared "I am for it, because I hope to see the day when the American flag will float over every square foot of the British North American possessions clear to the north pole! They are people of our blood. They speak our language. Their institutions are much like ours. . . . I do not have any doubt whatever that the day is not far distant when Great Britain will see all of her North American possessions become a part of this Republic. That is the way things are tending now."

The speech caused a storm in Canada. Taft was forced to issue a statement saying that "no thought of future political annexation or union was in the minds of the negotiators of either side. Canada is now and will remain a political unit."

Two days later, on February 16, the president of the Canadian Bank of Commerce Sir Edmund Walker (a Liberal) told a meeting organized by the Toronto Board of Trade that the proposals put continentalism ahead of the British connection. On February 20, an anti-reciprocity manifesto was issued by eighteen prominent Toronto Liberals, denouncing the proposals as the worst blow to Canadian nationality. And the same day, Sir William Van Horne said he was "out to bust the damn thing." Then, most dramatic of all, on February 28, Clifford Sifton told the House of Commons that he would be leaving the Liberal Party to fight the agreement.

"Now . . . when we can be of some use to the Empire that gave us our liberty and our traditions of citizenship – at the first beckoning hand from Washington we turn to listen; the first time anyone beckons we turn from the path that leads to the centre of the Empire and take the path that leads to Washington," Sifton told the House. "So far as I am concerned, I say, 'Not for me.'"

Robert Borden met with Sifton and three other opponents of the reciprocity deal, including Zebulon Lash, a Toronto lawyer who had organized the Canadian National League to campaign against reciprocity. They set out a number of conditions for their co-operation: Borden was to agree that if he won the ensuing election, he would not be subservient to Quebec or "Roman Catholic influences in public policy or the administration of patronage," he should resist American pressures, run a firmly Canadian fiscal policy, consult a group of three including two Liberals about his cabinet appointments, create a Civil Service Commission and a Tariff Commission, reorganize the Department of Trade and Commerce, and name some outstanding men of national reputation to his cabinet.

"Borden had no difficulty in concurring with these points," Brown wrote. "He himself had advocated identical positions on fiscal policy, the civil service, and a tariff commission many times. He had no sympathy or subservience to any religious interest, Catholic or Protestant, and that, too, was a matter of record."

But while his biographer defends his agreement to consult the Liberal rebels on his new cabinet, veteran Tories in the caucus were furious when they learned of his meeting with Sifton. Their anger precipitated the second attempt in twelve months to force Borden to step down as leader. In April 1910, caucus unhappiness with Borden had burst out into the open as members complained that he had been distant, inaccessible, moody, and had not consulted them. Borden successfully organized his extra-parliamentary support, which rallied to him, and his opponents in caucus were weak and disorganized.

A year later, in March 1911, the scenario was repeated. "Incredibly, just at the moment when the party had its first real chance to gain power, the malcontents again challenged Borden's leadership," Brown wrote. "They denounced his agreement with the Liberals. At a stormy caucus they forecast the destruction of the party." Again, Borden threatened to resign and mobilized support from provincial premiers: letters begging Borden to stay were presented to him on March 28.

On July 29, after his return from the Imperial Conference and the coronation of George V in London, Laurier called an election for September 21 in which it was clear that reciprocity would be the central issue, except in Quebec, where the Naval Bill of 1910 loomed larger. As Richard Jones noted, there was a paradoxical element in the 1911 election that ensued. For while in the other provinces the Conservatives succeeded in convincing voters that Laurier was insufficiently loyal to the British Empire, in Quebec Henri Bourassa was arguing that the Naval Bill proved that Laurier was too much of an imperialist. In a by-election in Drummond-Arthabaska on November 3, 1910, the Bourassa nationalists had claimed that the Naval Bill was a prelude to conscription – and won the seat.

In Simcoe, Ontario, on August 15, Laurier told his audience that Sir John A. Macdonald was the Moses of reciprocity who had been unable to bring his people to the Promised Land. "I am the Joshua who will lead the people to their goal." He claimed he was unconcerned about the opposition to reciprocity from the manufacturers. "On Thursday I will beat them and on Friday I will support their just interests," he said. "The manufacturers must understand that there are men who are not as magnanimous as we are, and forces will be aroused which it will be impossible for me to control. . . . They are preparing themselves for a rod which will some day fall across their shoulders."

The next day, he told a rally of ten thousand in Trois-Rivières that there was "nothing more important for the country than reciprocity." But he also dealt with the attacks from Henri Bourassa and the nationalists on the Naval Bill. "The day when England's supremacy on the sea is destroyed, your national and religious privileges will be endangered," he said. "And where is the French Canadian who will say 'No, I will not participate in that war?'"

Henri Bourassa had been more ambivalent on the subject of reciprocity. At the beginning of 1911, he wrote, "I believe in the superiority of Canadian-American reciprocity over Imperial reciprocity," and told the Canadian Club in Montreal in April that it was "ridiculous" to claim that reciprocity would result in the national, political, and economic ruin of Canada. In Saint-Hyacinthe during the campaign he reiterated his support, but in Saint-André-Avallin, he said to the farmers, "What advantage can there be for you to sacrifice your market to the Americans?"

There was similar confusion among other Quebec nationalists: Armand Lavergne, a Conservative, supported reciprocity, while the Quebec federal Tory leader F.D. Monk opposed it.

To the distress of some Tory leaders, and the satisfaction of Borden himself, Monk and Bourassa had come together with English Quebec Conservatives to form an alliance to defeat Laurier. Borden responded by virtually staying out of the province during the campaign.

At the same time as this coalition of Quebec nationalists to defeat Laurier, business interests were mobilized to defeat reciprocity by the Tariff Committee of the Canadian Manufacturers' Association, which took the name of the Canadian Home Market Association, and worked discreetly to produce anti-reciprocity tracts, and to support publications opposed to reciprocity.

In his campaign, Borden painted the choice in stark terms: reciprocity would lead to commercial union, and political annexation. "We must decide whether the spirit of Canadianism or of Continentalism shall prevail on the northern half of this continent," he told his last campaign rally. In the last hours of the campaign, Rudyard Kipling urged Canadians to reject reciprocity, much to the frustration and anger of its supporters.

"If mounting imports from the United States had not brought annexation, how could mounting exports bring it?" complained Skelton, a decade later. "How could the Canadian banker with reserves in Wall Street, the director seeking terminals in Chicago, the manufacturer joining in an international merger, ordain 'no truck nor trade with the Yankees'? If Mr. Kipling could sell his poetry for hundreds of thousands of American dollars without injuring the perfect bloom of his patented patriotism, could not a Saskatchewan homesteader sell a beef or a load of wheat without selling his country and his soul with it?"

On September 21, Borden's Conservatives won 134 seats (including 27 autonomistes in Quebec), while Laurier's Liberals won 87 seats. Laurier's campaign for reciprocity got 47.8 per cent of the popular vote, while Borden's crusade against it won 50.9 per cent.

The parallels with the campaign of 1988 are uncanny: a negotiated agreement on trade with the United States, an opposition leader contested in his own caucus, a passionately emotional debate on Canadian identity and Canada's relationship with the United States, the heavy involvement of business interests on one side of the issue, a subsidiary debate on naval expenditures (the Naval Bill in 1911, and nuclear submarines in 1988), and finally, a coalition between Quebec nationalists and the English-Canadian business community.

The difference was crucial: the Quebec nationalists and the English-Canadian business interests had changed sides.

———————

When Mulroney became leader of the Progressive Conservative Party, there was no hint that he would be pointing to free trade with the United States as one of his accomplishments after a first mandate. For in the 1983 Tory leadership campaign, Mulroney was arguing against the pro-free-trade stance adopted by John Crosbie. "This country could not survive with a policy of unfettered free trade," he told the *Globe and Mail* reporter John Gray. "I'm all in favour of eliminating unfair protectionism, where it exists. [But] this is a separate country. We'd be swamped. We have in many ways a branch-plant economy, in many ways, in certain important sectors. All that would happen with that kind of concept would be the boys cranking up their plants throughout the United States in bad times and shutting their entire branch plants in Canada. It's bad enough as it is."

However, he stressed that he favoured improved relations with the United States, saying that he wanted to get Congressional approval for a new Canada-U.S. fishing treaty and for an improved auto pact.

"I'm pretty sensitive to this issue," he said. "Good relations, superb relations with the United States of America will be the cornerstone of our foreign policy. That doesn't mean dependency, that means good, good relations. There's a price to be paid for good relations on both sides. The Americans have to pay a price for having such a tremendous country and people, such as Canada, as their neighbour. There's a price to be paid for that. And things like auto pacts and fishing treaties, to name but two, is a small price to pay to have a wonderful country like Canada sitting on your doorstep. And so I limit my free-trade concept to strictly bilateral issues that benefit Canada and serve the relationship with the United States too."

Asked five years later how he made the transition from that position to endorsing the idea of free trade with the United

States, Mulroney began by commenting on the context of the remarks in 1983.

"You have to view leadership campaigns as important challenges, and they're not without their pitfalls and their traps," he said. "I mean, you have to understand that this is a political contest, and you've got ninety or a hundred days in which to make sure that you don't generate the kind of debate that is going to bring you down and thereby deprive you of any chance of national leadership."

Mulroney favoured increased trade, opposed protectionism, favoured better relations with the United States, and favoured more American investment in Canada: positions he had made clear in his collection of speeches published as *Where I Stand*, and in the leadership and the 1984 election campaigns. His remarks five years later don't foreclose the possibility that his opposition to free trade with the United States was more tactical than strategic, since John Crosbie was strongly supporting free trade. Other Mulroney supporters have argued that the key phrase in Mulroney's remarks to John Gray was "unfettered free trade," and that the Free Trade Agreement is not unfettered.

However, Mulroney pointed to three elements that lead him to move from opposing to endorsing the idea:

"First of all, the terrible swing to protectionism in the United States, which threatened to pick off Canadian industries one by one. [Secondly] the move in Europe to 1992, to a much greater trading bloc. Thirdly, the excellent and thoughtful Macdonald Royal Commission Report with its exhaustive examination of Canada's economy and its future prospects."

When he came to office, Mulroney became convinced for the first two reasons that some arrangement had to be negotiated with the United States.

For the Canadian government had already been exploring the idea of sectoral free trade with the United States. External Affairs had been developing a strategy towards the United States, and the reorganization of the department in September 1983, bringing the trade and diplomacy sides together, gave new clout to the assistant undersecretary of state for external affairs in charge of relations with the United States, Derek Burney.

Burney had been active in the attempt by the Liberal minister of international trade, Gerald Regan, and the regional industrial expansion minister, Ed Lumley, to negotiate sectoral free trade. In February 1984, Regan had met the U.S. trade representative, William Brock, to discuss the possibility of free trade in four sectors: urban mass-transit equipment, steel, agricultural equipment, and computer services.

However, the Americans were not very interested, since it was difficult to find mutually balancing sectors with advantages for both.

On September 17, 1984, while the Mulroney cabinet was being sworn in, Burney was in Washington, starting to lay the groundwork for the first Mulroney-Reagan Summit, to be held in March. While the most publicly memorable event of that summit was Brian Mulroney singing "When Irish Eyes Are Smiling" with Ronald Reagan on the stage of the Grand Théâtre in Quebec City, the agreement to "halt protectionism" made it clear how much work Burney had done. For Reagan and Mulroney announced that Brock and James Kelleher, minister of international trade, would establish a mechanism to "chart all possible ways to reduce and eliminate existing barriers to trade."

Reagan and Mulroney also agreed to deal with national treatment of government purchasing and funding programs; the standardization, reduction, or simplification of regulations; the reduction of obstacles to competition among airlines; the reduction of trade restrictions in the field of energy; the reduction of trade barriers; measures to make business and commercial travel easier; the elimination of trade barriers to high-technology goods; and co-operation in the area of copyright law and intellectual-property rights.

That list was a substantial preview of what would emerge, two and a half years later, as the Free Trade Agreement. It was also an indication of how much of the initial work was prepared by Derek Burney and his officials.

But on September 5, 1985, came the final encouragement. The Macdonald Royal Commission, headed by a Liberal former finance minister, Donald Macdonald, was a political gift to Mulroney. It provided a clear policy direction at a time when the government was beginning to run the course of public consultation, and it was headed by a Liberal. Its advocacy of a Canada-U.S. free-trade agreement as "a leap of faith" captured the optimism and the entrepreneurial spirit that Mulroney had been trying to articulate, and translated it into a policy option.

From the outset, Mulroney was certainly aware of the potential problems involved in negotiating such a deal; he knew what had happened to Laurier in 1911. In Chicago, on December 4, he said that "our political sovereignty, our system of social programs, our commitment to fight regional disparities, our unique cultural identity, our special linguistic character – these are the essence of Canada. . . . They are not at issue in these negotiations."

The negotiations began in Washington in June 1986 after an initial meeting in Ottawa in May. They proved to be complicated and difficult. Relations between Simon Reisman and the American negotiator, Peter Murphy, were prickly; Reisman, an abrasive veteran of trade negotiations, seemed offended to be dealing with a more junior official, while Murphy didn't seem to enjoy being condescended to in public. American politicians made it clear that Canada's goals of a binding dispute-settlement mechanism and exemption from U.S. trade-remedy laws were unlikely to be achieved.

On September 23, 1987, Reisman walked out of the negotiations, and it looked like an impasse. It appeared that nothing acceptable to the Americans could be palatable politically in Canada, and vice versa. However, a final session started on October 2 after a last-minute intervention by Mulroney's chief of staff, Derek Burney, and Reagan's Secretary of the Treasury, James Baker.

On October 4, the deal was announced. A Free Trade Agreement had been negotiated. The subsidy question had been deferred for seven years of further negotiations; Canada had not succeeded in getting a true, binding dispute-settlement mechanism, but only a binational panel which would examine disputes to see if the United States had breached American law, or if Canada had broken Canadian law. Similarly, Canada had not won exemption from retaliatory trade measures.

The agreement reduced all tariff barriers in ten steps over nine years, granted "national treatment" to the goods, individuals, and corporations of both countries, and laid the groundwork for harmonization of technical regulations in a wide variety of fields. It gave American banks access to Canadian markets, but didn't provide reciprocal access to Canadian banks as long as banks are regulated by the states rather than the U.S. government. It also limited the power of the Canadian government to control energy exports to the United States, making it impossible for any future Canadian government to restore the National Energy Program. But, as Ian McDougall of Osgoode Hall Law School pointed out, "it also may reduce dramatically the provinces' control over their resources."

A Decima Research Ltd. poll conducted in early December showed that 51 per cent of Canadians supported the deal and 42 per cent opposed it. According to a Gallup poll taken in early January, just after the deal was signed on January 2, 1988, by Reagan and Mulroney, 48 per cent supported the deal while 32 per cent opposed it.

———

For the next six months, the opposition parties attacked the government almost daily on the Free Trade Agreement, accusing it of having failed to achieve its goals, and having capitulated in the negotiations. Parliament still had to approve the legislation before the agreement would come into force, and the opposition parties were making it clear that they would fight it every step of the way.

The union movement mobilized its resources against the deal, as did a large part of Canada's cultural community.

Margaret Atwood spoke for many in the artistic community when she told the Parliamentary Committee on Free Trade on November 3, 1987, that Canadians had real fears about the deal that had to be addressed.

"We would like to think we're about to get the best of both worlds – Canadian stability and a more caring society, U.S. markets – but what if instead we get their crime rate, health problems and gun laws, and they get our markets or what's left of them?" she asked. Dismissing the accusation of anti-Americanism, she said it was equally foolish to accuse critics of the deal of using emotional arguments, since almost all the arguments had been emotional. "Fear is an emotion, yes, and love of country is an emotion; but greed is an emotion too."

Similarly, the playwright and novelist Rick Salutin wrote that many artists were devastated by news of the deal.

"It pains us to see our country put on the block, our energy resources put out of our control and those of future generations; our ability to behave independently in the world curtailed," he wrote. "As writers, what are we supposed to write our books about, and play our plays and sing our songs – when there is no distinctive Canadian society left? Culture is not about culture, or literature, or art; it is about the way a people lives. What is the point of being a writer or artist in Canada, when Canada is no longer distinctive and in real control of its destiny?"

He argued that Canadian culture was already being severely affected by the deal, because cultural activities exist in a larger context: "the atmosphere in which we live, imagine and express ourselves." This "cultural air" was being altered. "We are inundated with a new imagery. Mr. Wilson says that opponents of the deal are 'dominated by fear and weak of will.' Former Finance Minister Donald Macdonald, who was chairman of the Royal Commission on the Economy, beats his chest like Tarzan and howls 'I don't see Canada as a sort of sheltered workshop for the inefficient, the incompetent or the less than capable.'

"This imagery is Ramboesque and Nietzschean, the image of tough, lean and mean; of winners and losers – and it comes to us from the America of Ronald Reagan. It is the cultural atmosphere of the U.S. marketplace in which all of us, and especially younger Canadians, will increasingly be forced to formulate our thoughts. . . . In the end, free trade is *entirely* a question of culture, because it is a matter of the kind of society we and our descendants will inhabit as a result of the deal."

The pleas by Atwood and Salutin for the rejection of the agreement in the name of a fragile independent society were themes that would be heard for the following year. But, ironically, one of the traditions of Canadian society that made it harder to defeat the deal in the election the opposition parties called for was the three-party system.

In fact, both the Liberal and the New Democratic strategists concluded that a one-issue election might be fatal and, in similar ways, planned their policy announcements during the campaign as a way to try to deflect the campaign from becoming a referendum on free trade.

However, there were indications of public unhappiness about the issue. In early June 1988, a seventy-two-year-old retired Alberta family-court judge, Marjorie Montgomery Bowker, sat down at her desk at home with the eleven hundred pages of the Free Trade Agreement, and spent four weeks, eight hours a day, reading, analysing, and writing about it. What emerged was a fifty-eight-page typescript analysis, which, on July 20, she sent off to a variety of politicians, professional associations, journalists, and private citizens.

"I began and ended my study as a supporter of freer trade," she wrote in her introduction to the published version. "I ended as an opponent of this particular Free Trade Agreement."

She concluded that the agreement would result in job losses in Canada because of the closing down of branch plants, an increase in American takeovers of Canadian firms, and the creation of new firms in the United States rather than in Canada in order to take advantage of the absence of minimum-wage laws in nine states, and the absence of employer contributions to premiums for health care, unemployment insurance, or pensions.

Mrs. Bowker interpreted the chapter on services as meaning that it would be possible for private American chains to operate Canadian hospitals, health services, and commercial blood banks, pointing out that they would be intended to operate at a profit.

"This can only be achieved by reducing staff, lowering wages, and compromising on standards of patient care," she wrote. "While the trend towards privatization may have already begun in Canada, the effect of the Free Trade Agreement is to speed up the process."

She also expressed concern that the negotiations over what constitutes a subsidy would focus on health care, since the American legislation allowed the U.S. to monitor all Canadian subsidy programs in search of unfair subsidies. "No other country is subject to such scrutiny," she wrote. "It is unlikely that Canada's health care system will escape close review. It is equally unlikely that the United States will elevate its system to the level of that in Canada."

Jim Coutts described the brief as "urgent reading for all Canadians" in the *Toronto Star* on July 31, and a month later, just as debate was ending on the agreement in the House of Commons, Roy MacGregor wrote a column in the *Citizen* in which he called her "a free-trade thinker for the average citizen." Marjorie Nichols of the *Citizen* followed up a week later with a column in which she wrote, "I think that Marjorie Bowker is what ordinary Canadians have been looking for: an impartial source who can assist them in making one of the most important decisions of their voting lives."

The articles provoked an extraordinary response, as people tried to get copies of her brief. When a printshop owner in Ottawa volunteered to make them available for four dollars – the cost of reproduction – he was swamped with requests, and by the end of September had distributed two thousand copies.

At the end of July, after the Liberal decision to ask the Senate to delay passage of the legislation until an election was held, an Angus Reid poll was published which reiterated the June findings: if an election were called, 35 per cent would vote Tory, 34 per cent Liberal and 28 per cent NDP; however, if the election were fought on the issue of free trade, 40 per cent would vote Conservative, 39 per cent would vote Liberal and only 20 per cent would vote NDP.

It was a clear indication of the dilemma facing the NDP – and opponents of the Free Trade Agreement: the Liberals gained support in the context of the free trade debate, but not enough support to prevent the Conservatives from winning.

At the end of the first week of the election campaign, the Pro-Canada Network published an effective pamphlet challenging the Free Trade Agreement, written by Rick Salutin and illustrated with cartoons by Aislin, the Montreal *Gazette* cartoonist Terry Mosher, which, at a cost of some $650,000, was inserted in newspapers across the country. Candidates campaigning door to door found that the pamphlet had a dramatic effect on the questions they were asked. But when Turner's performance in the debate triggered an overwhelming response from corporate Canada, the Pro-Canada Network did not have the resources to muster another volley.

Worse, although they were able to urge Canadians to vote strategically, they were not able to tell individual voters in specific ridings how they could vote most effectively to stop the trade deal. And they were not able to reach Quebec with their appeal to essentially English-Canadian cultural nationalism.

When John Turner performed as well as he did in the debates, he was able to reach out and stimulate anxieties which had already been aroused by the opposition criticisms of the bill, and by the various critics of the agreement. As part of their artillery, the Conservatives were able to deploy two important spokesmen: Emmett Hall in English Canada, and Claude Castonguay in Quebec.

On November 3, Emmett Hall, a retired judge of the Supreme Court, spoke to a news conference in Saskatoon. At

THE PARTING OF THE WAYS

eighty-nine, he was best known for having headed a royal
commission on health services which in 1964 recommended
the introduction of a national medical-insurance program.
He was widely viewed as the father of medicare.

"I am here to tell you there is nothing in this agreement
damaging to medicare in Canada," Hall said. "If I had found
there were in this Free Trade Agreement provisions which
would damage medicare or would destroy it . . . I would have
opposed the agreement because medicare is perhaps one of
the things I hold dearest in life today."

He said that he had got a copy of the deal to check the
allegations made by Turner and Broadbent. "After a complete
study of the document, I could only conclude they were not
being truthful about what is in the document," he said. "If it
had [affected medicare] I would have been out there lambast-
ing the agreement too, but search as I could and did, I could
find nothing in this agreement to support the arguments
being made."

Claude Castonguay, who had introduced the hospital-
insurance system in Quebec in the early 1970s, made a similar
statement. They provided the response that Tory candidates
needed. John Bosley, campaigning in Toronto, could feel the
mood change almost immediately; he had an answer to the
questions about medicare, and he gave it again and again.
Lucien Bouchard could feel the same thing in Lac-Saint-Jean.

CHAPTER FOURTEEN

Sovereignty-Association Upside Down

"Secret of political success in Canada – that of keeping Scottish Presbyterians and French Canadians in the same party."

Harold Innis

Brian Mulroney, as everyone around him knew, felt more comfortable campaigning in Quebec: he was looser, more relaxed, and got an energy from the enthusiasm of the crowds, which was striking in comparison with the response he got in the rest of the country. Moreover, the two principal accomplishments of his first mandate, Free Trade and Meech Lake, had a political resonance and consensus in Quebec that had no counterpart in the other provinces.

In fact, in symbolic terms, Mulroney had succeeded in turning the Parti Québécois formula of sovereignty-association – political sovereignty and an economic association with the rest of Canada – upside down. He never mentioned the words. He never made the connection overtly. But with the Free Trade Agreement, he was offering Quebec the ideal of economic independence; with Meech Lake, he was offering a political association with the rest of Canada. It was a powerful symbolic combination, which enabled him to recreate the coalition of 1984, marrying the traditional Quebec nationalists with the upwardly mobile middle class, enamoured of the entrepreneurial spirit.

As a result, much of his campaign in Quebec sounded strangely reminiscent of René Lévesque's unsuccessful Yes campaign during the 1980 referendum on giving the Quebec government a mandate to negotiate sovereignty-association. Lévesque tried to create a non-partisan coalition, easing Quebeckers' fears of political and economic uncertainty by seeking a mandate for political independence and economic association. He tried to bring together all the nationalist forces to reach out beyond the Parti Québécois ranks for support, presenting former Liberal and Union Nationale ministers who endorsed the Yes position.

Mulroney was able to point to the fact that the Liberal Premier Robert Bourassa, the Parti Québécois leader Jacques Parizeau, and Mayor Jean Doré of Montreal all supported the Free Trade Agreement, not to mention the new stars of the business class, and all the major French-language newspapers. The sense of identification with free trade was overwhelming; the three-party consensus in support of Meech Lake was solid, with the only criticisms coming from the Parti Québécois and the Quebec NDP, who said that it did not go far enough, and did not give Quebec enough powers.

In fact, Mulroney's skill in building support in Quebec was a crucial element, not only in the election campaign, but throughout his leadership of the Conservative Party, and his first mandate as prime minister.

When Mulroney ran for the leadership of the Conservative Party, he promised that he would deliver support from Quebec; the key rhetorical element of his campaign was the argument that the Conservatives could never win if they conceded the hundred seats with populations more than 15 per cent francophone. Then, in 1984, he set out to make good on that commitment by running for a seat in Manicouagan, the Lower North Shore constituency where Baie-Comeau was located.

Interestingly, the fact that Mulroney decided to run in Quebec not only helped ensure the wave of Tory support, it indirectly guaranteed him more sympathetic news coverage. For once he became a candidate in Quebec it meant that between 30 and 40 per cent of the campaign would be in Quebec. This meant that major news organizations had to assign bilingual reporters to the Mulroney campaign, at least for the time it was in Quebec. Almost inevitably, the bilingual anglophone reporters senior enough to be on the leader's campaign plane had worked in Montreal in the 1970s; almost equally inevitably, they knew Brian Mulroney. If they had not actually met him, they felt a private pride that an Anglo-Quebecker was doing so well. The francophone reporters responded to him simply as a Quebecker. The result was an environment of positive response.

In contrast, with few exceptions, the reporters covering John Turner knew him only as a former finance minister whose lunches at Winston's were celebrated by columnists who treated him as a crown prince. The reaction was vigorous skepticism among the reporters accompanying him.

Coming into Sept-Îles in early August 1984, Mulroney was relaxed and comfortable. Asked about whether he was concerned about the fact that his federal riding included two provincial ridings that had elected Parti Québécois members and had voted Yes in the referendum in 1980, Mulroney gave a revealing answer. "That was in 1980 – a lifetime ago," he said. "People want federal-provincial co-operation, they want change, they want realistic attitudes. They know we can't afford seventy-two strikes a year. Nobody owes us a living, and people have finally realized that."

It was a hint of the new direction he was about to take with regard to Quebec and federal-provincial relations. In the pre-referendum period, Mulroney had been a member of the Pro-Canada Committee, and gave every indication that he shared Pierre Trudeau's view of Canada and the constitution. During the leadership campaign, he had both criticized Joe Clark for "cosying up to the separatists" – and hinted that he would be more co-operative and less confrontational than Trudeau in his dealings with the provinces. But he had scrupulously avoided specifics.

At his nomination meeting on August 6, he delivered what became known as the Sept-Îles speech, in which he laid out his idea of federal-provincial conciliation and vowed to make it possible for the Quebec National Assembly to sign the constitutional agreement "with honour and enthusiasm." It was a passionate appeal to Quebeckers who voted Yes in the 1980 sovereignty-association referendum, and a vigorous attack on the Liberal government for its handling of the constitutional question after the referendum.

"In Quebec – and it is very obvious – there are wounds to be healed, worries to be calmed, enthusiasms to be rekindled and bonds of trust to be established," he said. "The men and women of this province have undergone a collective trauma."

Mulroney spoke of the motivations of those who voted in the referendum, suggesting that "very few of those who said 'Yes' to Quebec said 'No' to Canada, and not one of those who said 'Yes' to Canada said 'No' to Quebec. One thing is certain," he continued. "Not one Quebecker authorized the federal Liberals to take advantage of the confusion that prevailed in Quebec following the referendum in order to ostracize the province constitutionally. My party takes no pleasure in the politically weak position in which these events have placed Quebec. If Quebec is weakened, then Canada is weakened. If Quebec is strong, then Canada is strong."

It was a remarkable appeal to nationalist sentiment in Quebec, given his previous criticisms of Joe Clark for his tolerant attitude toward the Parti Québécois. The speech was full of code-words aimed at those who voted for the PQ in 1981, and who were angry at the way Quebec was left out of the constitutional settlement the same year. He stressed that he would deal with the "duly and legitimately elected" Quebec government – meaning the Parti Québécois; he referred to his proposed federal-provincial council as an organization for permanent "concertation," a term used frequently by the Quebec government and the PQ; and he referred to the "eleven

first ministers," (a careful use of the equivalent to premier ministre, used for both premier and prime minister in French) rather
than describing the provincial premiers in a way that would
suggest that they were part of a junior level of government.

The speech was important at several levels. It sent a message to Parti Québécois supporters that if they wanted to get
rid of the Liberal Party, Mulroney represented a palatable
alternative; it laid the first stone in his long-term objective of
reaching a constitutional agreement with Quebec; and it sig-
nified in public terms the message that he had been delivering privately.

Mulroney was all too aware that he did not have a party
organization in Quebec. He had to be able to bring together
people who not only had never worked together before, but
had fought on opposite sides. He had moved a long way
himself on the constitutional issue, largely under the influence of Lucien Bouchard, the Chicoutimi lawyer he had got to
know at Laval, and whom he had brought in to work as a
counsel on the Cliche Commission.

"Brian matured in his attitude towards Quebec," Bouchard
said. "In his development, he reflected the development in
English Canada."

He argued that Mulroney grew to understand the need for
conciliation in Quebec, the desire for an end to conflict
between Quebec and Ottawa, and the need to draw the province into acceptance of the new Constitution to make it legitimate.

There were political and organizational imperatives
behind such an approach. For when Mulroney became
leader, the party was virtually non-existent as an organization
in Quebec. "We were a small group – and I include myself in
this – of losers," the veteran Conservative Gary Ouellet said.
"We had the lowest employees in every company. We had the
janitors, while the Liberals had the company presidents and
the general managers."

The Conservatives had to convince people in Quebec that
they could be winners, and they had to convince people in

the other provinces (and in the party) that this was occurring.

Mulroney began by naming Jean Bazin as co-chairman of the national campaign with Norman Atkins, and the advertising man Roger Nantel co-chairman of the advertising and communications campaign. But, as he always did, Mulroney relied on a core group of friends which included Bouchard, Michel Cogger, and the Quebec City lawyer Gary Ouellet. He named Bernard Roy as director of the party, and relied on the experience of Rodrigue Pageau, a veteran Union Nationale organizer who had been Joe Clark's Quebec communications director in the 1979 election, but had joined the Mulroney forces in 1981. (Pageau, at that point, was ill with cancer, but would come to Baie-Comeau from his hospital bed to enjoy the election victory.)

"It's really a mixture of old-time Tories, university friends – all the network of people that Brian has established over a period of thirty years," Cogger said in an interview after the election. "He called upon his old schoolmates, friends in the business community, friends from St. Francis Xavier and Laval. . . . You bring them all together and you begin to have quite a bunch of people to roll with."

The construction of a credible, effective party in Quebec that could appeal to Quebeckers had three aspects: the building of an organization, the search for and selection of strong candidates, and the development of an effective message.

At the organizational level, Bazin, Roy, and Pageau set out to replace a group that had been a mixture of weary loyalists and young, rather eccentric former Créditistes. "All our energies were focused on the creation of an organization on the ground, which did not exist," Bazin said.

The organizers began a membership drive and a fund-raising campaign that, combined with Mulroney's two-month dry-run campaign tour in March and April, enabled the party to develop and test the machine. At the same time, work was begun to find candidates. In October 1983, the party established a candidate-selection committee, which met in Montreal every week. It consisted of Fernand Roberge, the manager of the Ritz-Carlton and a friend of Mulroney's; Roy, Pageau, Bazin, Ouellet and Jacques Vasseur, who was in the personnel management business. Later, Michel Cogger and Marc Lefrançois joined the committee.

The committee would meet, usually at the Ritz, and go over the ridings. "We'd take every riding," Ouellet said, "and go through a list of five or six people: 'He's interested, he's not, he's thinking, he wants to meet Brian.' Whenever we ended up recruiting three people, we would hold a nominating convention – at which point others would often jump in." Then, during the week, members of the committee would scout out more people – sometimes setting up subsidiary committees for different regions.

Often, prospective candidates would meet Mulroney, who sometimes told them bluntly that he was working eighteen hours a day and that this was what it would take to win.

"I can bring you 40 per cent [of the vote] – you're going to have to get the last 10 per cent yourself," he would say. Some would-be candidates expressed disbelief, asked for time to consider – and were dropped. Others dismayed the organizers by their determination.

In many cases, conventions became key morale-boosting events, and the timing was chosen for the maximum effect. In the Beauce, four thousand people showed up at Gilles Bernier's nomination meeting in November. Other key nomination meetings were held in Trois-Rivières – where five thousand people showed up in the spring to choose Pierre Vincent – at Jean Charest's hotly contested nomination in Sherbrooke, and in Mégantic-Compton-Stanstead, where François Gérin was chosen. All were successful events that added to the Conservatives' sense of momentum in Quebec. More important than simply the machinery of the party was the evolution of the message being delivered in Quebec. As in the rest of the country, the party sensed a desire for change. In Quebec, this was interpreted to mean a new conciliatory attitude toward the Quebec government and nationalist sensibilities.

This conciliatory attitude became a requirement for Tory organizers, many of whom grumbled that they were working with people they had fought tooth and nail. After the leadership convention, some Mulroney supporters had looked forward to a blood-letting, and one of the principal targets was Suzanne Duplessis, a Clark supporter who was already a nominated candidate in Louis-Hébert, a suburban Quebec City riding, and had presided over the Oui campaign in the provincial riding in 1980. "One of the things I like about Brian is that he bears grudges," chortled one organizer gleefully. "As he always says, 'Let us all gather together and settle old scores!'"

But Mulroney had learned to stop saying that. It was, in the phrase he used in the Sept-Îles speech, a time to heal old wounds, not settle old scores. Péquistes, provincial Liberals, Clark supporters, Mulroney supporters, former Union Nationale veterans, even former Créditistes, all worked together in Quebec while, across Canada, English Canadians turned away from a Liberal Party that had become tired and ineffective.

For months after Mulroney's Sept-Îles speech, there was little indication that he was moving to deal with the constitutional issue. Pierre Marc Johnson, René Lévesque's minister of justice and minister responsible for Canadian intergovernmental affairs, presented a sweeping proposal in the spring of 1985, which summarized every idea for increased power and jurisdiction Quebec had ever had. But the proposal never went very far, since Lévesque resigned a month later.

But there were some preliminary steps being taken. In the fall of 1984, Mulroney named Lucien Bouchard ambassador to Paris, with a mandate to clear the roadblocks that had prevented Canada, Quebec, and France from reaching an agreement on terms for a Francophone Summit. At the same time, he hired a Laval constitutional-law professor, Gil Rémillard, as his constitutional adviser. Rémillard had argued, in a two-volume book on Canadian federalism, that the formula for opting out of constitutional changes with financial compensation, which René Lévesque had endorsed in 1981, did not protect Quebec from changes in federal institutions.

In the fall of 1985, Rémillard resigned as an adviser to run as a Liberal candidate in the Quebec election. Bourassa was campaigning explicitly on a five-point Liberal program of conditions for accepting the constitution: participation in naming Supreme Court judges, powers in immigration, the limitation of federal spending powers, the recognition of Quebec as a distinct society, and a veto for Quebec on constitutional changes.

Five months later, in May 1986, Rémillard, now holding Pierre Marc Johnson's former portfolio, presented those terms to a conference at Mont-Gabriel, a ski resort in the Laurentians. They were the same terms, but with some interesting nuances. Rémillard pointed out that a veto was necessary for Quebec because it could not opt out of the Supreme Court or the Senate: a hint that Quebec might be prepared to accept a limited veto on changes to federal institutions.

That conference attracted some of the veterans of two decades of constitutional debate: a former deputy minister of justice, Roger Tassé; an Alberta constitutional adviser, Peter Meekison; a former clerk of the privy council, Gordon Robertson; Quebec Senator Arthur Tremblay; and various federal and provincial civil servants. When they rolled up their sleeves and examined the Quebec proposal, the consensus that emerged was clear: there was the chance of an agreement on the basis of Quebec's five points, but the issue had to be carefully handled, and limited to that list alone. Any additions would kill it.

Some of the older, wiser heads around the table suggested that the process should be carried on very discreetly. For, they said, a failure would be worse than no attempt at all. Gordon Robertson, who had played a key role on the federal side in the past, argued very forcefully that the time was appropriate for an agreement between Quebec and the rest of Canada, and that the result might be serious over the long term if the opportunity was missed.

There was little public reaction from the federal government to the Rémillard speech. But in June Mulroney named Senator Lowell Murray as the minister of state for federal-provincial relations and, when he gave him the job, also gave him a copy of the Sept-Îles speech. In his view, Murray was the only person who could do the job, because the minister dealing with the issue had to be an English Canadian who knew Quebec and spoke French, and was not in the House of Commons facing the barrage of Question Period every day. Lowell Murray, the usher at Mulroney's wedding who had hurt his feelings so badly when he did not support his leadership campaign in 1976, was that person.

The next piece on the chessboard had to be a senior civil servant. Mulroney believed that, despite their competence, there was a reservoir of distrust in the provinces for the officials who had worked on the issue. To reduce that, he sought out Norman Spector, a bilingual Montreal-born civil servant who had worked in Ontario and British Columbia, and made him secretary to the cabinet for federal-provincial relations. Spector, who had advised British Columbia during the 1981 constitutional negotiations, set to work on the details of a federal counter-proposal.

Finally, in a gesture that attracted little public attention but sent a powerful signal to the provinces, Mulroney named Murray to the crucial priorities and planning committee of cabinet. It meant that Murray was an extremely important member of the government: a message that provincial officials picked up immediately.

Together, Murray and Gil Rémillard began sounding out and briefing premiers and provincial officials. Gradually the elements of a deal began to emerge. However, there was a growing problem in Western Canada. The collapse of the economy from the simultaneous crises in oil and grain prices focused Western discontent on Senate reform as a way of giving the provinces a stronger voice in Ottawa.

While the federal government was discussing the issue privately with the provinces, the Liberals and the New Democrats were wrestling with Bourassa's five points in public and, with greater or lesser difficulty, passing resolutions at their conventions endorsing the idea of recognizing Quebec as, if not a distinct society, at least something different. This established a tri-partisan climate of support for negotiations.

On April 30, the premiers met Mulroney at Meech Lake, ostensibly to discuss whether or not there was a possibility of pursuing discussions further. At ten o'clock in the evening, they emerged with an agreement: the Meech Lake Accord. Mulroney agreed to restrict his power to name senators and Supreme Court judges, by limiting the choice to lists of names submitted by the provinces. Quebec would be recognized as a distinct society, and its agreement with the federal government on immigration would be entrenched in the constitution.

Going to Meech Lake, Mulroney and his advisers faced two firmly held positions, which had to be reconciled in some way. On the one hand, Quebec was determined to avoid ever again being ganged up on by nine other provinces, and insisted on some form of self-protective veto. On the other hand, Alberta and Newfoundland in particular were determined to maintain the principle of equality of provinces.

What emerged was a shrewdly layered deal. The premiers agreed to require unanimity for changes to federal institutions – in part because it was clear politically that Ottawa would veto a proposal unacceptable to it or Quebec – and, at the same time, they agreed to a commitment to discuss Senate reform. Premier Don Getty of Alberta had proposed that, in the meantime, provinces be able to name senators. Brian Peckford of Newfoundland offered a compromise. A federal counter-offer had already suggested that Supreme Court Judges be named by Ottawa from lists proposed by the provinces, he pointed out; why not do the same thing with senators? The agreement was struck and the premiers rose and gave Brian Mulroney an ovation.

For a month, the agreement was debated; Pierre Trudeau emerged from private life to denounce it as a betrayal of the federal government's authority. In a passionate article published in *La Presse* and the *Toronto Star* at the end of May,

he tore into it with the verve and invective that had characterized his writings twenty-five years earlier in *Cité Libre*.

His central point, which he repeated before the joint committee of the Senate and the House of Commons, and later at a
hearing by the Senate, was that the accord would mean the
end of a bilingual Canada.

"Those who have never wanted a bilingual Canada – Quebec separatists and western separatists – get their wish right
in the first paragraphs of the accord, with recognition of the
'existence of French-speaking Canada . . . and English-
speaking Canada,'" he wrote. "Those Canadians who fought
for a single Canada, bilingual and multicultural, can say
goodbye to their dream: we are henceforth to have two Cana-
das, each defined in terms of language."

Further, he argued, those who never wanted a Charter of
Rights had won a victory, because the "distinct society"
clause would mean that the Charter would have to be interpreted so that it did not interfere with Quebec's "distinct
society."

But, while Trudeau's analysis struck to the heart of the
arguments against the accord, it had little direct impact on
the premiers when they gathered at the Langevin Block on
June 3 to approve the legal text of the agreement – except in so
far as his words had put some pressure on Ontario's Liberal
Premier David Peterson. Perhaps partly as a result of that
pressure, there was a change made to the "distinct society"
clause.

At Meech Lake, the premiers had agreed that "(1) The Constitution of Canada shall be interpreted in a manner consistent with

"a) The recognition that the existence of French-speaking
Canada, centred in but not limited to Quebec, and English-
speaking Canada, concentrated outside Quebec but also
present in Quebec, constitutes a fundamental characteristic
of Canada; and

"b) the recognition that Quebec constitutes within Canada
a distinct society."

Further, Parliament and the provincial legislatures were committed to "preserving" the fundamental characteristic described in 1a) while Quebec was given the role to "preserve and promote the distinct identity of Quebec referred to in paragraph 1b)."

At the all-night session at the Langevin Block, a slight change in wording was hammered out, so that it was not the existence of French-speaking Canada and English-speaking Canada that was recognized as a fundamental characteristic, but "the existence of French-speaking Canadians" and "English-speaking Canadians."

All three federal party leaders endorsed the accord, so that no true national debate on the question could be held in the House of Commons, or in the election campaign. But, while the issue was not a formal part of what separated the parties in the 1988 election, the problem it represented would haunt both the Liberals and the New Democrats and be a central part of Mulroney's success. However, it remains to be seen how the ambiguities of the accord will be interpreted as the debate over the nature of the country continues.

With Marcel Côté's strategic analysis, the advertising campaign was fairly straightforward. The campaign began with ads showing Mulroney talking about job creation and economic growth; one showed a black and white photograph of a decrepit factory with Mulroney's voice saying, "Remember what it was like four years ago; the country was in a state of uncertainty." Then, sitting behind his desk in full colour, Mulroney says, "You then gave us a mandate to change things. We kept our word, and now things are better."

The slogan for all the French-language commercials was "Continuons dans le bons sens" – a pun meaning both "let's continue in the right direction," and "let's keep up the good sense."

When it became clear that free trade was the central issue, and that there were substantial worries about social programs, one commercial said that those who claimed that the Free Trade Agreement affected social programs were flatly distorting the deal. Mulroney then said, "Never will our social programs – unemployment insurance, health insurance – be touched by the agreement. Never. To oppose free trade is to compromise our prosperity."

A particularly powerful commercial showed a woman's hand, in front of three lights, similar to the buttons in a game show, with a digital clock flicking past. A voice said that on November 21, people had to choose the government. Who was the person best suited to lead the country? "John Turner, who lied to us on free trade, and is unable to lead his own party?" the voice asked. "Surely not."

In the first week in November, when it looked as if the victory was slipping away because of the Liberal onslaught on the Free Trade Agreement, Lucien Bouchard was losing patience. He had been questioned by senior citizens, and the people whom pollsters identified as shifting from the Tories to the Liberals: those over fifty-five, earning less than $20,000, and most vulnerable to threats to pensions, unemployment insurance, and medicare, and in Quebec the people who voted No in the 1980 referendum.

"I was beginning to get fed up, watching Quebec get frightened, when we know very well it's in Quebec's interest as much as the rest of Canada's, or at least that was what I thought," he told me later. "We could see Ontario attacking the idea, and I was getting a bit discouraged."

He decided to speak out on the issue at a local press conference on local issues when a reporter asked him about it. "Here is Ontario, which almost invented the idea of trade with the United States, and they are acting as if Quebec shouldn't do the same thing," he recalled saying. Radio-Canada picked up the tape from a local station that had covered the press conference, and reporters began calling him. Bouchard's argument was that opposition to free trade was basically a plot by the Ontario establishment to retain its wealth and privileges at the expense of the rest of the country, particularly Quebec.

"When I see David Peterson and John Turner congratulating one another in joy in Toronto because they might regain power in Ottawa, I say the rest of the country should think again," he told Benoît Aubin. "The West, the Maritimes, Quebec don't seem to be part of their cause to celebrate."

Bouchard drew a parallel between the free-trade debate in 1988 and the referendum on sovereignty-association in 1980, saying that in both campaigns, "Liberals, Ontarians, intervened heavily to scare a fraction of the Quebec population into preserving the status quo." He thought it significant that the opposition to free trade in the name of the Canadian identity came principally from Ontario.

"The Americans are worried because their market is flooded with Japanese products, but Ontario alone sells more to the United States than the whole of Japan. Ontario is the pipeline through which Canadian and American wealth are traded," he said. "And all of a sudden, Ontario says 'Be careful, you guys in Quebec; don't trade too heavily with the United States, it is bad for our Canadian identity.' I find that very peculiar.... Look at this debate with the eyes of a Quebecker from the Yes side. In 1980, Ontarians came to Quebec to tell us: 'You are ghettoizing yourselves. Don't do that. Open up to the world instead. Do like us.'

"Well, they convinced us," he continued. "Quebec chose not to separate, and to become an active partner in Confederation and to open up to the world. Now, they want us to stop? That happens every time Quebec is on the verge of a breakthrough. Quebec has decided to do things right, and to play the game by the book. We have become a vibrant, aggressive partner in Confederation. And now, Ontario tells us: 'Hold it. You, in Quebec, just stay at home, and just be an economic ghetto vis-à-vis the United States. We'll do the trading with them, and you'll get the equalization payments.'

"It gives me the impression that Quebec is the one playing straight inside Confederation and that Ontario has become the separatist force, the one that wants to go it alone. That makes me angry."

It was an emotional outburst that expressed how deeply the free-trade issue had captured both traditional nationalists in Quebec, and the new believers in the entrepreneurial ethic.

The next day, Bouchard received a lot of calls from worried Tories, convinced he had made a gaffe. But he was convinced that he was right, and that it had been a political coup, not a gaffe: Quebec had been losing its nerve over free trade, and he wanted to get the message to English Canada that voting against free trade would be interpreted as voting against Quebec.

"I felt that Ontario could not accept the idea of Quebec electing a government without also participating in that government," he said. "I was certain that if we stressed the strength of the party in Quebec, and showed that Quebec was getting ready to support the government massively and re-elect the government, Ontario could not be left outside the government, and there would be a split in the anti-free-trade reaction to the government's benefit."

The idea was shared by some of the people on the Mulroney plane, and, by the end of the campaign, by the Tory organization as a whole. A major part of the last weeks of the campaign was a plan to drive home to English Canada the strength of Tory support in Quebec.

The Liberals in Quebec could see the situation as clearly as the Quebec Tories could. Starting in September 1987, André Morrow had begun examining the opinion polling done by Marcel Giner, and very much the same picture had emerged. The NDP had soared to artificial heights, but closer examination revealed that, while people liked Ed Broadbent, they didn't know much about the NDP, which did not have an easily identifiable group of Quebec candidates. Mulroney's popularity had been affected by the conflict-of-interest scandals, but he remained personally popular. Turner was regarded as a weak leader, at the head of a divided party.

In the spring, Turner had performed extremely well at the convention in Montreal, walking about the stage with a hand-held microphone, taking questions. But a few days later, the caucus revolt became public. André Morrow felt that one hour's worth of newscasts on the revolt had destroyed a month of work.

There were deeper problems, however. Morrow, after all, had worked successfully with Robert Bourassa in 1985 in a similar situation: Bourassa was personally unpopular and viewed as weak, while Premier Pierre Marc Johnson was personally popular. The unfortunate difference was that in 1988 the federal Liberals had a divided party in Quebec: Raymond Garneau had not been able to neutralize Bourassa's tacit support for Mulroney; the top level of Trudeau lieutenants in Quebec like Chrétien and Lalonde were gone, and replaced by the second level: André Ouellet, Francis Fox, and Serge Joyal – and it was unclear whether Fox and Joyal would run. Deeper than personalities was the problem of the issue: the federal Liberals had become separated from their natural constituency in Quebec – the business community and the middle class – over free trade. Turner could not easily stand on a platform surrounded by the leading figures in Quebec who were opposed to the Free Trade Agreement: union leaders. And the Meech Lake Accord separated Turner from the Quebec heritage of the federal party: Trudeau, Lalonde, and Chrétien.

However, the Tories did have weaknesses, and the strategy decided on over the summer was to focus on those weaknesses, and emphasize pollution and the environment.

In the Liberal advertising campaign, there were three phases: a negative phase, a teamwork phase, and a Turner phase.

"In the first phase, we had to attack the credibility of Brian Mulroney and his government," Morrow told me later. "Lucien Bouchard had already set the tone in Lac-Saint-Jean: election goodies, an element of party renewal, and the disappearance of Tory ministers. So in the first phase of the campaign, we set out to attack the outgoing government, above all on its weak points: integrity, and its poor record on pollution and the environment."

In focus groups, the slogan "C'est clair et net" (literally, it's clear and clean; the phrase also suggested the idea of perfectly straightforward, quite obvious, a clean sweep) made people think of transparency in government, integrity, and precise political ideas: suggesting that, while things were murky under the Conservatives, the Liberals were preparing something very clear.

The first set of commercials, which were designed to attack the credibility of the Mulroney government, were rough: as negative as anything in Quebec politics since the 1979 Tory ads, which had been punctuated by what sounded like the slam of a prison door. One thirty-second Liberal commercial, in black and white, showed the sombre façade of a pillared courthouse.

"In 1984, Brian Mulroney had us believe that his government would be honest and trustworthy," the announcer's voice said. "That was a lie. Never has a government known so many scandals." Then, just as the names flashed on the screen, the voice intoned "Robert Coates, John Fraser, Roch LaSalle, Suzanne Blais-Grenier, André Bissonnette, Michel Côté, without forgetting Sinclair Stevens and Michel Gravel." Then a judge's gavel slammed down with a bang, and the voice said "Enough! We want a trustworthy and honest government. Let's vote for the Liberal team, because a Liberal government is open and clean (clair et net)."

Other commercials showed shots of an actor intended to be Mulroney, with glimpses of his cufflinks (B.M.) as he sat at what was represented as the prime minister's desk, complete with a photograph of Mulroney and Reagan. "Ah, that salesman and his promises," the announcer's voice said. "He tried to reduce old-age pensions and family allowances. He did nothing for women, young people, the elderly. He favoured the rich and over-taxed low-income earners. And he offered us some beautiful scandals . . . "

Other ads showed polluted riverbanks, dying forests, empty factories, and a farm with a for-sale sign on it as a huge trailer truck labelled "U.S. fresh" whizzed past. One showed two flagpoles, with a Canadian and a Quebec flag; the flags were lowered, and two American flags were raised as an announcer said that while the Liberals favoured freer trade, they did not want it at the expense of sovereignty.

The second phase of Liberal advertising stressed team-work. This was a theme that Morrow had used in the television advertising for the Quebec Liberals in 1985: shots of candidates sitting around a table with the leader, all of them in their shirtsleeves. Different ads picked up different candi-dates speaking about different issues: youth unemployment, agriculture, free trade; none of them had Turner actually saying anything.

Only in the final phase of the campaign, after his success in the debates, did any of the commercials use John Turner.

One Liberal candidate in Quebec who succeeded in keeping his campaign relatively independent of the central Liberal campaign and the free-trade debate was Jean-Claude Malé-part in the Montreal riding of Laurier – Sainte-Marie. At forty-nine he had been a Liberal MP since 1979; before that, he had been a Liberal member of the National Assembly from 1973 until 1976, when he was defeated by Guy Bisaillon of the Parti Québécois. Short, round, gravel-voiced and energetic, Malé-part was a tireless campaigner on behalf of the east end of Montreal, the elderly, and those on social assistance. He spoke almost no English and, as a result, was little known outside Quebec; however, his opposition to the government's plan to de-index pensions in 1985 had won him a substantial following in the province.

Big-bellied, double-chinned, Malépart echoed the streets of east-end Montreal with every word he uttered, every gut-tural vowel and rolled r. He was an enthusiast: a populist who, once elected in 1979, worked effectively with the former union organizer who had defeated him provincially, lobbying and pressuring, speaking out for the working class of Mon-treal. Before being elected, he had worked to get a variety of senior citizens' homes established; he continued doing so in office, pushing youth groups and senior citizens' groups to get established, get organized, apply for grants. In his biographical sketch in the *Parliamentary Guide*, he described himself in French as an administrator and an *animateur* – a word with no equivalent in English, meaning community organizer. The English translation given was "promoter" – which, of course, he was, in a way.

On October 19, he held a meeting in his riding to announce his commitment to senior citizens – and, to endorse him, he was accompanied by Solange Denis, the feisty little pensioner who had told Brian Mulroney that he had lied to them, and that at the next election it would be "bye-bye Charlie Brown."

When he spoke in his committee room, full of people from senior citizens' groups and community organizations, Malépart used the language of the union organizer, telling them how they had forced the government to back off on its plan to de-index pensions, tax medicine, and cut off unemployment insurance from those who had taken early retirement.

"After seventeen months of struggle, the government reimbursed forty-five thousand people on early retirement," he said. "I will continue the struggle to end discrimination against workers."

Like any effective union organizer, he knew the details of the social programs that mattered most to his people, and told vivid stories to illustrate the injustice of the system.

"Take three people living alone," he said. "Each one is sixty-two; they live in the same building, pay the same rent; all three are on welfare. They go to the pension office to enquire about the supplement. Are you a widow or a widower? Yes? You get it. Are you separated? They don't give it to you. Are you single? Sorry – you should have married, and he or she should have died."

They laughed and applauded, and clapped some more when Malépart said that the Liberal Party was going to look at making people eligible for pensions at sixty, beginning with those in need, regardless of their marital status.

Malépart had withstood the Tory wave in Quebec in 1984 by 2,749 votes – a squeaker compared to 1980, when he had won by 15,582 votes, and 1979, when he had won by 12,371. This time, he was facing Charles Hamelin, the former MP for Charlevoix who had stepped aside to make room for Mulroney, and François Beaulne, a former diplomat and executive at the Banque Nationale running for the NDP.

"I don't come from the North Shore like a hair on the soup," he told his audience. "I don't come from Ontario like the candidate for the NDP (Beaulne had once run for the NDP in Ottawa-Vanier), who arrives here two weeks before the election and discovers that he loves you. I've spent my whole life in the riding, I go door to door every year, and this year we did twenty-nine lunch-encounters to find out the needs of the elderly. And I can tell you, the first suggestion you made, which I am going to struggle for, is that we will establish with the provinces a real program of support for the elderly at home, and we will offer some services, not only medical services but housekeeping services for the elderly at home. I can tell you, there will be projects like that in the riding."

It was classic grass-roots politics: while Malépart was denouncing the government in the House of Commons for its heartlessness, mobilizing demonstrators on the Hill, and fighting for more funding for social programs, he was also using his discretionary funds and applying for grants to enable community groups to organize specific programs to help the elderly stay in their homes.

"You are the generation of the Depression; there were no Registered Retirement Savings Plans then; everyone had to put a little bit aside, and buy Canada Savings Bonds, or invest something," he said. "Previously, the first thousand dollars was deductible from your income tax. Unfortunately, in the last budget, the Conservative government eliminated this completely, without taking into account the fact that, for a whole generation whose only way to prepare for their retirement was to put money aside, they were being penalized."

Heads nodded, and when he said that the Liberals were committed to restoring this deduction and improving it slightly, there was applause.

He finished his speech, pointing out that the people of the riding had always voted for the man rather than the party, and that there were people there who had worked for the provincial Liberals and the Parti Québécois, who normally might have supported the Conservatives or the NDP; that representatives of seven unions had endorsed him.

"The day after the election, if you have a problem, is it the prime minister you'll go to see? The headquarters of the Liberal Party or the Conservative Party?" he asked. "Or is it the MP you'll go and see? Jean-Claude Malépart has proved, in power and in opposition, that he was able to deliver the goods. If you want me to remain your MP, it's simple – on November 21, vote Jean-Claude Malépart."

When the applause subsided, he introduced Solange Denis. A perky, tiny little sparrow of a woman, she bounded onto a chair and enthusiastically endorsed Malépart, who she clearly thought was cute as a button.

There were a number of things worth noting about Jean-Claude Malépart's meeting, that Wednesday morning in his committee room, a few minutes' walk from the Frontenac Métro station. It was a more militant vocabulary than many Liberals, English- or French-speaking, would have been comfortable with: politics for Jean-Claude Malépart is a struggle, an exercise in collective bargaining. As always, his remarks were vivid and colourful, dealing with few abstractions, and many of the nitty-gritty details of the forms, applications, wrinkles, and disappointments of the realities of social programs, as seen from a second-floor balcony or a government office waiting room, where policy is dealt with across a counter, to people who have waited all morning.

In his remarks, he never referred to John Turner. And he only referred to the NDP candidate (who had, in fact, been living in the constituency for some time) as from Ontario.

CHAPTER FIFTEEN

The Eggshells Crack

"The errors which proceed from a spirit of benevolence are the worst."

Von Clausewitz

After the television debate, Ed Broadbent felt that he had done pretty well. Indeed, the transcript shows that he hammered away effectively at the trade deal. In a memo to Broadbent after the election, ruefully signed "Vic, your evil and benighted erstwhile American pollster," Vic Fingerhut pointed out that the criticism that Broadbent had shied away from labour and the trade deal was clearly unfounded.

"Any review of the debate footage makes it clear that Ed took every opportunity to blast the trade deal . . . and he did it not just in narrow terms (i.e. Medicare) but from every conceivable angle, including a broad defence of Canada's sovereignty and a distinctive Canadian way of life," he wrote. ". . . It is clear that Ed's position in the debate – rightly or wrongly – was precisely the position everyone is accusing him of not taking throughout the campaign. It was a broad and all-inclusive critique of the trade deal . . . and an unblinking and unhesitating defence of labour and his support from labour."

But the French debate had tired Broadbent, and it showed; at times during the debate, he seemed testy and irritable. And, while he insisted that he had done well, senior campaign staff felt that he had psychologically taken a pounding, and, in the words of one who saw him the next day in Toronto, "Ed was in terrible, godawful shape."

That day, Wednesday October 26, going into London, Ont., the party was expecting a large crowd of about a thousand people from eight ridings in the London area. The federal office of the party did not expect great things from these ridings, where the NDP had consistently finished third in the past, but the Ontario provincial office felt there was some momentum. But there was also anxiety that the news coverage would focus almost exclusively on the aftermath of the debate.

The briefing note pointed out that there were three plants in the area where people had lost jobs. Two hundred jobs had been eliminated at Fleck Manufacturing Inc. earlier in October, and, at the end of the month, two other firms had announced that layoffs were coming – the Wilton Grove Bendix Plant in London, and the D.G. Trim Products Ltd. plant in Petrolia. Fleck was particularly à propos: it had closed abruptly after a strike vote on September 30; in the middle of the night, equipment was being shipped to a new location in Mexico. The plant was partly owned by James D. Fleck, who had been deputy minister of industry, trade and tourism under the Davis government, and a member of the Mulroney government's advisory committee on the trade talks.

"The real irony: Fleck is also author of a 1985 book called *Canada Can Compete*," the briefing note said. "It called for freeing up the market, lowering the deficit, lowering wages for public sector workers to provide a model for the private sector, low differentials between Canada and U.S. interest rates and a 70-cent dollar."

The note added that the Canadian Auto Workers union was holding a rally at the plant on Friday, and Bob White would be there. "This closure is a good example of how the trade deal will do nothing to stop the loss of Canadian jobs," the note concluded. "It in fact encourages them by giving access to Canada through the back door of the Maquiladora free-trade zone on the U.S. – Canada border."

All three closures seemed relevant. However, one of Broadbent's staff checked with the Canadian Auto Workers, and the union felt only one lay-off other than Fleck should be mentioned in Broadbent's speech.

This information was passed on. However, Broadbent made no mention of any of them. This became a question of some symbolic importance when Bob White lashed out in disappointment about the election results, after the election. But the impression made on most people following the tour was that Broadbent had had a successful evening: the crowd of well over a thousand had exceeded expectations, and was one of the largest the NDP had enjoyed in that area.

However, that particular failure in communications became a kind of symbol of the NDP's failure to hold its ground with union members in Ontario, or move forward in a province where the party had always had some substantial strength. As the resources had been dedicated to making the campaign "the first truly national campaign," as New Democrats kept telling one another, Ontario seemed to slip as a priority for the party. There were fewer prestigious candidates, and a slightly grumpy feeling in parts of the party in Ontario that too much energy, time, and money were being spent in trying to get a breakthrough in Quebec, and too little on building on the existing strengths of the party in Canada's largest province.

In the days that followed, a series of problems occurred which, in addition to stretching the nerves of the campaign staff, revealed some of the weaknesses in the party's development, and in Broadbent's leadership and political management style. Some of these problems were extremely damaging, while others merely proved annoying to key figures in the party. For, paradoxically, despite the shift in the polls and some of the internal difficulties in the campaign, Broadbent continued to perform well and the tour had some of its best days of the campaign.

On the week that began on November 1, he started his swing west with a stop in Thunder Bay, where two New Democrats had been elected in 1984. As he so often did, Broadbent began his speech by telling the crowd how well the campaign was going, and how well it was going in areas that had traditionally been cool to the NDP.

He told how the campaign had begun in Montreal with a successful rally. "We went from there to Edmonton, where in 1984 they had a nominating meeting in Edmonton North – not in a hall like this, they had a nominating meeting in someone's living room with thirteen people to pick the candidate," he said. "This time, the nominating meeting in Edmonton North alone had thirteen hundred people out – and they are going to be electing New Democratic MPs right across Edmonton."

Whoops and cheers greeted this.

"And last week, we were in southwestern Ontario, in the city of London, of all places, where we had the largest meeting in the campaign for the New Democratic Party, the largest New Democratic turnout in the history of London – twelve to fourteen hundred people turned out in London last week, and we're going to be elected in the city of London."

More whoops and cheers.

"And the subsequent evening, we went back to a colleague's riding, in St. John's East," Broadbent continued, reminding the audience how, the previous July, for the first time in history, the NDP had elected a member from Newfoundland, Jack Harris.

He told how he had bet John Crosbie's wife Jane a cigar that they would win that by-election. It was one of his favourite warm-up stories: sometimes he would tell how they met in an elevator, sometimes he would mimic her Newfoundland accent betting the NDP could never win a seat on The Rock, sometimes he would say "She is the nice Crosbie," or "She is the Crosbie who's read the deal!"

"I'm going to phone Jane Crosbie up and say 'I want another – but this time I want a box of them, because we're going to do that well in Newfoundland!'"

Cheers, shouts and chants of "Ed! Ed! Ed!"

This election, he said, was about controlling our own future and our own destiny. This was the code he had adopted at the beginning of the campaign for talking about the trade deal in symbolic terms.

"Not only do we have to get control, but we have to use that control to make sure that the benefits, just for once in Canadian history, as a matter of rule and not the exception, went to the average family," he said. "That's what this election, for us, is about." He pointed out that the Canadians had obtained an exemption to allow continued subsidies of energy projects, but that there was no exemption for the environment, for culture or for social programs.

He then began to talk about Mulroney's broken promises, and threw out a challenge to the prime minister. "It was not Ed Broadbent, it was Brian Mulroney who scared pensioners in 1984 when he promised to increase their pensions before the election, but right after, he tried to reduce them, and we stopped him in his tracks. He's the one who scared pensioners," he said.

"And I say to Brian Mulroney tonight, Brian Mulroney, I challenge you to a debate with any pension group, any place, any time in Canada, on the issue of pensions and this trade deal, and I will let the pensioners of Canada decide who is telling the truth, Brian Mulroney or Ed Broadbent. And I rest confident that they will know who is really on their side."

That was the new element of the speech, the news clip – and, in case anyone hadn't identified it as such, the giveaway hint was that he repeated it in French for the French-language radio and television crews. In some halls (but not all of them) there was no mumbling in the crowd during his remarks in French, suggesting either that the audience was sufficiently partisan to understand the ritual of repeating the key paragraph for the cameras, or that New Democrats wished they spoke French, or that Broadbent's heavily accented French was easy for an English-speaking person to understand.

The challenge was the new element of a speech that dwelt on what Broadbent described as a pattern of betrayal by Mulroney, who had said one thing before the election in 1984 and something else afterwards – a repetition of what he called "the old Liberal way: he promised us change . . . and people believed him."

"Canadians don't expect miracles, they don't expect perfection, but what they do want is some fairness, and what they have every reason to expect from politicians is straightforward honesty, to deliver after elections what they promised they would do before elections," Broadbent said, to a chorus of chants of Ed! Ed! Ed!

He went through a litany of contradictions: promises to improve the environment, followed by lay-offs of people whose job it was to clean up the environment; promises to help families followed by a cutback on family benefits; promises to end Liberal patronage, and its replacement with Conservative patronage. Canadians, he said, were fed up.

"They're saying, 'It's time we had politicians in Ottawa who say what they mean, and mean what they say' – and that's the way they're going to vote in this election!"

This led him to the central theme of the New Democratic Party's campaign. He said that one word summed up what the party was about: fairness. New Democrats, he said, could be relied upon. Canadians had trusted Brian Mulroney, and were now paying $1300 more in taxes than they had in 1984. "Canadians have a right to know now what the bill will be and who will pay it."

After stressing that Canadians wanted independence from the United States, and that no party had fought harder than the NDP for independence, Broadbent concluded.

"Canadians want both frankness and fairness," he said. "They want a government they can count on to say the same things before, during and after an election. This time Canadians will be saying No to Mulroney's trade deal, Yes to honesty and fairness in government; this time they will be saying No to the Conservatives and Brian Mulroney; No to the Liberals and John Turner, and Yes, this time, to the New Democrats from coast to coast."

From Thunder Bay, he headed west to Kenora, Moose Jaw, and Weyburn, where, on Thursday, November 3, he paid a

visit to a virtual NDP shrine: the Tommy Douglas Calvary
Baptist Church, where the late premier of Saskatchewan and
first leader of the New Democratic Party had served as pastor
from 1930 to 1935. At a cost of $300,000, the community of
Saskatchewan farmers was restoring the church and converting it into an arts centre as a tribute to the diminutive
preacher who had brought medicare to Saskatchewan.

Symbolically and emotionally, it was a return to the roots
of the NDP: the church where both Tommy Douglas and Stanley Knowles had preached in 1929, two young ministers who
helped weave together the threads of the social gospel and the
labour heritage of the Winnipeg General Strike of 1919 to call
for social justice. The tradition of the Winnipeg strikers – for
whom J.S. Woodsworth had produced a newspaper – and the
outrage among farmers created by the Depression combined
with the Fabian socialism of the intellectuals of the League
for Social Reconstruction to produce the Regina Manifesto:
the manifesto of the Co-operative Commonwealth Federation,
and the blueprint for "a Co-operative Commonwealth in
which the principle regulating production, distribution and
exchange will be the supplying of human needs and not the
making of profits." (The manifesto was both holy writ, and as
M.J. Coldwell, Woodsworth's successor as leader, later put it,
a millstone around the neck of the new party, with its ringing
final declaration that "No C.C.F. Government will rest content until it has eradicated capitalism and put into operation
the full programme of socialized planning which will lead to
the establishment in Canada of the Co-Operative Commonwealth.")

Weyburn was Douglas's home, and where he was elected
first to Parliament and then to the provincial legislature; it
was also where Bill Knight had taught school. Knight had
joined the tour suddenly to replace George Nakitsas, whose
father had died that week. When Knight was an MP, his riding had included Weyburn.

The church is on a hill, overlooking the flat farmlands
around, and Broadbent used the visit to warn that big business's commitment to profit would guarantee that Canadian

social programs would not be improved or expanded under free trade. However, on the long bus ride south from Regina, the reporters had been reflecting on the Free Trade Agreement, and the impact of the two clauses that Broadbent had been quoting, 1601 and 1402. Some had been on the phone to trade lawyers, and had concluded that those clauses did not quite have the specific impact that Broadbent said they did. At the news conference, they questioned him closely, and he conceded that his concern was broader and less specific than the particular clauses of the agreement.

"If we tried to have denticare, to add new services, you watch what the business community will say," he said. "The business community will be telling governments and the people of Canada 'We can't afford it because we are in this trade arrangement with the United States.'"

Since medical services are funded by federal and provincial governments and contributions from employers and employees, Broadbent said that Canadian companies would want their tax contributions for social programs reduced to allow them to compete with American companies that do not have to make such payments.

"They will be saying to Canadian governments, 'Ease off on social programs, cut back on social programs, don't expand social programs, because we can't afford it if we're going to compete,'" he said. "Well, thank you very much. We have created a framework for social policy that is light years ahead of the United States and I don't want it to be threatened by this deal." But after this press conference Broadbent stopped citing specific clauses in the Agreement.

Social programs remained a highly emotional issue in Saskatchewan. Tommy Douglas had introduced many social programs and laid the groundwork for others as leader of the first CCF government in Canada; now the Conservative government of Grant Devine was in the process of cutting back and selling off a considerable number of the government initiatives introduced by previous CCF and NDP governments. Two days later, on Saturday morning in Saskatoon, Roy Romanow, the provincial leader of the NDP, struck all those chords in a moving speech introducing Broadbent, reminding his listeners of the fight to introduce medicare in Saskatchewan in 1962.

"And who of us in this room can forget that struggle? I'll never forget that fight in 1962, led by people like Tommy Douglas and the late Woodrow Lloyd, and Allan Blakeney. These men stood alone. Well, not alone – they had you. They had the people, thousands in Saskatchewan with them, but they stood alone against all of those who, in 1962, would kill the idea of medicare, who would see it dead. We remember the opponents very vividly: they were, in 1962 as they are in 1988, the Chamber of Commerce; they were and are the leadership of the Progressive Conservative Party."

Throats tightened as he said, "I look around this room and I see many faces – people like Betsy Naylor and George Taylor and Walter Smishek and Bill Davies, and Ed Whelan, and others too numerous to mention: you were there at the time of this dispute. I was there." He paused, after this litany of people who had set up community clinics, and former ministers who had been there for the battle. "But I want to tell you, Grant Devine and Brian Mulroney were not there, and neither was the Canadian Chamber of Commerce – they were with the American Medical Association, to defeat medicare in Saskatchewan in 1962!"

When the applause died down, Romanow continued, pointing out that the Conservatives, big business, and the Americans were out to stop medicare, reminding them of how the doctors had struck, and the American Medical Association moved up with money and ad men and public-relations people, to fight the first publicly funded medicare program to be established anywhere in North America. "The AMA said No to publicly funded medicare because it was not the way that they did business in the United States, and they fought, and the doctors struck for twenty-one days, and the people of this province were terrorized. Yet we fought back and the people won!"

It was a speech that caught the collective memory of combat and social solidarity that was part of the heritage of the party. He sounded almost like a prairie Martin Luther King, naming the New Democrats who were there, and the Tories who were on the other side.

"And then, for five years after 1962, my friends – think about it" – and his voice rose to a shout – "for five years no one in Canada helped us! We funded medicare exclusively, right here from this small province of a million people, without a penny of assistance from Ottawa, and with no help! And for five years we did that. We did it even after they tried to close down the hospital privileges, and even after they tried to attack our doctors, and even after they tried to put on deterrent fees on medicare. We stood together as a people, and five years later, the rest of Canada discovered medicare."

With that emotional record laid out, Romanow turned to the present, and the debate over free trade, pointing out that some of the people who led the fight against medicare were now Conservative appointees in the Senate.

"Now they say to us, those opponents, they say to us 'Trust us!' Brian Mulroney says 'Trust us!' Senator Staff Barootes, head of the doctors' association in 1962, says 'Trust us on medicare!' The Canadian Medical Association says 'Trust us, we also believe in medicare!'"

Romanow's voice lowered. "I say to the people of this province, and I say to the people outside this province who may not have lived through what we lived through – you may trust the Canadian Medical Association and Brian Mulroney and Grant Devine for medicare – we in Saskatchewan know first hand that you can never trust them for medicare! It can only be safe with us in the NDP."

Romanow went on to say that he wanted to tell Canadians in other provinces that, while they had not had the experience of a Conservative government seeking a second mandate, people in Saskatchewan had lived through Grant Devine seeking a second mandate in 1986. "He said, 'Trust us, we're not going to attack medicare, it's safe in our hands.' And what did he do? Of course, the very moment that we trusted him and we re-elected him in 1986, the first thing we see is the abolition of the finest drug-care plan in all of North America. We see the privatization of the dental program, the finest one in all of North America. We see a bitter nurses' strike, because there is no money for the medical system. We see ten thousand people in Saskatoon alone waiting for a hospital bed. We see coverage in medicare being cut back every day. We see deregulation and privatization because this Conservative in Regina said, 'Trust us with medicare.' We in Saskatchewan know you can never trust any Tory anywhere with medicare, ever!"

It was the kind of speech that New Democrats were making in Saskatchewan, and which New Democrats running in British Columbia like former Premier Dave Barrett, former Finance Minister Dave Stupich, and the former president of the B.C. party, John Brewin, were making in British Columbia, where Social Credit Premier William Vander Zalm was making ferocious cuts in medical and social services.

However, Broadbent would later complain that, while he could campaign against Devine and Vander Zalm in Saskatchewan and British Columbia, he had a much harder time campaigning in Ontario. For in Ontario, Liberal Premier David Peterson had come to power after forty-two years of Tory government as the leader of a minority government in 1985, governed by an accord negotiated with the NDP. On the basis of a progressive two-year agenda, set by Bob Rae's New Democrats, Peterson had won a strong majority in 1987; Broadbent felt that the NDP-Liberal accord, which he had opposed at the time, gave the Liberals a progressive allure that made it very difficult for him to gain ground in Ontario. (In fact, Broadbent's federal NDP did not get as many votes in Ontario as Rae's provincial candidates had.)

On Thursday November 3, Broadbent had a large rally in downtown Calgary – particularly elating for him, given the traditional failure of the NDP in Alberta – and, on Friday morning, after announcing a housing policy in front of a suburban house being constructed on the outskirts of Calgary, he flew west to Nanaimo, on Vancouver Island.

After the Calgary event, before the plane took off, I phoned my paper's national desk to check in, and was told that seven NDP candidates in Montreal had given a press conference in the morning on language rights. A quick call to the *Globe*'s Montreal bureau confirmed this: the candidates had said that the Charter of Rights should not have priority over the concept of a distinct society. On the runway, and then, as the bus travelled from the Nanaimo airport to the hall where Broadbent was speaking, Radio-Canada correspondents used their cellular phones to call Montreal and get a summary of what happened. When Broadbent finished his speech and spoke to reporters, they would have a better sense of what had happened in Montreal that morning than he did. The result was a situation that dramatically heightened the tensions in the NDP campaign, and highlighted the contradictions of the party on the critical question of Quebec.

In recent years, Broadbent's problems in Quebec had been, paradoxically, growing with the party's apparent popularity in the province. For, while the polls showed a growing number of people turning to the NDP out of dissatisfaction with the other two parties, its development on the ground, in terms of party officials, organizers, and members, was very different.

Broadbent and the people around him in Ottawa wanted desperately to reach out to people who could appeal to the Quebec middle class. Thus, there was considerable delight in Broadbent's entourage at the involvement of Rémy Trudel, a university administrator with a Ph.D. in academic administration – a man of considerable talent who fitted easily into the pattern established by a whole generation of New Democrats like Broadbent himself: middle-class intellectuals, journalists, academics, lawyers and social workers, people like Michael Cassidy, Steven Langdon, Bob Rae, Michael Harcourt, and Alexa McDonough. Trudel was one of a number of candidates like this who had been recruited by Broadbent's office in Ottawa.

However, organizationally, NPD-Québec had been building its organization from a more militant, left-wing constituency: the teachers' union, the veterans of various small left-wing groups in Quebec, and the labour movement. Inevitably, there was conflict between the people who had been attracted to the party by Broadbent or by George Nakitsas, and those who had joined NPD-Québec. The people in Ottawa around Broadbent felt that NPD-Québec consisted either of well-meaning people who were simply incompetent ("decent human beings who don't have a clue how to build a party" muttered one) or of people who had an axe to grind: former members of far-left groupuscules, who had become intensely passionate about the language issue. This attitude of the people in Ottawa tended to encourage newcomers to the party in Quebec to view the activists in NPD-Québec as loony extremists.

The people who had been working to build NPD-Québec, on the other hand, felt that these various people – such as Trudel, Gourdeau, Donald Houle, or Phil Edmonston – were middle-class ego-trippers who were not prepared to get involved in the collective exercise of building a party.

In this tension, Michel Agnaïeff was in a particular, and eventually quite awkward position. He felt that Broadbent's understanding of Quebec was limited: that he believed that the decline of the Parti Québécois meant the decline of the importance of Quebec nationalism. Agnaïeff was convinced that the future of the party in Quebec depended upon its absorbing, rather than avoiding, the national issue. As a result, he endorsed Harney's idea of "national affirmation": a formula that was taken over by Pierre Marc Johnson when he led the Parti Québécois, and made the federal NDP extremely uncomfortable. But there was a deeper dilemma than this disagreement.

On the one hand, Agnaïeff was the most effective organizer the NDP had. As a senior official in the Quebec teachers' union, he was tough-minded and experienced, with a range of contacts across the province. He was working at building a long-term organization, trying to build alliances with the environmental activists and community groups, and dealing with the federal party officials in Ottawa, whose knowledge of Quebec he had some doubts about. He saw the coming election as a preparation for a breakthrough in the following election, while people in Ottawa felt that the breakthrough had to happen more quickly.

George Nakitsas, on the other hand, had staked a great deal psychologically on having the breakthrough happen as soon as possible. A McGill-educated economist who had come to the NDP research office from the Canadian Labour Congress, Nakitsas had grown up in Montreal. Intelligent and intense, and inaccessible in some ways, he brought to the job of chief of staff a very different style and set of skills from Bill Knight. Knight was a former MP who had worked for Allan Blakeney in Saskatchewan; casual, easy-going, and apparently relaxed, he was adept at managing the leader, countering his tendencies to solitude, balancing Broadbent's professorial approach with his own gregariousness. Nakitsas, on the other hand, tended to reinforce Broadbent's intellectual, solitary qualities.

In some ways,Nakitsas and Agnaïeff had a fair amount in common: both were immigrants, one of Greek and one of Russian parentage; one had joined the English-speaking community and the other the French-speaking community; both were intellectuals from the labour movement; both had reputations for toughness.

But in 1987 a cloud came over the relationship between Agnaïeff and the Broadbent people. There was a story in the *Journal de Montréal* that he had been under surveillance by the Canadian Security and Intelligence Service throughout the period he had been working in Quebec, and even before. Michel Auger, an investigative reporter, had obtained a leak from the security service, and interviewed Agnaïeff before writing the article.

Agnaïeff was not surprised: he was of Russian background, he had been involved in every major Common Front strike for fifteen years and had been the teachers' union director of the general strike of 1972; he had been very active in the peace movement, he had travelled to conferences in East Bloc countries, he had visited the Soviet Union; it was the classic profile to set an alarm bell ringing in any Western security service.

As soon as he knew an article would be appearing, Agnaïeff phoned Broadbent, who asked him the classic question: "Were you or were you not ever a Communist?"

Agnaïeff said that he had never been a member of the party, but explained how the security service might have thought so. Broadbent assured him that he believed him, and that he had acted properly, and told him to launch a complaint with CSIS. He did so, and received an investigation, an interview, and as close to an apology as any security service can ever give. He came away from the experience feeling that both Auger and the people at CSIS had acted entirely properly, and very professionally.

However, after the incident, he felt there was uneasiness in his relationship with Broadbent, and the people around Broadbent. There were never any specific accusations, or specific disagreements; simply a series of lip-pursing doubts that added up to a loss of confidence in the man who had been originally seen as the key organizational figure in the building of a new federal party in Quebec.

In January 1988, just at the time that George Nakitsas became Broadbent's chief of staff, Bill Knight became federal secretary and Arlene Wortsman succeeded Nakitsas as director of research, Donald Houle started as the chief organizer in Quebec: a retired Quebec Provincial Police officer and former Liberal who had worked on security for the Pope's visit and was a friend of Rémy Trudel's. Agnaïeff began to realize that he was no longer being consulted about decisions, and that Broadbent's office was dealing directly with Houle.

In May, at a federal council meeting, Agnaïeff submitted his resignation, and was persuaded to withdraw it; at the end of June, after a stormy meeting with Broadbent before a Saint Jean Baptiste day event in Laval, he quit again, and again was persuaded to stay. But the tensions were already considerable. Hopes continued to be high for some kind of breakthrough in Quebec, but there was an uneasy recognition of how fragile the party was there. "We were building on egg-shells," Bill Knight acknowledged later.

As Trudel emerged as the man on whom Broadbent and Nakitsas pinned their hopes, and Houle became the organizer, there were other problems with other people who had previously been seen as possible party-builders, like Éric Gourdeau, the crusty engineering consultant and former senior civil servant in Lévesque's government (who insisted on being allowed to join the federal party and not NPD-Québec), and Phil Edmonston, the consumer activist.

Part of the tension arose from the language issue. Under Harney's leadership, NPD-Québec had adopted a policy of strong support for Quebec's language law, Law 101, under which French was the only language permitted on signs. A group of candidates had come to Ottawa before the debates, pushing for Broadbent to take a very clear position on language and the Constitution, making it clear that the NDP endorsed the "notwithstanding" clause in the Charter of Rights and Freedoms, allowing Parliament or a provincial legislature to pass laws that infringe on parts of the Charter. There had been some careful negotiating, phrase by phrase, over what Broadbent would say.

On October 19, in an interview in his committee room in Montreal, François Beaulne indicated some of his hopes and expectations. "There is no ambiguity on the issue in the NDP, but Broadbent's statements have been interpreted in a nebulous fashion by the French-language press," he said. "The position of the NDP is clear. The Meech Lake Accord, which we support, recognizes the 'notwithstanding' clause as the only juridical guarantee that Quebec has now to preserve its cultural authenticity. As long as no other mechanisms have been found, we support the 'notwithstanding' clause and its use by the Quebec government to protect its gains on the language issue."

This was, in fact, quite wrong. The "notwithstanding" clause had been introduced in 1981 at the insistence of Western premiers; one of the few times when there had been a public debate on the role of a Charter of Rights in a parliamentary democracy had occurred at a first ministers' conference in September 1980, when Allan Blakeney, then premier of Saskatchewan, had argued strenuously for the primacy of Parliament, and of the legislature in areas of provincial jurisdiction – taking as an example the question of the right of a province to preserve local moral standards by film censorship. Nevertheless, although it had been used in Ontario and in other provinces, it had become identified with Quebec when the Parti Québécois government used it systematically as a way of expressing its rejection of the new Constitution, and, explicitly, to infringe on fundamental rights in its conflict with the public-sector unions in 1982-83.

During the debate in French, Broadbent was asked point-blank, "Should the 'notwithstanding' clause have priority over the Charter of Rights?" He responded that Canada had included two different democratic traditions in the Constitution: the tradition, on the one hand, of parliamentary supremacy, and, on the other hand, of a Charter of Rights. "I have a great deal of respect for the two traditions which are in the present Constitution," he said, adding that, while he had had some problems with the "notwithstanding" clause because it made it possible for governments to take actions like those taken against Japanese-Canadians during the war, the clause did protect Quebec francophones.

"I have stressed the Charter of Rights in the past," he said, referring to the debate he had had in 1981 with Allan Blakeney on the Charter. "But I discovered during the discussions in 1981 that we must, if we want to have a Canada with all the provinces, we must probably accept the two traditions, the two rights. I hesitate to change this arrangement."

This round-about, backhanded acknowledgement of the clause was hardly the ringing endorsement that Beaulne and a number of other Quebec candidates had been looking for. In the week that followed, there were a few consultations on the question. Beaulne had sounded out Éric Gourdeau on the idea of a declaration on language and the Constitution six weeks earlier; Gourdeau thought that it was crazy.

"It's out of the question," he said. "Bill C-72 [the revised Official Languages Act] has been passed; once you're elected an MP, you can try and get it amended, but it's not the time to talk about it now."

Gourdeau was well aware that the "notwithstanding" clause was not an issue; it was in the Constitution, it existed, and it could be removed only if all ten provinces and the federal government agreed that it should be removed. Thus, any debate over it remained highly hypothetical.

However, as the mood began to change in Quebec after the debates, some of the NDP candidates were increasingly eager to proclaim their nationalist position. A statement was prepared, and Donald Houle succeeded in reaching George Nakitsas, who had left the campaign to come home to Montreal for his father's funeral, and reading him the statement.

In the ensuing controversy, a number of things remain unclear – for example, whether or not Robin Sears received a copy of the statement at NDP headquarters the day before the press conference. However, some things are certain. Some candidates – but by no means all of them – had been discussing a declaration on language and the Constitution for weeks. Michel Agnaïeff, among others, believed that the statement that was prepared had been cleared by Broadbent's staff. And Ed Broadbent had no knowledge of it.

In the middle of Monday night, October 31, Nakitsas had woken Bill Knight to tell him that his father had died, and that he had to go to Montreal. On Thursday night, Nakitsas rejoined the campaign in Calgary, somewhat to the shock of the other people on the plane. But Nakitsas said little; when asked about the funeral, he said tersely, "The event went well."

The death of a parent was so personal a matter that Broadbent and the other senior campaign people hesitated to tell Nakitsas that he shouldn't rejoin the tour; there had been four deaths among people close to the party in Ottawa in recent months, and each one had taken its emotional toll. Broadbent himself had agonized when his own mother died, and other people in the entourage remembered the tugs and pulls of conflicting duties when their parents had died. "For George to lose his father at a time like that was obviously extremely difficult," Broadbent told Judy Steed later. "In Greek culture, there's so much ritual around death, and George was the only son. God only knows how that affected his psyche."

His loyalty to Broadbent was so intense that no one felt they could tell him that he should not, or could not get back on the tour. Later, some people would feel that Broadbent, as the only person he reported to, should have done so, since he wouldn't take himself off. "When George was on the plane, the tour didn't work. When Bill came on, it worked," Rob Mingay told Steed. "Those of us on tour lost confidence in George. He should have taken himself out of it, but he didn't."

However, others argued that the problem was not Nakitsas, but Broadbent's dependence on him, and the fact that his principal adviser reinforced rather than countering his tendency to withdraw, and to avoid conflict.

On Friday morning, November 4, seven NDP candidates held a press conference in Montreal, including Michel Agnaïeff, Jean-Paul Harney, Hélène Lortie-Narayana, François Beaulne, and Giuseppe Sciortino. The statement was clear enough: the press release began with three principles that it claimed "NDP candidates stand for": "The Charter of Rights must not have priority over the concept of a 'distinct society'; Yes to the 'notwithstanding' clause to defend and promote the collective rights of Quebeckers; Bill C-72 must not be used to diminish the effectiveness of Bill 101 or provincial jurisdiction over language."

The statement went on to say that the candidates believed "that when the NDP supported the Meech Lake Accord, it recognized that the concept of a 'distinct society' for Quebec meant that collective rights have priority over the Charter of Rights." That was substantially more than Broadbent had said ten days earlier, when he tried to maintain the equilibrium of the two traditions.

Then, the statement broke dramatically with anything Broadbent had said, claiming that no other province should have recourse to the "notwithstanding" clause. "However, the NDP only supports the use of the 'notwithstanding' clause to defend and advance the collective rights of Quebeckers, and does so because these rights are not recognized in the Charter of Rights," the statement said. "Aside from this specific exception, the NDP is against a 'notwithstanding' clause in a Charter of Rights."

Finally, the statement criticized the use of the Official Languages Act to spend money to support the English-language minority in Quebec or, as the candidates put it, "to promote the English language in Quebec in sectors within which the federal government has no jurisdiction. This is a threat to the French fact in Quebec. Years of effort to promote the French language in Quebec are in danger of being lost."

The law included provisions, the statement said, that showed blindness to the realities of the two languages in Canada. "French is threatened in Quebec and in Canada, not English."

In addition to the written statement, a number of candidates expressed those thoughts in more dramatic fashion. Jean-Paul Harney said that francophone Quebec needed new tools to "keep the wolves at bay"; Michel Agnaïeff said "You would have to be blind not to see that the only language threatened in Canada and Quebec is French"; Hélène Lortie-Narayana, who had been a reporter for Radio-Canada in Edmonton, said that the rights of anglophones in Quebec didn't need protection.

A few hours later, when Ed Broadbent emerged from giving a speech at a community hall in Nanaimo, he was clearly unaware of how far the candidates had gone, and repeated the position he had so carefully articulated during the debate: we have a balance in our Constitution between Parliament and the Charter and if this is changed, it should be done in a co-operative manner.

"Those elements are in the Constitution now, and no federal government should try unilaterally to change that balance that we have," he said. "Co-operative federalism requires full discussion with all the provinces, and respect for existing rights, including the 'notwithstanding' clause that is available to all provinces."

There was, perhaps, a different nuance to that position being expressed in Quebec, he said. "I haven't seen the exact wording of what my colleagues in the province of Quebec have said, but I would assume that what they would say would be consistent with party policy."

It wasn't. Broadbent didn't see the statement until the plane flew to Vancouver to enable reporters to file their stories. When the statement arrived, Hilarie McMurray, Broadbent's speechwriter who was also a policy adviser on constitutional issues, was incensed. She was furious that the statement had been made, and even angrier that Broadbent had been allowed to comment on it without knowing what it was.

That night in Saskatoon, there was a meeting of staff at eleven in a hotel room at the Relax Inn. Nakitsas was angry with the staff, which he felt was whining and complaining, and folding under the stress; McMurray was in a rage at Nakitsas for what had happened in Nanaimo; Ann Carroll and Rob Mingay were finding Nakitsas was being rigid and authoritarian.

It's November 4; we've got just over two weeks to go, Nakitsas said. Anybody who can't take it can leave now. Voices were raised, and doors were slammed. McMurray and Mingay decided to quit; at 2 a.m., McMurray booked a morning flight home before reconsidering. After finishing the bottom of French press secretary Christine Dyck's bottle of Glenfiddich, she wrote a memo for Broadbent to use the following morning to respond to the Quebec statement.

"Hilarie said she was going to quit, and I said I'd quit if she did, but we realized that we couldn't do that to Ed, so we agreed to stay on. We hung on for Ed and Ed only," Mingay told Judy Steed later. "We had decided that this was a tour through hell, we'd checked in for the duration and couldn't jump ship. So we stuck it out. But it wasn't a lot of fun."

By next morning, Broadbent had heard from Bill Knight, who was also angry about the Quebec statement. Ironically, Knight had been on the other side of the argument about the "notwithstanding" clause in 1981, when he was working for Blakeney; he knew what price Broadbent had paid in the party for his commitment to the Charter of Rights, and he told him that he should feel free to blow the Quebec candidates out of the water if he wanted to. At a nine o'clock press conference, Broadbent was much more definitive. Questioned about C-72, he said that the party's position was clear; it supported the law – although he conceded that there were "nuances" and differences in a federal party, pointing out that there was a difference in opinion between Mulroney and Bouchard on the question of the "notwithstanding" clause. Questioned further, he said that anglophones and francophones had the same rights.

"But that is not the approach of your candidates at a press conference in Montreal," said Chantal Hébert of Radio-Canada. "It was not an interview on their personal opinions, it was a press conference to unveil the language policy."

"I am the leader of the party, yes?" replied Broadbent, his awkward turn of phrase in French making his annoyance clear. "I have the responsibility for the program, for the approach. And I don't say one thing in Saskatchewan and something else in Quebec."

The controversy caused a furore in Quebec. NDP candidates in English-speaking ridings complained bitterly that they had not been consulted; on the other hand, when Broadbent's statement was reported, Émile Boudreau, a former NDP executive member and long-time steelworker, wrote to Le Devoir to say that for the first time in years he would not be voting NDP. Sears and Nakitsas remained defensive. Sears had told reporters on Friday that the statement was consistent with the party's position, and then angrily accused the Gazette of distorting it in its report on Saturday. Nakitsas said in annoyance when he got off the plane in Ottawa that only the Westmount Rhodesians were complaining.

It was the worst kind of campaign problem: it was self-inflicted, it highlighted weaknesses in the party's approach, and it focused on the glaring failure to integrate the Quebec party into the party as a whole. The francophone Quebeckers in the NDP remained foreign to the culture of the party as a whole – as unrepresentative, and unconnected to the party's sense of itself, as anglophones in the Parti Québécois.

And the problem also exacerbated the tensions among the tour staff on the plane, and between the plane and the ground. The campaign had reached a crisis.

At the regular Sunday meeting, there were discussions of the problems, and the latest television ads were presented, as various ways of turning the sliding campaign around were discussed. But campaign strategists were astonished that, despite all that had occurred, the tour would be going into Quebec for an event in Lévis with Jean-Paul Harney. The plans were announced, were inflexible, and would not be changed. Then, after the meeting, a special delegation went to Broadbent's house for a meeting to discuss how bad things had become. That night, Bill Knight's relaxed, laid-back manner cracked; he vomited blood from the strain.

CHAPTER SIXTEEN

The Final Days

*"I believe that he will be successful who directs his actions
according to the spirit of the times, and he whose actions do
not accord with the times will not be successful."*

Machiavelli

On November 1, when Brian
Mulroney flew west to Vancouver, he was starting a new campaign, in which he was no longer protecting a lead, but fighting hard to regain momentum. The television crews felt the difference first. On the flight west from Ottawa, Luc Lavoie went to the people from the networks, and suggested that they have a pool cameraman on stage, behind Mulroney, for the first two minutes of the speech.

It was a sign that the Tories wanted to loosen up. Until then, cameramen had been confined to cordoned areas, much to their annoyance. The other campaigns had allowed them more freedom to move. The Tories didn't want the TV shots cluttered up with reporters, security men, RCMP agents in dark glasses; the result had been flashes of hostility between cameramen and tour organizers. On October 15, in Prince Edward Island, Scott Troyer, a CBC cameraman, had put his tripod on the floor beside the riser which had been placed there for the cameras at an old-age home – and when Mulroney had started singing a song, had grabbed his camera and run up through the crowd to get a better shot. The security people were angry, and even angrier when, later the same day, he ducked around the corner and hid in a potato warehouse to get a better shot of Mulroney.

"It was a beautiful shot," Troyer recalled on the flight. "It was the shot that told everybody where he was that day. It was the perfect shot, which situated him with potato workers in PEI."

But Art Lyon was furious, and berated Troyer afterwards. "'I try really hard to do things for you guys,' he said to me," Troyer said. "'If you're going to play the game that way, what's to say your tripod doesn't get lost, or you don't get your hotel key?'" Troyer shook his head. "I mean, you don't threaten a network cameraman that way."

But now it was a different campaign, and the rules had changed. The crews from the networks huddled, and decided not to go along with the new proposal. "They've restricted us to risers – which means the cameramen have to use long lenses," Doug Small of Global explained. "That produces grainy shots and jiggly shots. Now they want to let us move around more – but still under their control. Too bad. Either let us move around the way we want – or not."

Normand Rhéaume, the reporter for the French-language network TVA, violently disagreed with the suggestion that television was a superficial, uncritical medium; he argued that it was a total medium, which brought together the intellectual and the emotional. He said that he worked to bring together the idea, the sound, and the image, and looked for something that would visualize the context (and, preferably, make fun of the message that the organizers were trying to get him to deliver whether he wanted to or not).

He gave as an example the report he did on Mulroney's trip in southwest Ontario on October 28. The bus had broken down, Mulroney had visited a high-tech plant, and, that night, the Canadian flags had fallen on him. Rhéaume delivered the following text that night: "On the way to Cambridge, the well-oiled Conservative election machine had its first breakdown. A single rubber belt almost delayed the day, which had been dedicated to high technology. The Conservative leader visited a successful firm, Com-Dev, and didn't hide that he was there to improve his image."

Then there was a seven-second clip of Mulroney saying, in English, "I am here because you are winners."

"Later, in front of Technology Method, everything was in place for a $400-million announcement – which had been made nine months ago," Rhéaume continued. He had finished his text and done his stand-up and was waiting for Mulroney to start his speech before rushing to Toronto to cut, edit, and send his item – when the Canadian flags fell over on top of Mulroney. His cameraman got the shot – so he rewrote the last part of the item to match the symbolism of the sight.

It was a mischievous retort to the desire of the campaign to control the pictures, as cameramen and TV reporters tugged and pulled with tour organizers over whose preferred pictures would be on television that night. But, in the final analysis, the tug-of-war would be to Mulroney's benefit; as he became more combative, the interests of television cameramen and campaign organizers began to coincide. Thus, reporters might comment on the fact that Mulroney gave his speech on November 2 in Victoria in front of a huge Canadian flag (Stuart Murray had been able to borrow one from a Husky dealer) – but no comment would deflect the impact of the image.

Mulroney had a stormy meeting in Vancouver on the night of November 1 before heading to Victoria and arriving very late at the hotel. After the morning strategy meeting, a two-page memo had been prepared for Mulroney, suggesting that the theme of culture planned for the following day in Victoria be modified in order to give stronger attention to what the strategists called "the NDP lie on pensions and health care." "Your objective therefore should be to nail the NDP (and Turner) firmly for their unsubstantiated fears regarding pensions and health care in the senior citizen capital of Canada," the memo said. "This should be the bite line of the day."

The next day, after *Tartuffe* at the university in the morning, the speech to the Chamber of Commerce at lunch, and the ensuing debate with the hecklers, he had done a half-hour interview with local television, spoken at Pat Crofton's riding headquarters, and then driven for an hour and a half for an evening rally in Nanaimo.

Vancouver Island was full of strong support for the NDP, with a substantial pocket of support for the Reform Party among retired Albertans who had moved to the Victoria area. When Mulroney visited Crofton's headquarters in Saanich-Gulf Islands, there was a noticeable number of grey heads and military blazers in the audience – and a strong burst of laughter when Mulroney made fun of Svend Robinson, saying, "Wouldn't that be something? Svend as minister of defence? I'll tell you, that would make one fine ministerial meeting!" (Later, he would insist that he was attacking Robinson as the man who had heckled Ronald Reagan and who had criticized the NDP's defence policy as too moderate, and was not intending to attack his homosexuality; his chortling audience wasn't so sure.)

Crofton, the member in the last House and a former businessman and retired naval officer, felt he was running second to the NDP's Lynn Hunter, the Vancouver Island co-ordinator for Oxfam, but it was clear to Hunter that the Reform Party was making inroads into Crofton's support. The Reform candidate was a retired military doctor, Robert Slavik, who had been astonished himself to see the membership in the party swell to eleven hundred in the weeks leading up to the election. At the first all-candidates meeting, almost half the crowd wore Reform buttons.

"It shook all of us up," Hunter told a reporter later. "A lot of those heckling [Crofton] at the meeting had worked for him in 1984."

Crofton conceded to the *Vancouver Sun* reporter Keith Baldrey that he was concerned that Slavik – not to mention the Western Canada Concept candidate, Douglas Christie, the lawyer who had defended James Keegstra and Ernst Zundel – might drain away enough votes to allow Hunter, or even the Liberal candidate Kathryn Clout, to win.

"It's a worry, I'll admit that," Crofton said. "There's an anti-French bias out there, no question. I just have to convince those people that they could be electing a socialist MP if they vote for the Reform Party."

While some of the Tories on the plane were uneasy about Mulroney's crack about Robinson, feeling it had been due to the fatigue of such a heavy day, the strategists in Ottawa were delighted by the results of his speech in Victoria and his debate with the hecklers: it was a symbol of the new campaign that had begun.

The next day, November 3, the campaign plane flew to Penticton, where Mulroney spoke to supporters at the airport, and had a scrum with reporters; he flew to Castlegar and drove up to Trail where he spoke to workers at the Cominco plant, drove back down to Castlegar for a rally, flew to Edmonton where he spoke to the same senior citizens' home where Ed Broadbent had spoken at the beginning of the campaign, met with representatives from the Lubicon Indian band, and then spoke to a party rally before flying to Winnipeg.

The pace was unrelenting – six, seven, and even eight events in a day – and Mulroney was on the offensive. If Turner had made a comeback, he could now be attacked, and Mulroney, out of the cage with a vengeance, was hammering him. For many of the people on the plane and at Tory headquarters in Ottawa, Mulroney's debate with the hecklers in Victoria was a turning point in the campaign; a signal that he was prepared to take high risks, and that what Jeffrey Simpson had called the "stuffed pigeon" phase of the campaign was over. From November 1 until November 10, Mulroney fought a new, separate, different campaign.

It was, in fact, a campaign with two fronts: a public campaign in which an aggressive and punchy Mulroney led the attack on the Liberals and the NDP almost alone, while the Conservative ads were being reorganized and shot and the business community was mobilizing; and an internal campaign, keeping nerves from cracking, and stopping confidence from breaking in the ranks.

All three campaigns had internal crises during the election: the Liberals a crisis concerning leadership, and the NDP a crisis concerning Quebec and the tensions on the plane. But the Conservatives also had a crisis to deal with: the growing pressure from the ranks of the party to cut the free-trade issue adrift, and promise a referendum on the issue.

On November 1, John Tory was in the hospital in Toronto with his wife, who was in labour, when he was called to the desk on the maternity floor; Peter White was on the phone. "There's some talk floating around about a referendum," White said. It was the first that Tory had heard about it.

As the polls began to show how the Liberals had taken the lead after the debate, the idea began to percolate up through the ranks of the party: if the Tories were going to be defeated on a single issue, cut it away: promise a referendum on it. The most prominent proponent of the idea was Robert Coates, the former defence minister who had been on the secret strategy committee. In one impassioned meeting with Lowell Murray – who opposed the idea – he tore open old wounds, reminding Murray of the other campaign platforms the Tories had adopted in the past, over Coates's objections and with Murray's support: in particular "deux nations" in 1968, wage and price control in 1974, and the strategy dealing with the Crosbie budget of 1979 which led to the election defeat in 1980.

It was true that, over the years, the Conservatives had a record of boldly adopting, and then fiercely clinging to, policies that proved to be electoral weaknesses. The Liberals had proved to be adept at campaigning against Tory policies rather than for their own. In 1968, the Conservatives had reached what they felt was an accommodation with Quebec nationalism in what was known as the "deux nations" policy; Pierre Trudeau had skilfully demolished it. Similarly, in 1974, Trudeau had ridiculed the Stanfield proposal for wage and price controls with the tough line "Zap, you're frozen" – and then had gone on to introduce it himself. Then, the Clark government had fallen on the Crosbie budget proposal for an eighteen-cent-a-gallon tax on gasoline – and, partly on Murray's urging – gone into an election, which the Liberals won. Tories like Coates saw the spectre of defeat-on-unbudging-principle rising from the ashes, and haunting the party again.

It was a horrifying prospect to many Tories, and Coates told Murray, in a very emotional encounter, that he was going to tell Mulroney that Murray was the only person he had talked to who was opposed to the idea. While that might have been true, as the word circulated that it was a possibility, other Conservatives were just as adamant that the idea would have shown fatal weakness and loss of nerve. Barbara McDougall phoned Ottawa to say how upset she would be ("I'll quit! Honest to God, I'll quit!") if such a policy were announced. The strategists who discussed the idea on November 1 urged Mulroney to "knock this one down."

But the idea was settled definitively by Mulroney, who killed it personally. He was convinced that if he were seen to waver in his support for free trade, the Conservatives would lose. The only way he could use the strengths he had was to show determination, campaign flat out against the criticisms of the deal, and attack Turner and Broadbent. If he was seen to be losing his nerve, he was convinced that defeat was inevitable.

By Thursday, November 3, the strategists were pleased with the whirlwind. "The basic strategy for today is more of the same," the memo said. "The exclusive target is John Turner's credibility, competence and motivation (not Broadbent). You can do this by re-emphasizing the distortions Turner has generated on Free Trade, especially regarding health and social programs, explaining patiently that these are without foundation. Your meeting with seniors in Edmonton – the same ones Broadbent frightened – offers an ideal opportunity to nail this down firmly."

The strategists felt that by then, the election was being seen as a referendum on free trade. "Your main objective continues to be to demonstrate your own conviction and knowledge of the Agreement at every opportunity – by listening and responding to seniors or real Canadians (not necessarily hecklers who are committed and who will likely be even more orchestrated in the future)," the memo said. "Our target is the confused or concerned Canadians, not the committed NDP nationalist."

Broadbent had raised some concern by issuing a challenge for a debate earlier that week in Thunder Bay, and repeating it as he headed west. "Bearing in mind that you and Broadbent are in Saskatchewan together on Saturday it is essential that his renewed call for a debate be killed," the strategists wrote. "You might say that Broadbent is wrong again, he owes the seniors a clear apology, that you intend to take your message directly to seniors and other Canadians and have no desire to give Mr. Broadbent or anyone else a podium for more lies or distortions."

Late that afternoon in Edmonton, at the Kiwanis Lodge, Mulroney made social programs almost a central, emotional element of citizenship, using Emmett Hall's statement that afternoon in Saskatoon.

"What Mr. Justice Hall said about pensions and medicare is the same for a senior citizen seventy years of age whose background is French or English, whose background is Ukrainian or whose background is Jewish, whose religion is Catholic, whose religion is Protestant," he said. "We are all Canadians, all of us are entitled to the same benefits, and as Mr. Justice Emmett Hall said, nothing in the Free Trade Agreement in any way impacts negatively on your benefits, on what you have worked so hard to achieve. And as prime minister of Canada, I conclude by repeating simply this: under the Free Trade Agreement, a prosperous Canada will be doing more. More. Mr. Justice Hall points out that all of your benefits are preserved, and they are. But what Canada will be doing for you, as a grateful nation, all of you who have done so much for us and for Canada, and I feel as if I were speaking in the company of friends of my own mother, who is in your position, who raised a family, and in her own way was a tremendous nationbuilder. . . . "

After talking about how she raised six children on an electrician's salary with his father holding down two jobs, and how hard it was, Mulroney said, "I give you the assurance that I gave my own mother, and that I would give my mother if she were on the blower to me right now, I would say "Mr. Justice Emmett Hall is probably the finest and most authoritative source that anybody can [be] . . . he is the father of medicare, he gave birth to this magnificent instrument called medicare. I would tell my mother, 'Ma, your medicare is O.K., your pension is O.K., everything is protected. What free trade is going to do is give Canada more money so we can do more for all of you.' And God bless you all."

It was Mulroney at his most sentimental, delivering a message of hope: free trade and a Conservative government would not mean cutbacks in social programs, but expanded social programs. Not fewer benefits, but, with greater wealth, greater benefits. Not less, more.

That night in Edmonton, November 3, after his brief meeting with the Lubicon Indians, Mulroney gave his pep-talk speech to a partisan rally of supporters, surrounded by most of the Tory candidates from Northern Alberta – except Joe Clark, who was at an all-candidates meeting in Barrhead, where he was determined to recover from an embarrassing evening three weeks before, in Whitecourt, when he had been heckled and booed by Reform Party supporters.

Clark had been scorned in some Alberta circles as a non-Western Westerner ever since he won the Tory leadership in 1976, but the grumbles in his constituency of Yellowhead – stretching west and north of Edmonton to the Rockies – had become more audible lately. Over the previous two years, some of the members of the Conservative riding association had become disenchanted, drifted away, and joined the Reform Party. In the spring, after the magazine *Alberta Report* published a story about this, there began to be a sense that there was a split in Clark's riding association.

"There is a belief that five directors got up from the table and walked out," Keith Chisholm, the riding-association president, said in an interview. "That's not the case. They were not comfortable with the policies of the PC Party of Canada. Fair enough."

It is a reflection of how monolithic the Conservative Party had been in Alberta that the Yellowhead riding association had eighty-two directors altogether, each representing an area or community in the vast riding. Cliff Breitkreuz, a farmer outside Onoway, had joined the Conservative Party in 1983 and become a director; gradually, he had become disillusioned with the party, and with Clark. Breitkreuz had taught school before deciding he wanted to farm; he was involved in the community, served on the local county council, and was increasingly convinced that Western Canada was being ignored in favour of the East, and that the government was perpetuating a series of mistakes that should have been corrected: mistakes, in his view, like official bilingualism.

"I suppose I felt betrayed by the election promises, and what we all anticipated would happen if the Tories came into power federally," he said, adding that he became disillusioned with Clark at the meetings of the riding association. "He would relate to us all the things that were happening in Ottawa, but it was a pretty-one-way street. Joe was representing Ottawa to us, instead of representing us to Ottawa."

About two years earlier, Breitkreuz had begun talking with Preston Manning. He let his Conservative membership lapse, joined the Reform Party, and became a vice-president.

Back in April, Breitkreuz had no illusions that Clark would be an easy target for the new party. "He's a formidable foe; he's been elected ever since 1972. But if Preston Manning ever ran against him, the chances would be about even."

His explanation spoke volumes about the wistful idealism that he felt, and the sense, less of anger than of confusion and disappointment, that was felt in rural Alberta over the recurring debates on bilingualism, capital punishment, and high taxes.

"For people over fifty, senior citizens, the name Manning makes them think of another time," he said, alluding to the fact that Preston Manning's father, Ernest Manning, had been Social Credit premier of Alberta from 1943 to 1968. "Things were a lot less complex, and life was simpler. Most of all, there was stability."

Joe Clark was well aware of the discontent in his constituency, and in the West generally. In September, in a speech in Calgary, he summed up the guiding purpose of voters in Western Canada in federal elections in a phrase: throw the rascals out, and their policies with them. "We voted against FIRA, against the National Energy Program, against freight rates, against tariffs," he said. "We were usually in opposition, and we acted that way, and came gradually to have a negative view of politics and, worse, a sense of grievance about the country, and a suspicion of its institutions."

But like so many Tories in Western Canada, Clark had to remind grumpy Western voters again and again that a substantial number of their grievances with the previous Liberal government had been ended: the National Energy Program, the Petroleum Gas Revenue Tax, and the Foreign Investment Review Agency; privatization had begun; Michael Wilson had reduced the deficit; contracts of the Canadian International Development Agency had been diverted to Alberta at a rate proportional to its population.

But these measures had little impact on the many Western dissidents, who, often with a kind of earnest intensity, wrestled with what they considered to be the unfairness of government priorities; people like the directors of the Waskada Co-operative Elevator Association in Goodlands, Manitoba, who spent their regular board meeting on May 3 discussing Meech Lake and Bill C-72, and concluded they were unanimously opposed to both of them. "We object strongly to part of our society being distinct," Hilton Wallace wrote in a letter to the editor of *Western Report* on June 13. "As well, we feel this makes the rest of society second-class citizens."

Preston Manning, an Edmonton lawyer, was the most articulate and moderate spokesman for these views. Although he lived in the suburbs north of Edmonton, he decided that he would run against Clark, and used the campaign to stress many of the issues dear to *Alberta Report*: an end to the Meech Lake Accord, support of Alberta's demand for a "Triple E" (elected, equal, effective) Senate, a reform of the tax system to favour Western Canada, and a lowering of interest rates.

Clark had known Manning for years; in the late '60s, he had even approached him to discuss his being a candidate for the Tories. Manning considered the suggestion, and declined. Manning struck a chord with the dissidents in the constituency, and Clark, who became convinced that Manning was using polling, got a rough ride at the first public meeting. On October 6, in Whitecourt, he was heckled and booed, as critics in the audience of three hundred shouted, "Where do you live, Joe?" and "Baloney!", drowning out his defence of the government's record, Meech Lake, and bilingualism. Losing patience, Clark ended his remarks, jabbing his finger towards his tormentors, shouting, "There is fear here . . . fear of Quebec, fear of Eastern Canada. . . . We have nothing to be afraid about!"

"I have fought for Canada and I have fear when you are in charge!" a middle-aged man shouted back.

Manning, on the other hand, was cheered when he told the audience to send the old parties a message, and that his election would be a warning to MPs across Canada. "If you will not faithfully represent those who elect you, you will be replaced by someone who will!"

This was the issue people questioned Clark most closely about. They opposed bilingualism and favoured capital punishment; he had supported bilingualism and voted against capital punishment.

"How can we vote for you if you don't vote for us?" one member of the audience asked. It was a well-crafted line, and one of the things that made Clark believe that Manning was not simply well organized, but was also using careful and sophisticated polling.

"Members of Parliament are supposed to exercise their best judgement," Clark replied.

After that meeting, Cliff Breitkreuz became more and more hopeful. Clark did better in Hinton, where he won strong applause, but his opponents focused on his lack of preoccupation with local issues. "You have just as much chance of bumping into Elvis Presley on the streets of Hinton as you have of bumping into Joe Clark," said the Liberal candidate, John Higgerty, a crown prosecutor and the only candidate who lived in the riding.

However, although Clark had been taken by surprise in Whitecourt, he was determined not to let it happen again. In Barrhead, on November 3, he succeeded in putting Manning on the defensive. The Reform Party had a proposal to take away a leader's power to disallow someone from running as a candidate – and, despite this, Manning had exercised that power in preventing Doug Collins, a vociferous proponent of a racist immigration policy, from being a candidate in British Columbia.

But the key issue Clark dwelt on was the danger of splitting the Conservative vote and electing the NDP.

"I had the feeling Manning was going to win," Breitkreuz told me later. "But all of the issues for which the Reform Party came into existence, all of those policies were sideswiped by the whole Free Trade thing. Everything else went by the wayside. People here wanted Free Trade, and there was only one party to vote for."

On Sunday afternoon, November 6, Brian Mulroney was at 24 Sussex Drive going over the situation with Lowell Murray, Norman Atkins, and Derek Burney. Mulroney was tired; the tour had finished a punishing week with a long day through rural Saskatchewan the day before, and had arrived back home in Ottawa at three a.m. (About two-thirty a.m. John Tory had called Harry Near at home from the plane to say cheerfully that he didn't know if Near was still awake, but he wanted him to know that they were.) They knew that a Gallup poll would be published the next morning, and Peter White had been asked to try to get an advance look at the numbers.

Reports began to come in about four-thirty. First, Harry Near called – but not with the Gallup numbers. He had managed to get an advance tip on the CTV poll that would be announced that night. He called first with the good news that the poll showed the Tories at 39 points and the Liberals at 35 – but phoned back to say that the news was bad, that those numbers were reversed, and the Liberals were four points ahead.

Worse was to come when Peter White called. The Gallup numbers were astonishing: the Liberals had soared to 43 per cent, the Tories had dropped to 31, and the NDP was at 27. "The phoenix-like ascension of the Liberal Party, if it is sustained through voting day, will certainly be recorded as one of the most astounding rehabilitations in Canadian history," the Gallup organization would say the next day.

"Look, I think this poll is wrong; they occasionally are," White said. "But nevertheless, if it's right, I think there's only one thing we can do, and that is to go down fighting for what we believe in – free trade and Meech Lake. There's one thing we can be sure will not happen: a Liberal majority government."

"If these figures are right, there will be," Mulroney replied, and asked White to call the key organizational people in Quebec to warn them that the numbers were coming out. By that point, Atkins had left, and was off having supper with a group of campaign workers in an apartment in Ottawa. Mulroney called him.

"Norman, I have the results of the Gallup," he said. "They're not very good."

He gave him the Gallup figures, and Atkins said "I don't believe that." Mulroney agreed. "Neither do I. They also indicate we're behind in Quebec."

"That just cannot be the case," Atkins said.

"Why don't you think about it for a while and call me back?" Mulroney said.

Atkins hung up the phone, stunned. While the numbers didn't feel right, he knew they would be extremely demoralizing to Tory workers across the country. In the bedroom of the apartment, Atkins sat on the bed, thinking, "Jesus, what do I do next?" He called Allan Gregg, and told him the Gallup numbers. Gregg had polled during the same period, and found the Liberals and Conservatives tied at 34 per cent with the NDP at 22 per cent, and 9 per cent undecided.

"I don't believe those [Gallup] numbers – they're not correct," Gregg said. "You're absolutely sure of that?" Atkins said. "I'm absolutely sure of that."

"Do me a favour," Atkins said. "Pick up the phone and call Mulroney."

"You can be absolutely certain that's a bad poll," Gregg told Mulroney. "Our overnights are really responding to the campaign; it's completely leader-driven, and our numbers are starting to come back."

For the next three hours, sitting in the apartment bedroom as campaign workers ate supper and chatted, Atkins was on the phone, across the country, warning, reassuring, conveying the news. The Network was being set to work. In the next room, one of the tour staff, who had been skeptical of Atkins and the Big Blue Machine, marvelled at how he set to work, soothing, stroking, and encouraging.

Even his admirers quickly conceded that Atkins was not a strategist or a strategic thinker. But part of his skill – and the part that infuriated those Tories who felt that the Big Blue Machine was an exercise in mutual congratulation and self-promotion – was his ability to create a sense of mutual loyalty, the feeling of belonging to a club. His critics argued that it excluded as much as it included, but the sense of kinship could prove invaluable in a crisis. Atkins often conveyed anxiety; he fretted, and Allan Gregg complained jokingly that he whined. But, at the same time, he created a code for running campaigns: a diffidence about his own role, a sense of respect for each person's authority, and a kind of patience for each person's concern. (Derek Burney was new to the environment, and didn't know the rules; at one strategy meeting,

Lowell Murray, Dalton Camp, and Atkins went on for about half an hour about what should be done for Atlantic Canada. Burney lost patience, and began to shout and swear that they should get their own self-interest off the table. Everyone at the meeting was horribly embarrassed for Burney; he had broken the club rule: never criticize your own.)

Marcel Côté had got the Gallup numbers in Quebec, and, equally convinced they were wrong, phoned Harry Near; as the circle of knowledge spread, the phoning intensified.

The next morning, the large weekly meeting was held; before it, Atkins pulled aside Gregg – who had taken the seven a.m. flight up – for more reassurance that the Gallup numbers were wrong. When Gregg reconfirmed this, Atkins said, "In that case, I'm going to open this meeting, make an opening statement – and then you're on."

"It's wrong, take it to the bank," Gregg told the meeting. "It's wrong." At the same meeting, Hugh Segal announced that commercials using Emmett Hall's statement from the previous week and Simon Reisman's interview with Douglas Fisher were both ready, and would be going on the air that week. Near had not gone to the meeting, but remained at headquarters, still calling people across the country, pumping out the message that the Gallup numbers were wrong.

In the afternoon, Atkins felt overwhelming relief when Mulroney told reporters in Hull that the Gallup figures were wrong, and that he had confidence in the Conservative campaign. That day, the decision was made to leak the Decima numbers.

In Montreal, Marcel Côté had received the Gallup numbers about four o'clock, and had provoked a similar containment exercise, notifying Tory organizers and leaking the Gallup numbers to Radio-Canada in order to diffuse their impact. On Monday morning, Côté asked people to check out how the Gallup had been done. When he was at the Ottawa weekly meeting, he got a call from someone who had checked with one of the people who had done some of the interviewing for Gallup. After Côté reported some of the details, an additional message was pumped out: not only were the numbers wrong, the methodology was flawed. The interviews had been done at home in the afternoon, thus weighting the poll heavily towards the elderly and housewives – both groups being more likely to vote Liberal in Quebec. Monday night, Côté ordered an overnight poll; the next morning, he passed on the news to the organization that things were looking good, and, waiting until five p.m. so as not to scoop Mulroney's visit to Montreal, called in reporters and gave them their numbers in Quebec: Tories, 43.6 per cent; Liberals 32.9; NDP 12.2. With the undecided voters reapportioned, this worked out to Tories 49.2 per cent, Liberals 37.1 per cent and NDP 13.8 per cent.

But the strain and panic being felt in some parts of the campaign were palpable, and pressure began to increase on the campaign leadership to cut loose the trade issue, and promise a referendum on it. On Tuesday evening, November 8, Atkins was at the American Embassy for a party to watch the American election results. People there were struck by how exhausted he was, and how candid he was about the difficulties of the Tory campaign. For several people at the heart of the campaign, those few days, when the Gallup came out, represented rock bottom. But in an interview on November 9, on the French-language radio station CKAC in Montreal, Mulroney publicly dismissed the possibility of a referendum on the free trade issue, which killed the idea once and for all.

On Wednesday November 9, Mulroney intensified his attack on Turner in Quebec, saying that a Liberal victory would have the effect of killing not only Free Trade but also the Meech Lake Accord.

"The stakes for Quebec are particularly historical. . . . If Meech Lake and free trade were to disappear, Quebeckers would be the big losers," Mulroney told fifteen hundred workers at Canadair in Saint-Laurent, in the north-east industrial suburbs of Montreal. "Their children and grandchildren will pay for a long time the price of the sabotage of our two instruments of dignity and prosperity."

Michel Cogger, the co-chairman of the campaign, told reporters that Turner had made his support of Meech Lake conditional on the reintroduction of eight Liberal amendments. This was not true; Turner had said that although it "has areas that I believe can be improved, I wouldn't reopen the accord. I believed and still believe that with all its faults, the Meech Lake Accord has an overwhelming purpose, bringing Quebec fully into the Canadian family."

But Mulroney spelled out the accusation even more clearly in the interview with CKAC, broadcast the next day. "A Liberal vote is a vote to kill free trade and kill the Meech Lake Accord."

It was an unfair attack, and Turner denied it immediately. "That statement by Mr. Mulroney is totally false. . . . I'm committed to supporting Meech Lake," he told reporters in Southern Ontario. "I promise again to support Meech Lake, not reopen it."

Mulroney began developing a rhetorical attack, accusing the Liberals of having celebrated the exclusion of Quebec from the constitutional agreement of 1981, which was close to what the Parti Québécois had said at the time. For those who remembered how critical he had been of Joe Clark in the early 1980s for "cosying up to the separatists," and the degree to which he had been identified with Pierre Trudeau's view of the Constitution, it was a considerable irony to hear Mulroney adopt the nationalist rhetoric of those who had attacked the constitutional agreement of 1981-2.

This was a tactic the Conservatives had been considering for some time. Months before the election, Cogger had told a Liberal at a party that if the Liberals opposed Meech Lake, "By the time we've finished with you, people will think you hanged Louis Riel." The suggestion that a vote for the Liberals was a vote against Meech Lake was all the more unfair since Turner had turned his party inside out over the question of Meech Lake. Loyal Liberals, including some in Turner's entourage, squirmed at the fact that Turner had renounced what they saw as the heritage of Pierre Trudeau, brushing it away as "Trudeau orthodoxy." Mulroney had been skilful enough to drive a wedge through the heart of the Liberal Party with the Accord: a wedge that led André Ouellet to accuse his former cabinet colleague Don Johnston of being a "Westmount Rhodesian" for rejecting Meech Lake; a wedge that made it impossible for the Liberals to bring Trudeau and Chrétien to the same platform as Turner to attack free trade, since both men made it clear that they would not avoid reporters' questions about their opposition to Meech Lake; a wedge that virtually ensured the failure of the Liberals to build any unity in Quebec.

When Mulroney was planning his visit to Saint-Laurent, he was still nervous that the campaign was slipping, and asked Bourassa to join him at the Canadair factory in his own riding. Bourassa, who had done so much to ensure Mulroney's victory – to the extent that Liberal Senator Pietro Rizzuto had become convinced early in 1988 that Bourassa was only maintaining a façade of neutrality to ensure that Turner's leadership was secure, so that he would be an easier adversary for Mulroney – drew the line at that. Nevertheless, he was prepared to introduce a resolution in the Quebec National Assembly in support of free trade, intended to win unanimous support. While this ultimately did not occur, Bourassa made a final plea on behalf of free trade in the National Assembly on November 16, only a few days before the election, calling it "Quebec's and Canada's ultimate insurance policy against any protectionist whim by the government of the United States." Then, he forbade his ministers to attend Turner's rally in Quebec City the following night. However, by then Mulroney knew that he had won the election.

On November 10, Ed Broadbent was in Quebec City. Despite vigorous opposition from some of the NDP strategists the previous Sunday – who argued that the declaration on language the previous week proved once again that Harney could not be trusted, and that Broadbent should stay away from Quebec – the visit was carried out as planned. The campaign took buses from the hotel across the river to Lévis, where everyone climbed onto a boat to head out into the St. Lawrence. At the end of a news conference on the boat, the CTV producer Barry Kliff asked Broadbent whether he thought the Quebec language law, Bill 101, was still needed.

"I'm not a Quebecker," Broadbent said. "It's Quebec legislation, and I can't decide as an outsider whether the bill is needed or not. Neither can I make a judgement on that – in terms of the sociological reality – because I don't live here. It's not up to me to do it. It's up to the people of the province of Quebec."

That was it; Broadbent's staff quickly ended the news conference. For the rest of the day, reporters pursued him on the question, pointing out that he had not taken this position when Saskatchewan passed legislation abolishing the French-language rights that had been recognized by the Supreme Court as part of Saskatchewan's historical obligation to its French-speaking minority. When Broadbent met reporters on the tarmac back in Toronto, late in the afternoon, he said that his position had been totally consistent, and that he had been a supporter of the objectives of Bill 101.

"But when I'm asked, as I was asked this morning, do I think certain legislative action is required in a province, quite literally that is not my responsibility as a federal leader," Broadbent said. "That's up to the province."

While constitutionally correct, the answer was politically disastrous. The last thing that the New Democrats needed was a series of reminders – which virtually every story provided – of the embarrassing divisions caused by the news conference of the week before, and of Broadbent's sense of being an outsider in Quebec. "If John F. Kennedy could say 'Ich bin ein Berliner,' surely Ed Broadbent could say 'Je suis Québécois,'" quipped one senior New Democrat gloomily. As had been the case with his remark about Canada moving to a two-party system, the error was Broadbent's alone.

That same day, November 10, Mulroney was in the Toronto area. In the late afternoon, reporters were told that they would be given a briefing on the cost of the Liberal promises – and, somewhat to their surprise, had a press conference with Finance Minister Michael Wilson. Wilson laid out his calculation of what the Liberal promises would cost, arriving at the figure of $37 billion for twelve of the forty promises. But, to the astonishment of reporters, when asked what Tory promises would cost, he said there would be no cost, as the Tory plans were not promises, they were government commitments. The distinction seemed so specious that reporters were left shaking their heads.

The question of the costs of promises would prove to be tricky. The Conservatives simply avoided it: the $15 billion worth of "commitments" – megaprojects, literacy, the cleanup of the St. Lawrence, etc. – had been announced before the writs were issued, and so, they claimed, were simply part of the government's record. The New Democrats had gone to enormous trouble to announce a price-tag with every promise, and, at the same time, the tax or deficit increase that would pay for it. On November 12, Broadbent announced the total package: $5.13 billion in promises to be paid for with a $1.4-billion increase to the deficit, and increased taxes on large corporations and upper-income people to pay for the balance. The Liberals had been refraining from announcing the costs of their promises; Kirby told Turner in early November that the polling suggested that the cost issue was not very important. But ten days into November, it was clear that the issue was hurting the Liberals, and that the Conservatives had succeeded in stirring up fears of the economic consequences of tearing up the trade deal.

It was also on Thursday November 10 that the Liberals finally won a court order requiring the television networks to run the commercial they had made of the most dramatic moment from the television debate, of Turner nose-to-nose with Mulroney. Combined with the commercials of Turner facing the camera, talking about the threat of free trade, they constituted the final Liberal attacks. (When he filmed his own last commercials, Turner commented that he was under some pressure to change the campaign and move away from free trade – but that he was going to stick to it.)

But, dramatic though the debate commercial might be, it was no match for the Tory onslaught. The Tory campaign had organized its advertising strategy so that the bulk of its television commercials would appear after the debates. At the time of the panic, when the Tories slid in the polls, everyone attacked the first batch of television commercials. The Network was negative from the beginning, and the tone of the daily notes became ever more strident, calling the ads weak and evasive, saying they did more harm than good, and, as the days passed and the ads were still on the air, saying they were getting worse instead of better, and describing them as corny, diffused in message, and totally ineffective. But the Network was not alone: Don Mazankowski began to call for booking TV time for him in Western Canada, Wilson in Ontario, Bouchard in Quebec, and Crosbie in the Atlantic Provinces, a reflection of his dissatisfaction. Individual Conservatives began to type up their own scripts for negative ads and fax them to the campaign.

But when the negative ads began to be shown, they were shown very heavily. With the advantage of Decima's research and constant and intensive focus groups (the cost of which is exempt from the Election Expenses Act), they were able to zero in on Turner's weakness, and hammer away at his credibility. The Tory placement strategy was also important.

For, while the Liberals and the New Democrats had bought heavily at the beginning of the month in which TV commercials were permitted, the Tories had concentrated their commercials in the last ten days. "We bought very very heavily in day ten to fourteen [counting back from Election Day], because that's when people make up their mind in disproportionate numbers," said Allan Gregg later. "Something like 16 per cent of the electorate make up their mind in the last two weeks."

The Tories also focused their advertising time in order to aim at the group they wanted to reach: a group which Gregg and his colleagues at Decima called "the open-minded con-fused," or, less charitably, "the urban stupid."

"These were people who believed there was a threat to sovereignty and social programs – or they didn't know about social programs – but they also believed that no free trade would probably hurt our economic prosperity," Gregg said. "This represented 30 per cent of the electorate. These were people who were . . . disproportionately older or younger, downscale, poorly educated, and urban."

The polling and focus groups found that these people were suddenly much more conscious of the negative message about the effect of free trade on social programs than they were of warnings about the possible impact of losing free trade. This enabled the Conservatives to aim their commercials at those concerns, and at that audience.

"What happened when that general anxiety about change and the future became a very specific and focused anxiety, when the debate came, these people said, 'When was the last time we participated in prosperity anyway?'" Gregg said later. "I mean, if you're a cleaning woman . . . 'But boy, losing my social programs, I understand that!' The negative side of the double argument they were prepared to buy all of a sudden took on a salience which overarched the threat side of no-free-trade.

"So we also bought *The Young and the Restless*, and all the soaps and everything," he continued. "A very very heavy non-public-affairs-buy. Normally, when you buy media for a political campaign, the el primo spot is in news adjacency spots because you're dealing with the learned consumer of public affairs and current information, who you want to influence. But we didn't. We wanted this other group."

Their concerns were probed with careful testing of messages. This refined the negative advertising to aim at the specific doubt about what Turner was saying. So the Tory map ad, which showed the 49th parallel being drawn back, had a voice saying firmly, "John Turner says there is something in the Free Trade Agreement that threatens Canada's sovereignty. That's a lie. And this is where we draw the line.

[Hand draws back border.] There's not one word in this agreement [book is shown, opened, and pages are turned] that affects our independence, our social programs, our health care, our pensions, or our culture: all those things that make us unique. John Turner is misleading the Canadian people. That is the biggest threat of all."

Other commercials were made quoting newspapers saying that John Turner was lying, quoting Emmett Hall and Simon Reisman, giving an excerpt of an interview with Reisman, and quoting people who gave the appearance of being random individuals stopped on the street. They weren't, in fact: they were Conservatives, staff people, or local volunteers. In one ad, a young woman said, "I think that he is more interested in saving his job than he is in saving mine." Since the woman, Sheila Meagher, was a political aide to Harvie Andre, the remark was almost certainly true. However, the sentiment flowed out of Gregg's research: when pushed, as the ads were pushing and as the people in the focus groups had been pushed, people were prepared to believe that Turner was saying what he was saying because he was a politician. This was a line that Gregg gave Mulroney: the only job John Turner is trying to save is his own.

However, while the focus groups proved responsive to some negative advertising, they resisted other ads. One commercial of the perhaps fifty that were made (only thirty-four were used) showed a man tearing up a document with a voice saying, "If John Turner gets elected, he'll rip up the Free Trade Agreement." "Currency will flee the country," the voice said, and a hand snatched money on a table, "and tear the heart out of Canada," and a hand ripped up a map of Canada. The strategists in the Langevin Block loved the ad; Decima's focus-group members said, "Now you're lying. John Turner lied before about social programs, and now you're lying." Such ads were never shown.

By the end of the campaign, the Tories were running four times as many ads as they had at the beginning of the campaign. Combined with the weight of the third-party supporters of free trade, the impact was very heavy. The Canadian

Alliance for Trade and Job Opportunities organized a $1.3-million advertising campaign in support of free trade. The *Toronto Star* alone received some $550,000 in additional advertising, almost entirely from the free-trade advocacy groups.

As the NDP campaign was fading, there was a desperate attempt to get Broadbent back on track. The campaign returned to the theme of the 1984 campaign: Main Street and Bay Street. Rob Mingay had the idea that the campaign should fly to New York and add Wall Street to Bay Street, for an innovation with more visual impact. Robin Sears became convinced that it would be worth doing, and the campaign strategists became embroiled in a debate over the wisdom of this. Finally, it was agreed that the complications were too great and the logistics too complicated, and those opposed to the idea prevailed.

The new commercials that had been discussed at the Sunday meeting on November 6 were prepared, produced, and broadcast. However, they got lost in the sweep of pro-free trade commercials, and had little or no impact.

Hugh Segal had been feeling very isolated from the cultural community in Toronto in his position as the Tory ad man. He was convinced that he had been unable to get decent studio times to shoot Tory ads because the Toronto cultural community was so united in its opposition to free trade. When he picked up the Saturday *Globe and Mail* on Sunday November 20, and saw an ad urging people to vote for the party that would help defeat the deal signed by many artists including Margaret Atwood, Pierre Berton, Timothy Findley, Gordon Lightfoot, Michael Ondaatje, Rick Salutin, Kate Trotter, and Sylvia Tyson, he was not surprised. But five pages further on, there was a second ad endorsing the agreement, entitled We Are Not Fragile, signed by even more Artists and Writers for Free Trade, including Alex Colville, Ken Danby, Robert

Fulford, W.P. Kinsella, Irving Layton, Mordecai Richler, and Harold Town. When Segal saw it, he began to weep.

The result of the polarization over free trade was a degree of class-based politics which the country had only rarely seen before; a division of opinion could be seen forming on the basis of class and income. In a poll published November 11, Environics found that 51 per cent of those Canadians questioned opposed the Free Trade Agreement, 39 per cent were in favour of it and 11 per cent were undecided. But 52 per cent of those who supported free trade earned over $60,000 a year, while 57 per cent of those opposing it earned less than $20,000. In addition to being wealthier, the minority that supported free trade had another major advantage over the majority that opposed it: they had only one party to vote for, while the opponents had two.

On Thursday night, November 10, the CBC reported in its poll that the Liberals and the Conservatives were almost tied: the Liberals had 38 per cent, the Tories 37.5 per cent, and the NDP 21 per cent. But on Friday morning, Mulroney got the numbers from Allan Gregg from the latest Decima survey: an extra-full survey which had been undertaken after the scare about the Gallup the previous Sunday. Gregg told him that he had his majority. In the solemnity of the Remembrance Day ceremony, Mulroney could hardly keep from grinning from ear to ear. That same day, in southern Ontario, canvassers for Perrin Beatty would feel the mood shift in their favour. The turnaround was complete. The new campaign Mulroney had undertaken when he went west on November 1 was now over.

John Turner began the last week of the campaign with a tour through part of Quebec, before heading east to the Maritimes. In Saint-Jérôme, he lashed out at the businessmen who had endorsed free trade at a press conference at the Ritz-Carlton on Thursday November 10.

"Les boys du Ritz-Carlton say they are ready to meet the competition," he said. "But on one condition: that the workers pay the price."

This became one of his themes for the last days of the campaign in Quebec: "les boys du Ritz." It was punchy, populist – and represented an out-dated reading of the mood of Quebec. The "boys du Ritz" rhetoric sounded inappropriate from a former Bay Street lawyer who had had his table reserved at Winston's for lunch, and echoed the militant rhetoric of the labour movement of a decade or two earlier. Quebeckers who might have supported the General Strike of 1972 and chanted "Parti Québécois, Parti Bourgeois" were likelier, sixteen years later, to be checking the progress of their portfolios of tax-exempted Quebec Stock Savings Plan stocks and hoping to go to the Ritz than to be denouncing those who did.

The last Liberal efforts in Quebec were marred by the fact that, later that day, a Tory demonstrator at the Liberal rally in Pierrefonds was beaten up. The Tories had sent a Santa Claus to the rally to symbolize Turner's promises, but the Tory hecklers had got inside, and Santa Claus withdrew, unnoticed. When there were television pictures that night showing Graham Gleddie with blood all over his windbreaker, Tories were delighted. It added to the general impression that the Liberal Party was rowdy, disorganized, and out of control, an impression reinforced by scenes at the nomination meetings in the summer, the disruption of the launching of the Quebec campaign by William Dery, and now the beating of a heckler.

Turner resumed his populist message when he returned to Quebec on Wednesday November 16. That evening, both Mulroney and Turner were in Montreal, speaking to slightly smaller crowds than expected (the Elections Canada officials were briefing the scrutineers of all parties that night), as Mulroney made his final appeal to Montrealers to help him maintain the "new climate of investor confidence" and "harmonious federal-provincial relations," and Turner addressed a crowd in a church basement in Marcel Prud'homme's riding.

Turner reminded the audience of Solange Denis, the pensioner who had confronted Mulroney on the proposal to de-index pensions, the woman who had come to endorse Jean-Claude Malépart a month earlier.

"She said 'Brian, you lied to us; the next time, Goodbye Charlie Brown,'" Turner said, adding that Mulroney was refusing to discuss the proposed national sales tax. "He doesn't want Mrs. Denis to know that he will impose a 16 per cent tax on everything she buys for the rest of her life," he said. "Sixteen per cent not only on her dentist, her cleaning, her bus ticket to Ottawa, but her personal needs, her phone calls, her cable TV, and her bingo game. Then, at the end of our lives, we will have to pay the Mulroney tax on our funeral and our will."

Turner then launched into an attack on Mulroney for cowardice in refusing to be straightforward about the effects of free trade.

"Brian Mulroney knows full well that the textile workers, the garment workers, and our food workers will be sacrificed on the altar of free trade," he said. "That's the initial cost of free trade, and the largest share will be paid by Quebeckers, above all the workers of Quebec."

"Obviously the big shots, the big guns, the bosses of the multinationals, les boys du Ritz will gain," he shouted. "They will get their profit at the expense of the workers of Quebec! Every dollar they invest in propaganda for free trade is an IOU that they will collect from Brian Mulroney, and it is again the real people who will pay the bill!"

The line won applause and chants of "Turner! Turner!" but the people in the Turner entourage knew that the crowd was too small, too old, and too ethnic to reflect anything but the hard-core Liberal support in central Montreal. Jean Riley, who travelled with the Turners on the tour, assessed the crowd that night, and knew the election was lost.

The next night in Quebec City, there was a good crowd, but only because people had been bused from as far as Rimouski. Turner used a vivid local image to capture his opposition to free trade, comparing the trade deal to the proposed sale of the Nordiques hockey team. "A few weeks ago . . . all of Quebec mobilized against the sale of the Quebec Nordiques, to be sold to unknown interests. Theoretically, it was a commercial transaction, with a buyer and a seller," he said. "But for the people of Quebec, the Nordiques are more than a hockey team; they are part of their tradition and part of their collective pride."

After a trumpeter in the crowd led it in a hockey chant, Turner added, "The Mulroney-Reagan deal is the same thing . . . it goes to the very heart of our identity."

Listening in the press room, Rick Salutin groaned in frustration at the irony of it. As a novelist, playwright, and journalist for *This Magazine*, working to the left of the NDP, Salutin had been engaged in the culture of national identity for years. He had written a prize-winning play, *Les Canadiens*, which dealt with the theme of hockey and Quebec nationalism, arguing that, when the Parti Québécois came to power, Les Canadiens became just another hockey team and lost their mythic status as the representatives of a people defending a nation's honour on the ice. He had written the pamphlet on free trade that had helped lay the groundwork of concern about the issue before the debate, and was writing a book about the election. Now, the leader evoking his themes of nationalism and popular culture was not Ed Broadbent but John Turner.

Earlier in the day, Turner had ruled out the possibility of a coalition with the NDP, saying flatly that there would be "no fusion, no coalition, no sharing of ministerial responsibilities." It was a shift in tone from a position he had expressed before the election, when he had told an interviewer from Southam News that it would be "a major victory" if the Conservatives were reduced to a minority, suggesting that he was considering some form of coalition with the NDP.

Ed Broadbent spent that Thursday in Edmonton, where he spoke to fourteen hundred people: an indication of the NDP's new strength in the Edmonton area. When asked by reporters about the possibility of a coalition, he was cautious. "We're not talking about forming an alliance," he said, dismissing Turner's remarks as irrelevant since, the previous year, he had said he would consider working with the NDP to form a government.

The dancing around the hypothetical question by both leaders was understandable, since neither could afford to convey the impression to his supporters that he was doing anything less than campaigning to win. In fact, before the debates, the former Manitoba Minister of Health W.D. Parasiuk had been given the task of checking with New Democrats across the country to consult on what the party should do if there were a minority government. It was a prickly question: in the minds of New Democrats, each formula the party had tried in the past had led to electoral disaster (and certainly no electoral breakthrough) in the subsequent election. From 1963 to 1968, the NDP had kept the Liberals in power, as it had in 1972-4; in both cases, the following elections were bad for the party. Provincially, the NDP had suffered from its attempt to set the agenda for the Peterson government in Ontario in 1985 without sharing cabinet seats. If there were a minority government in 1988, there would be enormous pressure to insist on cabinet positions.

However, after the debates, the consultations lost their priority as the Liberals surged ahead. Nevertheless, some New Democrats were unclear through the campaign what the party's real strategic goal was. There was a sense that resources had been spread too thin to make a serious breakthrough possible.

On November 17, in a speech in Washington, Ronald Reagan made a careful, three-paragraph reference to the Free Trade Agreement. "Even as we have been working on lowering trade barriers around the world, we have sought to eliminate most barriers with our most important partner, Canada," Reagan said. "As far as the United States is concerned, the free trade agreement is an example of co-operation at its best. It is a testament to the commitment of our two governments to the principles of the open market and to economic co-operation. It is also, as the leaders of the major industrial economies concluded at the Toronto summit, a catalyst for the rest of the world trading system."

Turner jumped on this remark as an example of what he called "unprecedented interference," saying, "It's a case of a lame duck trying to rescue a dead duck." It was a good line; unfortunately, it was delivered on Jean-François Bertrand's interview program in Quebec City. Even francophone Quebeckers who spoke English had to have the pun explained – that since the election of Bush, Reagan was known as a lame-duck president. But the next day, reacting to a comment by Margaret Thatcher in the *Washington Post* to the effect that it would be "very difficult for any prime minister of Canada to negotiate another international agreement with another country," Turner had his best line in French. He commented that Thatcher was still treating Canadians like "colons." While the word literally means colonists, it is a popular and powerful insult in Quebec, meaning someone who is ignorant, stupid and naive. When he uttered the phrase, there was an audible gasp from French-speaking reporters.

Broadbent, on the other hand, welcomed Reagan's remarks.

"It will remind every Canadian how close Brian Mulroney is to Ronald Reagan, remind every Canadian that the Americans got virtually everything they wanted in the deal, whether it's . . . access to our resources, moving in on our service sector, threatening pensions, or threatening medicare," Broadbent said in Edmonton. The next day, however, in Winnipeg, he was more critical of Margaret Thatcher. "Quite bluntly," Broadbent said, "It's none of her business."

In the last week or ten days of the campaign, John Gormley could feel things slipping away. As Conservative member for The Battlefords – Meadow Lake, northwest of Saskatoon, he felt he had worked hard, and, despite his reluctance to make a personal appeal to people on the basis of the work he had done, he found he couldn't help himself. In conversations on the doorstep, he was taking the slide in support very personally.

"Why aren't you voting for me?" he would say, point blank.

"It has nothing to do with you – I don't want free trade," he heard, time and time again.

"When you're an incumbent, it's that much more pathetic, because you start to take it personally," Gormley ruefully recalled later. He found himself reminding people of the work he had done for them. "Don't you remember the time when Grandma's cheque got lost?" he would ask. Later, he wondered if it was a sign of his desperation that he kept trying to dig deeper for a sense of identification with them; he had never liked the kind of politics where the politician reminded people of the service that they had received, and he found himself resorting to it, particularly when he knew the family.

"Did Uncle Harry tell you about –" he would ask.

"We all appreciate what you did," they would reply. "But I think free trade is going to mean we lose medicare."

On Sunday November 20, Dennis Mills, the Liberal candidate in the Toronto riding of Broadview-Greenwood, looked at the sheer tonnage of advertising. His background was marketing, he knew something of the impact the avalanche would have, and he figured it was all over. He phoned a business partner in the middle of the night to tell him to expect him back in the office after the campaign. The partner dropped everything, and joined the campaign for a final push in the last week.

In London-Middlesex, the Tory candidate, Terry Clifford, was trying desperately to reach some of the twenty thousand people he had talked to before the debates, when free trade took over the campaign. One of his people suggested live radio ads: an invitation on Saturday morning to drop around and get some straight talk on free trade from Clifford. So, for the last two Saturdays of the campaign, he got on the radio with an open mike, like a disc jockey at a furniture warehouse, urging people to drive on over and ask any questions they might have about free trade. Some two hundred undecided voters accepted the invitation; he would win by fewer than ten votes.

In La Prairie, Pierre Deniger could see his support collapse, as Quebeckers closed ranks to support the free-trade deal in middle-class constituencies like his own. Even friends told him they couldn't vote for him; people who had contributed money to his campaign. The voters were friendly – a hundred times politer than they had been in 1984, he would recall later – often wishing him good luck. Ruefully, he reflected that they were wishing him luck in another line of work. The Gallup poll that showed the Liberals in the lead had jolted the middle-class supporters of free trade in Quebec; the Quebec business community had launched a $600,000 advertising campaign with a powerful slogan: "Laissez-nous grandir ensemble" – allow us to grow together. It was a message of hope and enthusiasm; the Liberals' negative campaign was falling on deaf ears in Quebec.

On Saturday November 19, Pat Binns, running for re-election in Prince Edward Island, realized that he had lost when he knocked on a door, and a woman told him: "I have six sons; I guess they're going to have to fight in the American army."

As the campaigns wound down over the weekend, a kind of relaxation came over the leaders' planes: a mixture of relief and resignation, and a feeling that nothing could change the results. On Friday, when Mulroney was in Yarmouth, N.S., the word was whispered to the staff people and the advance men that they were home free: the latest poll on CTV that

---

431 ---

night showed their majority was safe. It was a matter of flying into Quebec for a few more triumphant rallies to send this message booming out one more time to the rest of the country, and then cruising home to Baie-Comeau.

That night, November 18, Mulroney arrived in Montreal, exhausted after events in Fredericton and Yarmouth and an evening speech in Longueuil. Gary Ouellet dropped by to see him in his hotel room. Ouellet had been left off the tour plane because, as the president of the consulting firm GCI, which since 1984 had become the most successful lobbying firm in Ottawa, he was a symbol for many in Ottawa of friends of Mulroney who were doing well financially because of their relationship with the new government. However, while he decided Ouellet should not be on the plane, Mulroney respected his street-smart political sense and enjoyed his earthy sense of humour, and kept in close touch with him. Working the phone from the hotel room, Ouellet somehow managed to obtain the Angus Reid polling figures to be published in the Southam papers the next morning. They showed the Tories with 41 per cent, the Liberals with 33, and the NDP with 23: the Tories doing very badly in the Maritimes, but surprisingly well in Ontario. Mulroney looked at the numbers: intuitively, he thought they were more prescient than Allan Gregg's. (In fact, the CTV poll broadcast that night had the exact numbers: Tories 43 per cent, Liberals 32, NDP 20.

Ed Broadbent campaigned in Toronto on Saturday, in a final rush of events in Toronto ridings, ending the campaign in Welland. As they arrived at the committee room, Rob Mingay called Ann Carroll over the cellular phone. "Hey, kid, last event."

It was the end of a long road for Ann Carroll. She had gone to work for Broadbent on September 1, 1975, and had been his secretary, his watchdog, his strategist, the tour's wagonmaster, and his most fiercely loyal adviser. Chiefs of staff had come and gone, research directors had left to pursue other careers, press aides had left, speech writers had changed; only Carroll had been there from the beginning of his leadership, and had never wavered in her commitment. She had had difficulties with some of the other people on staff at various times (they were not reduced when Judy Steed quoted her as having said that George Nakitsas would be chief of staff over her dead body), but no one ever questioned her loyalty, or her priorities. Ed Broadbent's interests came first.

Inside the hall, standing watching him give his last speech of the campaign, Rob Mingay reached over, grabbed her hand and held it. She started to weep from sheer pride. Broadbent saw, and quickly looked away; he didn't want her to get him started.

On Sunday, John Turner was back in Vancouver. A feeling of serenity had come over him. The events over the last few days had been extremely successful: wildly enthusiastic rallies in Hamilton (where, to the vast amusement of the press corps, Sheila Copps had made a Freudian slip of the tongue, and in listing off the Tory ministers who had disgraced the government and the country, had included the Liberal Party president, Michel Robert; the clip of Copps shouting "André Bissonnette! Roch LaSalle! Michel Robert!" was played again and again on the plane), Toronto (a strikingly multi-ethnic crowd, in which the only group of homogeneously white faces were the reporters and aides from the leader's plane), Belleville, and Winnipeg (where the enthusiasm of the crowds revealed something of the Liberal strength that would emerge in both eastern Ontario and Manitoba). On the flight west, cowboy hats were handed out, and the Turners mingled with the reporters as Geills took photographs.

Turner had succeeded in winning not only the respect but the affection of the reporters and camera crews on the plane; a striking contrast with 1984. As he headed west, he felt he had done everything he could. There was an admiration that would have been unimaginable eight weeks earlier for the man's courage in carrying on through the brutality of the campaign and the physical pain from his back.

On Sunday, the campaign bus went down to the Granville Island Market for one of the last events: a walk-about through the crowd with Liberal candidates. Standing waiting for Turner at one corner, Tex Enemark was still hopeful. He felt that Kim Campbell had suffered from losing her temper with a heckler at a meeting; the TV clip had been repeated constantly. He had been able to feel the surge of support after the debates, and he thought it looked like a three-way race with Johanna den Hertog.

Half a block away in the market, a group of NDP candidates were also campaigning: den Hertog, Turner's opponent Gerry Scott, and Svend Robinson. Robinson was nervous; it had been a tough campaign. At his Tory opponent's nomination meeting, Chuck Cook, the Conservative MP for North Vancouver, had said, "You're running against a publicly declared homosexual. That may sound dirty, but it's true. If Svend can say it, I can certainly say it. Now then, is that really what you want as a role model for your children?" John Bitonti, the Conservative candidate, told John Lownsborough in an interview that most of the people he met raised the question of Robinson's sexuality.

"What they're saying is that Mr. Robinson's being a homosexual is his concern," Bitonti said. "The point they don't like is that he came on the media and came out of the closet, not only in his own living room but in *their* living rooms. Crusading to their kids was seen as presenting his moral view on the whole riding."

It was a revealing remark; Bitonti sensed that television had introduced an additional restraint, an extra level of prurience for politicians: the public forum was now in the most intimate of private locations. As Lownsborough pointed out in *Saturday Night*, the word "family" became "a not-so-subtle code word in Bitonti campaign literature."

That Sunday afternoon, going through the market, Lownsborough watched as Robinson was campaigning from table to table in a restaurant, and stopped to make his pitch to an elderly woman and two elderly men.

"The woman, scanning the faces of her companions, turned to him," Lownsborough wrote. "'Oh,' she said, 'I vote for a *man*.' Nothing sarcastic. The tone was deadly because it was so lightly dismissive. He tried to josh her around the point. Smiling sweetly, she insisted: 'But *you're* not a man.'" Taking the measure of the table, Robinson decided to move on."

That night, the Turner campaign had a dinner for the reporters. It was a cheerful affair, full of teasing good humour, songs, and a mock news report put together from lines in speeches and scrums from the campaign. David Lockhart, whose imitations of the CBC radio reporter Jason Moskovitch had become one of the running jokes of the tour, performed, doing an affectionate imitation of Turner. He concluded with a vowel-perfect performance of John F. Kennedy's inaugural address; more than one person present was struck by the paradox that this would be part of the repertoire on the last night of one of the most passionate and nationalistic campaigns in recent memory. But it was also part of the paradox of Turner himself, a man who had served on the Board of Directors of Bechtel Corp., who considered George Shultz a friend, who had walked the ground of several battlefields of the American Civil War out of intense interest, who had campaigned in 1984 on the need to cut the deficit in half – and had campaigned in 1988 on guts, flags, Canadian identity, expensive promises, and social programs. Turner ended the campaign convinced, win or lose, his view of free trade and the threat to Canada would be proved to have been prophetic.

CHAPTER SEVENTEEN

Election Night

"I have never known an important issue in Canadian politics which has not been deeply influenced and sometimes determined in its result by factors of the most purely personal kind."

John W. Dafoe

As dusk gathered in Baie-Comeau, and the last voters were making their way to the polls, Brian Mulroney began to work on his speech for that night, sitting in the upstairs bedroom of the guest house at Le Manoir. Peter Newman was there to interview him for a history of his government, and when L. Ian MacDonald dropped off a draft of a text for Mulroney's statement, and paused to jot down a few notes, Newman glared at him in annoyance.

At eight o'clock, the polls closed in Atlantic Canada, and Mulroney began to get a few phone calls; one of the first bits of news he received was of Ross Reid's victory in St. John's East, followed by indications that Stewart McInnes had been defeated in Halifax and Tom McMillan was going down in Prince Edward Island.

Downstairs were Mila Mulroney and the children, Michel Cogger's wife and children, Bonnie Brownlee, Rick Morgan, John Tory, and Marc Lortie from the campaign plane. Mila Mulroney had prepared a family supper of ham and pineapple. After the polls closed and the results began to be announced, Mulroney and his wife had agreed that she would stay downstairs with the guests, and he would watch television upstairs, alone with Michel Cogger, watching two TV sets, one in English and one in French.

Downstairs, family and friends watched the results with mounting excitement and tension as the Atlantic results shifted and changed: it was 19-7 for the Liberals, 20-8 for the Liberals, 20-12 for the Liberals. Then the first indications of results from Quebec and Ontario.

In Vancouver, shortly after five p.m., John Turner was getting the same results over the phone at the Hotel Vancouver, but Liberal strategists knew that the solid lead in Atlantic Canada could crumble quickly when the results came in from Central Canada. The Liberals held their lead until about 8:20 Eastern Time. Then the Conservatives began to surge ahead as the wave of seats in Quebec began to be reported. At about 8:37, CTV projected a Conservative victory; a minute later, Radio-Canada made the same projection, and at 8:39, both CBC networks predicted a majority Conservative government.

Mila Mulroney and the four children headed up the stairs to embrace Mulroney, and met Mulroney and Cogger at the top of the stairs. John Tory, Marc Lortie, and the official photographer Bill McCarthy waited at the bottom of the stairs, and when the children came down, they went up, uncertain whether they should enter the room or not. McCarthy opened the door, and beckoned the others in to congratulate the prime minister.

"Marc, I am filled with a great sense of history," Mulroney told Lortie. "It is very rare in the history of our country that a government has won two successive majority governments, and even rarer for a Conservative government, for my party. Only Sir John A. succeeded in doing it. Et mon Marc, I can tell you – Sir John A. would be proud of his pony tonight!"

It was a line he repeated to his friends as he came downstairs – grinning with glee: Sir John A. would be proud of his pony tonight. It was classic Mulroney: part political historian, part racetrack tout.

Cogger, Tory, and Lortie then left to head over to the arena to give initial comments to the networks on the victory, and gradually old friends gathered to celebrate what they had been sure would be a victory: Terry McCann, known as Ace to his friends from St. Francis Xavier, a lawyer and engineer who had become the mayor of Pembroke; Mulroney's brother Gary, Fred Doucet, the Toronto lawyer Sam Wakim, and a few others.

Mulroney, casually dressed in a sweater and a yellow shirt, mingled with his friends, periodically withdrawing upstairs to watch the results alone, jotting a few notes, making and receiving telephone calls. He talked to all the Conservative premiers, to Robert Bourassa, to his mother, to a few personal friends.

He was delighted by the seats the Tories were winning in Ontario. Barbara McDougall kept her seat in St. Paul's, Terry Clifford was winning his in London-Middlesex, Michael Wilson, Doug Lewis, and John McDermid were all winning, although Flora McDonald was going down to defeat.

Mulroney then watched with interest as the results began coming in from the West. The Liberals were doing well in Manitoba. In Saskatchewan, Ray Hnatyshyn lost his seat to the NDP candidate, Chris Axworthy, by almost 5,000 votes, 19,669 to 14,689. Mulroney's first thought was that this was a result of right-wing splinter groups; however, they had no candidates in Saskatoon – Clark's Crossing. New Democrats later claimed that it was natural NDP territory; the remarkable thing was not that Hnatyshyn had been defeated, they argued, but that he had kept his seat for so long.

Dan Mazankowski, Harvie Andre, Lee Richardson, Jim Hawkes: almost all the Tories were winning in Alberta, although the New Democrat Ross Harvey was going to take Edmonton East from Bill Lesick. Joe Clark won re-election in Yellowhead, but it was a much closer thing than it had been in 1984. Clark beat Preston Manning by 6,711 votes, compared with his 30,000-vote margin in 1984; from 74 per cent of the vote then, he had dropped to 45 per cent.

In British Columbia, Kim Campbell succeeded in keeping Pat Carney's riding, but all the Tories on Vancouver Island lost: Pat Crofton and Ted Schellenberg were losing their seats to the NDP as were, on the mainland, Gerry St. Germain, Bob

Brisco, Fred King, and Stan Graham. Svend Robinson won his seat, and at his victory celebration someone shouted, "Svend Robinson for minister of defence!"

In Oshawa, Ed Broadbent came on stage with his wife Lucille, holding her hand in the air and waving as the crowd sang "For he's a jolly good fellow." Broadbent congratulated Mulroney on his mandate, saying that "the democratic will has been expressed" and that the NDP would continue to fight hard on the issue of taxes, the environment, and jobs. "We will stand up strongly to protect the interests of average Canadians, wherever they may live." Then, in the inverted sentence structure he sometimes adopted, he said, "It would not be accurate to say I am not somewhat disappointed. Of course I am."

For the NDP, despite winning a larger number of seats than ever before in the history of the party, had lost its only seat in Atlantic Canada, with Jack Harris falling to Ross Reid in St. John's East. None of the candidates in Quebec had won a seat, and Broadbent was particularly disappointed that Rémy Trudel had lost. Michael Cassidy, Lynn McDonald, and Marion Dewar had lost their seats in eastern and southern Ontario, and Ernie Epp had lost Thunder Bay – Nipigon – all to Liberals – although Cid Samson had won Timmins-Chapleau, and Steve Butland had defeated James Kelleher in Sault Ste. Marie. The other bright spots were that Steven Langdon and Howard McCurdy had kept their seats in the Windsor area.

In Manitoba, the NDP had lost historic seats: Cyril Keeper had lost Winnipeg North Centre, J.S. Woodsworth's and Stanley Knowles's old seat, and the veteran David Orlikow had lost Winnipeg North. Howard Pawley, the former NDP premier, had failed in his attempt to win Selkirk.

"There was an upsurge of Liberal support in urban Manitoba," Pawley told a television interviewer. "Certainly, it affected me in my constituency. There was no question about it – they had improved their standing a good deal."

In Saskatchewan, the news was much better. All the five New Democrats who had won in 1984 held their seats – Vic

Althouse, Les Benjamin, Lorne Nystrom, Simon de Jong, and Stan Hovdebo (two of whom, through redistribution, were running against Tory members of the last House) – and five more were elected, Ray Funk in Prince Albert – Churchill River, Ron Fisher in Saskatoon-Dundurn, Chris Axworthy who defeated Ray Hnatyshyn in Saskatoon – Clark's Crossing, Len Taylor who defeated John Gormley in The Battlefords – Meadow Lake, and Rod Laporte who defeated Bill Gottselig in Moose Jaw – Lake Centre.

In Alberta, a small NDP breakthrough occurred when Ross Harvey, the former research director for the NDP in the province, won Edmonton East. And in British Columbia, the news was very good. Svend Robinson had held his seat, as had Nelson Riis in Kamloops, Ray Skelly in North Island – Powell River, Jim Fulton in Skeena, Margaret Mitchell in Vancouver East, and Ian Waddell in Port Moody – Coquitlam. Even more impressive were the new members from B.C.: two former provincial leaders, Dave Barrett and Robert Skelly; a former finance minister, Dave Stupich; and members who had defeated sitting Tories, or taken Tory seats: Sid Parker had won back Kootenay East from Stan Graham, and Lyle Kristiansen, Joy Langan, Dawn Black, Jack Whittaker, Brian Gardiner, Lynn Hunter, Jim Karpoff and John Brewin had all won ridings away from the Conservatives. The single disappointment for Broadbent was that Johanna den Hertog had failed to win Vancouver Centre.

The result produced very mixed feelings for Broadbent. While the NDP had never done so well before, it had, for the first time, fallen well below its own expectations. There were no tangible results to show for the enormous amount of time, effort, and money spent in Quebec, or for Broadbent's support of Meech Lake. The party had tilted substantially to the West, and there would be lingering internal bitterness and resentment about the way the campaign had been run. The dream that was believable at the beginning of the campaign, of Broadbent's moving to Stornoway or even negotiating the terms of a minority government, had dissolved.

Before leaving for the arena, Mulroney spoke briefly to Turner, who had only recently received his own results in Quadra, and told him that he was going to make his speech. Shortly after midnight, Mulroney and his family arrived at the Baie-Comeau arena for a triumphant entry. It had been agreed that the speech would be a message of reassurance: a time for healing. The speech would be, until the Speech from the Throne in April, the only formal statement of what the mandate represented.

The crowd was much more subdued than it had been in 1984; pleased, excited, but with none of the frenzy of the previous shocking wave. After thanking the voters of Charlevoix, congratulating the elected Conservative MPs, expressing sympathy for his defeated candidates, commending those of all parties who ran, and congratulating Turner and Broadbent on "a hard-fought campaign," Mulroney then said what he thought the victory meant.

"Because the issues were historic, the campaign was especially challenging. But, however impassioned the debate, this campaign has shown that Canadians agree on what it is that we most cherish in our national life," he said. "Our sovereignty, the protection of minority rights, our unique social programs, our concern for the environment, our commitment to regional development – these have their source in a Canadian tradition of tolerance and sharing. It is something we expect of each other and of our governments.

"The election, then, has been not about those values, but about the means to give them greater effect," he continued. "So now, it is a time for healing in this land. For in the end, irrespective of party preference, we are all Canadians, we all love our country, and we all put the national interest first."

His mandate, he said, was to affirm those Canadian values. Canadians across the country had joined in a national affirmation of confidence, and given him a second mandate.

"The margin is decisive and the mandate is clear: to implement the Free Trade Agreement, which holds the promise of new opportunities and new prosperity," Mulroney said. "To ratify the Meech Lake Accord, which returns Quebec to the constitutional family on terms that are honourable for all concerned."

The rest of the mandate was general in the extreme: creating wealth and "the administrative breathing room we need" in order to generate new and improved social programs. "Administrative breathing room" was a delightfully suggestive phrase: a euphemism for who knew what kinds of cutbacks in staffing, slashes in funding, or tax increases in the name of efficiency or deficit reduction.

Political and economic growth was the only way to achieve unity, Mulroney said, adding, "Without a doubt, therein lies the true meaning of the mandate we have been given. It is a mandate for unity, for fairness, for tolerance and for openness to the world."

The country, he said, was taking on the demands of the future.

"And so, our fellow citizens have decided to give themselves the economic tools necessary to assume their responsibilities – for the security and welfare of all, for the environment, for sound management of public finances," Mulroney told the crowd and the country. "We pledge to Canadians a competent and caring government and a vision for a competitive and compassionate society."

With a few more ringing phrases filled with the abstract nouns he liked to use so often – vision, greatness, unity and prosperity, promise, tolerance – Mulroney ended the speech, and, amidst the euphoria of the crowd, kicked the large balloons into the audience, and danced with glee. On the way out, he crossed the barricade to shake hands with the crowd, and then headed back to Le Manoir.

It took a while for Turner to start getting ready to leave the Hotel Vancouver, and to make his way across town to the cultural centre where his election-night headquarters was established. Making his way through the crowd to the platform, he spoke briefly, saying how he had promoted his view of a strong, independent and sovereign Canada.

"I have done so with everything I had – with all my heart and all my strength and I have no regrets at all."

There was almost a Biblical cadence to the words; indeed, in the campaign, Turner had almost come to see himself as much as a prophet as he did as a politician. He had seized upon this campaign to redeem his honour, to lift himself above the sordid squabbles that had been such a constant plague to his leadership. He had shown himself to be, as he said with some rueful self-pity to a friend in the weeks following the election, a magnificent failure: propelled forward, but ultimately crippled by his personal flaws, insecurities, and weaknesses.

"Despite the fact that the Conservatives have a larger percentage of the popular vote, Canadians have certainly expressed their wish to keep this country strong, sovereign, and independent," he said. "They've also chosen to give the Conservative government another mandate. I believe, fundamentally, that the people are always right."

Turner pointed out that the voters had also doubled the number of Liberals elected to the House of Commons.

"We will fight for our ideals, and our vision of the country. We'll make our presence felt. We'll be vigilant, and we will be loyal to the principles of justice and equality and compassion for which this party has always fought."

He thanked his family, and deservedly so: they had rallied around him with grace and good humour, swallowing whatever distaste they felt for the media and being outgoing, cheerful, and friendly with a planeful of people who had been, for most of his tenure as leader, a constant problem. (In a gesture that singularly impressed the media people travelling with the tour, his four children spent the rest of the night drinking with the press corps, smuggling them into their hotel when the bars closed.) Turner thanked his fellow Liberal candidates, he thanked the people of Quadra, and concluded by saying, "I will uphold the confidence you've placed in me. I will honour that trust, and I will continue to hold my country first and foremost."

It was a speech which sounded as if it had been written with chunks of the Book of Common Prayer beside texts by

Lord Baden-Powell. And yet he never congratulated Mulroney. Then, after making his way through the crowd shaking hands, Turner returned to his hotel.

Back at the guest house, Prime Minister Takeshita of Japan was on the phone, with his congratulations. A few minutes later, Rajiv Gandhi, the prime minister of India, called.

At Le Manoir, a party was under way for the local organizers in Charlevoix and the people from the plane. About 2 a.m. the Mulroneys arrived at the party. There was a small band there, and, for about twenty minutes, Mulroney took the microphone and sang, accompanied by the accordionist, the romantic popular songs of his youth like "Volare," songs of Gilles Vigneault, the Irish songs he sang so often: corny, romantic songs he could sing out in the pure, unvarnished pleasure of victory.

CONCLUSION

"Politicians are people who truly make something out of nothing. They have few concrete gifts to offer. They are not engineers or artists or makers. They are manipulators: they offer themselves as manipulators. Having no gifts to offer, they seldom know what they seek."

V.S. Naipaul

Three men staked their careers on the outcome of the election; only one would remain leader of his party. Within six months, both Ed Broadbent and John Turner had resigned, and the New Democrats and the Liberals both embarked on the exhausting process of choosing their successors. The prospective new leaders would face enormous challenges in defining responses to the defeat their parties had suffered, and in correcting the flaws that had helped contribute to defeat – in a political environment which was very different, and yet still charged with the issues which had been so difficult in the past: free trade and Meech Lake.

The 1988 election was a turning point for Canada in many ways. As had happened in the past, in 1911 and in the 1940s, a coincidence of the interests of large corporations and Quebec nationalist sentiment had created an effective coalition that acted powerfully on behalf of the winning party.

As is so often the case in an election, what appeared to be a debate over a substantive issue became, in fact, a symbolic struggle. The Free Trade Agreement became distorted by both sides so that it became increasingly difficult for any citizen to have a better understanding at the end of the campaign than at the beginning of whether, in fact, Canada's medical system was threatened by the agreement.

For, when it suited their arguments, both sides would treat the document as a text in some cases, and as a symbolic blueprint for the future in others. When it was useful for the defenders of free trade, they described it in broad-brush terms as an example of Canada's ability to compete, its entrepreneurial spirit, and its commitment to growth, employment, and prosperity. However, when the details of the agreement were challenged, it became a limited legal contract. "The free-trade agreement is a commercial document that begins and ends with trade," said the advertisement "Straight Talk," produced by the Canadian Alliance for Trade and Job Opportunities; it is "a document that is cancellable on six months' notice," Mulroney said in the TV debate.

Yet the agreement limits the ability of the Canadian government to intervene in the economy as it has in the past, guarantees that Canada will never have another National Energy Program, would make it almost impossible for the federal government to nationalize industries and establish new Crown corporations, and ensures that foreign investors cannot be restricted in ways that Canadians took for granted in the past. And even one of the agreement's most vigorous critics, Marjorie Bowker, pointed out that the cancellation clause was a red herring, since the damage and disruption caused by cancellation might well be greater than the harm done by the agreement itself.

In his speeches and commercials, Mulroney took pains to say that social programs, unemployment insurance, pensions, and medicare, were not mentioned in the agreement. While this is technically true, there was little that he said in the campaign (other than arguing that greater prosperity would enable the government to improve social programs) that would restrict him from cutting back on social spending in the name, not of the free-trade agreement, but of deficit reduction. Indeed, although Mulroney had said quite explicitly that unemployment insurance would not be affected, Michael Wilson in his budget of April 1989 eliminated government contributions to unemployment insurance.

The critics of the Free Trade Agreement, on the other hand, failed in serious ways. Because their interests were so diverse, they were unable to propose a believable alternative, and keep the support of all the different groups opposing the deal.

The opponents of the deal were caught in a number of paradoxes. To begin with, neither of the parties committed to an activist role for government appeared as competent to govern as the party committed to reducing the role of government. Secondly, neither of the parties opposing free trade was able to develop an approach as coherent and believable in French Canada as it was in English Canada; the nationalism of the anti-free-trade crusade had no effective echo in Quebec. Finally, under pressure, both opposition parties indicated, without acknowledging it, that they would rather be the official opposition to a majority Conservative government than hold the balance of power during a minority government.

This is not shameful or surprising; to have done otherwise would have been to challenge the traditional assumptions of the Canadian parliamentary three-party system that has developed over the last half-century. The very existence of the three-party system meant that it was possible for one party to form a majority government with less than 45 per cent of the vote – just as the Conservatives in Ontario had done for many years, and as the Parti Québécois succeeded in doing in Quebec in 1976.

The results themselves were interesting. The Conservatives did poorly in Atlantic Canada, winning only two seats in Newfoundland, five in Nova Scotia, five in New Brunswick, and none in Prince Edward Island; the Liberals, on the other hand, won twenty seats, while the NDP was wiped out. However, John Crosbie won 62 per cent of the vote in his riding of

St. John's West. Four of the Liberals in Nova Scotia received over half of the vote (Francis LeBlanc, Coline Campbell, Russ MacLellan, and David Dingwall) as did three of the Liberals in New Brunswick (Douglas Young, Maurice Dionne, and Fernand Robichaud).

In Quebec, the Tory tidal wave of sixty-three seats ran deep: forty-seven of the Tory candidates won half the vote or more, and Mulroney won an overwhelming 80 per cent of the vote in Charlevoix. Only two Liberals in Quebec – Alfonso Gagliano and Sheila Finestone – won half the vote or more.

In Ontario, the Tories won forty-seven seats of the ninety-nine, the Liberals won forty-two, and the NDP only ten. While this represented a loss of twenty seats compared with 1984 for the Conservatives, it was an increase of nine seats over 1980. However, the Conservatives suffered historic setbacks in eastern Ontario, losing ten seats of the eighteen east of Oshawa. But the Conservatives retained their strength in the prosperous Golden Horseshoe, holding even constituencies in the Niagara Peninsula that many thought would inevitably be lost because of the fears of free trade. The results showed that Tory support in Canada's richest province was moving from poorer, rural ridings to the affluent suburban constituencies. Of the twelve urban ridings with an average family income of over $50,000, the Tories won nine.

But the periphery was largely Liberal: eastern Ontario, civil-servant Ottawa, ethnic Toronto, parts of Northern Ontario. The precariousness of the NDP in Ontario can be seen by the fact that Ed Broadbent received only 44 per cent of the vote in Oshawa – and, proportionately, only John Rodriguez did better, with 45 per cent.

In Manitoba, the Liberals gained from the slump of the New Democrats; it was the only Western province in which the NDP vote dropped from the 1984 level, from 27.3 per cent to 21, and from four seats to two. That slip in NDP support helped the Liberals win one of the two Winnipeg seats they took.

In Saskatchewan, the Tories dropped from 41.7 to 36.4 per cent of the vote, and went from seven seats to four, while the

NDP went from five seats to ten and from 38.4 to 44.2 per cent of the vote. The Liberals remained unchanged, with 18.2 per cent of the vote and no seats.

The Tory strength in Alberta was dented, but unshaken; Conservative support slipped from 68.8 per cent in 1984 to 51.8 per cent in 1988. The New Democrats won one seat, with an increase of only 3.3 per cent of the vote; the bulk of the Tory loss in support went to Preston Manning's Reform Party, which received 15.4 per cent of the vote. When John Dahmer, the victorious Conservative in Beaver River, died of cancer five days after the election, the Reform Party was in a solid position for the by-election. On March 13, Deborah Grey, a thirty-six-year-old schoolteacher who had finished fourth on November 21, won it with 11,154 votes – 7,000 more than she had received in November.

Tories analysing Preston Manning's vote in Yellowhead found that, while he came second to Joe Clark with 28 per cent of the vote, he got 22 per cent in the four towns in the riding with populations of more than five thousand, 25 per cent in the next three largest towns, and 31 per cent in the smaller towns and rural areas. The discontent with the government – or, perhaps one should say, government at all – was clearly greatest in rural communities.

In British Columbia, the Conservatives lost eleven seats to the NDP, and dropped twelve points in the popular vote from 46.6 per cent to 34.4 per cent, while the NDP went from eight to nineteen seats, but gained only 2 per cent of the popular vote, from 35 to 37 per cent. The Tories were bled both by the Reform Party – which had not been a factor in 1984, and got 4.9 per cent of the vote in 1988 – and also by the Liberals, who increased their share of the popular vote by 4.9 percentage points, from 16.4 per cent to 21.3 per cent.

The initial response of many observers was to identify the Reform Party as the factor which led to the dramatic increase in NDP seats. However, the increase in Liberal support was identical. Moreover, British Columbia was a particularly intense forum for debate over free trade, since the province had already suffered losses as a result of the softwood-lumber dispute with the United States, and was naturally polarized between left and right, environmentalists and loggers, peace activists and retired naval officers. Leaning away from the Tories, the province elected New Democrats, substantially strengthening the NDP caucus in terms of experience in government.

Overall, the results showed a degree of polarization in the country between rich and poor, urban and rural, French and English. The Tories had become, like the Borden government of 1911, representative of a blend of affluent English Canadians, largely of British Isles ancestry, and French-speaking Quebeckers. The Liberals had become a coalition of minorities: Maritimers, Montrealers, ethnic Torontonians, eastern and northern Ontarians, urban and ethnic Manitobans. And the NDP had become even more Western, without a seat east of Oshawa, and over three-quarters of the caucus from west of Ontario.

In the weeks and months that followed the election, it became clear that fundamental differences remained in the country about language, and that the private sector was about to engage in a process of "rationalization": within a week in January, there were four major mergers. The new environment of Meech Lake and free trade began to look less certain, and the mood of regional conciliation was gone, as was reflected in anger over language in Quebec, and the election of a Reform candidate in the Beaver River by-election in Alberta.

For the New Democrats, the dashed expectations were frustrating. Bob White of the United Auto Workers delivered a stinging rebuke to Broadbent and the party strategists, first at a meeting with the CLC executive, and then in a letter that was leaked to the press. It was a bitter, angry, and quite unfair attack, since the labour leaders had known about, and accepted the NDP strategy. Broadbent took some time to reflect on his future, and then told the NDP federal council in March that he would not be a candidate for re-election at the party's convention. The recriminations continued, with the publication of the paperback edition of Judy Steed's biography of Broadbent – which included some bitter remarks by some of the campaign strategists and tour people: a wounding breach of tradition for a party which had traditionally kept its upper lip stiff, and its criticisms internal.

The post-election malaise was reflected in the early months of the leadership campaign to choose Ed Broadbent's successor. The strength and stability of Broadbent's leadership seemed even greater in retrospect, as none of the members of caucus who declared their candidacies seemed able to capture the imagination of the public or the party. Those New Democrats who did enjoy national stature, such as Stephen Lewis, made it clear they would not be candidates.

The Liberals also began a process of soul-searching, as Paul Martin and Jean Chrétien both began to position themselves to succeed John Turner. Turner's decision to step down from the Liberal leadership seemed to liberate him from some of the partisan burdens he had been carrying: he began to speak out even more eloquently about the divisions and resentments that seemed to have been exacerbated in the country. The future of Meech Lake began to seem more doubtful, as its supporters wobbled and its critics grew even more resentful after Robert Bourassa's decision to invoke the "notwithstanding" clause to exempt his law restricting the use of English on signs from the application of the Charter of Rights. Turner began to sense, and speak about, a deterioration in the mood of the country. He was proud that he had won an accolade from the conservative philosopher George Grant, the author of *Lament for a Nation*, before he died, for his attack on the Free Trade Agreement, and, after the election, from the long-time NDP supporter Pierre Berton, who told a University of British Columbia audience that he had voted Liberal for the first time.

The months that followed November 21 showed that the election was clearly a turning point for Canada: an end of an era, and a parting of the ways.

What can be learned from the election of 1988? Certainly, within a few months, a certain cynicism was possible. The deficit was barely mentioned during the campaign; yet the election was barely won before Michael Wilson was calling deficit reduction the number one priority. Having stated that nuclear submarines were part of Canada's commitment to her allies, the government eliminated the nuclear-submarine program. After arguing that the government was committed to social programs, and that these would not be affected by free trade, the government eliminated its contributions to unemployment insurance, postponed the implementation of its child-care proposals, and drastically cut the budgets of Via Rail and the CBC.

Almost immediately after the election, it became clear that the government was committed to only one aspect of the rather limited election campaign: the approval and implementation of the Free Trade Agreement. Once that was done, the government was bound to little else.

At one level, very little happened during the election campaign of 1988. When Brian Mulroney went to Rideau Hall on October 1, the Decima polling showed him enjoying the support of 43 per cent of the voters. On November 21, he won a second mandate with 43 per cent of the votes. So, at one level, everything occurred before the writs were issued. In addition, the election became a virtual referendum on the Free Trade Agreement, and, with one party supporting it and two parties opposing it, the party that had a monopoly on one side of the argument was able to win the election with a minority of the votes cast.

At another level, the campaign was an extraordinary test of the political leaders and the political parties. It was an immensely complicated cycle of information generated by speeches, comments to reporters, leaflets, television commercials, and TV debates; all of it absorbed by voters – largely through television but also from newspapers, radio, leaflets, and canvassers – and tested by politicians or canvassers going from door to door and by sophisticated opinion-sampling techniques, which altered the flow of information into the cycle.

At one level, what I have tried to do in this account is to convey as many of the elements as I could in this extraordinarily complex cycle: how decisions by government or by political parties contributed to strategy; how strategy shaped political discourse; how the discourse was generated, through reports, speeches, and commercials; how polling, focus groups, and door-to-door canvassing picked up the public reaction, and then had an impact on reshaping decisions, changing strategy, and altering discourse for another cycle. The complexity is such that I do not pretend to have grasped every element, or necessarily to have given the appropriate weight to those elements that I did succeed in identifying.

But from that cycle, a number of things emerge. The election proved to be a supreme test of political management, and political leadership. All three campaigns had rocky periods, and all three had internal tensions and crises that verged on panic. All three faced internal dissensions, and vigorous pressures to adopt different strategies. Mulroney succeeded in keeping the divergent elements of his party working together rather than at cross-purposes; his success was a triumph in political management. Turner and Broadbent did not; their failures reflected cumulative errors in judgement. All three men were playing for keeps. They were staking their careers on victory. Turner and Broadbent lost, and stepped down. Mulroney won, and stayed on.

Part of that success came from a mixture of good luck and good management. Mulroney had the advantage of being severely underestimated by his opponents, and by the media. The relative scarcity of English-Canadian political observers comfortable in French meant that the political mood in Quebec was often ignored or misinterpreted. In addition, the delay in the decision of the Supreme Court on the constitutionality of article 58 of law 101, dealing with the language of signs, meant that the highly emotional reaction, both in Quebec and in the other provinces, to the judgement and to Robert Bourassa's use of the "notwithstanding" clause to pass Bill 178, occurred only after the election.

In addition to learning not to underestimate Mulroney, there are other lessons that can be drawn from the successful Conservative campaign. The expensive mixture of opinion polling, testing of campaign themes, taking advantage of strong support from the business community, and intensive advertising all worked. Public opinion changed. In the past, public-opinion polling was used to test the wind, to develop a sense of direction. The Mulroney government learned, in the 1988 election, not simply to sound out public opinion, but to shape it, manipulate it, and change it. They learned, in the jargon of marketing, "to move numbers." Thus, for the six months from the election to the budget, there was a constant chorus of warning about the deficit and the public debt.

If the Wilson budget suggested that the government had been selective to the point of duplicity during the election in its discussion of what it planned to do, the Speech from the Throne of April 3 nevertheless indicated the government's new priorities: changing the unemployment-insurance system, and putting more emphasis on the environment. But tucked away at the end of the speech was a small indication of what Mulroney and his advisers had learned from the run-up to the 1988 election. In a section entitled Canada's National Identity, the speech said that Canadians have placed a high value on the qualities of tolerance, compassion, and fairness, that Canadian society cares about "the quality of its national life, its health, education, human welfare and the environment," and that Canadian values had produced "a unique national identity of which Canadians are justifiably proud."

Then, virtually unnoticed, perhaps because it was hidden in the wash of civics-class prose, was the indication of the lesson learned. "My government has invited the participation of all the provinces and territories in planning Canada's 125th birthday in 1992," Governor General Sauvé read. "The same year will mark the 350th anniversary of the founding of Montreal."

The same year may well also mark an election, when the pinch of the deficit-reduction budgets is a fading memory, and the warm glow of celebration is still felt. By then, it will be clearer which of the three leaders was prophetic in his 1988 predictions about the effects of the Free Trade Agreement on Canadian sovereignty and social programs.

Graham Fraser

Ottawa, July 4, 1989

ACKNOWLEDGEMENTS

This book had its origin in a chat with Doug Gibson and Hugh Winsor in the fall of 1986, when I expounded at some length on the degree of insanity that was involved in writing a book, and how I felt cured of that particular disease. Almost from that moment forward, I was infected, once again, with the bacteria. My wife began finding scribbled ideas and odd notes, like the hints of an illicit affair.

Peter Livingston played an important role in making me ask myself the right questions, and, once I had answered them, in making the necessary arrangements. Doug Gibson, as always, provided confidence, trust, and infectious enthusiasm. Ivon Owen's care and professionalism meant, as always, a pleasurable collaboration. Geoffrey Stevens, then managing editor of the *Globe and Mail*, gave me leave to write the book, and imposed only one restriction: that I do no interviews exclusively for the book while still writing for the *Globe*. I kept to that: the interview with Prime Minister Brian Mulroney in June that is central to chapter two was the basis for a number of articles for the *Globe*, and other parts of the book appeared as part of my daily coverage of the election.

I am grateful to the leading members of all three parties: candidates, leaders' staff, advance people, tour organizers, strategists, advertising people, aides, volunteers. People in all three parties were forthcoming with explanations, documents, speeches, and videotapes; in many cases, people patiently made themselves available again and again to go over incidents in the campaign, some of which included unpleasant memories. In each party, there were people who went far beyond mere duty, and helped me track down details, confirm theories, and simply shared my interest and enthusiasm for trying to understand the mysterious dynamics of an election. I emerge from this process with an even greater respect for those who engage in the very difficult, often thankless task of trying to get the political party they support elected. Whatever criticisms I have of people who were involved in this election, and whatever errors I may have made in fact or interpretation, I hope that I have been able to convey that respect.

I am particularly thankful to my colleagues at the *Globe and Mail*. Geoffrey Stevens granted me the leave to do the book; Tim Pritchard, his successor, extended it. Rick Mackie, national editor during the election, was always helpful, as was Sylvia Stead, the election editor. Both during the campaign and afterwards, as I tried to reconstruct it, my colleagues in the Ottawa bureau continued to be invaluable in their friendship, encouragement and support: Chris Waddell, Jeffrey Simpson, Hugh Winsor, Paul Koring, John Kohut, Ross Howard, Susan Delacourt, and Richard Cleroux all contributed memories, theories, notes, tapes, advice, enthusiasm, and wisdom. My brother, John Fraser, read the page proofs with a sharp eye. Many thanks. They deserve part of the credit for the texture of the book, and none of the blame.

A significant number of people in all three parties who proved to be most helpful were the most desirous that they not be mentioned. I hope that I have lived up to their confidence. But as a result, to list all the other people I spoke to would be unfair. My only fear and regret is that I have not been able to do full justice to all the people who gave me so much time and assistance.

In addition, as always, friends provided particular support and accommodation as I travelled: Anne Uteck in Halifax, Benoît Aubin and Claire Viens in Quebec City, Stephen Bornstein in Montreal, and Bob and Arlene Perly Rae in Toronto. François Desrochers did crucial work for me in organizing election clippings, and Maureen Harrison, Maureen Cullingham, Katherine Miller, and the staff of the Parliamentary Library were all extremely helpful.

My deepest gratitude is to my wife Barbara Uteck and my two sons, Malcolm and Nick. Confident when I was nervous, cheerful when I was grumpy, they were patient, understanding, and supportive. Thanks.

Graham Fraser

CHRONOLOGY

1983

June 11: Brian Mulroney is elected leader of the Progressive Conservative Party, defeating Joe Clark on the fourth ballot.

August 29: Mulroney is elected in a by-election in Central Nova.

October 6: Mulroney speaks in favour of the Liberal resolution on the Manitoba language question, establishing Conservative unanimity on bilingualism.

1984

February 29: Pierre Trudeau announces he is resigning as prime minister.

June 16: John Turner is elected Liberal leader on the second ballot, defeating Jean Chrétien and Don Johnston.

July 9: With an 11-point lead in the public-opinion polls, John Turner calls an election for September 4.

July 13: Brian Mulroney announces he will be a candidate in Manicouagan, in Quebec, rather than in Nova Scotia.

July 24: Debate between the three leaders in French; Mulroney is considered the winner in Quebec.

July 25: Debate between the three leaders in English; Mulroney attacks Turner on patronage.

August 6: Mulroney promises a new era of federal-provincial co-operation in a speech at his nomination meeting in Sept-Îles.

September 4: Election. The Progressive Conservatives, led by Brian Mulroney, win 211 seats and 49.9 per cent of the vote. The Liberals, led by John Turner, win 40 seats and 28 per cent of the vote; the New Democrats, led by Ed Broadbent, win 30 seats and 19 per cent of the vote.

September 17: The Mulroney cabinet is sworn in.

November 8: Michael Wilson announces *A New Direction for Canada: An Agenda for Economic Renewal*.

1985

February 12: Robert Coates resigns as minister of national

defence after publicity over his visiting a nightclub in Lahr, West Germany.

February 15: Mulroney says that he will proceed with the idea of negotiating a trade agreement with the United States.

Quebec Liberal Party position paper, *Mastering Our Future*, is published, laying out the party's five conditions for signing the constitutional agreement.

March 17–18: "Shamrock Summit" in Quebec City with Ronald Reagan.

June 19: Solange Denis berates Mulroney, and tells him he lied about protecting old-age pensions.

June 27: Wilson announces that Old Age Security payments will be fully indexed to the consumer price index, and the government backs down from its plan to de-index pensions after an outcry from senior citizens.

Pierre Marc Johnson presents the Quebec government's twenty-four conditions for signing the constitutional agreement.

August: There is a vigorous nationalist debate when the U.S. Coast Guard icebreaker *Polar Sea* enters disputed Canadian Arctic waters without permission.

September 1: The Canadian Commercial Bank fails.

September 5: The Macdonald Commission Report is released, recommending a free-trade agreement with the United States.

September 9: Mulroney announces conflict-of-interest rules.

September 23: Fisheries Minister John Fraser resigns after controversy over his role in approving the sale of tainted tuna against the advice of his officials.

September 25: Communications Minister Marcel Masse resigns when he learns that the RCMP is investigating his election expenses.

September 26: Mulroney tells the House that Canada will try to negotiate a trade agreement with the U.S. to reduce tariff and non-tariff barriers.

September 30: The Northland Bank is closed.

November 28: Masse returns to the cabinet, exonerated.

December 2: The Liberal Party, led by Robert Bourassa, wins the Quebec election.

December 31: Suzanne Blais-Grenier resigns from the cabinet to protest the closing of a refinery in Montreal.

1986

March 7: Andrée Champagne admits urging that government funds be used to recruit young people to the Progressive Conservative Party.

April 23: The U.S. Senate Finance Committee approves the request to begin free-trade negotiations on a 10–10 vote.

May 9: Gil Rémillard presents Quebec government's five conditions for signing the constitutional agreement in a speech at Mont-Gabriel.

May 12: Sinclair Stevens tells the House of Commons that he has resigned as minister of regional industrial expansion, and has asked Mulroney to establish an investigation into the allegations of conflict of interest against him.

May 15: Michel Gravel is charged with ten counts of bribery or attempted bribery, thirty-two counts of defrauding the government and eight of breach of trust.

June 13: An interview with John Turner is published in Le Devoir, in which he gives cautious support to Bourassa's five conditions.

June 30: Mulroney makes a major cabinet shuffle; he names Mazankowski deputy prime minister.

August 12: The premiers issue the Edmonton Declaration, saying that their top constitutional priority is to embark on a constitutional process, with Quebec's five points as the basis for discussion.

October 31: The government announces that the CF–18 maintenance contract will go to Canadair in Montreal, rather than to Bristol Aerospace Ltd. in Winnipeg.

November 11: Marc Lalonde urges Liberal delegates to vote for a leadership review.

November 30: Turner wins 76.3 per cent support from the Liberal convention.

1987

January 18: André Bissonnette is fired from the cabinet following a report in the Montreal Gazette of a land-flip in his riding involving the sale of land to Oerlikon Aerospace Inc.

February 11: An Angus Reid poll is published, showing the Conservatives with 23 per cent, the New Democrats with 33 per cent and the Liberals with 42 per cent. Of those polled, 60 per cent disapprove of Mulroney's performance as prime minister.

February 19: Roch LaSalle resigns from the cabinet: the seventh minister to leave the cabinet since it was sworn in.

April 16: The *Globe and Mail* publishes a story showing that renovations to 24 Sussex Drive were paid for by the PC Canada Fund.

April 30: Mulroney and the ten premiers unanimously reach a constitutional agreement in principle at Meech Lake.

June 2–3: The formal Meech Lake Accord document is negotiated at the Langevin Block.

June 23: The Quebec National Assembly approves the Accord, which starts the clock for the three-year deadline for Parliament and nine other provincial legislatures to ratify it.

July 20, 1987: The NDP wins by-elections in St. John's East, Hamilton Mountain, and Yukon.

September 23: Simon Reisman breaks off free-trade negotiations.

October 13: The Liberals win every seat in New Brunswick, and Frank McKenna becomes premier.

October 3–4: The Free Trade Agreement deal is struck in Washington.

October 26: The House of Commons passes the Meech Lake Accord.

December 3: The Parker Report is tabled in the House of Commons; Chief Justice William Parker finds that Sinclair Stevens violated the conflict-of-interest code fourteen times.

December 10: The final text of the Free Trade Agreement is presented to the House of Commons.

1988

February 2: Michel Côté resigns from the cabinet, telling the House of Commons that he did not declare a large loan from a Quebec businessman.

March 31: Lucien Bouchard is sworn in as secretary of state.

April 25: Senator Pietro Rizzuto tells Turner he has letters from twenty-two Liberal MPs urging him to step down.

April 27: Turner tells the caucus he is staying as leader.

April 29: Mulroney calls Lac-Saint-Jean by-election.

June 19–22: G–7 Economic Summit in Toronto.

June 21: Lac-Saint-Jean by-election: Lucien Bouchard is elected.

June 22: The House of Commons takes the final vote on the Meech Lake Accord, which was sent back by the Senate.

June 23: Bernard Roy resigns as principal secretary.

July 14: Peter White is named principal secretary.

July 15: Priorities and Planning meeting at Meech Lake.

July 18: Announcement of agreement in principle to develop Hibernia.

July 19: Turner agrees on strategy to ask the Senate to delay its vote on the Free Trade Agreement until after the election; he announces his decision the next day.

August 28: Mulroney tells Peter Mansbridge that the election will be in the fall.

August 31: Bill C–130, the legislation implementing the Free Trade Agreement, is passed by the House of Commons.

September 19: The U.S. Senate passes the Free Trade Bill.

September 28: President Reagan signs the American Free Trade Bill. The Liberals hold a special caucus meeting, and announce the forty-point election program.

WEEK ONE

Saturday October 1, 1989: Brian Mulroney visits Rideau Hall, and the writs are issued. John Turner is campaigning in Toronto, and Ed Broadbent responds to the election call in Ottawa.

Sunday October 2: Mulroney visits Tory headquarters, and announces that Sinclair Stevens will not be a candidate for the Progressive Conservative Party; Ed Broadbent opens his campaign in Saint-Basile-le-Grand; John Turner attends a strategy meeting in Ottawa.

Tuesday October 4: Turner announces a housing policy in Toronto. Broadbent tells senior citizens in Edmonton that free trade is a threat to medicare. Mulroney says in Calgary that free trade will create thirty-thousand jobs in Alberta.

Wednesday October 5: An Angus Reid poll is published showing the Conservatives with 45 per cent, the NDP with 27, and Liberals with 26 per cent. Mulroney predicts good times for the B.C. lumber industry in Prince George, B.C. Broadbent announces a $580-million pollution clean-up program in Richmond, B.C. Turner announces a child-care policy in Montreal.

WEEK TWO

Tuesday October 11: Broadbent says that Canada would gain from the evolution to a two-party system: the Tories and the NDP; Environics poll is published showing the Conservatives with 42 per cent, the NDP with 29, and the Liberals with 25.

Wednesday October 12: Turner speaks to Confederation Dinner in Toronto; peace activists are dragged out of a Mulroney meeting in Toronto; Broadbent unveils part of a tax-reform package to help families.

Friday October 14: Liberal strategists meet, and prepare the weekly memo telling Turner how bad the situation is.

Saturday October 15: Turner is told that the strategists think he should step down.

WEEK THREE

Wednesday October 19: The CBC broadcasts a report that Liberal strategists have discussed the possibility of Turner's stepping down.

WEEK FOUR

Monday October 24: Leaders' debate in French.

Tuesday October 25: Leaders' debate in English.

Wednesday October 26: Broadbent speaks in London, and neglects to mention Fleck Manufacturing Inc. layoffs, infuriating Bob White of the Canadian Auto Workers.

Saturday October 29: An Angus Reid poll is published showing the Tories and Liberals tied with 35 per cent, and the NDP with 28 per cent.

WEEK FIVE

Monday October 31: Michael Wilson accuses Turner and Broadbent of "peddling outright lies" about free trade, and says the auto pact is threatened if the Free Trade Agreement does not go ahead.

Tuesday November 1: An Environics poll is published suggesting the Liberals could form a government; the Liberals have 37 per cent, the Tories 31, the NDP 26.

Wednesday November 2: Mulroney debates with hecklers in Victoria.

Thursday November 3: Emmett Hall says there is nothing in the

Free Trade Agreement damaging to medicare. Mulroney speaks at the same senior citizens' home Broadbent addressed on Oct. 4. Turner attacks a four-page ad endorsing free trade by the Canadian Alliance for Trade and Job Opportunities. Broadbent says in Weyburn that free trade will stop social programs from being improved or expanded.

Friday November 4: Seven NDP candidates in Quebec hold a press conference to declare that the protection of French should have priority over the Charter of Rights.

WEEK SIX

Monday November 7: A Gallup Poll is published, showing the Liberals with 43 per cent, the Conservatives with 31, and the NDP with 22.

Thursday November 10: Broadbent says he is not a Quebecker, and cannot comment on whether Bill 101 is still needed. The Liberals win a court order requiring the TV networks to run the commercial of the dramatic Turner-Mulroney exchange in the debate. Turner attacks "les boys du Ritz." CBC-TV broadcasts its poll results: the Liberals and the Conservatives almost tied with 38 and 37.5 per cent respectively, and the NDP with 21. An Angus Reid poll is published showing the Tories with 39 per cent, the Liberals with 35, and the NDP with 24.

WEEK SEVEN

Monday November 14: Broadbent speaks to 1,500 people at Paul Sauvé Arena in Montreal, and says he has worked almost all of his political career for this moment after he receives a strong ovation.

Wednesday November 16: Turner rules out coalition with the NDP.

November 17: Ronald Reagan calls the Free Trade Agreement "an example of co-operation at its best."

November 18: Margaret Thatcher is quoted in the *Washington Post* as saying that if the Free Trade Agreement failed, it would be "very difficult for any prime minister of Canada to negotiate another international agreement with another country."

November 19: A Gallup Poll is published showing the Tories with 40 per cent, the Liberals with 35, and the NDP with 22. An Angus Reid poll shows the Tories with 41 per cent, the

Liberals with 33, and the NDP with 23. A CTV poll shows the Tories with 43 per cent, the Liberals with 32, and the NDP with 20.

November 21: Election Day. The Progressive Conservatives win 169 seats, and 43 per cent of the popular vote. The Liberals win 83 seats and 32 per cent of the popular vote. The NDP wins 43 seats and 20 per cent of the popular vote.

NOTES

Most of this book was researched personally, through reporting I did on the campaigns of the three parties during the election, or in interviews after it. However, where I have taken quotations from published sources that are not self-evident in the text, I have tried to attribute them here. Full references to the books cited will be found in the Bibliography that follows.

Chapter One: Election Day

James Bryce's comments on parties are found in his *Modern Democracies*, vol. 1, p. 528. The conclusions of Clarke, Jenson, LeDuc, and Pammett on the nature of Canadian brokerage politics are on p. 172 of *Absent Mandate*. André Siegfried's discussion of "the arguments that really weigh in Canadian elections" is found on pp. 130–42 of the Carleton Library paperback edition of *The Race Question in Canada*, which was originally published in French in 1906. The book by Richard Brookhiser is *The Outside Story*. He presented a similar argument in an essay in *The American Scholar* published in the spring of 1989. The comment by George Will that politicians' words should be taken seriously is from *The New Season*, p. 56.

Chapter Two: Mulroney Rounds the Edges

The Mulroney remarks about giving Pierre Trudeau a head start and seeing a roomful of senators are quoted in Martin, Gregg, and Perlin: *Contenders*, pp. 84 and 85; the comments about bureaucrats' offices, pink slips and running shoes, and living, breathing Conservatives are in Robert McKenzie's article in the *Toronto Star*, April 23, 1983. Details about the planning and development of Baie-Comeau can be found in Wiegman: *Trees to News*, pp. 189–92. Most of the following biographical information is drawn from L. Ian MacDonald's *Mulroney* and from Murphy, Chodos, and Auf der Maur: *Brian Mulroney*.

Peter Newman describes Mulroney's relationship with Diefenbaker on p. 283 of the 1964 paperback edition of *Renegade in Power*. The reputation of Mulroney as one of the candidates on the left of the Tory Party in 1976 is described in Brown, Chodos, and Murphy: *Winners, Losers*, p. 101. The revealing interview with Stephen Kimber was published as "After Joe, Who?" in the *Financial Post Magazine*, June 1978. Robert McKenzie's observations are in the article published in the *Toronto Star* on April 23, 1983. The reference to the June 1984 SORECOM poll that showed the Conservatives with 28 per cent support in Quebec and the Liberals with 62 per cent can be found in MacDonald's *Mulroney*, pp. 277–8.

A useful account of the debate over universality is in chapter 6 of Bercuson, Granatstein, and Young: *Sacred Trust?*

The embarrassing incidents are described in Jeffrey Simpson's masterly analysis of patronage in Canada, *Spoils of Power*, and summarized in Claire Hoy's *Friends in High Places*. The Sinclair Stevens story is recounted in Coyle, Fulton, Hurst, and Polanyi: *Sinc*, and Stevens's own reaction is shown in Robert Mason Lee's *One Hundred Monkeys*, chapter 5. The February poll results can be found in the *Gazette* and the *Citizen*, February 11, 1987.

Pierre Trudeau's article on Meech Lake was published in the *Toronto Star*, May 27, 1987, and reprinted in *With a Bang, Not a Whimper*, edited by Donald Johnston.

Stephen Clarkson describes the new trade strategy in *Canada and the Reagan Challenge*, pp. 328–40. For a favourable analysis, see Lipsey and York: *Evaluating the Free Trade Deal*; for a critical analysis, Cameron, ed., *The Free Trade Papers* and *The Free Trade Deal*.

Chapter Three: Potlatch Politics

Art Eggleton's remark about the 1996 Olympics is quoted in the *Financial Post*, June 20, 1988; MacDonald's phrase, "from somewhere between Queen's University and the United Church," is from his *Mulroney*, p. 303; "The Diplomat as Buddy" is Simpson's column in the *Globe and Mail*, July 9, 1985; Bouchard talks about how the remarks hurt in an interview with the author, *Globe and Mail*, February 13, 1986; the Val Sears article on the cabinet shuffle was in the *Toronto Star*, April 2, 1988; editorial comments on the Lac-Saint-Jean by-election: *Globe and Mail*,

June 16, 1988; *Vancouver Sun*, June 18, 1988; *Financial Post*, June 20, 1988.

Chapter Four: John Turner Hones the Speech

"Perhaps he read them, and was distracted": "Bourassa rabroue Turner," *La Presse*, le 13 août 1988. "Mulroney and Bourassa then turned and looked at each other with knowing grins": "Bourassa Says Turner Was Wrong on Trade," David Vienneau, *Toronto Star*, August 14, 1988. "Mr. Bourassa is intelligent enough to know what is good for Quebec": "Bourassa se moque encore de Turner," *La Presse*, le 15 août 1988. "Bourassa merely nodded but did not smile": "Turner and His Pal as the Odd Couple," Deborah McGregor, *Financial Times of Canada*, August 22, 1988.

Mayor Leonard Jones as "a national symbol of anti-French prejudice": George Perlin's article, "The Progressive Conservative Party in the Election of 1974," in Penniman, ed., *Canada at the Polls: The General Election of 1974*, p. 115.

For biographical details on John Turner, see Jack Cahill's *John Turner*, Christina McCall-Newman's *Grits*, Ron Graham's *One-Eyed Kings*, and "Born to Run," by Valerie Gibson, *Vancouver* magazine, September 1988. Turner referred to having "the whole experience" at Oxford in Cahill, *John Turner*, p. 57. The comment, "He just wouldn't say anything he figured would offend," was quoted by Christina McCall-Newman in "Turner, the Once and Future Contender," *Maclean's*, May 1971, and in *Grits*, p. 244. Stikeman's "He seemed to be in need of a father figure": Cahill, p. 72. "But he eventually showed I was wrong": Cahill, p. 82. Turner's account of his "rough time" in the "kitchen of government" is quoted by McCall-Newman in *Grits*, p. 245. Martin Sullivan described Turner as "sounding like the champion of the underdog" in *Mandate '68*, p. 251. Keith Davey's comment "If Turner had been nothing more . . ." is from McCall-Newman, *Grits*, p. 245.

Turner's "heart and gut" is quoted by Sullivan in *Mandate '68*, p. 336; his memorable "mellow men" phrase at the convention is also in Sullivan, p. 348, as well as in Cahill, p. 27, and Peter C. Newman, *The Distemper of Our Times*, p. 466. His epithet "young tigers" is quoted by McCall-Newman, *Maclean's*, May 1972; the Mulroney comment is quoted in the same article and in *Grits*, p. 249. Turner's statement that he was "bitterly disappointed because I thought we had an incomes-control situation" is from Cahill, p. 176. His comment about giving more powers to the provinces is from the same book, p. 193. William Macdonald's opinion that Turner was not going to run in 1980 was quoted by Thomas Walkom in "Chance to Lead Beckons Turner from Exile," *Globe and Mail*, June 18, 1984. Jeffrey Simpson's comment that "he was dealt a bad hand and played it poorly" was in the *Globe and Mail*, September 6, 1984. There is no shortage of grim post-mortems of the Liberal campaign in 1984: Ron Graham's *One-Eyed Kings*; Norman Snider's *The Changing of the Guard*; "The Dauphin and the Doomed: John Turner and the Liberal Party's Debacle," by Stephen Clarkson, in Penniman, ed., *Canada at the Polls, 1984*; "The Vincible Liberals," by Jeffrey Simpson, in Frizzell and Weston, eds., *The Canadian General Election of 1984*. Turner's replacing of Bill Lee with Keith Davey was told first by Linda Diebel in the *Gazette*, then by Keith Davey in *The Rainmaker*, by John Sawatsky in *The Insiders*, and finally by Greg Weston in *Reign of Error*.

"It provided some tangible evidence . . .," Hugh Winsor, *Globe and Mail*, December 1, 1986; "the most rewarding moment of his life," Valerie Gibson, "Born to Run," *Vancouver*, September 1988. André Ouellet denounces Don Johnston as a Westmount Rhodesian: *La Presse*, le 12 mai, 1987. "My mother had not been actually present in life for the last five years": Gibson.

Gregg's comments on the differences between his approach and Goldfarb's are quoted by Jeffrey Simpson in "The Most Influential Private Citizen in Canada," *Saturday Night*, July 1984.

"People see a degree of sovereignty being sacrificed . . .": "Sovereignty Issue on the Rise," by Martin Goldfarb, *Atlantic Business*, vol. 6, no. 6, Nov.-Dec. 1987.

Chapter Five: Ed Broadbent: the Family Gathers

Broadbent "inherited the mantle of Woodsworth, Coldwell, Douglas and Lewis": Morton, *The New Democrats, 1961–1986*; "the first mere mortal to lead the party": Charlotte Gray, "The Importance of Being Ed," *Saturday Night*, March 1988; "Ed is a difficult person to work with . . .": Norman Snider, "Ol' Brown

Eyes: the Sentimental Love Song of J. Edward Broadbent," *Toronto Life*, February 1988; "He has the protective veneer . . . ": Steed, *Ed Broadbent*. Jim Laxer's report was quoted in the *Globe and Mail*, January 10, 1984, and by Terence Morley in "Annihilation Avoided: the New Democratic Party in the 1984 Federal General Election," in Penniman, ed., *Canada at the Polls, 1984*, p. 120.

Caplan's memo is quoted by Nick Hills in "The NDP Survivors," in Frizzell and Weston, eds., *The Canadian General Election of 1984*.

Chapter Six: Issuing the Writs

Arthur Ford talks about A. D. McRae's addressograph mail system in his memoir *As the World Wags On*, p. 146. John Sawatsky describes Tory mistrust of Allan Gregg in *The Insiders*, pp. 159–61, 171–6.

For biographical details of Peter White, see Peter C. Newman's *The Establishment Man*, pp. 48–54. The computerized system of names is described in Bercuson, Granatstein, Young: *Sacred Trust?*, pp. 64–7. Simpson's account of the shredding of memos is in *Spoils of Power*, p. 362. Fulford's description of White is in *Best Seat in the House*, p. 245.

For biographical details on Mazankowski, see "Mazankowski: a Reputation for Fairness, Decency and Hard Work," by Andy Ogle, *Edmonton Journal*, June 26, 1988; "Check It with Maz," by Charlotte Gray, *Report on Business Magazine*, October 1988. Simpson's observation about Mazankowski as minister of transport is from *Discipline of Power*, p. 95. Mazankowski's role at the 1983 convention is described in Martin, Gregg, and Perlin: *Contenders*, p. 185. He talked about helping the prime minister in an interview on February 9, 1989; he said the job of deputy prime minister was to "sort of run the shop" in an interview published in the *Lethbridge Herald*, January 16, 1988. "You want to talk about CF–18? Let's talk about it . . . ," *Edmonton Journal*, June 26, 1988. For a lengthy and detailed compilation of government spending commitments, see Christopher Waddell's piece "Tory 'Commitments' May Face Budget Axe," *Globe and Mail*, April 10, 1989.

"Mrs. Thatcher has fought this creeping isolation over the years," Tyler, *Campaign!*, p. 172.

Chapter Seven: The Tories Cruise

Christina McCall-Newman describes Colin Kenny's campaign expertise in *Grits*, p. 352. Bruno's book is Bruno and Greenfield: *The Advance Man*. Martin Schram, *The Great American Video Game*, describes the use of television by the Reagan campaign in 1984.

Chapter Eight: Stumbles

The bulk of this chapter is based on my observations on the Turner plane. Paul Martin's remark about coaching was quoted by Greg Weston in the *Citizen* ("Top Grit Contender Emerges Quietly from Shadows"), August 29, 1987; his description of CSL as the quintessential Canadian company was quoted by Robert McKenzie ("Rising Liberal Star Sees Federal Party Rebirth"), *Toronto Star*, August 30, 1987.

Terence Morley's comments on the British tradition in the NDP leadership and membership are to be found in "Annihilation Avoided" in Penniman, ed., *Canada at the Polls, 1984*, p. 120.

Chapter Nine: A Very Canadian Coup

The events described in this chapter have been debated by journalists and political organizers on a variety of platforms, most specifically at a conference at Queen's University on February 24 and 25, 1989, and at the annual convention of the Centre for Investigative Journalism in Ottawa on June 3. They have been described and analysed by Alan Frizzell and Anthony Westell in *The Canadian General Election of 1988* and by Robert Mason Lee in *One Hundred Monkeys*.

The quotations from Axworthy and Goldfarb: *Marching to a Different Drummer* can be found on p. 127.

The comments that I attribute to Michael Kirby are from Caplan, Kirby, and Segal: *Election*. The book was actually written by David Stewart-Patterson on the basis of interviews with the three party organizers.

William Johnson's argument, which he repeated at the CIJ convention in June, was published in a column in the *Gazette* on October 22, 1988.

Chapter Ten: The TV Debates

This chapter was based on interviews, and transcripts of the two debates.

Chapter Eleven: The Ground Moves

The comment "When you're leading a nation, you're playing for keeps" was quoted by Heather Bird in the *Toronto Star*, October 27, 1988.

Chapter Twelve: Bombing the Bridges

The Lesley Stahl anecdote is told by Martin Schram in *The Great American Video Game*, pp. 23–6, and by Hedrick Smith in *The Power Game*, pp. 412–15. David Ogilvy's comments can be found on p. 130 of the 1976 edition of *Confessions of an Advertising Man*.

The description of the 1942–5 business-community campaign against the CCF is in David Lewis's memoirs, *The Good Fight*, pp. 306–19.

Chapter Thirteen: The Parting of the Ways

I watched the debate between Mulroney and the hecklers in Victoria, and then watched the TV coverage of that debate on CBC and CTV.

O. D. Skelton's description of the reaction to Fielding's announcement of the reciprocity agreement is in his *Life and Letters of Sir Wilfrid Laurier*, vol. 2, pp. 369–70. Craig Brown's comment on the "full assault" on the agreement is in his *Robert Laird Borden*, vol. 1, p. 177. Lawrence Martin quotes Taft's phrase "parting of the ways" on p. 74, and the famous Champ Clark speech on p. 72, of *The Presidents and the Prime Ministers*. The statements of Sir Edmund Walker, Sir William Van Horne, and Clifford Sifton are quoted by J. M. Beck in *Pendulum of Power*, pp. 122–3. Brown discusses Borden's agreement with them on p. 179 of vol. 1 of *Robert Laird Borden*. Laurier's speeches are quoted in Skelton, *Life and Letters*, vol. 2, p. 379. The first Henri Bourassa comment is quoted by Richard Jones in

Vers une hégémonie Libérale, p. 110; the second by Craig Brown, p. 192. Skelton's complaint is on p. 376. The results in seats and votes of the 1911 election are cited by Beck in Pendulum of Power, p. 135.

Mulroney's comment on "unfettered free trade": John Gray, Globe and Mail, June 1, 1983. Ian McDougall's point about reduced provincial control over resources was in the Globe and Mail, February 23, 1988. Margaret Atwood's and Rick Salutin's remarks were published in the Globe and Mail on November 5, 1987. A selection of the press reaction to Marjorie Bowker's paper was printed as an appendix when it was published as a book, On Guard for Thee. The Angus Reid poll was published in the Toronto Star on July 30, 1988.

Chapter Fourteen: Sovereignty-Association Upside Down

For more background on sovereignty-association, see my book PQ.

Pierre Trudeau's interventions were collected in Johnston, ed., With a Bang, Not a Whimper. In addition to the Trudeau polemic, the Meech Lake Accord is also analysed by Peter Hogg in Meech Lake Constitutional Accord Annotated, and attacked by Bryan Schwartz in Fathoming Meech Lake. Quebec's support of it is discussed in Forest, ed., L'Adhésion du Quebec à l'accord du Lac Meech.

Chapter Fifteen: The Eggshells Crack

The remarks made to Judy Steed are taken from the preface to the 1989 paperback reprint of her 1988 biography Ed Broadbent, entitled "Shattered Dreams: the 1988 Election Campaign."

Chapter Sixteen: The Final Days

For details of the campaign in Saanich – Gulf Islands, see Keith Baldrey's story in the Vancouver Sun, November 10, 1988, the Victoria Times-Colonist, October 20 and 22 and November 13, 1988, and the Globe and Mail, November 18, 1988.

The debate in Whitecourt was covered in detail in the Edmonton Journal on October 7, 1988.

Svend Robinson's campaign was described in detail in "Svend Robinson, MP," by John Lownsborough, Saturday Night, May

1989. For coverage during the campaign, see "Burnaby-Kingsway Battle Shapes Up," Larry Pynn, *Vancouver Sun*, November 12, 1988, and "Sexual Politics Big in Burnaby" by Andrew Ross, the *Province*, November 16, 1988.

BIBLIOGRAPHY

Axworthy, Thomas, and Martin Goldfarb. *Marching to a Different Drummer: An Essay on the Liberals and Conservatives in Convention*. Toronto: Stoddart, 1988.

Beck, J. M. *Pendulum of Power: Canada's General Elections*. Toronto: Prentice-Hall, 1968.

Bercuson, David, J. L. Granatstein, and W. R. Young. *Sacred Trust? Brian Mulroney and the Conservative Party in Power*. Toronto: Doubleday, 1986.

Bowker, Marjorie. *On Guard for Thee: An Independent Review of the Free Trade Agreement*. Hull: Voyageur Press, 1988.

Brookhiser, Richard. *The Outside Story: How Democrats and Republicans Re-elected Reagan*. New York: Doubleday, 1986.

Brown, Patrick, Robert Chodos, and Rae Murphy. *Winners, Losers: The 1976 Tory Leadership Convention*. Toronto: Lorimer, 1976.

Brown, Craig. *Robert Laird Borden: A Biography*, vol. 1. Toronto: Macmillan, 1975.

Bruno, Jerry, and Jeff Greenfield. *The Advance Man*. New York: Morrow, 1971.

Bryce, James. *Modern Democracies*. London: Macmillan, 1921.

Cahill, Jack. *John Turner: The Long Run*. Toronto: McClelland and Stewart, 1984.

Cameron, Duncan, ed. *The Free Trade Papers*. Toronto: Lorimer, 1986.

Cameron, Duncan, ed. *The Free Trade Deal*. Toronto: Lorimer, 1988.

Caplan, Gerald, Michael Kirby, and Hugh Segal. *Election: The Issues, the Strategies, the Aftermath*. Toronto: Prentice-Hall, 1989.

Clarke, Harold D., Jane Jenson, Lawrence LeDuc, and Jon H.

Pammett. *Absent Mandate: The Politics of Discontent in Canada.* Toronto: Gage, 1984.

Clarkson, Stephen. *Canada and the Reagan Challenge: Crisis and Adjustment, 1981–85.* Toronto: Lorimer, 1985.

Coyle, Jim, E. Kaye Fulton, Robert Hurst, and Margaret Polanyi. *Sinc.* Toronto: Fitzhenry and Whiteside, 1987.

Davey, Keith. *The Rainmaker: A Passion for Politics.* Toronto: Stoddart, 1986.

Ford, Arthur. *As the World Wags On.* Toronto: Ryerson, 1950.

Forest, Réal-A., ed. *L'Adhésion du Québec à l'accord du Lac Meech: points de vue juridiques et politiques.* Montréal: Éditions Thémis, 1988.

Fraser, Graham. *PQ: René Lévesque and the Parti Québécois in Power.* Toronto: Macmillan, 1984.

Frizzell, Alan, and Anthony Westell, eds. *The Canadian General Election of 1984: Politicians, Parties, Press and the Polls.* Ottawa: Carleton University Press, 1985.

Frizzell, Alan, Jon H. Pammett, and Anthony Westell, eds. *The Canadian General Election of 1988.* Ottawa: Carleton University Press, 1989.

Fulford, Robert. *Best Seat in the House: Memoirs of a Lucky Man.* Toronto: Collins, 1988.

Graham, Ron. *One-Eyed Kings: Promise and Illusion in Canadian Politics.* Toronto: Collins, 1986.

Hogg, Peter. *Meech Lake Constitutional Accord Annotated.* Toronto: Carswell, 1988.

Hoy, Claire. *Friends in High Places: Politics and Patronage in the Mulroney Government.* Toronto: Key Porter, 1987.

Johnston, Donald, ed. *With a Bang, Not a Whimper: Pierre Trudeau Speaks Out.* Toronto: Stoddart, 1988.

Jones, Richard. *Vers une hégémonie Libérale: Aperçu de la politique canadienne de Laurier à King.* Québec: Presses de l'Université Laval, 1980.

Lee, Robert Mason. *One Hundred Monkeys.* Toronto: Macfarlane Walter and Ross, 1989.

Lewis, David. *The Good Fight: Political Memoirs 1909–1958.* Toronto: Macmillan, 1981.

MacDonald, L. Ian. *Mulroney: The Making of the Prime Minister*. Toronto: McClelland and Stewart, 1984.

Martin, Lawrence. *The Presidents and the Prime Ministers: Washington and Ottawa Face to Face: The Myth of Bilateral Bliss, 1867–1982*. Toronto: Doubleday, 1982.

Martin, Patrick, Allan Gregg, and George Perlin. *Contenders: The Tory Quest for Power*. Toronto: Prentice-Hall, 1983.

McCall-Newman, Christina. *Grits: An Intimate Portrait of the Liberal Party*. Toronto: Macmillan, 1982.

Morton, Desmond. *The New Democrats, 1961–1986: The Politics of Change*. Mississauga, Ont.: Copp Clark Pitman, 1986.

Murphy, Rae, Robert Chodos, and Nick Auf der Maur. *Brian Mulroney: The Boy from Baie-Comeau*. Toronto: Lorimer, 1984.

Newman, Peter C. *Renegade in Power: The Diefenbaker Years*. Toronto: McClelland and Stewart, 1963.

Newman, Peter C. *The Distemper of Our Times*. Toronto: McClelland and Stewart, 1968.

Newman, Peter C. *The Establishment Man: A Portrait of Power*. Toronto: McClelland and Stewart, 1982.

Ogilvy, David. *Confessions of an Advertising Man*. New York: Atheneum, 1963.

Penniman, Howard R., ed. *Canada at the Polls: The General Election of 1974*. Washington: American Enterprise Institute, 1975.

Penniman, Howard R., ed. *Canada at the Polls, 1984*. Durham, N.C.: Duke University Press for the American Enterprise Institute, 1988.

Sawatsky, John. *The Insiders: Government, Business, and the Lobbyists*. Toronto: McClelland and Stewart, 1987.

Schram, Martin. *The Great American Video Game: Presidential Politics in the Television Age*. New York: Morrow, 1987.

Schwartz, Bryan. *Fathoming Meech Lake*. Winnipeg: Legal Research Institute of the University of Manitoba, 1987.

Siegfried, André. *The Race Question in Canada*. Translation revised by F. H. Underhill. Ottawa: Carleton Library, 1978.

Simpson, Jeffrey. *Discipline of Power: The Conservative Interlude and the Liberal Restoration.* Toronto: Personal Library, 1980.

Simpson, Jeffrey. *Spoils of Power: The Politics of Patronage.* Toronto: Collins, 1988.

Skelton, O. D. *Life and Letters of Sir Wilfrid Laurier.* New York: Century, 1921.

Smith, Hedrick. *The Power Game: How Washington Works.* New York: Random House, 1988.

Snider, Norman. *The Changing of the Guard.* Toronto: Lester & Orpen Dennys, 1985.

Steed, Judy. *Ed Broadbent: The Pursuit of Power.* Markham, Ont.: Viking, 1988, paperback edition Penguin 1989.

Sullivan, Martin. *Mandate '68.* Toronto: Doubleday, 1968.

Tyler, Rodney. *Campaign! The Selling of the Prime Minister.* London: Grafton, 1987.

Weston, Greg. *Reign of Error.* Toronto: McGraw-Hill Ryerson, 1988.

Wiegman, Carl. *Trees to News: A Chronicle of the Ontario Paper Company's Origin and Development.* Toronto: McClelland and Stewart, 1953.

Will, George. *The New Season: A Spectator's Guide to the 1988 Election.* New York: Simon and Schuster, 1988.

INDEX

Laxer, Jim, 110, 112, 117, 118
Le May, Norm, 337, 338
LeBlanc, Francis, 448
LeBreton, Marjory, 138, 139,
    148, 264, 299, 321
Lee, Bill, 80, 82, 215
Lefrançois, Marc, 360
Leley, Richard, 58
Lesick, Bill, 438
Lévesque, René, 120, 280, 355,
    361, 362
Lewis, David, 77, 111, 112, 113,
    327
Lewis, Doug, 438
Lewis, Stephen, 108
Liberal Party, in 1988 election
    abortion policy leaked, 241-
    42
    advertising, 311-16, 370-72,
    419-20
    campaign team, 234-36
    childcare policy, 210-13
    cost of campaign promises,
    419
    debate strategy, 241, 265
    election strategy, 101-3
    malaise after election, 451
    nomination fights, 162-66
    public opinion of, 41-42, 150,
    227-28, 303, 321, 424
    and Quebec, 369-75
    strengths and weaknesses,
    135-36
    See also individual Liberals
Lloyd, Woodrow, 384
Lockhart, David, 210, 435
Loiselle, Bernard, 221, 222
Lortie, Marc, 51, 180, 186, 187,
    195, 332, 436, 437
Lortie-Narayana, Hélène, 394,
    395
Lougheed, Peter, 143, 144, 160,
    188, 189
Lumley, Ed, 346
Lundrigan, John, 192
Lyon, Art, 180, 400

MacAdam, Patrick, 23
McCann, Terry, 23, 160, 438
McDermid, John, 216, 438
MacDonald, David, 112
Macdonald, Donald, 280
Macdonald, Finlay, 264
MacDonald, Flora, 25, 288,
    302-3, 438
Macdonald, John A., 10, 12, 15,
    341
MacDonald, L. Ian, 37, 44, 84,
    180, 300, 436
McDonald, Lynn, 9, 297, 439
MacDonald, Pierre, 141
Macdonald, William, 79
McDonough, Alexa, 387
McDougall, Barbara, 45, 51,
    264, 405, 438
MacEachen, Allan, 74, 94, 98,
    234, 250
McIlroy, James, 324
McInnes, John, 267
McInnes, Stewart, 194, 305, 436
MacKay, Elmer, 21, 28
MacKay, Neil, 337, 338
McKenna, Frank, 92
McKinnon, Ian, 138
McKnight, Bill, 153
Maclaren, Roy, 163
MacLellan, Russ, 92, 171, 448
McMillan, Charles, 38, 189
McMillan, Tom, 194, 436
McMurray, Hilarie, 104, 220,
    267, 292, 315, 396
McMurtry, Roy, 48-49
MacNaughton, David, 138, 236,
    256
Macpherson, C.B., 108
McRae, General A.D., 136
Maheu, Shirley, 165, 259
Maillet, Antonine, 276, 279,
    280
Malépart, Jean-Claude, 59, 90,
    372-75
Maltais, André, 32
Manley, John, 203

INDEX